FREE
MAN
WALKING

ANDY NIEMAN

Produced by:

FriesenPress
Suite 300 – 852 Fort Street
Victoria, BC, Canada V8W 1H8

www.friesenpress.com

Distributed to the trade by The Ingram Book Company

TABLE OF CONTENTS

**I could not stop drinking! I could not stop
sticking that needle in my arm!**

**I could not get my life together!
No matter what I tried I always failed!**

Until... I learned the TRUTH!

I have lost most of my childhood friends to drug overdoses and alcoholic mishaps that claimed their lives. Friends that I have grown up with and have grown to love over the years. When they die they take a part of you with them when they go.

They could've found the freedom that I found but for whatever reason they didn't. I dedicate this book to them, to my mother's memory, my family and to those who will find freedom through this true-life story. That same freedom that I have found and have come to love. That beautiful freedom that I am not willing to exchange for anything this world has to offer. (AN)

When a prisoner has finished his time in the penitentiary, on his release day, as he is walking towards the last gate that separates him from freedom, a guard yells out, "Free man walking!"

Today... I am a Free Man Walking.

PROLOGUE

After ten years on skid row, ten and one half years in jail, twenty seven years of chronic alcoholism, three years in a residential school, twenty three years of heroin, cocaine and drug addiction, I found the true path of healing that allowed me to overcome the effects of Family Violence, Neglect, Sexual Abuse and become a new person. I went back to school, earned a University Degree in Social Work, ran my own counseling business for six years and became an Officer of the Yukon Legislative Assembly. When the suggestion was put forth that I should write a book on my life I thought with enthusiasm, "Yeah, I **should** do that!" At the time, I had no idea of the monumental task I was about to embark on. Monumental, in terms of not only fitting in the time to write, but also to deal with those emotions that would be re-lived and the scenes that would be re-played over and over again for the benefit of accuracy. The task is monumental in terms of deciding where to begin, what to include and what to leave out.

Like a painter dipping the tip of his brush into many different colors seeking to find that perfect hue, I now realize that I too, must "dip" my historical "paint brush" into the harsh colors of a jaded past and into the pools of my emotions in order to paint as accurate a picture as memory will serve. I have been given a new lease on life. I know that. It can't be argued. And along with that lease, comes a price tag. A price tag I'm grateful yet burdened to pay. Part of that price tag, are the memories which must be resurrected of loved ones long since passed-on. Memories, once thought to be so carefully tucked-away in a dark secret chasm of the mind they would never be disturbed again. Tucked away in a place where it seems not even hypnosis, or the strongest truth serum (if there were such a thing), could penetrate. Memories, still so very clear they seem to have been waiting for these precise moments to come alive once again.

There will also be scenes, complete with the sounds of skid row and prison life. Scenes that bring to life the muffled sound of a lonely heart breaking as the under-nourished body is stabbed repeatedly by the agonizing knife of drug withdrawal. There is sweat. There are tears. There is humor. There are scenes of drug overdoses and of prison violence. Scenes, like the time I stood on the steps of the Lower Post Indian Residential School, a ten year old boy with tears in my eyes, after being told I was not going home. I was 300 miles away from my mother, my father, my family and my friends. A child forced into a strange environment with people I did not know. Scenes, of that same ten-year-old boy smoking cigarette butts out in the wilderness, on a weekend outing at the residential school. There are scenes also of lasting friendships borne out of adversity. Friendships created through the necessity of survival. Scenes also, which depict the kind of courage it takes to admit you've suffered physical, sexual, emotional and mental abuse at the residential school. That you've done wrong to those who have treated you well and you need their forgiveness. Your mind's eye will view scenes of laughter, smiling faces, joy, triumph and trauma and most importantly. . .love.

This writer will give you a front-row seat. A real-life virtual tour, of the way it is in the life of a person living for over ten years on skid-row and ten and one half years behind prison bars. You'll have a glimpse into the life of a person who was a chronic, hopeless alcoholic for twenty-seven years and a drug addict for twenty three. You will walk through the seedy world of the cocaine addict and the heroin addict. You'll learn first-hand what it takes to come out of such a painful life as well as how to live an overcoming lifestyle that endures, after the drugs.

The writer will not have any trouble recollecting scenes or events for this autobiography. Just as a soldier will remember the sounds of war, or a rape-victim remembers the touch of cold steel on flesh, pain somehow has a way of triggering one's memory (or is it memory that triggers pain)? Neither will there be any need for exaggeration in this story. Reality has its own staying power and sings its own sour-sweet song, loud and clear. And truth. . . truth does not back down nor bedfellow with exaggeration, it has no need to. It is not my job to convince you of truth, it is merely my place to present the factual events of my past life, leading up to the present, where my life now stands. My criminal record is posted online as an establishment of truth at: www.freemanwalking.net.

As we embark on this journey together, it is this writers hope, that these pages will instill a hope into the hearts of those who are going through something similar and for mothers, fathers, sisters and brothers who may have family or relatives living on skid-row, in prison, or who are presently living in the throes of alcohol/drug addiction or other realities of traumatic despair. Please, and I say again. . . . . **Please**, don't *ever stop* HOPING, PRAYING, and BELIEVING in them. And NEVER STOP LOVING them. Simply because… **you just never know**… how they will respond, when the true love that only comes from above and from your heart, will break through into their darkness! As long as they are still breathing, there is hope for them.

As I look back on the days of my past now, the scenes are still so very clear, as though they had just happened last night. I honestly thank God, in fact I pray, that He would never let me forget those times, while I'm here on earth. It marvels me, how the human mind seems to store *in mint condition*, those memories that are the hardest on us. While the good ones seem to vanish like the quickly fading voice of a nurse counting backwards, after administering a final anesthetic dosage before wheeling you into the operating room. While I sit at this computer and write this autobiography, I find it hard to stifle the emotions that stir in me. I'm thankful many of those emotions are of sheer gratitude. Yet, many of them are not. The process, I now realize, is one that's both a burden and a blessing. Before we go any further, may I stop and say, "Thank you"? To spend these moments with you is a great privilege, and I want you to know how grateful I am for the opportunity.

I would like to write of a happy childhood where fond memories of love and nurture abound. In fact, I would even be satisfied to write of a somewhat normal childhood, but rality dictates otherwise. I am left with only one alternative… presenting the bare, unrelenting, traumatic, sometimes happy, sometimes sad, triumphant, never-a-dull-moment… truth. Truth that is complete with knarls, warts, bumps, bruises, velvety-smooth caresses and time-less endurance. This is not a sad story. It is one of triumph. It is my story and it may even be a part of your story. It is truth and truth lingers. I have paid the price for your ticket to this live event. Now it is time for you to get comfortable and enjoy your front row seating.

Not being one to stick to formalities and for the sake of sheer adventure, I sometimes like to just jump into the thick of things and explain later. This is where we will begin. Jump-in with me, as we take a first-hand look, or, should I say, a real-life tour, and examine how the life of a former alcoholic, cocaine/heroin addict and an ex-convict's life on skid row turned into a beautiful journey out of addiction and how I became a free man walking. Andy.

CHAPTER ONE

A GLIMPSE OF SKID ROW

"The Lighthouse"

The sun was setting in my life,
I couldn't last much more,
I watched as all my broken dreams,
Came washing up on shore,

As hope was fading from my heart,
I took another drink,
I stood in rags, I begged for food,
To the bottom I would sink,

I roamed the streets in dark of night,
I cried my silent tears,
As loneliness chained down my heart,
Cocaine brought me new fears

A. Nieman

I did not sleep well last night. This morning I wake up around 7:00 am. It is never comfortable on my flattened out cardboard box laid out on the concrete floor of an underground parking lot. The only time I didn't notice the discomfort, was when I passed out there. The underground parking lot was below the United Church on East Hastings St. and Gore Ave. This is Vancouver, British Columbia, Canada. What woke me were the muffled, angry, voices of heroin and cocaine addicts arguing in the dark. Someone complained that they had missed the vein. Another swore out a stream of profanities so loud it made everyone uneasy and caused each of them to take a quick nervous scan of the parking lot.

The one doing the swearing had just realized their so-called dope turned out to be nothing but Baking Soda. Still another practically shouted, "Hold the #&⋆% light still!" as he sought to find a vein in the almost-impossibly dim light of a flickering Bic lighter. The flame goes out, producing another string of profanities from the one desperate to get the syringe into a vein.

The one "keeping point" (watching for police) – usually called the "point-man" was normally the one who had already "shot-up" (injected) his/her drugs. And as always, depending on what their drug of choice was, they wound up doing a very poor job of "keeping point". The reason being, if it was heroin the point-man shot-up, he/she would be "nodding-off" or fighting off the opium dreams, and it would only be in-between nods, that they would garner a look to see if there were any cops around. Mind you a nod could last anywhere from ten seconds to two minutes so you were really taking your chances!

If the point-man's drug of choice was cocaine, he/she might be so high and paranoid they would quite easily suspect any and every person of being an undercover cop. A coca-nut, which is slang for a cocaine addict, when high on cocaine is always paranoid. A "coca-nut" is in such a state of deception and paranoia while high on the drug, that he/she would not believe anyone on this earth, that something is any different than **how they see it**! They would normally remain in this state, until the effect wore off and they came down off the drug. When cocaine-induced paranoia has an addict in its grip, there is *no way* another human being can "talk" them out of their paranoid state, simply because cocaine induced psychosis rules their thinking process. The addict has to come to a place where they convince their own self that the perceived danger has passed. A cocaine addict in this hyped-up state can be very dangerous, while at the same time be extremely scared of everyone and everything. I have been there thousands of times.

On this particular morning I am feeling very cold. A cold I just cannot shake. The wet, damp cold, the west coast of British Columbia's October night, normally brings. Vancouver, Canada is wet, cold and damp, even for those who *did not* live on the streets. I was also feeling another type of cold. This cold ran deeper than any rain-swept night. It is the cold reminder that I am "damaged goods", damaged, by the sexual perversion of a pedophile at the Lower Post Indian Residential School. I wished I had a blanket tonight. My sad reality reminded me that not even the world's warmest electric blanket would be able to bring some warmth to my icey-cold soul. Besides, I usually did not sleep with a blanket. I gave up the futile effort of trying to keep a sleeping bag. It was never any use trying to hide a blanket in this seedy run-down neighborhood. A neighborhood that was thick with drug dealers, prostitutes, ex-convicts, alcoholics, screaming sirens and mean police. This neighborhood was also crawling with homeless people, who always seem to know exactly where to look to find any type of stash. I would usually just pull my coat around me real tight in an attempt to be warm. I never really ever slept a good night's sleep while doing drugs and living on the street. It was usually a matter of laying my drug-riddled body down in sheer exhaustion. If I happen to catch a few winks while in the process, well…that was a bonus. Other than that, my only sleep came when I would pass out from an excessive amount of alcohol consumption.

This morning, the cold seeped deep into my bones and seemed to "push" itself into every fibre of my being. A wave of cold remorse and forlorn feelings of a failed life had settled into its familiar spot, smack-dab in the center of my heart. And, as was the norm, I struggled to keep it from draining my strength. Along with that wave of remorse, came a stream of familiar thoughts I had no control over. I thought of my many failed attempts trying to "get straight. I thought of the deep sheer contempt I had of myself for being such a two-faced person. I thought of my body's present condition, so undernourished, weak and drug infected. I thought of my mother and my family so far away, no doubt wondering how I'm doing and hurting for me. I thought of suicide again. It would be so easy to just buy a cap of "China White" (the most potent heroin on the streets at the time) and overdose myself. End it all. There was just one problem. I was too scared there might really be a hell, complete with flames, gnashing of teeth and eternal torment somewhere down below. This fear kept me alive. I had no choice but to fight on. What a contradiction this life of mine was. I was afraid of life and afraid of death. My only option was to struggle on. I dreaded my past, feared my future and despised my present.

In times like these, my thoughts always turned back to the one whose love for me I knew was so real. A love that I knew would never let me down nor ever leave me, the love of my mother Agnes (RIP). When I thought of my dear mother and the hurt I had caused her as a result of my alcohol and drug addictions, it always cut me somewhere deep down in the pit of my soul. I tried my best to avoid thinking of her as it made me lonely and made me feel regretful. I had become somewhat of a master at shutting off those thoughts and the sad feelings that accompanied them. This is what I called my "dead man mode". It was a skill I had developed over ten and a half years behind prison bars "doing time". A skill that was honed out of survival's necessity as a young boy on the loose, forging out my individual path of survival, self-destruction, criminal activity and addictive behavior. It was not a skill to be proud of. I taught myself to "shut people out", in a cold-hearted manner. I hated myself for it. It became too easy at times. But it was also very necessary. Necessary, because on the mean streets of Vancouver's skid row and in jail you just didn't allow your heart to get too close to anybody. And I mean anybody! Relationships in jail could be very shaky at the best of times and could easily end at the drop of a misplaced or misunderstood word to the wrong person. A friend could be with you one day and dead the next. Or be transferred to another jail. Or be "shanked" (knifed), make bail or overdose. I'm sure you get the picture. You just didn't "buddy-up" to every Tom, Dick and Harry who came along. You chose the ones you would associate with very carefully. It mattered, because other convicts judged you by the company you kept (just as people on the "outside" do). It mattered more if you were in for a long time or if you were a chronic convict. I was a chronic convict, meaning; I would always be coming back to jail until the day I died. In other words, I was doing life on the installment plan. Most of those in jail are addicts of one kind or another, not everyone, but most. As an addict, one is not as emotionally stable or developed as healthy people are. An addict usually carries a lot of "baggage". Society calls that baggage a dysfunction. In reality, that baggage is unresolved hatred, abuse (of all sorts), depression, mental illness, abandonment and childhood violence. These insecurities are usually hiding underneath a tougher-than-thou image. They could easily make a person very explosive and dangerous. Jealousy, hatred and violence, are also part of that baggage. Such character traits lingered just under the surface of the skin of this writer and most of the people I "did time" with in jail.

Rising from the flattened out cardboard box, I found I had to resort to my emotional dead man mode this morning. When thoughts of my mother were involved at these times, I especially hated myself. I missed her and always felt pangs of guilt when I was reminded of the grief I had caused her. My mother always felt so far away from me. My dead-man-mode did not always work and usually failed me when I really needed it the most. That is when depression would engulf my soul. It would turn everything gray. And the ills of the world, people's kindest acts and sincerest desires to help, would be viewed through a negative, untrusting, hateful, jealous, attitude. Alcohol and drugs were my only relief then. They were the only things that brought me close to feeling a sense of peace. Such relief was always short-lived and fleeting. Peace and strength were nothing but words to me then. They didn't mean anything. I couldn't comprehend the full depth of what they stood for, how they were achieved, or even if they really existed. Just words. They never really existed for me. Just words.

I stirred from my place of restless, fitful sleep. I had to start the day. There was no escape from it. I knew the "shakes" from needing a drink would soon be rearing its ugly head, in the form of dry heaves, a runny nose, shaking hands and watering eyes. I couldn't stay here much longer. My addictions were forcing me to move on. I dreaded the thought of walking on my blistered feet again. Walk? Who could enjoy the *luxury* of *walking*? Not me. Not this morning. Limping, was the only pace I could keep. I had been awake for four days straight, shooting cocaine and working any scam I could find prior to my laying down in the underground parking lot. Cocaine is an "upper". It stimulates you. Ninety percent of those four days was spent walking the drug dealer's beat on my feet, hence the blisters. Each time I took a shot of cocaine, I would gain about fifteen minutes of relief from the ache of those blisters. When I was drinking, the alcohol numbed the pain even more. It made me oblivious to the pain, which in turn caused me to do more damage to those blisters by walking on them. But there was no escaping it, the pain always found its way back with the inescapable dawning of another day.

This morning, I was somewhat relieved the soup line was just down the street. But what did it matter? I could not keep any food down anyway. That is, not until I got a few drinks into me. Some mornings, depending on where the alcohol and/or cocaine had taken me the night before - I could easily wake up miles from this area, and either had to walk back or would have to scam a bus ride. I'm thankful the walk is not so long today. The main reason I make my

7

way down to the soup-line, was not to eat, but to see if any of my buddies had anything to drink, or perhaps some valium or other pills to ease my suffering. This was my routine. I was hungry, sick, cold and as usual lonesome. Lonesome seemed to be my only constant, ever-present true companion. Long story short, I was not a pleasant sight. I was thirty-nine years of age and felt like I was going on eighty-nine! As I made my way down the street, I noticed the air was clear and cold. It had stopped raining. I caught the smell of fried bacon from one of the restaurants I passed by and it kicked my hunger pangs into gear to remind me that food needed to be a priority and *soon*. I almost gagged at the smell of food even though bacon was one of my favorite breakfast items. I also noticed that the soup line was longer than usual. My mind cleared enough to conclude that it was the day before welfare Wednesday. That meant people on welfare were out of money and groceries. They would be hitting the soup lines.

I searched the faces in the line to see if there were any of my drinking or drugging buddies there. I could not help but notice how despicably sad, dirty and unkempt the people in the line looked. People who looked exactly like me. What caught my attention the most was what I seen in their eyes. Rather, what I did *not see* in their eyes. They looked at me with eyes that were empty, sad and hopeless. Their eyes looked blank at first glance but if you continued to look just a little longer you would see the hurt in those eyes. There is no hope in those eyes. These are eyes saying, "I have all but given up. I do not have a future and it hurts." They looked like prisoners of war in a concentration camp. They looked like people from a war-torn, third world country in line for a ration. Heads hung down. Their shame was evident in furtive glances and restless feet. They didn't look you in the eye. If they did, it was only for a split second. You got the impression that if you looked at them long enough, they were afraid you might see their past. See their failure. See their pain. The only ones who let their eyes linger on you were the ones under the influence of alcohol or some other drug. This was the only way they could continue looking at you without feeling self-conscious.

The people in this line were mostly First Nation people, but there were also white people, Hispanics, Mexicans, Blacks, French people and others. They are real people. They have souls. They have a history. They are mostly people who live on the street. These are the homeless, the ex-convicts and prostitutes. They have feelings just like you and I. They do their best to survive. They are drug addicts. They are alcoholics. They are those who live in poverty. They laugh once in a while. They cry more than they laugh. They leant a helping hand whenever the opportunity arose in the past. They would still lend a helping hand, if they could. They could still be kind. They could still feel compassion. They have resilience. They feel remorse. They have come through more trauma than they care to remember or admit. Some never dared to dream anymore. Others once had dreams so bright. Dreams that were so real, they could almost reach out and touch them! That is… until the cruelties of life; sexual abuse and addiction took them by the hand and dashed those dreams upon the rocks of cruelty, failure and despair. Cruelties, which dragged them, against their will at first, down the road of alcoholism, violent crime, prostitution, stealing, lying, homelessness, panhandling, drug addiction and eventually an early grave. If not an early grave, then a hospital, a prison, a mental institution or a life of desperation on skid row streets. After a while they go along willingly accepting this as their fate because they now believe they have no choice. Their dreams are gone. This is now their lifestyle. It was all they knew and probably all they would ever know. To me, it was like looking in a mirror. All of this was evident in those eyes. It all hit home with me. Sadness once again stabbed my defenseless heart. I wished I could help them, but I needed help just as much myself, if not more. I tried not to look too long, I seen too much of my own reality and hurt there. When I was hung-over, as I was this morning, my defenses were down and it seemed I could notice nothing else but the pain and the heartache.

For the most part, most of them were sober. This was not a good sign for someone who desperately needed a drink. I didn't feel my chances of finding a drink were all that great, but I decided to take a peek inside the United Church anyway, after all it couldn't hurt. I was glad I did! For right there, not more than ten feet from me, was a sweet sight for sorry, sad, blood-shot, hung-over eyeballs! There was my best friend Gary Dawson! (RIP). Gary was a full-blooded First Nations man who had Tlingit (pronounced Kling — Get) blood in him. He was sitting there enjoying his cup of soup and his coffee. I limped up to his side and he glanced to see who it was that had come so close to him. I could smell alcohol on his breath. When he recognized that it was me, his eyes lit up, "Nieman!" he practically shouted. He smiled at me with that smile that always made me feel so important, no matter how sick I was. A smile that seemed to say everything was going to be all right because I had just come on the scene. Gary had that kind of a smile. He quickly perked up, "Well, if it isn't my good old side-kick. You sick? Looks like you need an eye-opener! Grab yourself some soup and let's blow this rat-trap. I'll fix your hangover." I didn't bother getting any soup, my feet and my head hurt too much. It wasn't worth the pain to wait in line. I needed a drink! I would think about my stomach later. I hobbled along beside Gary, grateful that he was slowing down to accommodate me. That was one of the reasons he was my lifelong best friend. He had real compassion. He cared for me. He always cared for me. Doesn't matter what I did or where I came from, Gary still cared for me. Gary did not do any hard drugs anymore. He used to shoot heroin with me and our other Yukon buddies, but he had given that up over fifteen years ago. The only drug he would allow himself to indulge in now was marijuana or hashish and of course alcohol. Gary had a cure for me this morning all right. He didn't like to drink that cheap Ginsing stuff, he had to have his good old fashioned, liquor store wine. I knew the wine had to have come from a bootlegger because it was so early in the morning. On this particular morning, being in the pain I was in, Gary was a knight in shining armor! I didn't care what kind of drink he had, or where he got it, just so long as IT HAD ALCOHOL IN IT! We made our way down Hastings Street to Victory Square, stopping in a doorway along the way to have a gulp. I was glad to see that the bottle of wine Gary had was almost full. It wouldn't cure my hangover completely, but it would definitely take some of the edge off so I could become somewhat functional. Then, I could start planning my scams for the day. I knew it would be more than enough to get Gary well on his way to being intoxicated. Gary always seemed to get drunk faster than me ever since he quit doing the hard drugs.

We sat down in Victory Square. Gary pulled out his harmonica and started to play his mournful, sweet blues that usually got people to stop and listen. On this morning, they were actually stopping and listening, even in this cold! If I had been one to use my brain for something other than dreaming up illegal scams, I would have thought to put a hat on the ground for a collection. Instead, I just sat there listening, the music caused me to roll over melancholy thoughts in my head as I reflected on my failures in life and my drug addict lifestyle. Oh the joys of a hung-over mind! My damaged, lonely, lost childhood memories came stealing back again and flooded me. When Gary stopped playing and the people clapped, he routinely asked if anyone had a smoke for, "Me and my buddy?" When cigarettes were passed out, Gary would then hone in on one of the spectators and ask, "Say, could you help a guy out? Me and my buddy are short. We're just trying to get enough for bus fare." Nine times out of ten he would get "bus fare". And I would always say, after the crowd had gone, "Gary, don't ask for bus fare next time, ask for money FOR FOOD! They'll give you more that way!" His reply would never change, "You ask next time then." That always shut me up.

As we sat there drinking the wine, Gary looked over at me and I could see he was starting to feel the effect of the booze. He was closing one eye to get a better focus. He was getting more talkative with people as they walked by. He began to wander around the park. He would play his harmonica and ask for smokes. He always had a joke to tell when he was "feeling his oats". And I could tell that's exactly what he was doing, because he was chatting with three ladies and they all burst into laughter. Three *white* ladies at that! Gary, like the rest of his family, had an awesome sense of humor. He saw the world through a different "lens" than most of us did. I always looked up to him. Gary was one year and ten days older than I. He was my best friend and always had been for as far back as I can remember. He was that type of friend, who you could not remember the first time you met them. It was as if they were always there. Someone, who just naturally belonged at your side. He was also one of the most respected fighters I knew. He may not have been the best fighter, but to me he was the most respected. I mean I've had friends who were very good fighters who were very bad news and you just didn't mess with them! They would shank you, or pipe you, shoot you or just plain beat you within an inch of death. But Gary was the fighter I respected the most because he didn't look for fights. Not only did he *not look* for fights, he always stood up for the little guy. If Gary felt someone was getting bullied, he would purposely take the place of the person being bullied, and challenge the bully by saying, "Why don't you pick on someone your own size, like me?" I can honestly say, I've never seen Gary lose a fight and I've seen him in many, many "scraps". Gary would never, and I mean never, back down from *anyone!*

This is Gary walking down the street in Vancouver. I believe he is 18 yrs. old in this photo. RIP my friend. I still miss you a lot.

I loved Gary because he was honest and had a big heart. Here he was, growing up with someone who knew nothing but stealing and lying (yours truly), and he still maintained a high level of honesty. The only time I ever saw Gary being involved in stealing or not telling the truth, was when I was influencing him. Gary looked up to me and I looked up to Gary. Gary found it hard to say no to me because I usually had a way of making money and of getting drugs and/ or alcohol, throughout our whole lives. That is…when I wasn't in jail. But even in jail it wasn't hard for me to get those things. I liked to get things the quick, easy, ready-at-hand way. Gary liked to do things the honest way. He only had a grade eight education, just as I did, but he was willing to work when work was available and whenever he was sober enough to work. I also loved Gary because he had such a tremendous sense of humor. That humor always showed itself true to form, especially when we were both down and out. I come from a frightening, wild, gloomy, traumatic, fight-for-survival lonely childhood. So it was always very refreshing to have someone around who could make me laugh. Gary could always make me laugh and so could his brother "Maddy" (RIP). I treasured Gary. I loved Gary. Gary was my secret role model. I didn't have to tell him any of this, he knew it. We were the closest of friends. We were the best of friends. We came through everything together. The Group Home, LSD trips, Magic Mushrooms,

11

MDA, Marijuana, Hashish, Drunk tanks, Heroin overdoses, Firefighting you name it! Whenever I felt the world was letting me down and no one cared how

I felt or understood me, I could always turn to Gary! We could be walking down an alley digging in garbage bin after garbage bin and we'd both be belting out the same Rolling Stones song in what we felt was perfect harmony singing real loud …"I can't get no, satisfaction. I can't get no girl reaction, but I try n' I try, n' I try…I can't get no!" That was Gary's lifelong favorite band. He didn't just like the Rolling Stones, he had a passion for them! And today in the park, once again, Gary would belt out a Stones' tune. And once again I felt like Gary was my knight in shining armor.

As Gary was joking and being friendly with other people in the park, my mind pondered the happenings of last night that lead me to today's present situation. My heart felt the cold stab as a lightning bolt of loneliness pierced it. A wave of melancholy and forlorn crept in. I wanted my life to be different. I wished there was some way out of this despicable world of ex-cons, alcoholics, rip-off artists, winos, addicts and drug dealers. I knew there wasn't. I had tried so many avenues; Alcoholics Anonymous, Narcotics Anonymous, Cocaine Anonymous, Native Spirituality, Eastern Religions, Philosophy, Psychology/ Self-Help Books and church after church after church. I tried to "straighten-out" for my mom, my family, my girlfriends, to keep a job, and to stay out of jail. As usual, nothing worked. Everywhere I turned for help, I always met with failure. I felt like I just didn't possess the moral fiber, the strength of character, or the sheer will-power, that I heard so many say is what it takes to beat the addiction. Every avenue I turned to, seeking some assistance to help me overcome this dreaded curse, would always lead me to the same pitiful result…utter disappointment and a deeper disdain for self and life. Was I to be forever doomed to this ball and chain of self-loathing, alcoholism, depression, hopelessness, homelessness, suffering and shame? My thoughts began to drift to last night's activities.

Not many people survive much less thrive, after spending over ten years on skid row, as a full-fledged alcoholic, wayward convict and a pill-popping, cocaine/ heroin addict. I'm one of the uncommon few who did. On more occasions than I can remember, my life on the streets of Vancouver's downtown Eastside, found me at 3 a.m. (or thereabouts), crouched in a darkened alley, underneath (what I was sure had to be the world's dimmest light-bulb), searching desperately for a vein in which to inject the cocaine-filled syringe. That's exactly what I was doing last night. As the cold west coast rain fell relentlessly around and on me, I was reminded how increasingly difficult it was to find a vein that wasn't collapsed. A collapsed vein is a vein that does not pump blood as fully as it used to, due to the overuse of a syringe, or some other impediment. A normal vein will usually puff-up when the blood flow is pinched, making the vein stand out, and it is easier to inject a syringe. A collapsed vein will not puff-up as much as it used to. It then becomes very hard to get the drug directly into the blood stream. When this happens, there is the risk of missing the vein completely, upon injection. When a vein is missed, the drug is injected directly into the muscle and flesh. This is a painful process and the drug takes much longer to take effect. If the vein is missed and the drug injected, there is the risk of initiating an abscess. This is one of the worst fears of an addict, besides spilling the drug, getting ripped-off or overdosing. An abscess is a very painful and I emphasize *very painful* infection. Within minutes, the pain starts. And it could turn into an infection that usually forms around the injection spot, into a large lump of increased swelling, redness, pain and it will eventually fill with pus. A full-blown abscess left untreated is an awful sight and the pain is second only to the smell. The combination of the two is an awful experience. The lump can become so large and painful one cannot bend the arm. The abscess can last anywhere from two to three weeks or longer, depending on the care that it receives.

In the back alleys of Vancouver's skid row, I would play out this scene of searching for a vein time and time again. While looking for a vein, I had to keep a wary eye on the alley for the police or any other threat that would attempt to keep me from my injection. Once the injection was complete, there is no real enjoyment. The pain, both physical and emotional is numbed for a while and goes away. Then when the effect of the drug wears off there is a lingering sense of being used and exploited once again by the drug. It's almost as if the drug purposely reminds that you have no control over it because it has complete control over you. You experience paranoia, mild hallucinations and suspicion. At times like this, one always feels that there is something, someone, a threat of some kind out there stalking you. The more cocaine in the injection, the closer the threat would come to overtaking you. I would repeat this very same ritual at least fifteen to twenty times on an average day or an average night. This had become "the norm" for me. It was all I lived for. It was all I breathed for. Just let me get that needle in my arm and well. . . quite frankly, you could take the world and do what you wanted with it. Why did I do it? The drug offered me a numbing effect. A numbing effect, that temporarily took away the physical and the emotional pain. It relieved the pain of childhood trauma and sexual abuse, the pain of a failed life and mile-deep valleys of death-like loneliness. This had become my life. There appeared no way out for me, or so I thought, other than in a pine box. I had resolved this in my mind and accepted it to be my fate, my reality. I had no doubt I would return home from Vancouver in a pine box. The only question remaining was not how, but where and when would I go?

I finished my injection. Gathering up my small bottle of water, my syringe and after taking a last look on the ground to see if I dropped or missed anything I was off into the big city night. A night that would pass by repeating this same ritual until the dawn arrived once again on the mean streets of Vancouver's downtown eastside. This was a typical night in the addict's life where drug dealers peered at you from under sweat suit hoods. This was an ordinary night where prostitutes with running mascara, could be seen occupying every street corner, giving you an expectant, hopeful look with eyes asking, "Are you a trick (client)?"

CHAPTER TWO

SLEEPY HOLLOW

"The Train"

Looked back down the road I came,
scenes of sorrow and pictures of pain,
Never wanna' go back there again,
where can I catch the Future Train?

Some have laughed and called me names
kicking a rock I carried the shame,
People can play the dirtiest games I need
to board the Forgiveness Train,

My love, my love was all in vain,
it left my heart with a scarred-up stain,
I carried a burden of bother and blame, I
missed my ride on True Love's Train,

A. Nieman

Vancouver's skid-row is a long way from the Yukon where I was born. How I got there, is really no different than how other First Nations people get there. We all seek to escape the trauma of the residential school, a life of violence at home, poverty and alcohol abuse. We run. We run and the only place we run to is a place where we temporarily exchange the hurt from a life of poverty, violence, desperation and loneliness for an alcoholic/drug addict's life of desperation on the mean streets of East Vancouver or any other major city. What's important is... **how I got out.**

I was born in Whitehorse, Yukon, Canada, into a relatively large family. I am the third youngest of nine children. I am of Native ancestry, Northern Tutchone((pronounced 'too-show-nee') on my mother's side and my father, Paul Nieman Sr. (RIP) was of Danish and German ancestry, (I think the Danish blood was thicker because he only strapped me once). He was a trapper, a prospector and a camp cook. He was also a bootlegger of moonshine. He was very rarely ever home. As a result, I did not have a male role model in my life. As a young man my dad was quite adaptable. In Edmonton, Alberta Canada, he wore the hat of a detective, a farmer and a short-lived career as a boxer. He came up north to escape a failed marriage and to make a new start. When he wasn't bootlegging, he made quite an honest living as a Camp-cook, Prospector and a Trapper. My father was away from home a lot, which left my mother Agnes, alone with nine children to raise single-handedly, poor woman. Looking back now, I can see how she really didn't have much of a chance to establish a strong defense, for what would later become her own personal battle with alcohol. She was raised in the bush most of her life and the year I was born in 1954, is when our family moved to Whitehorse. In Whitehorse she was no longer sheltered by the peace, the solitude and the healing qualities of the Yukon wilderness. She became exposed to the lure, the appeal, the easy access and the misery of alcohol. It was all too readily available and at her disposal.

My mother's maiden name was Jack. She was the second youngest daughter of Copper Jack (RIP). Copper Jack, my grandfather, was one of the five sons of Copper Chief, who came over from Copper Center, Alaska. My grandmother Jessie Jack, nee Tom Tom, (RIP) came from Ft. Selkirk, Yukon. My mother's family comes from the Snag/White River area in the Yukon and Copper Center, Alaska. In my earliest years, before I was taken to the residential school, we lived in a place called Sleepy Hollow in Whitehorse. Sleepy Hollow, (please don't ask me why they called it that, it was one of the rowdiest, loudest, drunkenest neighborhoods in town...who could sleep!) Sleepy Hollow was situated on what was then called the "outskirts" of Whitehorse along the banks of the Yukon River. Today, it would be located behind Boston Pizza towards the River bank. On the socio-economic ladder, Sleepy Hollow was in between the rungs of, not quite qualifying to be a Native Reservation and not quite qualifying to be a full-fledged part of taxpaying society, what we called the white man's world. It was a squatter's paradise and a ruffian's escape. It was no man's land. It was also home to a number of honest people, people who were hard-working, law-abiding, productive members of society raising their families as best they could. To say that most people in Sleepy Hollow liked their booze would be a gross understatement. The truth is a lot of them drank and drank **hard**! Most of us lived so far below the poverty line because of drinking, that even the mice in our houses took turns begging for food with tears in their eyes!

In those early years, there were many good people and families living in Sleepy Hollow. Some of these fine people have raised wonderful families, who are thriving today as lawyers, MLA's, Social Workers and the list goes on. There are many sons, daughters, nieces, nephews, in-laws, grandchildren and even great-grandchildren, who are descendants of this Sleepy Hollow generation. I'm guessing not many of these offspring are familiar with the humble beginnings, the sacrifice, nor the tremendous obstacles their fore-bearers had to overcome. They had to overcome more than the average person in order to ensure their offspring gained a better life than we had growing up there. I truly respect, love and admire each of these families and their descendants. Some mighty fine people came out of Sleepy Hollow. I know I have a lifetime bond with most of them

The people who lived in Sleepy Hollow were not rich or well-off by any-one's standards. On second thought, let me re-phrase that…we **were** rich! We were rich in our enthusiasm to survive and get out of there, and we **were** well off! Well off… on the road to poverty and alcoholism. At least *our* family was. This was due (not from a lack of effort on my father's part), but mainly to the ravages of alcoholism that haunted my mother.

Our home was a small house made partly of salvaged logs and partly of plywood and two-by-fours (pictures included). In essence, it was like any other typical Canadian half-breed home. It had the influence of two cultures, First Nation and European. To walk into our home, you would go through the only door in the house. If my mom was sober for more than three days your nostrils would probably be greeted by the lingering smell of fried moose meat, potatoes and onions. Your ears would catch the hissing of a full kettle of hot water on the old wood-fed cook stove. It would be nice and warm in the house. If you were to enter our house in the early morning you would catch the smell of Irish Spring soap in the air. There might be an old Hank Williams song playing softly on the radio.

To your immediate left, right beside the door, is a washstand with a wash-basin. The washbasin is usually half full with water that's been used. This water is used to wash your hands after going to the restroom. If you noticed it was quite dirty, you had to empty it and then refill it. If my mom or one of my sisters noticed that the water was particularly dirty, they would practically shout and ask in a mean voice, "Who washed their hands last and didn't change the water?" The basin is made of metal with a thick coat of white paint. On that white paint are brightly colored flowers painted on the inside. A few black spots catch your attention where the paint has chipped, peeled and fallen away. Beside the basin is an ordinary small diner's saucer. Inside the saucer is a tiny bar of old soap, dwarfed by a newer, larger Irish Spring bar. Nobody really wanted to throw any of the old soap away in case it might come in handy. On the wall above the washstand, is a square medium sized mirror. It has a cheaply designed wooden frame. The glass on the mirror is splattered near the bottom, with specks of dull white soap stains. A towel that appears somewhat dirty, hangs on a single nail beside the mirror. The towel despite its appearance is clean.

Were you to gaze around the 15 x 20 ft. house, you would notice on the north wall, a medium sized, brown wooden crucifix with Jesus hanging there. Blood is flowing from his hands and feet. It is near the ceiling. It appears the crucifix was not placed in a specific place. It was not placed in a carefully chosen spot, just placed on the first convenient nail that was high enough to keep it out of the reach of children. Below the crucifix is another mirror. There is a one and a half by one and a half foot window beside that mirror. The window is divided into four panes with the glass knocked out of the lower pane. A piece of cardboard held in place by a couple of tiny nails, covers the broken pane. A curtain to cover the window, hangs limply on a string strung between two nails. The once white curtain is heavily stained by the smoke that attacks it every time the wood stove is opened by someone adding more wood and the curtain's color is now more yellowish.

Behind the stove is a wood box full of dry split and small round spruce wood. Above that, are two nails about 2 feet apart with a thin string hung in between them, a poor man's dryer. On that string there were usually dish towels hung to dry. Sometimes there would be socks, insoles, mukluks or whatever else needed drying at the time. The floor has old linoleum that has seen better days. In high-use areas, such as by the washstand, around the stove and in front of the beds, the linoleum is worn clear through and exposes the plywood underneath. Against the east wall is a bunk bed. The bed is about five feet from the stove. The covers on the unmade bottom bed, indicate that someone simply threw them back, got out of bed, started the day, and never returned. There are two rooms shaped into squares with sheets of plywood for walls. The doors to these rooms are simply long curtains hanging between two nails.

Ours was a humble home to say the least, a typical northern poverty-stricken Canadian half-breed home. That is how my home looked when my mom was sober. When she was drinking, and brought others over to drink with her, the picture of our home would change dramatically. It would become a place of loud music (mostly Johnny Horton), loud lemon-gin induced laughter, feigned friendships and anger, my mother's anger that was usually directed at me and my sisters. After my mother started to feel the effects of the alcohol and would start to get quite inebriated, her anger at my dad would, without fail, show itself and was usually directed at me. She blamed him for making her feel so lonely. She blamed him for the jealousy she was feeling. She blamed him because she had to raise the kids alone. She literally blamed him for everything. And since I was the only male left in the household back then, I received the brunt of her anger. I had two older brothers, Paul (RIP) and Harold (RIP) whom we called "Buddy" and six sisters: Elsie (RIP), Eileen, Margaret (RIP), Elizabeth "Lizzy", to those of us who were closest to her and Kim and Frieda. Paul and Buddy left home as soon as they were able. I don't know what life at home was like for them. But I can certainly guess. Their childhood was before my time. I have a suspicion that it was not easy for them either. I'm the third youngest in the family and the youngest of the boys.

As a result of living with a mother who was very violent under the influence of alcohol, we lived a life of nervous tension. It was an emotional life of extremes. Extreme, because when she was sober, she could be extremely nice or extremely angry. And when she was drunk, she was **always** extremely angry and violent. This would keep us children in a state of uncertainty. The most vivid memories I have of my childhood at home, are ones of fear, violence and loneliness. However, there were also times of love and laughter, though very limited. My only regret is that those happy times were far too short, too few and too far in between. My father was away from home quite often. He was always, it seemed, out in the bush, cooking, prospecting or trapping. My mom basically raised us kids single-handedly.

Let my memory "paint" you a scene of a night in our house (when my mom would come home drunk). If mom did not come home right after bingo we knew **immediately**, without a doubt, without fail, that she was drinking. Once this was realized, it was routine for us, my sisters Liz, Margaret, Kim and myself to lay awake until she came home. We'd often drift in and out of sleep, trying our best to be awake when she got there, for fear of waking up with our hair being pulled, as we're dragged out of bed. One of the clearest memories I have of such nights and there were many, is laying there in bed, scared as could be as my mind raced and imagined the reality that was about to come. It was absolutely horrible and terrifying. There is nothing quite as traumatizing as knowing that a beating is coming your way and there is no escaping it. It is just a matter of waiting for it, all the while dreading the very thought of it. I'd be listening for the crunch of taxi cab tires on forty-below snow, which was a sure signal that she was home. We knew then, that it would only be a matter of minutes until one of us, or all of us, would be pulled from our warm beds and ordered to make her something to eat. It was for this reason that none of us wanted to be the one to sleep on the outside of the bed, away from the wall. For some strange reason, on these occasions when she came home drunk, I always hoped against hope that she would be in a good mood this time. And true to form, she never was.

I remember one night in particular when I had fought my best to stay away from being the one at the front of the bed and failed. Liz got the wall that night. I remember being very scared! As my sisters drifted in and out of a restless semi-sleep, I lay wide-awake listening for the crunch of taxi cab tires on frozen snow. I could not make my mind think of anything else because all circuits were overwhelmed by fear. When the taxi begrudgingly arrived, I braced myself as best I could for the ensuing scene I knew was going to come. . . being dragged from the bed (probably by my hair). She out-weighed me by at least 170 pounds. I was defenseless. I heard the car door slam shut and listened as the tires crunched the snow and the cab pulled away. Taking with it the cabdriver whom I felt was the only bit of safety available to me and the only one who could possibly help me at such a time.

I heard my mom's footsteps crunching snow under foot as she walked up the three steps to the front door. She opened the door and stepped in closing it. I heard the wheezing of her bronchial tubes as they fought to fill her lungs with air. She had chronic bronchitis. She paused, held her breath and listened to see if anyone was awake. I pictured her in my mind's eye, leaning on a chair for support as she gathered her bearings. Her extended sigh announced that she was satisfied she had made it home safely and all was well with the kids. It was as if she was talking to herself in a quiet way. Then there was the all-too-familiar "clink," as two bottles of alcohol rattled against each other, under the crinkling sound of a brown paper bag. I could hear her set the bottles in the bag on the table. She started to walk towards our bedroom. I turned my back to her, ducked under the covers and rolling myself into a tight ball. I braced myself. Her feet shuffled closer and her wheezing grew louder. She was right above me! Here it comes! I thought to myself. But no! Wait! Something different was taking place this night! Mom *wasn't* grabbing for the nearest person. In fact, she was reaching past me, as if for one specific person. That someone was Liz. She said, (and her voice was surprisingly gentle not as loud and mean as usual, but heavy with the smell of alcohol), "Lizzy! Where's Lizzy? That you Lizzy? Come here." Liz pretended she was just waking up and feigned shielding her sleepy eyes from the light. She climbed over me and went out to the kitchen with her. On this night, I didn't hear the usual loud orders being given, such as, "Make me something to eat." I didn't hear any slaps. And I didn't hear Liz crying and saying, "Don't mom!" In fact, it was uncommonly quiet. Not only was it quiet, it was quiet for what seemed like an eternity. What was going on? This raised my curiosity. And even though I knew there was a grave element of danger present, if I was to be caught, I just had to take a peek. I had to take the risk. I had to know what was going on, this was unusual! I slithered out of the warm blankets onto the floor in one fluid motion. I crouched down as low as I could go and laid on my belly at the bottom of the doorjamb. The floor was very cold. As I ever so slowly and carefully peered my eyeball around the corner, I witnessed a very strange scene. There was my mother, holding Liz tightly to her bosom, and sobbing heavily. She was crying silently, but so hard, that her whole heavy body was shaking. Shaking not only her and Liz but the table as well. They were deep gut-wrenching, silent sobs. And finally a high whine escaped that was meant to be held in, but no longer could be. That sound and that scene cut me deep to the marrow of my soul and burned itself into my memory. My mother was hurting something terrible. It had been a long time since I felt empathy for her, but right then and there, I felt deeply sad for my mom.

As my heart wrestled with what it was feeling, I could ever so plainly read the look on my sister Liz's face. It was like the whole scene before me was being played out in slow motion. Her look turned from surprise, to relief, to sadness and finally, gave way to tears. I watched as she cried big, silent tears that welled up and spilled out effortlessly appearing, as though out of nowhere, unstoppable tears that seemingly had a life all their own. They rolled silently and swiftly, like little rivers, down her face. Liz didn't look at me, but something inside seemed to tell me that she knew I was watching. Upon that realization, the exact same kind of tears began to flow from my eyes too. My mother was lonely and hurting. My sister was lonely, hurting and helpless to assist. And I too, was lonely, hurting and helpless to assist. I wanted to walk out and touch my mom. To lean my head on her arm and say, "It's going to be OK mom, please don't cry." But fear wouldn't allow me. Past experience reminded me that she could explode and change moods in a split second. I could only stifle my sobs, climb back into bed and wonder what was going to happen next. We did not acknowledge each other that night and never said anything about our feelings, but I knew deep down inside, that I would forever be connected to my mom and my sister Liz in way I would never be able to break for the rest of my life. It remains true to this very day.

My mother *was* an alcoholic. I don't think any of my family members would argue this fact. However, she was not the type of alcoholic who would drink for 1 or 2 weeks on end. She was what we would consider a "binge drinker." She would drink for 3-4 days in a row at the most, sober up for a time and then start again. However, the depth of anger and violence that we experienced and witnessed when she did drink, would take a long time for a heart to heal. In fact, it would affect me for life. I had severe separation anxiety from a very young age. An example of how severe that separation anxiety really was came to light on my very first day of grade school.

When mom left me at school for my first day of academia, I thought she was getting rid of me for good when I saw her walking away from the school. I honestly thought she wasn't coming back for me! I felt helpless, vulnerable and alone. Feelings that are all-too-familiar to me. Feelings I had come to deplore. That feeling of being left behind grew stronger and stronger the longer I sat in the strange surroundings of the classroom. I remember very clearly, that I could not hold my tears in. I had no control over the salty water that was running ever so swiftly from the dams of my eyes. I began to feel fear. Fear, like I had never felt it before. I could handle the beatings at home. I could handle fighting with my family members and neighbors. I could take running away from being beaten and sleeping by myself in an abandoned car. I could take a dare, almost any dare. I could fight almost any fight…but please, don't separate me from my mother and leave me alone! I'll do just about anything, but whatever you do, DON'T LEAVE ME ALONE! Don't leave me apart from my mother! Please! When the realization hit me that my mother had left me there, I felt warm liquid run down my pant leg. I pee'd my pants. I could not control it. This made me cry even harder. I was mad. I was scared. I was ashamed. And I felt trapped! The teacher took me out of the classroom and asked me what I wanted? I told her I wanted to go home. I told her I NEEDED to go home! In fact I didn't want her to think she had a choice of letting me go or not, and just to prove my point, I took off running as fast as I could! I ran most of the way home stopping only a few times to catch my breath and to glance back to see if anyone was coming after me.

I felt shame and fear as I approached our house. I also felt anger at my mom for playing such a trick on me. I already knew what I was going to say to her and I was angry enough to say it! I opened the door and the house was quiet. I could hear the kettle hissing on the stove, it was nice and warm in our home. I caught the smell of wood smoke as if the stove had just been loaded. One thing I noticed that struck me as being quite strange was…I couldn't hear the sound of the radio or any movement. I checked both bedrooms. No one. Fear started to grip my stomach, "Had she gone somewhere to drink with someone?" I thought to myself. I walked outside and just as I was rounding the corner of the house, I heard the loud screech of the outhouse door as it opened and my mom stepped out. The outhouse door screeched real loud again as it slammed shut behind her. She didn't see me right away until she was part way down the trail. She didn't appear mad when she spotted me. She looked more surprised than mad. "What you doing here? How come you're not in school?" She asked me in a surprisingly calm voice. I started to cry. "How come you left me there all alone?" I blurted out. She asked, genuinely concerned that they might have done something wrong to me. "They hit you? How come you're crying? What'd they do?" Her voice was becoming frantic. I sensed that she really cared about my welfare and that made me cry even more. In between sobs I was half-crying, half-shouting, "You left me there all alone! You didn't even tell me you were going! How come you took off on me!?"

It was if she knew then that I wasn't hurt *physically*. Upon that realization, she knelt down beside me, put her arms around me, drew my head into her bosom and said, "Azoowa, (this is Northern Tutchone for 'you poor thing'). I cried and I cried. Not so much because I was relieved, but because I was receiving REAL LOVE. Love that I had been starving for! Love that I had not felt for what seemed like an eternity. Love, from the one who's love mattered the most to me in the whole wide world. I wasn't about to let this moment slip by too quickly. I put my arms around her, actually they only reached part way around her, she was a big woman and I held on for dear life! Before too long, when I came back down to earth after relishing these short-lived moments of love, I remembered that I had pee'd my pants! One moment ago, I was hanging on for dear life. Now, I wanted to let go as fast as I could fearful that she would smell the pee and really give me a whipping! At that precise moment, I was hoping that the fresh unadulterated air, of this vast Yukon land, would be sufficient to stifle the smell of pee. Thankfully it was. Talk about a roller-coaster ride of emotions happening in a short period of time! I went from loneliness to anger, to relief to love, to hope to fear and to relief again, in a matter of minutes! I was thankful this roller-coaster ride ended on a good note today. It is a strange thing, but I found it very hard to be separated from my mom. Even as her drinking escalated and she beat me with any object that was within her reach. I still did not like to be away from her for *any* extended period of time. I longed to be back in her presence. Yet, as soon as I was back at her side, I could feel her anger rising towards me once she started to drink. I hated the alcohol. It stole my mom. I loved her and I loathed her. Such strange creatures we humans are. We love the ones we love and hate the ones we love with a hatred that is equal to match. I wanted to hug her and I also wanted to get mad at her for all the times she hurt me.

One day when I was seven years old in early November, the snow that was going to stay through the winter had just fallen and covered the ground. The river carried little patches of thin see-through ice it was very cold out. Today was one of the rare times when my older brother decided to come home and spend the night. He was quite drunk. I was relieved to see him come home because I knew then that I had some protection from mom because she was drinking today too. My brother would be able to protect us kids that is, if he didn't pass out before her. Well he didn't pass out and in fact what happened next made me sick to my stomach so much so that I wished he never came home! My mother was playing the record player and listening to "Your Cheating Heart" by Hank Williams when she decided to turn it up real loud. The music was blasting and my brother got mad. "Shut that   music down!" he had to shout to be heard over the music. Mom turned it a little louder. That incensed my brother and he let out a loud stream of profanities directed at my mom. He got up from the bed where he was sitting and staggered over to where she was sitting by the record player. He went to turn the record player down and she got to her feet and reached out to stop him. He quickly grabbed both her arms and pushed her out of the way and she fell to the floor! She fell backwards and landed on her butt. He then picked up the record-player and smashed it against the wall. He shouted at my mom, "I said to turn the   thing off!" and he walked back into the room he just came out of. I watched in horror! I could not believe what had just happened right before my eyes! My mother swore at him loud and continuously while Margaret and Lizzie struggled to get her to her feet. She stood up crying and swearing. Once she realized what had happened to her music, she swore at the top of her lungs and made her way to the door. She flung the door wide open and slowly started walking out into the cold afternoon air of early November. She had no coat on and we all scrambled to the window to see where she was going. My brother got up and closed the door. To our horror mom was walking slowly down towards the river!

I ran out quickly along with everybody else. I watched in desperation and terror as my mother made her way down into the water. She grabbed some willows that grew on the bank of the river to support her then she put her first foot into the freezing cold black swirling water. She felt around with her foot for a solid footing. The strong current quickly pushed small particles of paper-thin floating ice up against her lower leg as ice-cold water rushed up and over her ankle! She then took another step out farther into the swirling black water and she immediately sunk up to her waist, almost pulled under by the strong current of the mighty Yukon River! Only her grip on the healthy northern willows held her back from certain death! She was threatening to drown herself! She was mad and crying. She was being fuelled on by alcohol and deep anger, anger at my brother. "Mom don't!" we all shouted at the same time. Margaret was carrying Kim and Lizzie and I stood there crying and pleading with her as loud as we could as the tears started to blind my vision! "Don't mom! Pleeeease don't!" we cried in horror and fear. All we could do was stand there helplessly screaming and pleading with her. We were too small to help her. She looked back at all of us and said, "Tell him." (meaning my brother), "To get away I said!" I watched the water as it continued to rise past her hips and swirled around her waist as she fought to keep her balance. "Mom, STOP!" Margaret, Liz and I screamed in perfect unison again. I had never known or felt such complete SHEER TERROR! Panic gripped my throat. Fear was shaking my body. My knees went weak. I felt helpless, afraid yet somehow energized. Margaret, Liz, Kim and I all stood there out in the cold on the riverbank, crying and pleading with mom to, "Come back inside the house."

Just then, my brother came out of the house and spoke up. I wasn't sure who he was speaking to exactly, it seemed like he was speaking to all of us, and in particular, wanted my mom to hear. He said, "Ahh just leave her alone. She's not gonna do it. She's just faking it!" My seven year old brain and my freezing cold ears could not believe what they just heard! Those were the LAST words I needed to hear at that precise moment in time! Those were the exact words, my heart told me that would push my mother over the edge. I thought this was the last time I would see my mother! Panic once again shot through my system. My brother then turned around and started walking away leaving the yard, leaving the house and leaving all of us behind. I hated my brother right then more than any brother should. I swore deep in my heart that when I got older and big enough I was going to beat the living daylights out of him and make him feel some of the pain he was causing all of us! I then shot my gaze back to my mother. She was struggling to get back to the shore. The current was too strong for her! All she was holding onto was the tips of the willows and now they were slowly slipping from her grasp. Margaret, recognizing that mom was trying to get back to shore and that she was losing her grip on the willows, tossed Kim to the ground and quickly grabbed an old two by four that was laying on the ground! She ran down to the river's edge and extended the two by four to mom, "Grab this mom grab this! Here!" Mom was doing her best to hold onto the willows but it was useless as the current was too strong pulling her hand loose from the willows! And then somehow in her drunken state she managed to look over and saw the two by four Margaret was holding out to her. She grabbed it just in the nick of time as the willows slipped out her hand. Once she had a grip on the two by four piece of wood she was able to stabilize her footing. When she recognized that she was stable she took a step towards the shore. When she came out of the water her soaking wet dress had little clumps of thin broken ice that previously had been floating freely down the Yukon River, clinging to it. She starting walking back towards the house and it wasn't until I knew that she was safe that I felt the freezing cold air of the Yukon bite my ears at the exact same time I felt the warm caress of relief engulf my heart. Nothing in this world could possibly scare me as much as this incident did that just took place before my eyes! We all went back into the house and even though our lives were total messes back then the relief, the love and the appreciation we felt for each other that night was humongous! We did not have much in terms of material things or safety, but most importantly we still had each other and having each other was what mattered most of all that day. For a few treasured moments after the incident we experienced the peace that can only come after a near-death experience. That peace felt so good but I never want to pay the high price to experience it ever again.

CHAPTER THREE

STEAMING PANTS AND
POOR MAN'S HOCKEY

"WHO WILL...?"

Who will still the cry of a lonely child at night?
Who will show the love to take away his fright?
Who will feed the soul of a loved-starved little child?
Who will take away the fear when dreams are running wild?
Who will make him happy when all he feels is sad?
Who will reassure him that life is not so bad?
Who will take his hand when he's reaching out in pain?
Who will be there for him and make sure he's OK?

A. Nieman

Living so far north in the freezing cold Yukon our house by northern standards was cold. My dad didn't insulate under the house he just laid down the logs and built on top of them. His definition of insulation was to bank up the outside of the house with snow as soon as there was enough of the white stuff. As a result, in the dead of winter (with average temperatures of minus forty below lasting for three months straight without a break from December to February in those days), if nobody loaded the woodstove before going to bed just about everything in the house could easily freeze overnight. When this happened, when we woke up the next morning the water in the basin we used to wash our hands with would have a thick layer of ice on it! We had to put it on the stove to thaw out before we could wash up. We had no running water and in the middle of the night when it was too cold to go outside to the outhouse to relieve ourselves, we had to pee in a slop-bucket. Our slop-bucket was an old tin can, a ten gallon Chevron Oil bucket. Sometimes that froze too.

Well last night someone let the fire go out and needless to say everything froze. I awoke and blew my breath into the air to see if the fire went out last night and sure enough I could see my breath hanging like ice fog in the room after I exhaled. Under the covers of our ninety by ninety eider-down filled army issued sleeping bag, it was so warm and toasty that believe me you, nobody wanted to MOVE! Nobody wanted to make anything that resembled a move towards getting up and especially NOT ME because I had pee'd the bed! I knew that my wet pants would get very cold very fast once it was exposed to the freezing cold air. I am only six years old and I am both thankful and afraid that mom got up to start the fire this morning. Thankful, because I didn't have to start the fire in this cold and afraid because I did not want her to find out I had peed the bed. I can hear the odd clang of pots as my mom is tinkering around in the kitchen obviously getting breakfast ready for us. It is a school day and mom yells out our names one by one to make sure we are awake. Margaret, Liz and I each answer one by one to let her know we are awake.

Then mom asks me out loud point blank and everyone hears her, "Did you p—- the bed Andy?" I laid there as my mind raced to find an answer for this unexpected question. Why did she have to ASK this morning!? In an attempt to ward off any suspicion, I did my best to sound annoyed when I answered her question and said half-heartedly, "No." I had to say "No" even if the answer was supposed to be "Yes" because I hated feeling even the slightest bit of shame and would do anything to avoid it. Lying was never the right way but it came so naturally to me and it was always the easiest way out or so I thought, that I would never think twice about lying. I figured that if I was the first one to get out of bed, mom wouldn't suspect that I had pee'd the bed. Margaret and Liz learned a long time ago not to tell on me for peeing the bed because of the beatings they witnessed me receiving as a result. This morning is no different, I was sure they knew yet they said not a word. I did not pee the bed every night but on average probably once a week. When I finally muscled up enough courage to try and avoid getting caught with wet pants this morning I got out of bed. When I quickly slid my legs out of the nice warm sleeping bag and my socked feet hit the floor, the cold hit me immediately. Our room was icicle cold and the only heat was in the kitchen area close to the stove. I didn't even slip my shoes on but went right for my heating up spot close behind the piping hot stove. I moved as fast as I could so mom could not see the wet stain on the front of my pants. I stood there with my back as close to the stove as I could possibly get and let the heat wrap me in its warm arms as it gave me a great big "hug".

I noticed that mom had already "thawed out" and was busy doing other things and that she was not watching me so I turned around to warm the front of me. I stood there in heaven for about one minute feeling and absorbing the luxurious heat. Mom asked me again, "Did you p—- the bed?" This time I WAS ANNOYED at her asking and since she did not notice that I HAD peed the bed, I let it show in my tone of voice and said with anger louder than I should have, "No, I said!" "Then what's that coming from the front of your pants?" Her tone of voice told me she was not angry. I looked down and there was steam rising from the front of my pants and I became acutely aware of the strong odor the drying pee sent directly into my nostrils! Mom couldn't help it she burst out laughing and could barely talk but in between the laughter she managed to say, "Margaret, Lizzy look at Andy! Come here, look at your baby brother!" and she continued laughing. What a sight I must've been standing there in a cloud of steam trying to look innocent and serious as can be! This laughter caught me totally off guard! Margaret and Liz came out and took a sleepy look at me and once we all realized how funny the situation looked and that mom was not mad, all three of us burst into uncontrollable spontaneous laughter! I laughed as the steam would die down each time I turned away from the stove and would start up when I turned back! I did this a couple of times on purpose and we all killed ourselves laughing each time I turned towards the stove and the steam would start!

We all shared a few precious moments as spontaneous laughter filled our cold little home on a Yukon morning in mid-January, with new found warmth that touched our hearts! We laughed and laughed with laughter that we didn't want to let go because such a good laugh was a rarity. Once we gained our composure, mom went into her room and pulled out a pair of my pants she had finished sewing and gave them to me. The down side to all of this was, since we had no shower in our home, mom heated up the wash basin on the stove and then told me to go into our room (our cold room) and wash the pee off before I put my clean pants on. It was a morning and a lesson I never forgot. The lesson was simple, don't stand too close to the stove when you peed the bed.

Few things brought me real pleasure in life back then. Hockey was one of them. Playing hockey put me on another planet. It took me to another world. It was an escape for me. I didn't realize it at the time but hockey was actually very therapeutic for me. We were too poor to afford skates. The only skates I had to use were my sister Margaret's white girl's skates. Although they were just a regular white color, I was self-conscience when I put them on and it seemed like they became extremely bright white the second I put them on my feet! That is, until I got on the ice. Once I was on the ice, in my imagination, the lights of Madison Square Garden came on and they never shone brighter than they did at that moment! We loved to play hockey, my cousin Joe, Stanley and I. But hockey players need equipment and I couldn't afford any. Most of the people who played with us didn't have equipment either. So we had to become what being a true Canadian really means: playing bush-league hockey on a frozen pond, with rolled up newspapers, catalogues or whatever we could tie around our shins for protection. I probably looked like a real hockey player from all the bruises I received at home. I must've been quite a sight. If you can imagine, an eight-year old boy flying down the ice, stick-handling the puck (a small rock), with bright white girl's skates flashing in the powerful northern sunlight, a battle-scarred face, showing the biggest toothless smile this side of Vancouver and a thin stream of green mucous appearing and disappearing in and out of a cold, red nose as he bears down on the goalie. He deeks to the left, then to the right, back to the left and casually slides the puck in the net on his backhand. The crowd in Madison Square Gardens goes absolutely wild! The stuff only dreams are made of. My family members never ever came to scrimmage with us. If my sister Lizzie happened to stop by with one of her girlfriends, that was a real bonus. I had someone to show off to then. Most times though, it was just us rag-tag NHL wanna-bes, out there in the freezing cold being whatever NHL player we wanted to be. Nobody seemed to notice our lack of equipment thank God, we just wanted to play hockey.

Another event that brought us happiness and excitement back then is when our dad would come out of the bush from one of his cooking jobs and the company he worked for let him keep the leftover food. It was a very special event when our dad came out of the bush with boxes and boxes of groceries. A strange truck would pull up in front of our house and as we all watched wondering who this could possibly be, I was always afraid it was going to be someone who would start my mom drinking. When we saw it was our dad we all ran as fast as we could to be the first one to reach him! Dad was all business and got us to pack groceries never mind the hugs until later. There were about ten boxes! There was all kinds of canned goods. There was canned Klik, canned peaches, canned pears, strawberries, canned ham, sardines, corned beef, Red Robin baking flour, baking powder, sugar, Aunt Jemima pancake mix and syrup, boxes of salt, tins of strawberry jam, jars of peanut butter and the list goes on! Once we got everything packed away, mom would usually start cooking something and we would gather around dad and he would give each of some money. He'd put an unfiltered Export cigarette into the corner of his mouth and then he'd grab the box of matches. He'd take out a match and hand it to me to light his cigarette for him. It was one of those strike anywhere matches and I would use the zipper on my fly to light it. It made me feel special when he did that.

When my mother was sober, she could be so very loving and often was. She could also be very temperamental and often was. All of us kids liked her best though, when she was "hung-over." We liked her best then, because when she was in that state, she would be oh so kind to all of us and would let us have just about anything we wanted. In fact she would let us have *anything* we asked for, that is if she had it to give to us. Whenever I ran away from home for about three or four days in a row, I would do my best to coordinate my return home to coincide with a day I knew she would be hung-over. I admit, my actions did become quite sly and cowardly at times, but that's OK. When you have an inebriated mother who tips the scales at close to two hundred pounds and you're just a skinny little runt, - and you know a beating is in the wind - one learns sly and cowardly ways mighty quick! The longer my mother drank, the more the violence escalated. The violence did not have a starting point in my life. It was always there. Like an unavoidable bully who had a knack for showing up at the precise times you didn't want him to.

The violence at home made me feel isolated, violated, scared, lonely and resentful. I was resentful at my mom, then my family and eventually the world in general. I felt powerless. The only way and the only time I could be free and feel like I had some sense of peace and quiet, was when I ran away from home. So I ran away and I ran away a lot! I mean for days on end. Never just for one night, but two or three in a row. That is if I didn't get caught sooner. From the time I was five years old I started running away. Usually when I was home alone with mom and she wanted to go to the bar to drink, she'd take me up town with her. First, she would stop at Jamieson's Store and buy me a sucker. Then she'd sit me down outside the Whitehorse Inn bowling alley steps, which was right beside the entrance to the main hotel, the Whitehorse Inn. I guess she wanted to make it look like I was waiting for someone in the hotel and not the bar. She would then go and drink in the Whitehorse Inn Tavern. I had to wait there until she came out. Every time I waited for her outside that bar I got hungry. I had to scrounge for food. It was at the early age of five, and driven by hunger, that I began to look into vehicles parked outside the bar. I discovered another world where all kinds of surprises could be found. I started to steal from cars then and many times I found food in the vehicles. People would go shopping and then stop at the bar for a drink on their way home. Nobody, absolutely nobody locked their car doors in those days. Some days were great sitting outside the Whitehorse Inn or the Regina Hotel waiting for my mom because a lot of people from Sleepy Hollow went to drink at the bar. They would recognize me and stop to give me a penny, a nickel, a dime and if I got a quarter that was like hitting the jackpot! Back then everything was cheap. You could get 3 gum or 3 jawbreakers for one penny! Sometimes my sister Liz waited with me outside the Whitehorse Inn. I am still amazed to this day how the welfare did not catch us or our mother as we sat outside the bars.

I learned to survive from a very early age out of sheer necessity. I remember one night in particular sleeping in a ninety by ninety feather downed sleeping bag when it was forty below outside, in Johnny Tom Tom's abandoned car that sat in front of our house. Forty below weather is just too cold for any five year old boy to be sleeping in, even if you have a thick eider down-filled sleeping bag. When my mom was drunk and violent towards me if I could get away I would grab my boots and coat and sneak out the door and go sleep out in that car. I felt sorry for my sisters Margaret and Liz, I had no doubt my mom would turn on them with her anger since I was not there. My Sister Margaret would brave the cold to come out and check on me and would try to coax me to, "Come back in the house." I would not. I stayed awake most of that night and kept an ear open for my mom to pass out. She did not pass out until about 3 am. Margaret then came out into the freezing cold and called me into the house. It was like heaven to feel the heat once I got inside the house. Looking back, I sincerely believe running away helped me to maintain my sanity. Even though I knew I would get a beating upon my return home, the days free from violence and verbal abuse, made it all worthwhile. Running away from home became habitual, very habitual. Most of the time when I ran away from home and needed a place to stay, I would ask a friend to ask their mom if I could stay over because I was too scared to go home since my mom was drinking. That line worked so well

I even used it when my mom wasn't drinking, just so I could stay at a friend's place, or if I felt it was too cold to walk home. Often, my mom would send one of my poor sisters to various homes to check if I was there and bring me home, sometimes, even when the temperature was as low as minus forty below. It wasn't easy for them either.

Every time I ran away and I mean every time, I found one way or another to steal money. The serious stealing began when I was around six and seven years of age. I need to emphasize the deeply ingrained nature to steal that was so inherent in me. Most of you reading this, can probably remember quite easily, the very first time you ever stole something. Either you got caught or you didn't. If you were caught, you probably received a spanking and didn't return to stealing. The difference between you and I is this, I was stealing from such an early age I can't *even remember when I first started*! I truly believe that I must've been born with a thieving spirit that had latched itself onto me, long before I can remember. It became my second nature second only to the need for food, clothing, and shelter. I felt so trapped at home and so powerless with all the violence directed at me, that when I ran away, I entered a whole new world. It was an exciting world! It was a world where *I* could call the shots. This is when that thieving spirit that was in me came to life and was most active. By the age of seven, I became very fluent at lying and manipulating. Through my lying, I learned I could match wits and exercise a certain amount of control even over adults. And also in my lying, I found that I had a certain degree of power. Something I didn't have at home. On every one of my run away excursions, I felt free. The more I ran, the freer I became. It was like breathing new-found fresh air! I didn't have to answer to anyone. When I was free from the beatings and on the run, it energized me! My senses came alive. I was alert. I was "on point" for any opportunity and watched for any sign of carelessness that would present me with an opportunity to make some fast money or get some food. Alcohol had such a grip on my mother that the whole paycheck my dad sent her went to booze. We (children) were left without groceries so many times it was nothing new to us. Liz and I were left home alone one time for about three days. There was not a stitch of food in the house when mom left the house to go drinking. We thought she was going shopping. Liz and I got happy and started acting crazy as we played and teased with each other. We were looking forward to finally getting some good food in our stomachs. We were tired of bannock and watery moose-bone soup that had no meat in it. When mom didn't come home that first night we laid in bed fearful that she would return home drunk. We were also too hungry to sleep. On the second day, we had cleaned out every last bit of jam and peanut butter that was in the house. There was nothing left to eat. The only thing left in the cupboards was salt, sugar, some spices and a box of uncooked Quaker rolled oats. The rolled oats were high up on the top shelf and I had a difficult time reaching them. Liz helped me to balance as I put a chair on the table to stand on. As I strained to reach for the box I couldn't help but notice the man's picture on the outside of the box. It was a picture of a Quaker man who had long white hair with a hat on and he looked so healthy. I wished I was that man. At least he wasn't hungry! I finally grabbed the box of rolled oats and took it down. It was half full. We did not know how to cook and we were so hungry we didn't care about cooking! We dug right in like two ravished wolves and starting eating. It was extremely dry. But when you left it in your mouth long enough it started to form into something you could actually chew! (Try it sometime. Lol).

Liz and I eventually hit the jackpot in food when we learned to scrounge for food behind the Tourist Services Supermarket. There was a great big covered wooden box crate that had wheels on it parked behind the store. It was the supermarket's garbage bin. The store would throw out the fruit that was too bruised to sell or eggs that had a crack or meat that started to smell. On our first trip there, we climbed right into the bin so nobody could see us. Liz and I were like totally amazed that they would throw away such good food! I picked up an apple and showed it to Liz and with total amazement in my voice said, "Look at this! There was not even anything the matter with this! It just has this little rotten spot on it!" "Boy, how crazy," Liz said nonchalantly. We were both very excited! At least I was! Liz was more concerned about being seen in there than anything else. I was excited about all the food we had discovered! This was our jackpot! When winter came we still ate from the bin frozen food or not. I actually liked frozen apples and frozen pears.

CHAPTER FOUR

MY RICH UNCLE

"Dimmer and Dimmer"

I was raised on boot-leg liquor,
Didn't work when the hand was quicker,
Lived in Sleepy Hollow now that was a picture!
Had a mom it was hard to trick her,
She made me pick a willow for a switcher,
Went to Res. School became a sinner,
Got hooked on heroin grew thinner and thinner,
Skid row made me sicker and sicker,
At the end of the tunnel I saw a flicker,
When I obeyed the Bible, Jesus made me a winner,
On my cell phone I have a Gospel ringer,
When I feel God's love, my heart is a singer,
And I am really just a beginner,
Growing in God's love that eternal glimmer,
Someday I'll sit down at the Lord's great dinner,
Watch all my worries grow dimmer and dimmer,

A. Nieman

Money was somewhat of an obsession for me as I had learned that money gave me power. It gave me more respect than I could ever receive at home and it gave me more freedom. It got to the point where I no longer cared about the risk of getting caught, I HAD TO HAVE MONEY! I learned also that money made everyone want to be close to me. They wanted to be my friend. And if anyone ever needed friends, this little, love-starved, lonely boy sure did! I came to view money as something that came to me fast and as something that

I had to get rid of just as fast, in order to get rid of the evidence. To my seven-year old mind, I felt that if I bought things right away with the money I stole, this allowed me to get rid of the evidence and when the police checked me for that money they wouldn't find any. Therefore, it would be hard for them to prove anything. I got very good at breaking into houses and stealing. And since Whitehorse was so small back then it was only natural that I would become a prime suspect because I was hardly and I mean *hardly* ever in school. When the police did pick me up, I would sit there in the back of the police car, with all kinds of candies stuffed into the pockets of brand new clothes chewing a wad of gum big enough to choke a baby elephant.

I remember one particular time when I was nine years old and one of the more creative stories I came up with to justify the "new" clothes, was that "My rich Uncle Joe, who worked on the railroad tracks at Lake Bennett, (which he really did), came to town and bought me the clothes and the candy. He's on his way back to Lake Bennett so you can't talk to him right now. But I could let him know to call you the next time he comes to town!"

I don't believe the police ever thought a nine year old could be so fluent or creative in lying, because that story worked more times than I ever dreamed it would. That is, until Constable Falkingham came to town. The third time I tried to use that line on him, he had picked me up for a B&E (break and enter), and as I jumped into the back of the cruiser (careful not to scuff my brand new Beatle boots), before I could relay my story to him he said, "And which rich uncle did you run into today, Andy?" He thought he had me. However I merely switched stories on the spot and told him that two of the George boys older than I, from the village, had forced me to go into this building. And they had told me where the money was. He asked me their names and I said I didn't know their names but I knew what they looked like. I knew that Mr. Falkingham was somewhat new in town and hoped he didn't know the George boys too well yet. As it turned out he didn't. He asked if I knew where they lived and if I would take him there to show him who the two brothers were? With an eager voice that was almost a little too enthusiastic, I piped up, "Sure!" We drove down to the old village and actually went right to the George family's house! I was desperate. After all, I had just purchased the last pair of Beatle boots in my size that existed in Whitehorse (with the money that Mr. Falkingham was now trying so hard to find) and I wasn't about to part with the Beatle boots or the money that easily, Constable Falkingham or no Constable Falkingham!

After Mr. Falkingham explained why we were there, we walked through the house and luckily none of the boys were home. Just the parents were there. We then proceeded to drive around town as I assured Mr. Falkingham with all my heart (my lying heart that is), that I would certainly point the boys out to him. After all, I didn't want them to force me into *any other kind* of criminal activity now did I! And just wait until I tell my big brother Paul about them!" I was saying this all out loud to Mr. Falkingham trying to draw suspicion away from me. Later, back at the police station, I almost cried as I was taking off the only sacred pair of Beatle boots left in Whitehorse and probably in the world, or so I felt, that would fit me. Mr. Falkingham knew that I was guilty of doing the B&E but he didn't have any proof and as a result, he certainly wasn't going to let me keep those nice shiny boots. I was telling Mr. Falkingham that, "It just wasn't fair for me to have to give the boots back, because I had already worn them and the store would be in the wrong to try to sell shoes once they were worn wouldn't they?" And guess what? As it all turned out in the end, my dad wound up paying for the boots and I got to keep them! I got such a severe beating from my mom for it (after all I was cutting into her bingo money). I wore holes the size of silver dollars clear through the bottom front soles of those old Beatle boots. And the heels became so worn down at the very back they started to look like high-heeled shoes! I believe I even slept with them under my pillow one or two nights, just to make sure nobody stole them.

I learned to roll people (take their money) when they passed out at our home after a drinking party. You didn't have to be a detective to know the feel and the crinkle of a dollar bill in the jeans pocket of a snoring, passed out drunk. One day, one of my brother Paul's friends was passed out at our place. Maddy and I decided to roll him. Maddy was Gary's younger brother. Maddy had an amazing sense of humor. He could find the humor in simple things. His personality was such that he could burst into laughter even under the most extreme dire and dangerous situations such as when you are sitting in the Principal's office and you KNOW you are going to receive a strapping. Maddy could still make me laugh even in a situation like that! Maddy was also not afraid to fight anybody even if they were two sizes bigger than him. I told Maddy to watch the door and to let me know if anyone was coming. I called the man's name and shook him. No response. I shook him harder, still no response. I knew he would not wake up so I proceeded to feel around his pockets. All my senses were at peak performance as I was feeling and listening for the crinkle of money. The man was passed out on his stomach and when I felt around to see if he had any money, I felt a few crinkles in his front pockets which meant he had money. My heart started to pound faster as I got excited at the anticipation of finding out how much was there. As I start to squeeze my fingers underneath his belly to get at the bills, he let out a great big fart! It was so loud it scared both me and Maddy! We bolted out the door like two scared rabbits and ran around to the side of the house. Once we realized we were OK and he was not getting up, we busted out laughing. It was so funny! We decided to finish the job and as soon as we entered the house we smelled it! It was gross. "Whew! What was he eating rotten eggs?!" Maddy said pinching his nose. "Watch the door!" I said as I did my best to keep from cracking up laughing! I forced myself past the smell, found the crinkle and pulled out two twenty dollar bills, "Got it!" I said as I let the air I was holding in out of my lungs. We took off running and as we were running I said, "Here," and gave Maddy one of the twenties. We had many a laugh over that incident for many, many years after.

Things did not get any better at home. Although, I really had some good times with my mom and my family in the early years, they were always short-lived. I know mom loved me dearly it was just that she had a problem with the booze. I have memories of playing "Red Rover" on the pond with other neighborhood kids. And after coming home from the pond dead-tired, she would have potato pancakes warming on the stove, along with bannock and hot rabbit soup, chock-full of vegetables. When our family would all be together and mom was sober, (of course dad was out on the trap-line most of the winter), we would tease each other and make each other laugh. We didn't have a TV so we had to use our imagination to entertain ourselves. I would usually be the "clown", who attempted to make everybody laugh and succeeded! I liked to act as silly as possible and would do just about anything to get a laugh. I loved to get the attention. There was nothing more pleasing to me back then than to make my mom laugh. And I wasn't able to just make her laugh, she would in fact, laugh *real hard* at my joking around. Those were some of the happiest times I ever had at home. What baffled my young mind and what I could never fully understand, was how she could shower me with so much love when she was sober and then hate me with so much hatred when she was drunk. I didn't ever really want to believe she hated me, I just believed it had to be that rotten alcohol that made her that way. One time when she came home drinking, she called me over in a gentle voice and it was just that very afternoon that she had kissed me and given me such a warm hug. I did not realize she was drinking because I was so excited that she was home. I was expecting another warm hug so I walked as quickly as I could up to her, glad that she was still in a good mood I stretched out my arms to give her a hug. Then out of nowhere I got a hard stinging slap! My ears started ringing immediately and they rang very loud as I staggered in mid-step, falling to the floor! All I could hear in that ear was a piercing loud ringing. I burst into tears. I was shocked, dazed, and confused! I scampered on all fours trying to get away from her as fast as I could! "You get to bed right now, you rotten no good for nothing!" She yelled. I couldn't believe what I was hearing! She was too drunk to catch me as I scurried just out of her reach! I couldn't believe what was happening! How could I be so stupid to not see she was drinking!? I couldn't believe what had just taken place! What is going on here!? My mind was scrambling trying to make sense of what I had done wrong! I had a hard time seeing through my tears as I half-walked, half ran to the room. I was crying so hard I almost lost my breath! The ringing in my ear was still loud. I ran into the room in total shock. I was so scared. I was overwhelmed by the hurt and anger I felt. I was hoping she wouldn't come in after me. I wanted to hit her! Thankfully, she did not follow me into the room.

I would have run away right then and there, but it was extremely cold outside. I could tell it had to be at least forty below. The broken pane in our bedroom window was completely frozen over covered in ice and frost that was at least one inch thick. A dark cloud invaded my heart then, as I realized I was once again alone and trapped. I felt like nothing good was ever going to happen in my home or in my life. It seemed like nothing was ever going to change. Just when things were starting to feel better at home, it all came crashing down in an instant! Margaret and Liz were in the kitchen area with her now no doubt scared and wondering if I was alright. I knew they wanted to come to me to help me but they couldn't. They might wind up feeling her wrath as well.

As I listened to see if she would follow after me, I heard her put on a Johnny Horton record. I could hear, but didn't appreciate, the words to, "Whispering Pines." I laid down on the bed and buried my face in the pillow. I was wondering if there really was such a thing as true happiness in the world? Did it actually exist? All I knew in the reality of my short life was pain, fear, disappointment and despair. Why did it always come down to my mom hurting me? The end result when I came home and mom was drinking was always the same and without fail, she would wind up hurting me again and again. The only escape would came after she passed out but by that time the damage on me had been done. I was so exhausted now from all the crying. I was cried out. I just couldn't stay awake to watch for her anymore. I drifted off to sleep, vowing to never ever play a Johnny Horton record as long as I lived. And I never have.

Summer nights in the Yukon are not really all that warm, yet not too cold that one couldn't sleep outside with a thin blanket. It was nearing the middle of June as school was about to get out. I awoke in the old car in front of our house. Remembering the events of last night and how I had managed to run out the front door before my inebriated mother noticed I was home. I came awake to the cheerful sounds of Robins singing. There were no loud sounds coming from the house so I assumed it was safe to go in and opening the door ever so cautiously I caught the smell of fried bacon. My sister Margaret was making breakfast. She looked up from the frying pan and said, "Oh there you are. Better hurry up and get ready for school. Where were you over at the Dawson's again?" "No." I answered. "I'll put your breakfast on the table when it's done. Hurry up, wash up and get your school clothes on." Little did she know and I didn't want her to notice (which she usually did) was that I was wearing and had in fact slept in my school clothes! I hurried into the bedroom thankful that she was cooking and therefore didn't notice my clothes. She usually did most of the laundry with Lizzy's help the old-fashioned way with our old white ringer washer. One would wash, they'd both use the ringer and one would hang the clothes on the line while the other tackled a new pile. Margaret always seemed to pay much too close attention (for my liking), to my wardrobe, just to make sure I stayed as clean as possible. Not only because she had to do the laundry, but because she genuinely loved and cared for me. Margaret was always very, very special to me. She treated me with such love and kindness. It was as if she acknowledged the suffering she witnessed me going through, by giving me a little extra care. All of us children suffered because of our mom's alcoholism. But as I previously mentioned, my mother's anger seemed to be directed more towards me, probably because I reminded her of my father. I don't know. Margaret was four years older than I and two years older than Liz. Margaret had the soul of a caretaker. She was the type that liked school and was smart enough to not have any problems with the schoolwork and always did her homework. Liz had no problem with the schoolwork either. In fact other classmates would ask either Margaret or Liz to help them when they couldn't figure out a problem.

In our family when we got mad at each other, we had "bad" nicknames we would call each other because we knew that *for sure* it would get that person mad. We called Margaret "Big Bill," that was the name we called her when we wanted to get her mad. We named her that after this cop named Bill who had a larger than normal forehead. Margaret used to have her hair combed and pulled straight back exposing her forehead and she would tie it in a ponytail. If you called her "Big Bill" those were immediate fighting words! If I called her that I would risk being wrestled to the ground and sat on. I learned to not get Margaret mad because if I did, she would always get even with me. Her favorite trick to get even with me was to call me over to her and she would grab me and hold me and then let out a fart. I was too small to get away and she would burst out laughing then say, "Well, teach you to get smart with me, remember when you called me "Big Bill?" And when she said, "Big Bill" I couldn't help but laugh. If I called Maragret that name and mom was around I knew I could get away with it, Margaret would then give me that "Nieman look" that silently said, "I'm going to get even with you later just you wait!" It was a stare that could melt icicles! My sister Liz and I were even closer. Liz and I spent most of our lives together as kids. Of all the girls she was my best friend.

Back in those days as a small child I came to know fear in such a way that it would almost make me physically sick. It was only when I ran away from home that I could alleviate the sick feeling. I dreaded going home because a beating was inevitable. There are too many incidents of violence for me to recall all of them. I am only recording a few so that you the reader will be able to get an accurate sense of the violence that I had to endure from as far back as I can remember. One Monday evening Liz came over to Art Dawson's (RIP) place to see if I was there and to bring me home. The Dawson family had just finished supper and May Dawson (RIP) made sure that Gary brought me a bowl of stew and bannock. Art and May Dawson have probably saved my life and kept me from freezing more times than I can remember. They were two of the most beautiful people I've ever known! At that time I had run away from home for three nights and I slept up in the attic at the Dawson's house. When Liz came to get me, I heard a, knock, knock, knock on the door. Every time I heard a knock on the door when I was running away and staying at the Dawson's fear would grip my heart. I feared that it would be either my mom or one of my sisters come to get me. When the knock came Art shouted out in his big booming voice, "Come in!" The door opened and I heard Liz say in her shy voice, "Is Andy here?" I immediately scurried under the bed. "Ask those kids," Art said then he shouted, "Gary! Is Andy still here?" I think it was the "still here" that gave me away because Liz didn't wait for Gary to reply she just walked right into the room and looked under the bed. I was caught. "Mom said you have to come home right now Andy." I slowly clambered out from under the bed with my head hung down in utter humility and embarrassment. As I walked out I didn't look anybody in the eye and Gary said, "See ya' Nieman," and Maddy did the same, "See you at school Andy." Liz and I stepped out into the black night of a cold Yukon winter and started walking in a brisk pace wanting to keep a step ahead of the cold. As we walked, the fear that arose when I first recognized Lizzy's voice from under the bed began to grow worse. I tried to stem the fear by making idle conversation, "Is mom sober?" "You'll see," Liz was mad at me for two reasons, the first reason is because it was about thirty five below out and she did not appreciate having to come look for me in such cold weather and second, she knew I was going to get a terrible beating when I got home and when I got a beating it hurt her as well. "Is she mad?" I asked. I knew it was a dumb question as soon as it left my mouth. I had to ask a question, any question dumb or not in order to keep the fear from overwhelming me. "What do you think Andy?" Liz shot back obviously irritated by the sheer stupidity of the question. The sound of our boots crunching the snow in thirty five below weather was very loud and it seemed to get louder from the silence that was created as my mind struggled to find another question. "Is she sober?" "Yeah." "When did she sober up?" "Two days ago." *That*, was *not* what I wanted to hear. I was hoping against hope that she would be hung-over so I could avoid a licking. Liz continued, "Boy, you missed a good supper last night." I didn't care about what I missed, I was only concerned that mom was not hung-over this meant there was trouble just ahead. As we entered the house, the cold outside air meeting the hot inside air of the warm house instantly turned into a cloud of fog and rushed along the floor. I closed the door and my eyes quickly scanned the room. As soon as my mom seen that I was coming in behind Liz she asked, "Where was he?" "At the Dawson's," Liz said it in a way that showed she was irritated that mom had to ask her a question that she already knew the answer to. As I was about to remove my boots I noticed mom's hand reach into the wood box and she grabbed a piece of split wood and started to walk towards me. Our house is so small that she was on me almost immediately. I tried to make a dash into the room to get under the heavy blanket for at least *some* protection but my frozen boots slipped on the linoleum floor and I fell. "How come you never come home you rotten thing!" she yelled at me. She picked me up by the back of my parka like I was a rag doll and she started swinging immediately! She hit me anywhere she could as she held me with one hand! I could feel the pain shoot right through me as she hit me on the back of my legs, my butt, the side of my knees, my elbow and on the bone just above my butt. "You think you're the boss huh? You think you don't have to tell anybody where you are?" she yelled at me as she hit me as hard and as fast as she could. She never once hit me on the head it was like she made sure of that. It seemed like she was aware that she could not hit me on the head and to make up for it, she hit me extra hard on every other part of my body. And although it felt like an eternity it all happened in a matter of seconds and was over real quick. She then threw me on the bed, "You stay there too! I don't want to see you out here! That's all you're good for, to steal and lie and run away!" She turned the light out and went into the kitchen. I hurt all over and just lay there crying. I did not want to move or even try to move it hurt too much. I also knew that I better not move because it might cause her to come back in. After a half hour or so my breathing started to return to normal from all the crying and I pulled up my pant leg to see why my leg was hurting so much. The bruise on the back of my leg was gigantic! My whole calf muscle was purple and my ankle was swelled to twice its size. I did not notice it at the time she hit me because of my boot, but she had hit my ankle and it hurt with every little movement. I heard my mom in the other room tell Liz, "Give him some of that meat and rice." Food was the last thing I wanted right now. I needed some relief from the pain and from the constant fear of knowing that she might return at any time and hit me some more and I was totally defenseless. I wanted to run but with my ankle the way it was, there was no chance. Liz came in and asked in a genuine concerned voice, "Are you OK Andy? Andy? Are you OK?" I looked at her with eyes that were puffy from crying and she didn't want to look at me but when our eyes met, I seen that tears were starting to form in her eyes. She put the moose meat in gravy and rice on a stool by the bed and walked out. It was like Liz did not want *anybody* to see her cry or to know she was crying. In my heart I knew Liz was feeling sad for me. Luckily none of my bones were broken. I still hobbled to school even though it hurt terribly. That was better than feeling trapped at home. Even when mom was sober and at home, it was hard to relax completely, there was always the fear that one of her friends would pop by at any time and get her started drinking. If that happened, that was usually when I ran away.

I caught scabies somewhere when I was seven years old and I was sent home from school with a note. My mom was supposed to pick up some medicine for the scabies but she started drinking and never got around to it. The itch from the scabies got so bad that I scratched and scratched until my legs started to bleed. Sores developed from all the scratching and they would scab over. During the night I would scratch the scabs off and my long johns would stick to the sores. The itching was so persistent that I would pull the long johns free from the scab while scratching and then I'd twist the long johns so it would not stick back on the same spot. Twisting my long johns caused new sores to form and my legs became covered with sores and scabs all around the lower parts of my legs and the tops of my feet. I would wrap a cloth bandage around the sores and it itched so much that I would scratch right through the bandage. The scratching caused more bleeding and sometimes pus would seep through the cloth bandage. I soon learned not to put so much wrapping over the sores in order to be able to scratch them when they itched. I could not play any sports and I had to walk really slowly so I would not tear the bandage off. It was pure misery. I ran away from home so much that I never got the scabies attended to properly. I don't remember any of my sisters catching it. The itchiness was so bad that after I had a good scratch (it always felt so good when I scratched the itchy spots), the blood and pus would start seeping through the bandage and I would just leave it to dry. It started to stink after a while and one time my sister Margaret asked, "What is that rotten smell? It smells like something died! Is that you Andy?" she put her nose close to me and sniffed up and down, "It *is you*! What is that? Did you your pants?" She asked. Liz came over to investigate what all the commotion was about, "What?" Liz asked with real interest as her curiosity was aroused and she peeked her head in between us. Margaret replied, "That smell can't you smell it?" She said in a tone that made it sound like the smell was the most obvious thing on the planet! You knew Margaret was going to get to the bottom of it no matter what and find out what the smell was so she could fix it! I answered her question, "No I did not   my pants!" Margaret kept sniffing around me and sure enough she knew it was coming from my legs.

"It's coming from down there," she said pointing to my legs as she straightened up. "What's that from Andy? Let me see your leg." "It's nothing," I tried to lie. "It's just my feet I haven't changed my socks in a while that's all!" I wanted to quickly walk away but couldn't it was too painful. "Let me see your leg Andy, come here," Margaret meant business and I knew it was useless to try to hide it anymore. She continued, "Don't make me force you, . ." as her sentence hung in the air she had a warning in her voice that could not be denied. "Let me see," she ordered. I said angrily, "Man why don't you mind your own business?" I got mad because I knew I had no choice but to show her. I sat down on the bed and made sure my pants weren't stuck to the bandage before I pulled it up. I slowly raised my pant leg and looked at the fresh pus that had leaked out through the bandage. It was evident what was causing the awful telltale smell. "Ewww," Liz said grabbing her nose. Margaret was more curious than alarmed or shocked, "What in the world happened, did you cut yourself?" I pulled up the other pant leg and Margaret let out a small gasp. Liz said, "Eww that stinks! Does it hurt?" I felt suddenly brave and shook my head, "No." Margaret said, "We gotta' get those bandages off. I'll get some water. Stay there Andy don't move!" Margaret was a nurse that night and even though she wet the bandages down with warm water as much as they could be wetted down, it hurt like a hot branding iron taking the bandages off those scabs. I still have the scars to this day from my prolonged bout with scabies.

Back then, whenever I would run away and get some money I practically lived on candy. It was all I ate! As a result it rotted my teeth. I got such terrible toothaches and the pain was so great it felt like my head was going to explode! We had no aspirin and only God knows how many times I cried all night and could not sleep because of the pain. Many, many, times the whole side of my face would swell up from an abscess. I've had toothaches where more than one tooth would be hurting and it hurt so bad I would cry day and night continuously. The infection in my gums was so severe that with every throb from my heartbeat I felt pain. It was too cold out to go anywhere and we had no aspirin in the house so there was no way to relieve the pain and I would cry until I had no more energy to stay awake.

CHAPTER FIVE

BREAKING AND ENTERING

"COMING DOWN"

I lived the kind of life most men don't come back from,
I made my living doing crime and doing time,
I learned to steal to stay alive, I know I made so many cry,
And through this life alone I roamed, had no love in my own home
Res. School tried to kill me, suicide called out my name,
Found relief inside a bottle that left me in its shame
My momma always prayed, "Lord please forgive my family."
"Keep Your hand upon them especially on Andy."
I pushed the needle in my arm and soared among the clouds,
So wasted on the sidewalk I hate this coming down!

A. Nieman

The violence at home was a constant. My mother was always the one doling it out. If it wasn't physical violence then it came in the form of verbal put-downs like, "You no good for nothing! Or, "You rotten thing!" (I'm leaving out the curse words on purpose here) and the list goes on. The barrage of verbal put-downs came whether she was sober or not. This continuous abuse instilled an envious attitude in me. I imagined that other boys I knew at school probably went home to a safe, happy existence, where love, a full belly and restful nights were the norm. While the home I had to return to, was one of violence, alcohol, anger and fear. That envious attitude is one that I cultivated and carried with me into and throughout my adult life. As a young boy, I often felt that other children didn't have it quite as hard as I did. Self-pity comes easy to an abused child. I learned that lesson at a young age. Coming from a childhood of violence I learned to survive at an early age. You learn to fight very young. You learn nothing comes free. And you learn nothing comes easy. You have to make opportunities where no opportunity exists. Getting a licking (a spanking) didn't help me. I wanted to be away from the violence my mom was inflicting on me. I wanted to feel free from the fear and I would do just about anything to achieve that. And I did.

When I would see non-first nation boys at school, so clean cut, with nice lunches, clean clothes, always appearing so happy, I would get extremely jealous. Resentment festered in me and took up a permanent place of residence in my heart. I truly believed that all white boys had it better than me. As a result, I disliked most of them. That jealousy caused me to threaten them, intimidate them, fight with them and I would eventually wind up taking their lunches and their money. I would get physical and beat them up if they didn't give me their lunches and their money. I was often sent down to the principal's office where I would promptly receive either: a lecture, a strap, detention, or all three. None of these deterred me. It was easier than what I faced at home. The Principal's office became like a second home. Because of my lot in life, I developed the attitude that the world was against me and things were not going to get any better. I preferred to be left alone. I felt like nobody else knew or had my problems and that I had to fend for myself. In my heart, I was determined to find a place where I could feel I had some control over my awful life. A place where I could find a bit of freedom and feel safe no matter how short-lived it might be. A place where others could see that I was not such a bad kid after all, that I just wanted to have what the other boys had. I just wanted some love, some safety and some happiness. But where was that place? I would spend a lifetime searching for it.

The only advantage I had over other kids my age at school, that helped me bear some of the shame I constantly felt was my athletic ability. I found I was faster in sports than the majority of them. Whether it was soccer, dodge ball, tag whatever. That is, whenever I made it to school. As a result, most of them were scared of me. I remember trying to make an honest dollar when I was nine years old by selling the Yukon News. It was my first job. It lasted one day! I placed no real lasting value on money it was just something gained quickly and then gotten rid of just as quickly. When I wound up with all those nickels, dimes and quarters in my pocket from the newspaper sales, my brain told me; *I worked for it, so it's mine*! I had no one to teach me that that type of behavior wasn't acceptable. I never went back with the money. Three dollars was a lot of money then and the temptation was too strong. I guess I was just too used to doing things my own way. From that experience, I learned that other paper boys also had money and they became my next targets. I began taking their money. I was gaining a bad reputation in Whitehorse by the time I turned ten years old. Parents of other children were angry but they couldn't confront my dad as he was out in the bush all the time and they certainly didn't want to tangle with my mom nor could they beat me up, so they wound up complaining to the police. My bad reputation kept growing day by day worse and worse. I learned at a young age the benefits of stealing and living off the avails of crime. It brought me freedom, respect and acceptance yet in the end, it cost me my freedom.

My first real profitable B & E (break and enter) was when I was ten years old. There was a man who lived across the tracks from us and he was in the process of building a house. When he was half way through building it, he moved in. I could not help but notice this new neighbor. I also noticed that he went to work each day and that he lived alone. A new neighbor easily arouses the curiosity of a ten year old, especially a ten year old with a thieving heart. I soon learned his routine and could easily tell when he was not home. I also learned that he had a window with a pane that had no glass in it. I couldn't get as close a look as I wanted to, but upon closer inspection, I was almost certain I was small enough to squeeze through it. I felt excited. It was a secret only I knew of. What were the possibilities of finding something valuable in there? To my ten year old mind, the possibilities were endless. I decided that I would find out one of these days when I had some free time on my hands. I did my best to initiate some free time and two days later, I found myself skipping out of school, sneaking through the bushes behind his house. He had a dog chained outside of his place right near the front door. It looked like a cross between a Rottweiler, a Saint Bernard and a Lab. It was big, ugly, drooled a lot, and possessed a bark that sent shivers down your spine. I was sure you could hear it for miles. Lucky for me, the window was at the back of the house. The dog didn't even stir a muscle as I snuck through the bushes and approached the house. I prided myself on being so stealthy.

I was right. I fit through the window but it was a very tight squeeze, I scraped some skin off the sides of my hips. Once inside, my heart was pounding. There were many crazy thoughts racing through my mind; *what if he had someone living with him that I didn't know about? What if the dog heard me, broke the chain and attacked? What if the owner lent his car to someone and he was still in the house? Why didn't I think of these things before, instead of now? Calm down Andy, and be still, listen.* Silence except for the ticking of the clock on the wall. I noticed the pungent smell of fresh cut lumber and sawdust. Then I heard the gust of air forced from the dog's lungs in the form of a sigh, as it found a more comfortable laying position in order to sleep. I could not help but notice how easily sound carried in this house. I was in the kitchen and it sounded like the dog was right outside the door.

I really didn't know where to start looking and decided to check the bedroom. On my way there I glanced at the clock on the wall, it was one thirty in the afternoon. I had lots of time. There were pictures of the man on the dresser. I gazed at them for a long moment. He looked serious and mean like a criminal. He was big. He looked like he was a Russian or of European blood. I felt afraid of him. It almost felt like he was right there in the room with me not very far away. I stopped and listened just to make sure. Nothing. All I heard was the sound of my pounding heart and the clock on the wall. I decided I better look through the house to make sure I was alone. I had to move slow and be very quiet I didn't want to wake the dog. I checked each of the three rooms in the house. They were empty.

I had no idea what I was looking for, so I began rummaging through the closet. Nothing but shirts, pants, cowboy boots and hats. I went back to the dresser and atop the dresser behind the picture of an elderly woman, there was a gold watch and some cufflinks. There was also a small alarm clock. Behind the alarm clock there were some envelopes and to my amazement, I noticed there was money in one of the envelopes. Ten and twenty dollar bills! My heart skipped a beat. My mouth felt dry. I began to shake. There must be a lot of money here! I didn't bother to even think about counting it. I quickly grabbed the whole envelope and stuffed it down the front of my pants. It was precisely at that very moment, that I heard the dog give a friendly bark and I heard the sound of gravel crunching under car tires. Someone was coming up the driveway! There was no way I would be able to squeeze through the window in time! The car stopped and I could hear the owner call out to his dog in a thick European accent, "Hey Champ, you lazy old dog, sleeping again huh? Some vatch dog you are." What to do? My mind raced here and there as I glanced about the room! Get in the closet and hide behind the clothes! No, he might see my feet! The bed! Under the bed? Yes! That was my only alternative. I scurried under the bed and rolled to the very far end of the bed as close to the wall as I could get.

"What is he doing home so soon?" I angrily thought to myself. *"And what am I doing here anyway. How stupid can I get? What is he going to do if he catches me? What can I say to him? It's just him and I in here, what if he hates Indians and kills me?"* I remembered overhearing a past conversation where it was expounded that a man could legally shoot someone who was caught in the act of breaking into his home. Many panicked thoughts rolled through my ten-year-old mind at breakneck speed until in desperation, I decided I would tell him that some older boys put me up to it. They made me do it. Yes, that's what I'll tell him! If that line could work on detective Ralph Falkingham, it might work on him! I could hear him put the key in and unlock the door. A thought crossed my mind: *What if he brings the dog in? I'll be a goner! Wild thoughts raced through my mind, pictures of the dog attacking me. It was times such as these where having a vivid imagination really hurt! Please mister, leave the dog outside! I don't care what you do to me, but DON'T LET THE DOG IN PLEASE! And sure enough, he lets the dog stay outside.* Only now, he's walking directly towards me! His work boots grow larger and larger as they advance in my direction. He sits down on the bed. Springs squeek, the bed sags. The bottom of the bed pushes against my back, forcing me lower to the floor. Can he feel me? He begins unlacing his boots. He places them side by side near the bed. Goes to the closet and selects a pair of cowboy boots. He sits on the bed and proceeds to pull one on. Just then, another wild, panicked question flashes through my mind. . .*what if he goes to get the money from the envelope that used to be behind the clock, but is now stuffed in my pants and discovers its not there? Then what? He'll start searching for it. Surely he's going to look under the bed and find a little wide-eyed frightened native boy about to mess his pants! Stop that Andy! Calm down.*

The man finishes putting his cowboy boots on, rises to leave and on his way out stops to gather his out-going mail from the kitchen table. He steps out the front door, locks it, jumps in his car and I listen as tires crunch gravel and he drives away. That quickly, it is all over. Except for my pounding heart booming in my eardrums! Silence slowly creeps in. Nerve-wracking business this life of crime! I waited for what seemed like an eternity, not daring to move from my position. Finally, when I felt he really was gone, I slid out from under the bed. I re-scraped my hips as I squeezed out through the window and when I felt I was in the clear, I began to run. I ran hard. I ran like a frightened rabbit who just had a "Lunch" sign placed around its' neck by a hungry bobcat. I stopped after awhile and I looked down at the front of my pants, just to see if I was wet or dry. Surprisingly, it was dry! Too close for comfort! My take? I know you were wondering, $70.00.

Living in Sleep Hollow, the lower class of mainstream society, if I could compare it to anything, I would compare it to living on an Indian reservation. Although there were never any Indian reservations in Yukon, Sleepy Hollow could be classified as one step away from being one. As a result of living so close to the poverty level, most of my friends were of First Nations (Native), ancestry. Such were the Dawsons.

That year, the tenth year of my life, up to that point, was one of the busiest times of my short criminal career and not-so-sweet time on earth thus far. I skipped out of school alot. I always had the Truant Officer, Al Adams after me. It wasn't too hard to keep one step ahead of him I just had to stay off the streets as much as possible. It didn't take me long to figure out that most everybody went to school or to work, so I could roam about quite freely. I learned that it was only on the rarest of occasions that someone was home during school or work hours.

I liked to roam around by myself and explore places. I wouldn't explore places that were natural for ten olds like, the forest, ponds or cliffs. I would explore downtown and neighborhood homes, looking for an opportunity to grab something of value. If I was skipping out from school, one of the surest places I could get some fast money or some valuables, would be the teacher's residence. They always left their doors open back then. That is, until I started to visit too often. If none of them were home in bed from some kind of sickness, I knew the Teachers would all be in school. Doing a B&E, always involved a certain degree of risk. It was the risk that some criminals thrive on. They find it enticing and exciting. I was not from that breed. I strictly wanted to get in, get the valuables and get out.

On one particular day of playing "hooky" (skipping out of school), I decided to let my friend Maddy in on my little secret about the teacher's residence. I made him swear to never tell anybody, not even my friend Gary, (his older brother). He agreed. On this specific day, I found that the doors were all locked at the teacher's residence so I had Maddy boost me through a window. I told Maddy to go and hide in the alley and wait for me. As I looked through the apartment searching for valuables, I came across a Colonel Sander's piggy bank chock-full of quarters. I left it where it was, hopeful that I would find something of higher value and not so heavy. I remember looking through a stack of Gordon Lightfoot albums and thinking, "Life must be so boring for Teachers to have to listen to Gordon Lightfoot." [My apologies to all you Lightfoot fans. Hey, I was just a kid!] I looked in the fridge for any cooked food and found some bologna. I put it into a bag along with some bread. I didn't find anything more valuable than the Colonol Saunders piggy bank, much to my regret. I knew the piggy bank would be heavy and cumbersome to carry. In reality, the thing must've weighed 20 pounds! Although I struggled with it, I put it into a bag and managed to carry it out to the alley where Maddy was waiting. He peered into the bag, and I could see a strange look cross his face. Maddy wasn't sure if he should get angry or if he should laugh. "Colonel Sanders! Is that all you got? What'd you take *him* for?" The way he made it sound, you'd think I was taking the most treasured icon in the world! I responded, "There's nothing but quarters in it. I bet you there's quite a bit of money in there." Maddy replied, "Yeah but you didn't have to take the Chicken-man, that's somebody's piggy bank!" He sounded disappointed. I almost shouted, "If you don't want any of the money, you don't have to take any. I'll have your share, let's get out of here!"

We had to take turns carrying the piggy bank and sometimes we carried it together because it was so heavy. We took back alleys all the way down to the shipyards and climbed onto the abandoned, dry-docked ship named "Tutshi". We made our way to the bottom of the ship and in the semi-darkness, lighting match after match to see, we poured the contents onto our coats spread out on the floor. There were a lot of quarters there! A lot of quarters! When we counted out the money, we couldn't believe our eyes! One hundred and twenty-some dollars! We were rich! My heart started pounding. We were both very excited! We were also scared. The prospects! Just think of the prospects! Two nine-year-olds with a hundred and twenty bucks! That meant: new bikes, new clothes, showing off to friends and making your older sister jealous! (that is, if I decide to let her in on the secret). Those were just *some* of the possibilities! But in the meantime reality set in. Mistrust, fear and caution gripped our hearts mistrust of each other. Could we trust each other to keep a secret this big? Fear, that we would get caught having so much money. How would we spend it without drawing attention to ourselves? And caution, we had to be very careful from here on in this was a secret of the grandest proportions!

In our excitement Maddy and I made an agreement. I proposed that instead of dividing the money up, we should leave the money in the piggy bank and keep it stashed here down in the boat. And since we were such close friends, we could spend the money together. That way, we wouldn't "draw heat" on ourselves by spending too many quarters at the same places around town. We had to be in control of how many quarters we spent at all times, so as to remain inconspicuous. We were not to take any of the money on our own, we had to be there *together*, if we wanted to access it. And we would definitely NOT tell anyone else. I mentioned to Maddy, that if we told anyone else, they might steal it all from us. We both agreed vehemently that it was our secret and our secret alone and no one else was allowed in.

We had a harder time spending the money than we bargained for. In hindsight, we later realized that it would have been so much easier to just divide the money. As it turned out, in order to spend any of the stash, Maddy and I found that we had to devise a plan that took such careful planning, the military would have been proud of us! To spend our ill-gotten gains, we first had to agree to spend some of the money. Then, we had to decide what we were going to buy and then we had to devise a way to "put-the-ditch" on our buddies so we could go to our stash. Putting the ditch on our buddies was proving to be harder and harder as our popularity with them was growing in leaps and bounds since we were doing so much of the buying. And then to top it off, we had to hope nobody was playing on the boat so we could access our stash. Once all these obstacles had been overcome, we had to decide how much money we would take and the best part. . . which store to go to. I tell you, this early life of crime was not a walk in the park! One always seemed to be walking a tightrope of thinking, planning, watching, scheming and keeping one's mouth shut!

I remember one interesting night in particular. Maddy and I had accessed our stash and spent the day eating every sort of candy on the market, while we skipped out from school. That night, my mom was sober and stayed home from bingo, since she obviously didn't have any money. I came in the door with my pants hanging rather low as both pockets were half filled with quarters. I immediately scolded myself for having overlooked my usual practice of peeking through the window to see who was home, before I entered. I remembered my oversight as soon as I entered the door and seen my mom. I thought, "Oh, oh I'm in for it now!" Fortunately she was sober and in a good mood. She sat in her room with the curtain open. She was busy sewing. She simply glanced up at me from her sewing as I walked in, she was checking to make sure it was me. She said, "There's some rabbit in the frying pan on the stove and macaroni in the pot have some and save some for Lizzy." I was relieved that she was in a decent mood. Not too nosey and not mad, what a relief.

As she was engrossed in her sewing, (that's how she made some of her bingo money), she made reference as to why I didn't come home right after school. I lied and told her I was over at Daryl Lease's (RIP) place. I was so full from steadily eating candy most of the day, I felt like I didn't have a millimeter of space left in my stomach for food. I didn't want to draw attention to myself by not eating, as I was sure she would start to ask more questions, so I took my dish into the bedroom. "You see Lizzy at school?" She asked. My mind flashed to the old boat me and Maddy played on most of the day, skipping out of school. "No", I answered, listening for her next question. My mother continued, "She never came back from school yet, either. She must be over at Karen Darbyshire's I guess." "Must be", I answered, as I set the dish of food under the bed and pushed it as far back as I could reach, to keep it out of sight. I didn't want her to notice that I wasn't eating any of it. I pulled out my brand new "Archie and Jughead" paperback book that was tucked in the back of my pants and threw it on the bed. I then took off my pants with the pockets half filled with quarters and put the pants on the floor. I was so excited about reading the *new* Archie comic book I completely forgot to put my money in a safe place. I fell asleep reading the book. It wasn't long until I was awakened by my mother's angry, loud voice, "Andy! the police are here! They want to see you. How come they ask for you, what did you do?" "Nothing," I said as I shielded my eyes from the light. A policeman stuck his head in the door and said, "We'd like to talk to you for a minute out in the car Andy." "Who said you could come in here?" My mom half-shouted angrily at him. My mom was always angry at the police. She never did like them. In those days Indians were not allowed to drink and as the police enforced that law, they were deemed as prejudiced by the First Nation people, so there were a lot of bad feelings between them.

The policeman respected my mother's stance and said over his shoulder as he walked out the door, "We'll be out in the car Andy, make it quick." I was thankful that my mom was following right behind the policeman. She was exercising what little authority she could. "I'll be right out mom", I said. I came awake very quickly and remembered the money I had in my pants, thankful that my mom hadn't noticed it. I quickly picked up my pants and stuffed them under the mattress at the foot of the bed. I rummaged in the old beat up dresser drawer, to find another pair of pants. What a jumble of clothing! Everything was mixed together, both boys and girls clothes. There were, blouses, sweaters, briefs, tunics, everything else. . . .but none of my pants! The panic of the moment woke me up even more. I heard my mother's voice, "What do they want to see you for anyway? What did you do this time?" There was anger in her voice. She stood by the door and peered in. "Nothing", I answered. "Well how come they want to talk to you?" "I don't know". It was my turn to be agitated. I had to keep her busy, so I added, "You know how they always blame me for everything that happens. They always do that!" She thought about that and knew I was right. "What are you looking for... pants?" She asked. "Yeah." I replied. "There's some on the line by the stove." She answered.

I quickly dressed and after checking to see if my pants were noticeable under the mattress I stuffed them under farther and went out to meet the police. I stood outside the vehicle beside the front passenger window waiting for the officer to roll his window down. It was Fall time and the air was cold. The officer motioned for me to jump in the back. I stood there scowling at him. "What do you want?" I asked, without hiding the disappointment in my voice. "Jump in the back. We want to ask you a few questions. It should only take a minute."

Much to my relief, when they questioned me, it was about another matter I had no knowledge of.

It was easy to answer their questions as I was not guilty and it made looking in their eyes a breeze. However, this was a close call a little too close for comfort!

CHAPTER SIX

THE WOODEN BARREL AND COURT

"NEVER THE SAME"

I was forced to run while still so young
And I lived out on my own,
Slept out at night under starry lights
Too scared to go back home,
I learned to steal to get a meal,
Didn't ask to live that way,
With thieving hands, I made a stand,
Just to see another day,
Policeman came he called my name
Said, "You're not allowed to live that way."
Wound up in court freedom cut short
After Lower Post I was never the same.

A. Nieman

The final straw that broke the proverbial camel's back, came when I broke into a home and discovered that they had hidden the family savings in a small round wooden barrel in the freezer compartment of their fridge. A place no ordinary mind would look for money. However, I was no ordinary kid. I was in fact, a hungry, neglected, thieving little boy from the poor side of the tracks. If I couldn't find money, food was high on my shopping list. The apartments, there were three of them, were at the top of some stairs all in the same building. I knocked on each door before trying to turn the door knob. I already had a question in my mind to ask if someone answered. I was going to say, "Hi, is this where Mr. so and so lives? Obviously the answer would be, "No" and I would quickly say, "OK. Thank you" and be gone. It was the third and final door that the knob turned. Entering I said out loud, "Hello, anyone here? Bill are you home?" just in case someone was there. There was no one. I searched that apartment from top to bottom and did not find anything of value. I looked in the freezer for some food to take, because it became my habit to never leave empty-handed. When I opened the freezer, there it was, in the form of a small barrel that looked like it was a pirate's treasure chest standing on end. It was not locked. One quick peek inside and I could see it was stuffed plump full with bills of both Canadian and American money. I quickly grabbed it as my heart started to race even faster than it was before. I glanced around and found a plastic bag. I put the barrel in and that was all I needed. I headed for the door. Up to that point, this was the most money I had ever stolen. There was well over three hundred dollars in that little barrel! Most of it was American money. I scurried down the nearest alley and went to my friend Masons' house. There was a shack behind his place and I put the barrel under the shack. I was "money-bags" then to all my friends. We ate in the Whitehorse Inn restaurant and the Dairy Queen. I bought clothes and toys and didn't have to worry about a place to stay. I had plenty of friends who were willing to sneak me into their homes. On the fifth day of that spending spree, I got caught. Whitehorse is a small town and word gets around fast. Somehow word about my spending got out. I remember leading the police to my stash after they promised me it would help me in court. It never did. As I watched them take the money from the little barrel and begin counting it, I remember how the twenty dollar bills in American money looked so much like "play-money".

Well that last B&E really did me in. As I look back now, it was the beginning of the end for any chance I would ever have of leading anything that remotely resembled a decent life. Because of that B&E, as punishment, they sent me to the Lower Post Indian Residential School. I would spend three years there. The abuse in my young life was to continue in a whole different manner. It was about to take a turn… for the worse.

My parents attended court with me as I was being sentenced for the B&E. My mother was sober (after all this was a serious matter because of the amount of money involved) and my dad had come in from his Camp-cooking job to attend court. This *was* serious! I was nervous. Not because of the penalty that was about to come, I felt I could handle that. I wasn't afraid of my dad or my mom on that day either. I wasn't afraid of the court-induced shame that was about to come where I would be made the center of unwanted attention again. I wasn't afraid of the police. What really struck fear into my heart was the realization that I could and probably would be *separated* from my mom. This meant I would have to wrestle with the unrelenting demons of abandonment. The one thing I hated and dreaded the most. I was about to face the deep valley of separation and being alone again. Being alone that was not of my own accord. There was a big difference and that terrified me. Feelings of being abandoned began to incite suffocating fear into me. I could handle just about any beating and/or disgrace that was directed my way. I actually would, (if given the choice) prefer that, to being away from my mom. Strange creatures us humans; on one hand we have the ability to hate a person with a passion and on the other hand we have the ability to love that same person with the same amount of passion. The end result is an almost unbearable fear of being away from that person and yet not really enjoying being around them. Such was my relationship with my mom. I glanced back in the courtroom to where she was sitting hoping to make eye contact with her to let her know how sorry I really was for the whole situation. I also wanted to find out where I stood in her books. She did not even look at me. She had her own demons to deal with. Back in those days (early sixties), Native people felt very intimidated by the dominant society and what appeared to be shyness, on the Native person's part, was in reality, resentment, shame and anger directed at the white people. On that morning, it must have been very traumatic for my mother to have to sit in a place where she felt looked down upon, detested and shamed, only to witness her ten-year-old son being handled by an unfriendly, obviously-biased group of people who held all the power.

My dad on the other hand, was casually talking with an RCMP officer. When I caught my dad's eye, he winked at me as if to say; *everything will be alright.* That was my dad. These types of situations didn't really seem to have an effect on him as it did on the rest of our family. After all, there were times when he could just go back to his job in the bush and not have to face the consequences of our harsh dysfunctional violent lifestyle. This was one of those times. There were many other times however, that our dad had to stay and face the harsh consequences of my mother's jealousy, fueled by alcohol and a desire to get even.

I remembered very clearly, too clearly for comfort, how she kicked him out of the house in forty-below weather when all he had on was his long johns and socks. She had no trouble pushing him out because she outweighed him by about 100 pounds easily and besides that, he would never hit her back. After she pushed him out the door, he came around to the side window where one of our window panes was missing and there was a towel frozen into the hole. I can still hear him now, "Andy, are you there Andy? Can you reach my clothes and my boots? Don't let your mom see you. Ask Lizzy to get my clothes if she can." I hated seeing him like that. I hated my mom for doing that to him. I hated myself for being put into such a helpless position! One of the great mysteries of my young childhood life and one of the biggest questions that I never got an answer to was simply this; *Why didn't you ever fight back dad?* I have never witnessed my dad ever striking my mom. In all the years of abuse and physical torture she put him through, he never once hit her back. Not that I ever witnessed anyway. There was a time though, when I felt for sure he was going to get even with her physically.

He and my mom were drinking and my mom was getting quite drunk. They were arguing, or rather my mom was arguing and accusing him of fooling around with so and so. As she got angrier and angrier, her voice got louder and louder then she reached over and grabbed the iron (used for ironing clothes), off the stove and threw it in his direction. My dad was sitting on his bed in his bare feet and didn't see the iron coming, The pointed end of the iron landed on the top of his foot leaving a big gash that started spewing blood straight up in the air like a miniature garden hose. I had never seen anything like it. Like any normal person I don't like the sight of blood. But for some reason, I couldn't take my eyes off the blood at this particular time. What kept my eyes riveted to the scene was how amazingly straight the line of blood shot up. It looked as if someone turned on a miniature hose. My sister Margaret immediately grabbed a towel and placed it on the cut. While adding force to the wound she yelled out, "Someone run over to Betty's and call an ambulance!" (Betty Darbyshire was our neighbor). "Hurry up!" "Don't just stand there Andy! run over there, RIGHT NOW!" Margaret shouted. My mother, not realizing the extent of the damage she just caused picked up a piece of fire wood and threw it, just barely missing Margaret and my dad. "You rotten Germany dog!" she blurted out as she struggled to regain her balance and fell into her seat at the kitchen table. I wasn't just standing there. I was watching my mom reach for the piece of wood and she held my attention because I thought she was going to grab a knife. Once I realized it was just a piece of wood she grabbed, I sprang into action. I began to panic! "Dad might die!" I thought as fear pushed me into action. Grabbing my winter coat, I pulled it on and dashed out the door just inches ahead of my mother's hand as she reached out in an attempt to stop me.

Thankfully the Darbyshires were home and phoned the ambulance right away for us. They were always so kind, the Darbyshires. I have no doubt, they saved some of our lives by all the times they let us use the phone to call either the police or an ambulance. We were friends with them. George (RIP) and Betty, the parents, had six children. The oldest was Karen, then Francis, then Gary, Earl, Charlotte and Kathy. Long story short, the ambulance came and took my dad to the hospital. My dad made it to the hospital to receive stitches and told the police some made-up story as he usually did in similar circumstances in the past. If my dad had told the truth as to what really went on at home - for all the past dysfunctional incidents and violent acts of my mom - we would have been placed in Foster Care years ago. But as I said, Sleepy Hollow had some rough characters with unorthodox reputations. It was a no-man's land and only the most serious cases drew the attention of the police and the authorities down there. The police took my mom to the police station that night. We were left to clean up the mess. You'd think we would have been able to get some rest with our mother at the police station, but being so young, we had no way of knowing what was going on. We waited in fear for her return all the while worrying about dad and what his situation was. We all took turns Margaret, Liz and I looking out our frozen glass window to see if a taxi was coming. It was Liz who first seen it, "There's a car coming!" she blurted out in excitement mixed with anxiety. We were all in fear and we were also all excited. We were in fear because we did not know if it was mom returning and we were excited because we thought it might be dad. It was a police car and it was dad. The policeman had driven dad home from the hospital. Dad came into the house on crutches with his foot twice the size from all the bandages on it. There was quite a bit of blood on his pants and shirt. The policeman held the door open for him. Once inside, the policeman started talking first. "Well Mr. Nieman you make sure you take good care of that foot. Mrs. Nieman will be out in the morning. How you kids doing?" The clean, smart-looking policeman looked down at us. I wanted him to take me with him. I wanted the kind of home he was living in. "Fine." I said. Margaret spoke for her and Liz as Liz was quite shy back then, "We're OK." The policeman continued, "Is there anything I can get you Mr. Nieman? You have cigarettes, you're OK?" "Yes, I'm fine," my dad said in his voice so familiar to us kids. "I want to thank you officer for all your help," dad said with a smile extending his hand to the officer. While he was talking I was amazed to see a real live handgun and real handcuffs hanging from the policeman's belt. "OK then," the officer said, "If you kids need anything or if anything happens at all and you need our help, you call us, ya' hear? Call us anytime day or night ya' hear? Make sure now." He rested his hand on my head as he spoke then ruffled my hair when he finished speaking. "OK we will," Margaret said. My eyes were riveted on his gun as he pulled on his brown leather gloves. My dad said, "OK then, thanks officer. Thank you for the lift." When he left, our full attention went right to our dad. We didn't hug him, none of us did, but we had a lot of questions for him. We wanted to know first of all, "Are you going to be OK?' and "What did the doctor say?" I wanted to know, "Is mom coming back tonight?"

Back in the courtroom, people began to take their seats in unison as if by some unnoticed cue. I got the sense that court was about to begin. No sooner had that thought crossed my mind when I heard, "Order in court, all rise". The Judge walked in sat down then we all sat down. People started talking and I could not understand most of the big words they were saying and as a result my mind immediately drifted to another time and place. My mind and my heart began to be filled with memories. I remembered the time I woke up alone in a cold house. I had wet diapers on and I climbed out of bed. The shock of the cold floor on my bare feet almost captured my breath away. I couldn't talk yet and I could barely walk and on the verge of tears and anger from the cold floor, I made my way into the other room. I *had to* see if there was anyone there. There was no one. The house was empty and it was freezing cold. When I realized I was alone I could not stop the scream that filled the empty air. I cried until I almost choked losing my breath. Then my sister Margaret came bursting through the door and to my rescue.

My mind drifted in memory to the time I would sleep between mom and dad. It was the warmest spot on earth. Lizzy had her turn last night, now it was my turn. When it was my turn to sleep with mom and dad, I could smell nicotine on my dad's t-shirt. I loved that smell. I didn't know it was cigarette smoke at the time. I just loved it because it was dad. If I missed him too much when he was out working, I would make sure no one seen me and I would smell his suit jacket that was hanging on the wall. I wanted to smell and be near him so bad. It wasn't the same. The suit smelled more like wood smoke. After all, the suit was hanging there so long that every time the stove door was opened, there was a contribution of wood smoke made to the garment as if it's main purpose was to kill the nicotine smell. It succeeded. I also remembered how mom would carry me on her back in a warm, blanket rolled up on the ends so she could tie the ends together, creating a pouch. I could actually stand up in that blanket. It came right up to the back of my neck. I was as safe as safe could be. Still in diapers and not a care in the world!

My trip down memory lane was rudely interrupted and I was pulled back into the reality of the courtroom when the judge practically shouted my name, "Andrew! Did you hear what I just said!?" Startled, I came to my senses and it didn't take me long to realize every eyeball in the courtroom was focused on me. "Pardon me?" I asked sheepishly. I did not hear a single word he said! The Judge continued in a loud angry voice, "No wonder you're always in trouble young man, you don't know how to listen! Now stand up! And stand up straight! Right this minute!" I couldn't understand most of his big words as he passed sentence on me, but I did remember hearing the words, "Lower Post." I remembered those words because they didn't make sense to my ten year old brain. I thought to myself, "Lower Post, what in the world is that?" Sadly, I was about to find out and all too soon. When court was over and the Judge walked out, an RCMP officer came over and rested his hand on my shoulder. He said, "Just wait here Andrew until everyone leaves." I was not sure what was going on or what was happening. I looked back at my mom to see if she knew what was going on. She was bent forward with her head in her hands and I noticed the tears as they fell to the floor from behind her hands. She was crying. She was crying so quietly that no one noticed. No one seemed to notice her crying but me. The tears were easy for me to see. Tears then welled up in my eyes and I did everything I could to keep them down. I could tell she was forcing herself to not look at me. She kept her eyes on the floor and wiped her tears with a Kleenex. After most of the people had filed out and left the courtroom, she blew her nose, rose up from her chair and slowly walked out. She looked old and defeated. My dad, after shaking hands with a couple of people, did not even look at me but put on his hat and followed her. Just then a man named John Hoyt (RIP), a Probation Officer, came over and squatted on his haunches before me so he was at eye level and introduced himself. "Hi Andrew," he said in one of the friendliest voices. It was like he knew how sad I was feeling and was going to make it better. "Do they call you Andrew or Andy?" "Andy." "OK. Hi Andy. I'm John. John Hoyt and you will be spending the night with me in a hotel room tonight. Have you ever stayed in a hotel room before?" I hung my head down and shook it to indicate "No." "Not many ten year olds get to stay in a hotel room. I think you're going to like it." I'm staying in a hotel room tonight, I thought to myself. Good, guess I'm not going to jail after all. My heart started to feel a little better. Hey things may work after all. I started to get happier and questions started to formulate that I wanted to ask this new man in my life. He continued, "When I was your age I had never stayed in a hotel before either. How old are you?" "Ten," I said looking him in the eye for the first time. "Bet you're hungry huh?" I nodded my head. Well let's go get something into your tummy. Do you like hamburgers?" I nodded my head "Yes." "Great, we'll get us some burgers then."

CHAPTER SEVEN

LOWER POST INDIAN RESIDENTIAL SCHOOL

"I'M MOVIN' ON"

Can't call me a number I'm not there,
Can't make me eat nor cut my hair,
Can't put me down or silence me,
You tried all that yet I'm still free!
I don't let past hurts ruin my day,
I lay them down each time I pray,
You told me not to speak my tongue,
You said I'd never overcome,
But now that I have found my voice,
I'm movin' on, I've made my choice!

I've lived in sorrow, lived in shame,
I lived to tell, I overcame,
You could not kill this Native child,
You could not still my songs inside,
You could not end my will to live,
You could not steal these smiles I give!
Not many know how far I've come,
The bitterness I've learned to shun,
Yet through it all hope's found a way,
I'm movin' on to a brighter day!

A. Nieman

The sentence I received for my B&E placed me on a bus headed for the Lower Post Indian Residential School the very next day. Lower Post was 300 miles from my home. It all seemed to happen in a whirlwind. I didn't even remember hearing the Judge pass sentence. A ten year old boy's mind loses interest very quickly when listening to legal jargon. The night I spent in the hotel room with John Hoyt passed rather quickly and in the morning we had breakfast in the restaurant then made our way down to the bus depot. John had a way of deflecting all of my questions with a constant, "You'll see," each time I asked what was going to happen with me. We made our way to the bus depot and I did not get any of my questions answered.

My mom and dad were there. Mom had prepared a small bag for me and she placed it in my hand. "I brought you something to eat for your trip" she said very softly. I felt the hurt in her voice. I began to get fearful. "Where are they taking me mom?" I noticed my voice was shakey and sounded weak. "That man said they're going to keep you at Lower Post to go to school until summer time", my mom answered. "Where's Lower Post?" I asked looking at her seriously. Something told me she didn't know where Lower Post was either, but she didn't want to let on that she didn't know. "In B. C.," is all she answered. Because my mom didn't know where Lower Post was that made it seem even farther away. I started to cry. "Why do they have to send me away? I asked wiping the tears that fell from my eyes. "I won't get into trouble anymore! I promise!" My mother bent down and held me in her big arms. I could smell the aroma of our house on her clothes. The smell of freshly washed laundry, perfume, wood smoke and our dog "Trixie," all floated through my brain in a flash as I hugged her. I wanted to go home right then and there. The thoughts "triggered" by those smells, intensified the lonesome feeling that was settling itself into my stomach. I heard the bus driver yell, "All aboard! Please have your tickets ready." The probation officer grabbed my hand and said as gently and respectfully as he could, "Over here Andy." He walked me over to the bus driver and introduced me. "Larry, this here is Andy, Andy Nieman. And as I mentioned he'll be getting off at Lower Post. Andy, you do everything Mr. Brown tells you to do. He's going to take good care of you until you get to Lower Post. If you have any questions, or if you need anything, you just ask Mr. Brown, OK? Now go and say good-bye to your mom and dad." My heart and mind were in a whirlwind trying to grasp what was happening, "Say Good-bye?" I thought to myself. Nobody told me I would be leaving! I did as I was told and in a daze of unbelief and shock as though in a dream. I said my good-byes then returned to the bus. The bus was empty except for three other people, four including the bus driver.

I will always remember the horrible loneliness of that bus ride. A loneliness so overpowering it gripped my heart and threatened to choke the very breath out of me. As the bus began to pull out from the bus depot, I pressed my face up against the glass, straining to keep my mom within eye contact. Fighting back the feeling that tore at my heart and with tears blinding my eyes, I ran to the back window of the bus and jumped onto the seat straining to look through the small tinted window. The reality and the realization of what was taking place filled my mind and heart with so many heartbreaking thoughts: Wait! This can't be happening! There must be some mistake! No one told me it was serious enough to come to this! I'll change! Really I will! Why didn't anybody warn me this would happen? Please somebody stop this! I promise to change! I'll never steal anything again, NEVER! Just give me one more chance please! The bus picked up speed as the driver shifted gears and it headed to the south side of town. The last glimpse I caught of my mom that day would be the last time I saw her for almost a year. I felt panic! I felt grief. I felt totally defeated. Everyone and everything that mattered to me the most in my life was being left behind and there was not a thing I could do about it. I do not have an aggressive personality. I have what is called a passive/aggressive personality. That means when something bad happens to me, I turn my anger and hurt *inward* as opposed to *outward*. It also means I tend to suffer silently. I laid down on the back seat of that bus and cried until I had no more energy left. I cried and I cried and I finally fell asleep from total exhaustion.

I don't exactly remember falling asleep, but I do remember the bus driver waking me. "There, there Andy, you'll be OK. I'm going to take good care of you. Come with me, it's time you had something to eat. You'll feel better with some food in that little tummy of yours." He lead me into a restaurant, ordered a bowl of soup for me and asked if there was anything else I needed. I shook my head. I would later come to know this man's name to be Larry Brown. His kindness was never forgotten. I looked at the restaurant and it might as well have been from another planet. The place felt strange and it seemed to have its own atmosphere of loneliness. That atmosphere reminded me that I was miles from where I should be, at my mother's side. I couldn't stop the tears as they began to flow again. I had no appetite. I did manage to take a few sips of the Coke that Larry bought me. Even Coke didn't appeal to me. That in itself, is a sure sign that I was in a bad way. Back on the bus traveling down the road, I reached for the bag my mom had packed for me. Just seeing the bag made me miss my mom some more. The bag wasn't really a bag, it was one of my mom's head scarves and she had tied the four corners together to form a bag. I could smell her perfume on the scarf. Fighting back the tears, I could see she had packed me some dry meat, a couple of Fig Newtons, a package of Juicy Fruit gum, a Coke and a roll of assorted Lifesavers. I had no appetite whatsoever and didn't touch any of it. I just wanted to go home. I wanted my mom. I wanted my sisters. My thoughts drifted to home and my sisters. I imagined what they would be doing right about then. Margaret and Liz were probably just finishing off their homework and would be getting ready for a tickle-fight with Kim. But then, I wasn't there, so maybe they wouldn't. I wondered if they missed me. I sure missed them. My heart was overwhelmed with the reality that I was going to a strange place and that I would not see any of them for a long, long time. With a broken heart and an uncertain future, I tried to stifle my sobs but couldn't help it. My tears caused me to fall asleep again.

Our next stop was Lower Post Indian Residential School. Canada's Indian residential school system began officially in 1892. In hopes that the Aboriginal population would assimilate into European-influenced Canadian society, the government of Canada established residential schools. They were government funded boarding schools where Aboriginal children were sent to learn about European-Canadian culture. Attendance was mandatory, as removing the children from their communities was seen as essential to the assimilation process. The Government of Canada operated nearly every school as a "joint venture" with various religious organizations including the Roman Catholic, Anglican, Methodist, Baptist, United and Presbyterian churches. Residential schools were established in all provinces and territories across Canada except Newfoundland, New Brunswick and Prince Edward Island. The schools were built to house and assimilate Status Indians from the age of five years until they turned sixteen. All Status Indians of those age groups *had to* attend the residential schools *by law.* There were approximately 130 residential schools in territories and provinces across Canada Most residential schools ceased operation by the mid-1970s, although the government was no longer officially involved after 1969. Not all residential schools closed in the 1970s. Akaitcho Hall in Yellowknife, the last residential school in Canada, closed in 1996 Approximately 150,000 Aboriginal students were forced to attend the 80 Residential schools that were established through the country. Lower Post Indian Residential School opened in 1940 and closed in 1975 it was a Roman Catholic school. In the annuls of the Law Library at the Andrew Phillipson Law Building in Whitehorse, Yukon, public court documents show that there were a total of eleven pedophiles convicted of sexual crimes in the residential schools across the Yukon. Seven of those pedophiles were employed at the Lower Post Indian Residential School. The most notorious of all the convicted pedophiles was George Maczynski. He was at Lower Post the same time I was there. He was the pedophile that abused me. He arrives later in this autobiography.

When we arrived at the tiny village of Lower Post it was dark. I was in a deep sleep when Mr. Brown the bus driver shook me awake. "Andy, Andy, come on boy, this is your stop fella." The last thing I wanted to do was leave my warm spot on the seat where I was curled up. Yet I had to, as tired and cold as I was, there was no choice. Hunger pangs reminded me that I hadn't eaten my supper. I arose wiping the sleep from my eyes. I looked around for my bag. "I have your things right here Andy", Mr. Brown said, as he held up the only piece of baggage I had and the last treasure that connected me to my mom. "There's a man here that will take you to the school," Mr. Brown continued. I sensed sympathy in his tone of voice. He rested his hand on my head and tossled my hair as I brushed past him. "Everything's going to be alright son", were the last words Mr. Brown spoke to me on this trip.

Half way up the steps of the bus there stood a short man in complete black attire. I caught my first sight of a man I would soon come to regard with a great deal of fear, Brother Guy (pronounced 'Ghee'). Aside from the black attire, the first thing I noticed about this short be-speckled man with the big nose was his ears. They were huge. They seemed to have been made for a man three times his size! And at first sight, they appeared to be phony, as if they were part of a clown's outfit. He seemed to know that I marveled at his ears and did not appear agitated, perhaps he was used to it. He was all business and came right to the point. "Are you Andrew Nieman?" He pronounced it "Nee-man", as most people did. In our family we pronounced it so it sounded like "Ny-man." With my head down, I answered softly, "Yes." Either he didn't hear me or he wanted to show who was in command right off the "bat" because he asked sternly and his voice grew louder without shame, "What did you say? Speak up young man are you Andrew Nee-man?" I didn't like him from that moment on and answered him in a louder voice not hiding my anger, "Yes, I said, that's me!" "Alright then, look at me when you speak to me from now on", he said, staring at me with beady eyes through "coke-bottle" glasses. He spoke very good English and only the trained ear could detect the slight hint of French that carried his voice, "I'm Brother Guy. Where are your bags?" He then looked at the driver and asked in a kinder voice, "Does he have any luggage sir?" "Just what he has in his hand", Mr. Brown answered. "OK then Andrew, follow me," Brother Guy said as he turned and walked down the few steps of the bus. As he walked ahead of me, I noticed he was very, very "pigeon-toed". I began to reason that I now knew why he was so mean and belligerent. Who wouldn't be, when you have monkey ears the size of elephants ears, a Croucho Marx nose with beady eyes magnified behind "coke-bottle" glasses and to top it off you walk like an overweight duck on dry land! I felt sorry for Brother Guy. Silently, I felt shame for thinking so negatively about him. Then, as if to justify my guilty thoughts I decided; if he's nice to me, I'll be nice to him. If he's hard with me, I'll be hard with him. Boy, was I in for a surprise and a lesson on power and control! He was hard whether I was nice or not.

He walked like a man with purpose. It was like he was in a hurry and wanted to get this business over and done with as quickly as possible. Having sensed that, I followed behind him at a deliberately slow pace. I wasn't going to be ashamed at showing Brother Guy my displeasure with him. I *wanted* to get under his skin. How dare he show me such disrespect, he didn't even know me! Well, he is about to get to know me, I thought to myself. Although my anger at Brother Guy helped to get my mind off my sadness, it wasn't long before I realized that my sadness was still there and in fact was growing. I had no control whatsoever over the sadness that was to become my side-kick for the next thirty years. I made a mental point that I would do my very best to never let Brother Guy know the reality of my sorrow. I did not trust him.

The drive to the residential school was extremely short and the night was extremely dark. I couldn't see a thing out the window except for the fading lights of the restaurant where the bus had stopped. Lower Post was very small, just a gas station, a restaurant and a small village. Brother Guy asked me, "How old are you Andrew?" I hesitated to answer as I was going to show him I didn't just forgive and make up *that* quickly. Then I remembered that I would treat him like he treats me. He looked in the rear view mirror at me after he didn't receive a reply and just when he got halfway through saying "Andrew" again, I said "Ten. I'm ten years old." "Do you play hockey"? he continued on. "A little bit.""What position do you normally play?""Anywhere", I answered. It sounded strange after I said it and when I realized the silliness of my answer, Brother Guy said, "The boys like to play hockey here. If you listen and do as you're told, you'll be able to play some hockey." My mind wasn't on hockey. I didn't like this situation. There had to be some mistake! I didn't belong out here in the middle of nowhere with this stranger! "How far are we from Whitehorse?" I asked trying to hide the panic in my voice. "That kind of information is none of your business. Don't tell me you're going to be a trouble maker. Are you?" "Am I what?" I asked innocently. "Going to be a trouble maker I said!" he repeated loudly through clenched teeth. I could feel the anger in his voice. "No. I was just wondering that's all", I hoped I didn't draw suspicion on myself already. I could tell I had to be very careful around this man, Brother Guy.

Arriving at the school I clutched my mother's bright scarf that she made into a bag and held it tight. I followed Bro Guy up the concrete stairs and entered the building. The smell hit me right away it was so over-bearing. It smelled of mold and bleach and clean linen, a strange combination to say the least. I had never smelled anything like it and it was about to become a smell I would come to hate. Bro. Guy said, "Have a seat there," as he pointed to a wooden bench. I sat down my feet barely touching the floor. Bro Guy closed the office door and I could hear muffled conversation between him and the head priest. It was late at night around 11:30 pm and there was no one around. I looked around the building and could tell the building was not new. It was kept very clean but it was not new. It was very warm inside and I could hear a big clock ticking loudly as I sat there alone with my thoughts. I looked outside into the pitch-black night examining my chances for an escape. But where could I escape to? I did not know where I was or in which direction Whitehorse was. I decided that I would have to get more information before I attempted to run away.

When they were done talking, the door knob turned and Bro Guy and the priest came out. The priest gave me a big smile and his gold tooth shining brightly in the front row of his mouth caught my attention immediately. "Hi Andrew, I am Father Morrisette," he said in the softest and kindest voice I had ever heard. He extended his hand for me to shake and I caught the strong smell of cigarette tobacco. I then noticed the brown nicotine stains on his fingers. I reached out and my small hand got lost in his as he shook it and said, "Is your mother Agnes?" My ears perked up immediately and he seemed to become both a friend and a comforter just in the mention of my mother's name. "Yes!" I said with a new found keen interest in this man. How did this man know my mother? I couldn't help but ask myself. Seemingly as if he knew the question in my mind he answered, "I met your mother in Burwash Landing, do you know where Burwash Landing is?" he asked in his soft voice. Do I know where Burwash Landing is!? Well of course! I thought to myself incredulously. I only travelled there just about every summer with my mom on our way to Beaver Creek! I also stole some money when I was nine years old from a lady's purse on a trip to Burwash one time when the bus made a lunch stop at Haines Junction. After we arrived in Burwash and unpacked all our stuff at Aunt Jessie Joe's (RIP)

I wanted so badly to go back to Whitehorse that I ran away and I walked all the way (ten miles) through the bushes following the highway from Burwash to Destruction Bay. The police picked me up when I was buying some candy at the gas station in Destruction Bay.

I answered Father Morrisette as respectfully as I could, "Yes I know where Burwash is." He continued, "I know your mother Agnes. She always goes to visit Jessie Joe in Burwash." "How is she doing Andrew?" he asked. "My mom?" I questioned the question. It sounded like he was asking about Jessie Joe. "Yes, you're mom." "She's doing OK," I answered, my mind already creating some hope that I might be able to convince this man that there was a terrible mistake made and I need to be sent home as soon as time would allow. "Oh, that's nice to know," he continued. "Well, you must be tired and hungry. Bro Guy will take you downstairs for a shower and some food and put you to bed. Welcome to Lower Post Andrew. I'll see you in the morning. Good night" "Good-night," I answered as Bro Guy grabbed my arm and stood me up. "This way Andrew, follow me," he said. He pulled a bunch of keys out of his pocket and let them rattle at his side as we walked down the hall. This rattling of the keys sound was a trademark sign that I would learn all too well. It was a sound that let us know Bro Guy was coming.

We walked down the hall and it was obvious that most of the lights were turned off for the night. Bro Guy flicked on various lights as we walked down more concrete steps to the basement where the dining hall was and the Recreation Room. Bro Guy told me to undress. As I was taking my clothes off, he picked each item up off the floor and also grabbed my mother's scarf that she had filled for me. He said, "I'll put these away for safe-keeping." "I'd like to keep that. Can I keep it, please?" I asked pleadingly. "You can have it when you leave. I'll make sure it's well taken care of." "That's my mom's." I said hoping that it would make a difference. It didn't. "I understand. It will be well taken care of, don't worry. Now go shower," he said. I felt a stab of sorrow and a surge of hatred run through me. "I'll get even with you somehow you monkey," I thought to myself. I had a shower in what appeared to be a private bathroom as Bro Guy found me some pajamas and blankets and a pillow case. He gave me some de-licing shampoo and told me, "Be careful not to get any of this in your eyes be very careful." I finished showering and changed into pajamas. Bro Guy then put some clothes on top of my blankets and he told me to have a seat at the table. I sat down at the Staff Dining Room. Little did I know that in the future I would be sneaking down in the middle of the night to steal food from this very table because we got so hungry. Bro Guy gave me a sandwich of peanut butter and jam along with a glass of milk. I finished all of it and he left me alone. As Bro Guy walked with his rattling keys to the Rec Room office and went in loneli- ness started to creep into my heart as the "strangeness" of my new surroundings began to dawn on me. When he came back out he was carrying a flashlight and all he said was, "Grab you blankets and follow me. Do not say a word" We went back up the concrete steps and stopped at the door just outside the dormitory. Before we entered Bro Guy turned and with his finger to his lips said, "Shhh."

As soon as we entered I knew there was no need to be quiet. I could hear the sobbing of other homesick little boys and could feel the loneliness that hung in the air. It was heavy. I wished I could turn around and walk back out. I did not want to be here. I was already lonely and this room was making it worse. I did not want to hear and feel what I was hearing and feeling. Bro Guy led me to a bed and showed me how to fix the bed. He whispered to me, "There, now go to bed and no talking. Good night." I didn't say anything because a big lump had formed in my throat. I listened as I heard other little boys sobbing in the night. It is a memory I will never forget. I could not hold back and started crying as well. There was no escaping from how I felt. Crying myself to sleep was nothing new and tonight was no exception.

The next morning, my first morning at Lower Post Indian Residential School, I was rudely awakened by Bro Guy lifting my bed up and shaking it so hard I had no choice but to get up. "OK I'm up!" I said angrily. He stopped. I sat on the side of my bed trying to wake up. I was tired as my eyes started to adjust to the light and I remembered where I was. Heaviness gripped my heart this was a very strange place. Everyone was waiting for me. I looked around and observed all these stranger's faces, soon to become familiar, staring at me. All of their eyes seemed to be silently saying, "Well, what's taking you so long? You're holding us up from our breakfast?" I got dressed and walked to the sink where I saw another boy washing up. I washed my face and then got in line with the rest of the boys. Bro Guy came over and grabbed me by my arm with a tight-fisted iron grip. I felt his fingers dig into my arm. It hurt so much I dared not move. He forced me over to my bed and pushed me towards the wooden stand beside my bed. "Get your toothbrush," he ordered. I tried to rest my arm to ease some of the pain. "Well what are you waiting for?" he snapped. My arm hurt so much it was hard to lift it. I did not want to move it because of the pain, but I forced myself to move even though it hurt badly. I took the brand new toothbrush out of its plastic wrapping and stood there. The pain went into hiding whenever I did not move so I stood there motionless enjoying some relief. I do not know what Bro Guy interpreted my inaction as, but he exploded with a shout, "Get over to that sink and brush your teeth right this minute!" He then grabbed me by the ear and lifted me up on my tip-toes and marched me to the sink. My ear was hot with pain. I dared not touch it, I knew it would hurt more if I touched it. The tears ran out of my eyes with a life of their own. I could not stop them if my life depended on it. I stood there blinking and wiping my eyes trying my best to see as panic started to rise in me. Where in the world is that x#@*_ toothpaste?! my mind screamed. I had never brushed my teeth before. I knew Bro Guy was losing his patience with me for he shouted, "Don't you see you're holding up the line! Get busy right this minute!" "Where, where's the toothpaste?" I asked frantically, surprised that he didn't hit me again. He walked over grabbed the slim can of toothpowder and slammed it down on the sink in front of me, "Right in front of your eyes you idiot!" he shouted. I had never seen tooth powder before. I poured some powder on the toothbrush but because the toothbrush was dry most of it simply fell off or went right through the bristles.

"Someone help this idiot!" Bro Guy ordered. Two boys quickly stepped out of line at the same time and started towards me, "Just you Rupert," Bro Guy said sternly. The other boy got back in line. I did my best to look at Rupert through the tears and noticed right away that he was fairly light-skinned, much lighter than everyone else. I took a good look at him for I wanted to remember who he was because he was so eager to help me. I watched closely as Rupert ran the toothbrush under water and then poured some toothpowder on it. He handed the toothbrush back to me. My top three front teeth and other teeth in the back were extremely decayed. They were brown and black. My teeth in the front were all but gone. They were so rotten that they broke in half and started to decay right up to the gum-line. I looked toothless. Toothaches were a common thing for me as a child and as an adult. I don't know of any pain that is worse. I took the toothbrush and because I had never brushed my teeth before, I had some difficulty keeping myself from gagging. I finally made it through this ordeal, my introduction to the toothbrush as everyone watched me. I am a shy person by nature and I hated that everyone was watching me so intently. In my heart I was angry that so many eyes were on me. I gave the group a mean look and some looked away at eye contact, others looked back just as angry. The only face that looked familiar was Rupert's.

Bro Guy directed me to the back of the line, grabbed me roughly by the shoulders and said in a voice that had calmed down, "Now stand up straight, look straight ahead and no talking." The bell rang just then. It was a hand-held bell. Its ring was very loud and could be heard from a great distance and it would surprise you how far away you could be and would still hear it. Someone was ringing it from downstairs. You did not want to be too close to that bell when it was being rung. We walked single-file down the stairs and as we were walking, another line of bigger boys joined our line and fell in step right behind me. I was last in line. I noticed how everyone looked so very serious all the time and there was not a word spoken. My first introduction to the "No Talking Rule." The only sounds heard were the shuffling of feet and the odd cough here and there or someone clearing their nose. We all walked single file into the dining hall. Nobody said a word, not even a peep. There were rows and rows and rows of tables. As we were walking in single file, the girls were walking in single file on the other side of the room. The boys went to one end of the room and started filling up the seats and the girls went to the other end of the room and did the same. This was all so new and strange to me that I looked around in wonderment trying to take everything in. As I was looking around I stepped on the heel of the kid in front of me and I tripped and fell out of line. I fell almost at the feet of Bro Guy. Before I could get up he grabbed me by my ear, twisted it and lifted me to my feet by my ear! The line kept moving. The pain shot right through me and I thought he ripped my ear! I yelled, "Owww!" and put my finger to my ear to check for blood, there was none. He pulled me out of the line and stood me up beside him, "Stay here and be quiet," he said threateningly. I was too insulted to cry. He had insulted me right in front of the girls! I wanted to kick him so badly but I was no match for him. My ear was burning with pain.

After everyone had entered the dining hall, Bro Guy spoke to the group, "Good morning everybody give me your full attention please. This is Andy Neeman", I hated the way he pronounced it. "Can you say 'Hi Andy?' and they all responded in perfect unison, "Hi Andy". Bro Guy continued, "Andy is from Whitehorse and will be with us for awhile. Andy is still learning the rules and if you see him doing something he shouldn't be doing what are you going to do?' he waited for them to answer and they all answered, again in perfect unison, "Tell the supervisor." "Right," Bro Guy said. Bro Guy then turned to one of the Nuns, the nuns were always dressed in their full uniforms and said, "Sister Aleco would you please bring Andy some cutlery?" She never answered and with a nod of her head sprang into action. Bro Guy led me to a table and sat me down with the younger boys who were about my age. I was feeling hungry and forgot about my loneliness as I was taking in this new atmosphere. I looked around the table at the other boys and then looked at my food, cold porridge and a single piece of cold toast. I was just about to reach for my spoon when the boy next to me quickly grabbed my arm and pulled it down below the table. Just as he did that and as I turned towards him about to question him, Sis Aleco said in a real loud voice, "Close your eyes and bow your heads." I then understood why the boy had grabbed my arm. His name was Peter. I closed my eyes and bowed my head as the whole dining hall erupted as if in one voice saying grace, "Bless us, O Lord, and these Thy gifts, which we are about to receive from Thy bounty, through Christ our Lord. Amen." Sis Aleco then said, "You may proceed." The dining hall then filled with the noise of clanging dishes and cutlery and none said a word. I then looked at the boy who had grabbed my arm and I said, "Thanks." The boy acted like he didn't hear me as he reached for his spoon. I wanted to show him that I was thankful and said it again this time a little louder, "Thank you." I could tell that almost everyone heard me, for most of them turned to look at me. Peter did not look at me but kept right on eating. As I started to reach for my spoon, I heard the swooshing of Sis Aleco's dress behind me and felt the hair on the back of my head near my neck-line being pulled upwards and it hurt big time! I rose to my feet trying to relieve some of the pain as she made me rise to the tips of my toes. She held me there and said in a really stern voice as her hot breath blasted into my ear, "No talking in the dining hall young man! No talking AT ALL!" She let go. I grabbed the back of my head and put my hand over the spot she had pulled. "Now sit down, shut your mouth and eat," she said pushing me hard into my seat with both her hands on my shoulders. The tears came out of nowhere and I felt so hurt and ashamed that I hung my head and tried my best to not let anyone see my tears. I tried to see through the tears and wanted to act like nothing happened as I sought to pull myself together and tried to find my spoon. I wiped the tears with my sleeve and looked around at the others at the table. No one looked at me. No one said a word. It was as if they understood completely what I was going through. They kept eating. Every once in a while they would sneak a peek to see where Sis Aleco was. When she turned her back towards us I noticed one of the boys made his hand like a fist and stuck his thumb between his fore finger and the third finger and he pointed it towards Sis

Aleco for all of us to see. This gesture was the First Nation equivalent of flashing someone the 'bird'. We all understand the gesture and it brought a smile to our faces including mine. I was just about finished my food when I heard, "Cutlery down!" It was Sis Aleco again. Just about everyone was finished eating except for a few stragglers. I did not put my spoon down right away but instead reached for one more scoop of porridge and shoveled it into my mouth. Just as I did, I glanced up to see if Sis Aleco was watching and she was. We made eye contact. Only this time she gave me a threatening look and waved her finger at me as if to say, "Don't you try that again." I nodded "OK" to her. She looked away and said, "Table one." Like a well-oiled machine, those sitting at table one stood up and proceeded to leave. I watched as all the other children stood up and started to file out of the dining hall in single file the same way we came in. As we walked out I looked over at the girls and there was one girl looking at me. She was very pretty. I later learned her name was Louise Porter. She smiled when our eyes met and I quickly looked away, too ashamed of my rotten teeth to smile back. Louise would be my very first girlfriend. They marched us back upstairs to our dorm. Upon walking into the dorm, I noticed that my bed was the only one not made. I didn't like that. I didn't like standing out, especially in a place like this. I noticed that the boys wasted no time getting undressed and then getting dressed in church clothes. Some were rough-housing and teasing each other and the atmosphere was a little less tense. Bro Guy called me over to the little office at the corner of the dorm near the front entrance. "See how all the beds are made up and yours is not?" he queried. "Yes," I answered watching his hands to see if he was going to strike me. He had me on-edge. I would never again be relaxed around Bro Guy until the day I left Lower Post. He continued, "I didn't push you to make your bed this morning because it's your first day and you were running late. Your bed has to be made first thing from now on. First thing, even before you wash up or brush your teeth, you make your bed. Understand?" "Yes," I answered. "I'll show you later on this morning how we want your bed to be made every morning. It's time for Mass right now," he said. I knew what Mass was as I was a Catholic and attended Christ The King Elementary School back in Whitehorse. "Come with me and we'll get you some clothes for Mass," he said nudging me out the door as he pulled out his big batch of keys and locked the office door. He looked at his watch. I followed him and his rattling keys down the hall and we entered a room that smelled of clean linen and bleach. It had closets and closets full of brand new white shirts, dress pants, sweaters, ties, shoes and dress socks. I tried on a few white shirts, pants, sweaters, shoes and left there with everything I needed for Mass. I liked the tie he gave me, it made me look like Al Capone. I pretended I was Al Capone just arriving at a jail and Bro Guy was a guard. "Hurry up and get dressed it's almost time for Mass," Bro Guy said hurriedly. I liked the idea of having some brand new clothes to put on. Back in the dorm as I was getting dressed, I started to feel like I was one of them. Yet I also knew that I did not want to stay there. I thought of the man who called himself Father Morrisette that I had met at the front door last night. I wondered how I would go about asking to speak with him. I wondered if I could ever speak to him. I decided that I would wait for a bit in order to learn a little more about the rules around here and how to avoid getting my ear twisted and my hair pulled out of its roots. Then I would plan how I could meet him.

Bro Guy came over and was just about to show me how to make my bed when the bell rang again. That loud hand-held clanging bell that told us it was time to line up. They lined us up differently this time. We were lined up side by side in two rows. We headed off for Mass, each doing our best to keep in step with the person we walked beside. We proceeded to the chapel. As we entered the chapel I smelled the sweet incense that hung in the air and it was very pleasant. There was a thin veil-like wisp of grey smoke from the incense that hung in the air just above the altar at the front of the chapel. We took turns dipping our fingers into the holy water, making the sign of the cross as we genuflected and took a seat. As we sat there listening to the priest recite prayer after prayer, I was overtaken by the warmth in the room and the peace that somehow had found its way into my heart. I started falling asleep. I had a difficult time fighting off the tiredness that kept invading my concentration. I was falling asleep and my head would go from one side to the other resting on each boy sitting beside me. The boys took turns shrugging and bouncing my head up each time I rested on their shoulder. Well it wasn't long before I sprang completely awake as the pain of my ear being pinched and twisted brought me starkly back into reality! There was no escape from Bro Guy's ever-watchful eyes not even in chapel and I was soon to learn *especially* not in *the chapel*! He stood behind me and as he whispered in my ear, I smelled a strong odor of garlic on his breath and it was awful. "Get out of your seat and come sit in the back," he ordered. There was such a stern ring to his voice, I was almost certain he was grinding his teeth as he said it. I rubbed my tired eyes, got up and went to the back. He motioned for me to sit down beside him and put his finger across his lips signaling me to be quiet. When Mass was ended, I was sure Bro Guy was going to scorn me but to my surprise, he told me to get back in line beside the person I walked in with.

After we got back to the dorm and after I changed my clothes Bro Guy showed me how to fix my bed properly. It had to be done military-style. Everything measured just right and pulled tight. Real tight. Nothing less would be accepted. The bell rang and we all got in line. We proceeded to march downstairs. Once downstairs in the recreation room the boys started pulling out various toys and began to play. I just stood there and watched not sure what to do or where I fit in. Brother Guy came out of the office and signaled for me to come over. I walked towards the office and I couldn't take my eyes off what looked like a merry go round contraption in the middle of the rec. room. I couldn't understand how come none of the kids were playing on it, I would've been the first one there, if I knew how it worked! I wanted to try it but would have to wait. When I got to the office Brother Guy introduced me to a stocky man with glasses who had wavy black hair with lots of hair on his chest that showed at the opening of his shirt. He was handsome and looked like Clark Kent. He had a big toothy smile and kind sparkling eyes. I liked him right away. He was a supervisor and the hockey coach. "This is Mr. Roland, Andrew." "Hi Andrew or is it Andy, what do they call you?" "Andy," I said it loud enough hoping Bro Guy would notice and stop calling me "Andrew." I tried to sound smart and strong hoping Mr. Roland couldn't detect my sadness. "OK, Andy it is. Welcome to your home away from home. I see you're from Whitehorse. Do you play hockey?" "A little," I answered, "Good, we will get you some hockey gear after school today." Just then the bell rang and we all lined up again. "Okay, quiet now it's time for school boys. No talking," Brother Guy said in a loud voice. He grabbed me by the arm and pulled me into line. He then pulled me out and shoved me back into the line again at a different spot. He stood back to examine me. Then he pulled me out again and pushed me back into line at a different spot. He stood back and looked at me again. I wondered, "What is this guy doing!?" and then it dawned on me that he was placing me in line according to my height. When he was satisfied he pointed to the boy in front of me and said, "This is Robert," and to the boy behind me he pointed and said, "This is Walter, your place in line is between Robert and Walter, no other place. Do I make myself clear?" I nodded my head, "Yes." "I didn't hear you!" Brother Guy said sternly. I said in a disgusted voice, "Yes!" and gave him a dirty look. "Good!" he said. "Make sure you remember that!" he warned me. I did not like him at all. He had no kindness whatsoever. I did not like it here. I felt confined and trapped. I did not have any control or any freedom or any relief from my fear and loneliness. I was alone among strangers. I could not go home. I could not see my sisters. I could not see my mom. I could not run. I could not find any comfort. I longed for my mother. Even if she was drunk and mean and they let me go see her, I would have run a hundred miles an hour, gladly! The world I had come from, something told me inside, might as well have been as far away as the moon. It was unreachable. My heart got heavy as this reality sunk in. I felt the tears roll down my cheeks. What am I doing?! Stop it Andy! I told myself. Stop your crying! I wiped the tears away as quickly as I could, hoping nobody noticed. We marched single file through a long corridor that linked the main building with a wing which was the school. There were four classrooms on the main floor. They put me in grade four. Back home, I had failed grade one because I skipped out of school so much. The schoolwork was easy, it was the violence and the drinking at home that was hard to live with so I ran away and I ran away all the time! I ran away from school. I ran away from the Truant Officer (a Truant Officer is an employee of the government whose job is to make sure no kids are truant [skipping out] from school). I ran away from the cops. I ran away from anything I didn't like, that made me feel uncomfortable. I was ten years old in grade four. Sis Anthony was our teacher in grade four at Lower Post.

The reality that I would not be going home for a long time was beginning to sink in. I did not want to accept the truth that I would be here all winter and maybe longer. When I began to ask the other kids how long they were there, it was like I was rubbing a sore spot in them. I soon learned to stay away from that topic. I liked school though. School kept my mind busy and I liked to read. Reading was a strong point of mine. Sis Teresa must've noticed this because she called on me to read when no one else would put their hand up to read, which was a lot. When another student could not pronounce a word, or did not know the meaning of a word, or got stuck on a word, she would call on me. Sometimes I had the answer some times I didn't. I really liked to read and I liked it when she called on me to read. Even though I was very self-conscience because of all my rotten teeth in front, I looked forward to reading out loud for Sis Anthony and the other students. My passion for reading overpowered my rotten teeth shyness.

After school, Mr. Roland took me to the equipment room and I found me a pair of skates that fit. He then found me some shin pads. These shin pads had very little protection. All they had for protection were sticks sewn over some thick cloth. He also gave me a puck and a hockey stick. That was it for my introduction to hockey equipment. I walked out to the hockey rink for my first taste of playing hockey at Lower Post. As I got closer to the skate shack I noticed there were not many boys skating mostly girls. All the boys were standing on the side lines watching the girls skate. When I walked into the shack, I realized why there were so many girls on the ice most of the guys were still in the process of putting their skates on. The skate shack was just that, a shack. There was no heat. You changed as fast as you could in order to keep as warm as possible. Once I got my skates on, my hands were quite cold. I slipped them into the thin liner of the cowhide mitts they gave me and grabbed my puck. Sis Aleco blew a whistle and the girls all skated off the ice. I walked through the snow and almost fell as the snow turned into ice that was covered in snow and it caught me off guard. Once the girls were off the ice the boys dropped their pucks and began skating around and shooting their pucks against the boards. Mr. Roland asked a couple of boys to help him and they jumped over the boards and grabbed the goalie nets, setting them in place. Then Mr. Roland blew his whistle and shouted, "OK, scrimmage time! There's not much time so let's hurry. Line up if you want to play!" All the girls who came off the ice went into the shack, changed into their boots and came back out to watch us. Mr. Roland picked two guys for captains and they began to choose players. I was picked last. I didn't care, I just wanted to play. I had never played organized hockey before. All I had ever played was pick-up hockey on our frozen pond at the dump back in Sleep Hollow. Back home there were no colored lines, no whistle and no checking. You just did your best to score by shooting the rock between two tin cans. Here at Lower Post in this scrimmage game, when I got the puck, all I knew was to stick-handle and to keep the puck to myself away from the other players. It wasn't hard for me to stick-handle and keep the puck to myself. I stick-handled through just about everyone and was enjoying myself because it was so easy and then I heard other players yelling, "Pass the puck hey! Quit being a puck hog!" I had no idea what a puck-hog was. Then all of a sudden, I was checked real hard. The puck went one way and I went the other. My skate got caught in a crack in the ice and I went flying to my knees. Both knees hit the ice with a hard, "Thud!" and as I slid on both knees the pain felt like I was sliding on a red-hot stove. I could not understand why the guy had run into me so hard like that. It was like he did it on purpose! Some of the players laughed at me and then the whistle blew. Mr. Roland came skating over to me real fast and asked, "Are you alright Andy?"

I felt the anger rise in me as I turned around to see who it was that checked me as I sat on the ice. My knees felt like they were on fire and I clutched them while I looked around again trying to see who had checked me. I had no idea who it was. My knees hurt, but my pride hurt even more. Everyone was looking at me including the girls. I heard someone snicker, "Teach you, puck hog!" I felt a lump form in my throat as I realized I had not a friend in this crowd. I was hurt and these guys were mocking me, they were not interested in helping me. I felt like the only one who really cared was Mr. Roland. Mr. Roland was the only one besides Peter at the dining room table, to show me anything that resembled kindness since I arrived at Lower Post. "I'm OK," I said as I forced myself through the pain to stand up. I was glad I didn't cry this time because as I skated off to take a rest, I noticed that girl Louise was there watching. I quickly glanced away. I didn't play anymore that night. I couldn't. My knees were sore for a couple of days.

Back inside the Rec. room after the scrimmage as I was putting my things into my locker, Mr. Roland came over to me and sat down on the bench in front of my locker. "Where did you learn to stick-handle like that? You haven't played organized hockey before have you?" He asked in a gentle voice with a half-smile on his face. "What's organized hockey?" I asked. "Well organized hockey means knowing the game and playing by the rules. Do you know what rules are?" "Of course, everyone knows what rules are! If you break the rules you get in trouble," I said matter-of-factly, "Right!" Mr. Roland sounded delighted. "No, I have never played with any rules. The only rule we played with back home is you can't go out of bounds that's all." "Where did you play?" he asked, "On the pond over by the dump." I felt a lump starting in my throat as I pictured playing hockey on the pond with my cousin Joe and Stanley and my friend Darryl and the others back in Sleepy Hollow. He noticed the tears starting to form in my eyes. "OK, come here don't worry, you're gonna be fine. I know how you feel." As I held me close to him and gave me a hug, I caught a faint whiff of sweet cologne and cigarette smoke from his plaid shirt. It reminded me of dad. Because I was feeling something I had not felt for what seemed like years, real genuine kindness, I had a real good cry. I was thankful there was no one else in the room right then. Mr. Roland never did abuse me he just showed me genuine kindness, encouragement and respect. He wiped the tears from my eyes with a corner of his shirt sleeve and said, "OK now that that's over, I have a little surprise for you wait here." I heard his big batch of keys jingling as he pulled them out and I watched as he fumbled for a key, disappearing from the room. I continued to put my hockey stuff into my locker. When he returned he had an Oh Henry chocolate bar and gave it to me. As I grabbed it he held onto it not letting go until he looked into my eyes and said, "Now I don't want no more crying OK? This is the first and last time I'm going to give you anything for crying. I want you to keep this in your locker until canteen day which is Friday and do not eat it until then. Am I clear?" "OK I won't touch it. I promise," I said not taking my eyes away from his. I had just discovered a new-found warmth in my soul put there by this handsome man with a kind heart and a big smile. "We could use you on the hockey team Andy. Would you like to be on the team?" "Sure!" I almost shouted. He could've asked me to jump off a bridge right then and my response would have been the same! "OK. Fine, we'll have to teach you how to play the game according to the rules then."

My first week at Lower Post Indian Residential School was the toughest. I missed my mom something fierce! I had never been so far away from her before. Every other time I was away from her I knew where I could find her and could go see her when I wanted. Not here. Here I could not run from what made me uncomfortable. I had a difficult time accepting that truth. I did not sleep a full night and I only slept when I cried myself to sleep. My appetite, that first week was all but gone. There was no one here who showed me any sign of love or caring.

I soon learned that every day at the res. school was the same old cold, calculated routine. We did not have to think for ourselves. We were herded like cattle. Cattle are herded with an electric prod, at the school we were herded with a bell or a whistle. A bell rang to get you up, line you up, get you fed, go out to play, to go to school and to go to bed. Bells, bells and more bells. If it wasn't a bell it was a whistle. The same bell day in and day out. Don't think, don't talk, don't cry and do as I say or else! Each morning they woke us up at 7 am. We had to be silent and could not talk. We had to make our beds and they checked to make sure they were made right. They had to made perfectly just like in the military. If not, they pulled it all apart and you started again. If you pee'd in your bed you had to place the wet sheet on your head and walk it down to the laundry room. Then we washed up. We brushed our teeth with that awful tasting toothpowder. When the bell rang we lined up for breakfast. Breakfast was most always sticky porridge. We had to eat all our food or we would be punished. We ate in silence. We knew the Supervisors had bacon and eggs before we ate because we could smell it in the air. Students could see and eat in the same dining room as their biological brothers and sisters but could not talk or even look at them. If they did talk or were suspected of looking at their brother or sister, they would be grabbed by the ear, yanked around and told to "Sit up straight and keep your eyes to yourself ". Sometimes they were dragged to the front, had their pants pulled down or their dresses pulled up and they were spanked on their bottoms in front of everyone then sent to the dorm.

After breakfast we lined up again and were told what chores we had to do. When our chores were done we lined up and went to the chapel for mass. After Mass, we got in line and marched to school. We were not allowed to talk while we were in line, never. You were disciplined if you did. After supper, we were allowed to go outside and we had to play whatever they told us to play whether we wanted to or not. If you had a problem with one of the other boys you still had to play with him whether you felt like it or not. If you got into an argument with a fellow student, you had to put on boxing gloves and fight that student in front of all the other boys down in the rec room. I had to fight three times with those gloves. I won two and last one. If it felt too cold to play hockey, we still had to get out there and play. You had no choice no matter how cold it was. If they told you to get our there on the ice or out to the playground, believe you me, you had to get out there! I remember being forced to get out there and play on the ice when it was so cold the pucks kept snapping in half when we shot them against the boards. We had to skate through the ice fog and my feet got so cold I could not feel my toes anymore! I never froze them, but I know I must've come as close to freezing them without actually freezing them as is possible. When I went to take my skates off, the tips of my socks were frozen to the skate. When I finally got the sock loose I could see the frost on the sock. No wonder I couldn't feel my toes! Lower Post almost killed my love for the game, but my love for hockey was stronger than any rules, regulations or abuse. The girls were forced to go out and *play* too, even if it was too cold for them, they still had to go. After recreation, we would go to the dorm, brush our teeth, kneel down and pray, then go to bed. Sometimes at night they would play a record over the loudspeaker. It might be a Fairy Tale story or Marty Robbins. I heard a lot of Marty Robbins there. After the record stopped, without fail, every night you would hear someone crying for their mom. Sometimes, you just couldn't help it no matter how you tried and you cried too.

I didn't know how I was going to survive in this situation that I could not run from. Then I met Robert Niedley. Robert Niedley was also a student there. He had the biggest and the toothiest smile I had ever laid my eyeballs on! He was a real, true, bona fide jokester! He could make anybody laugh and I mean anybody! He could twist his face in so many directions you'd think his face was made of rubber! He'd stretch his mouth this way and then that way to the point we were all sure it was going to tear! He'd pull his eyelids this way and that and walk in such a distorted way it was like his legs were broken! Robert was from Fort Nelson and he was the same age as I was. Looking back now, Robert probably did more to help me keep my sanity than anyone else at Lower Post. My sadness and my sorrow and my loneliness were toxic! There were many times when I would get anxiety so bad from the loneliness that I thought I was going to lose my breath and have a heart attack! That is, until I met Robert. I first met Robert the second week I was there. After supper one night, we had all gathered around Bro. Guy as he read us a boring short story about Pinocchio. We sat on the floor and when Bro. Guy was done he said, "So if you don't want your nose to grow don't lie. OK, half an hour 'till bedtime fellas. It's too cold and too late for anyone to go outside. So no one goes outside, clear?" We all answered in unison (I was catching on to the routine), "Yes, Bro Guy." He continued once he heard our automatic response, "Inside rec 'til bedtime." Then Bro Guy walked in his pigeon-toed way into the canteen room. We all sat there motionless not sure what to do. Then, Robert Niedley stood up. He made this really funny face like a chimpanzee, bent over and hung his arms down and started half-jumping, half-walking around the room. We all busted into laughter immediately! He made it look so real and it was so funny we couldn't stop ourselves from laughing, especially me! Then Robert stopped. Then he pointed towards the canteen room that Bro Guy had walked into and he started acting like the monkey again! We knew exactly what he was doing, he was pretending to imitate Bro Guy and

THAT,...now that made us laugh even louder and harder and I thought I was going to pee my pants! Bro Guy stuck his monkey ears head out the doorway of the canteen room and checked to see what the sudden outburst of unusually loud laughter was about and we all just kept on laughing. When he saw it was Robert, it was probably like nothing out of the ordinary to him so he pulled his head back in. Then Robert put his monkey face on again and imitated Bro Guy again by pretending he was poking his head out of a doorway just like Bro Guy just did. I had never laughed so hard in such a long time! It was the perfect remedy for how I was feeling and just at the right time! I started to feel lighter. I had not felt this light in a long, long time. In fact, I had not felt this light in years. Something called hope began to rise inside of me. I felt like I was part of this group and it was not going to be all doom and gloom. It was like, we were all in the same boat and that boat was floating, it was not going to sink and it was going to take us all safely to a destination. We were in it together. Then Robert came over and sat down. There were little bits of left-over laughter here and there. Then, with this new-found hope bursting in my heart I got into the act. At the age of ten, I had a high-pitched voice (like all ten year olds). I discovered that I could make this laugh that sounded *exactly* like the witch in "Snow White and The Seven Dwarves." I could make that laugh sound perfectly and exactly like it did in the movie! I only did it to myself up to this point and prided myself in being able to do it, but I always thought to myself, "Yeah, big deal where's sounding like a witch gonna' get you?" But on this night fueled with the new found knowledge that I had the ability to laugh in this horrible place and seizing on the moment out of pure spontaneity, I let my witch laugh go and to my surprise everyone cracked up laughing! I cracked up too as I knew it sounded so real and so much like the real witch that it truly was funny! When I stopped, someone said in an excited voice, "Do that again!" And I did, again and again. Then Robert jumped up and started into his monkey act and we had a laughing party! And before we knew it, Bro Guy came out of the canteen room and said, "OK, it's BEDTIME!" That night, something great had happened in my life. Something changed for the better. I discovered for the very first time, that I could find laughter, even at the darkest hour of life. I found the bright light of hope that had never shone in my life before. I was like a kid in the proverbial candy store. And for the first time in Lower Post I went to bed feeling like I was part of something that I never dreamed possible! I could actually have good feelings in this horrible place.

Robert and I became very close after that. Everyone liked Robert simply because he was just naturally a humorous, funny guy. I became quite popular also just because I could do this laugh! Then Robert and I became popular together as a team. We invented what we called the "chicken walk." We did the chicken walk by walking in a jerky motion, humping our mid-sections as we walked, moving our necks forward and backwards and swinging our arms all at the same while walking forward! Just like a chicken. Then we invented this act where we'd pretend we were crazy by holding one hand up by the side of our eyes, and we'd look at our hand from the corner of our eye with our head turned the other way, and we'd make these silly sounds that didn't make sense and we'd act like two crazies who escaped from the crazy house! Then we'd switch into our chicken walk! Then we invented a short act where we acted and sounded like two little babies laying on our backs playing in a crib. At the time it was hilarious to all of us.

CHAPTER EIGHT

THE PEDOPHILE

(I named this chapter "The Pedophile" on purpose so that those sexual abuse victims who do not want to trigger bad memories can have the opportunity to skip it.)

"My Past"

If I could change my past what would I be?
I'd be someone else I would not be me
If I held onto my sorrow and shame,
I would live life bitter, beat down with blame,
If I hid my past like it was not mine,
I'd still be "lost" drowning in wine,
If I lived my life in the past each day
The peace I've found would fade away
Yet my past is mine and I'm not ashamed,
It's made me who I am today!

A. Nieman

He was introduced as "Mr. George" and that's what all of us kids called him. I did not know his real name until 30 years later. His real name was Jerzy George Maczynski.

[Author's Special Note]

30 years later in my life after I left the residential school and started my healing, the government of Canada decided to compensate former Indian Residential School students who had experienced sexual abuse, physical abuse and unlawful confinement (being locked in a closet or a room alone as punishment) at the residential schools. I had a valid claim of sexual abuse filed in 1995 against Mr. George and was compensated, $90,000 (ninety thousand dollars.) It was only then, when I filed my claim of sexual abuse against Mr. George, that I learned what his last name was. When I graduated from the University of Regina (in 2000) with a Bachelor of Social Work degree, I started my own Therapeutic Counseling Business called "BEAUTIFUL JOURNEY COUNSELING SERVICES" and specialized in counseling Residential School Survivors and their families to heal from trauma. With my business and because I had a degree, the Government of Canada put me on their list of approved therapists to assist former students who were filing a claim of sexual abuse, physical abuse and unlawful confinement against the Government of Canada and who chose to go through the Alternative Dispute Resolution (ADR) process to settle their claims. The Government of Canada invented the ADR process as an alternative to Civil Litigation. Civil Litigation is where a former students who wanted to sue Canada for the abuse they suffered at the schools went through an actual court trial and a Judge made a decision as to whether or not there was enough evidence to award compensation. If a former student wanted to sue the Government of Canada, and they won, they had the potential to be awarded millions of dollars. In the ADR process the most a former student could be awarded was $250,000 (two hundred fifty thousand) maximum. Once a former student decided to go through the ADR process and accepted the settlement amount, they could never go back and sue the Government of Canada. This was written into the Settlement once you agreed to take the amount offered and signed the agreement. For further information on the ARD process please check the Internet, the information is there.

As a Support Person for former residential school students going through the ADR process, I sat right there in the hearings beside them. Because most of the former students knew that I had attended Lower Post, they instantly had a high level of trust with me and many of them requested me to be their Support Person in their Hearing. As a counselor involved in the ADR process, I have sat through close to one hundred individual Hearings and the majority of those sexual abuse cases named Mr. George as the offender. Each Hearing I sat through, I thought I had heard it all in terms of horror. But to my astonishment, they only got worse. The stories of abuse I heard in those Hearings, every one of them, were horrific and extremely heartbreaking. The damage one pedophile can do in a room locked up with hundreds of helpless little boys is absolutely and totally devastating! The damage would last a lifetime. As a former student of the Lower Post Indian Residential School, I knew exactly what every one of these victims was talking about. And I knew they spoke the truth, no need for exaggeration, because I had been there. As a former therapist dealing first-hand in counseling with many of Mr. George's victims, here are some facts I learned about him. These are from my personal files and I heard the same or similar accounts in many of my counseling sessions:

-Out of 11 Convicted (I emphasize convicted in a Court of Law) Pedophiles employed in various residential schools throughout the Yukon 7 were employed at Lower Post Indian Residential School.

-I learned through counseling sessions and in the ADR Hearings that Mr. GEORGE was the WORST of the 11. HE had a SEXUAL APPETITE that was virtually insatiable. Many of the lawyers and other professionals I worked with in the ADR Hearings stated that Mr. George's sexual appetite and sexual prowess was "almost supernatural".

-His room, the supervisor's room, was located in BETWEEN the BOY'S DORM and the BATHROOM…many boys PEED in their beds, rather than risk going to the washroom and have Mr. George follow you in. As a result they were punished for wetting their beds.

-Mr George WOULD GROOM his victims by GIVING THEM the AFFECTION THEY CRAVED. HE PREYED ON THEIR LONELINESS of BEING AT THE SCHOOL

SO FAR FROM THEIR PARENTS. He gave them the FALSE AFFECTION they NEEDED and TURNED that AFFECTION into SEXUAL ABUSE.

-He would tell OLDER VICTIMS.."I'M GOING TO SHOW YOU WHAT TO SAY TO A WOMAN.. HOW TO TREAT HER RIGHT and WHERE to TOUCH HER"

If one of the STUDENTS was A GOOD ATHLETE or WON an AWARD and went on A TRIP He would GO as a CHAPERONE and ABUSE THEM.

ANDY NIEMAN

Jerzy George Maczynski (Mr. George) was convicted for his sexual abuse crimes at Lower Post in the mid 1990's. He was sentenced to sixteen years and died of a heart attack while in prison.

[END of AUTHOR'S SPECIAL NOTE]

Time passed and a few months went by. I made the hockey team. We played hockey regularly against Upper Liard and Watson Lake. We really looked forward to playing hockey outside the school in another community. It gave us a chance to get away from the foul environment of the school. I was a Junior Boy then. At the residential school there were three categories or age levels: there were the Junior Boys, Intermediate Boys and Senior Boys. This was the same for the girls. I believe the age groups were: Junior Boys, 5-10 yrs.; Intermediate Boys11-13 yrs. and Senior Boys 14-16 yrs. We were separated into one of these groups according to our age.

When I first met Mr. George he became my favorite of all the supervisors almost immediately. He had a Welsh accent and I liked it when he would pick me up, throw me up in the air and catch me then tickle me. I especially liked it when he would rub his stubble of whiskers on my face and on my neck. Just like my dad used to do back home. Every other weekend or so all of us boys would go for an day long outing to a place that was called "Boy's Town". Boy's Town was just a campsite out in the bush away from the school. Sometimes just the Junior boys would go, sometimes just the Intermediate boys would go and other times just the Seniors would go and sometimes we would all go together.

When we went on these trips with Mr. George, sometimes he would carry one of us boys on his shoulders. He couldn't do it all the time as he had a slight limp and sometimes used a cane to get around. He did not use his cane all the time. When Mr. George was on shift, and it seemed like he was always on shift, at least more then the other supervisors, I noticed there were more boys crying at night than usual. I also noticed that whenever a boy came out of his room, his room was situated in the dorm, between the dorm and the bathroom, each of them had a candy bar or a sucker. Well, to a ten year old who did not have any money sent from home and could not buy any candy, this was an interesting situation. One night, I couldn't stand it any longer. I was tired of watching in envy as the other boys ate the candy Mr. George had given them. I was going to get some for myself too! That night while we were preparing for bed, I waited for my opportunity. As soon as the next boy came out of Mr. George's room I decided that I was going to ask Mr. George if I could have some candy too. I waited and waited and watched the door that had the curtain pulled closed so tight that it was impossible for anyone to see in. I watched the door handle eager for it to start turning. When it did start turning, I thought to myself, "Finally!" The boy came out wiping tears from his eyes. I thought to myself, "What a cry-baby! Boy, if I had his candy, you wouldn't see me crying like that!" After the boy closed the door and left, I thought I better hurry before Mr. George came out and said, "Lights out!" I knocked on the door with a timid knock not wanting

76

the other boys to notice what I was doing because I thought they might get mad that I was invading their candy territory. There was no answer. I started to get impatient and irritated. I knocked again a bit louder this time. Then I heard his voice, "Come in." I turned the knob and wanted to rush in as fast as I could so nobody would see me, but I knew I couldn't. I had to let him invite me in after all it was his room. "Ahh, Andy," he pronounced it as "On-dee," what is it my boy, something wrong? Come in, come in." I entered his room and pulled the door part way closed behind me. I held the door partly open to show him I was ready to leave right away depending on his answer. "What is it On-Dee?" he asked putting his glasses on and looking at me. One of his eyes was a glass eye. It was hard for me to tell which one was real until I looked at him for a long time, "Hi Mr. George, I was just wondering if I could have some candy too please?" "Oh it's candy you're after. Well I have lots of candy and would be glad to give you some, but there's just one problem." "Oh, there is?" I queried, my heart beginning to sink. "Yes, and the problem is this, candy doesn't grow on trees and that means that candy does not come free, you have to work for it. Are you willing to work for it On-Dee?" "Yes. I'll work for it Mr. George. What do you want me to do?" "Come over here and sit on my lap." I went over in my pajamas and sat on his lap. I caught the smell of Old Spice aftershave. I liked how it smelled. However, in later years, it would become a smell that I hated as it reminded me of him. "The type of work you'll need to do is not work at all. In fact I shouldn't even call it work because it feels so good to you. I am the one who does all the work. Now does that sound like a good deal On-Dee or not?" "It sure does Mr. George!" I said enthusiastically. With those words, I entered the world of this pedophile and the hell of sexual abuse that would change my life forever. Jerzy George Maczynski then put his hand into my pajamas and so began the sexual abuse that would totally ruin my life for the next twenty seven years. I could never be that same little innocent boy that I was when I first stood on the other side of his door and knocked ever again. The abuse at the school went on for three years.

The sexual abuse I experienced by Mr. George was of course very painful yet some of it sad to say, was pleasurable. As a result, this created such tremendous shame and guilt in me that it made me extremely self-conscious. It became very hard and I mean very hard for me to look people in the eye in social settings. However it was a totally different story when it came to my survival and when it came to feeding my addiction. If I had to lie to get food or other necessities of life, or drugs I could look anybody in the eye and be whoever I had to be and do it all with a straight face to get what I needed. I became a master actor. I learned to mask my real feelings. I learned to bury my real feelings so far and so deep down in my heart that when I started my healing twenty seven years later, getting to those feelings was one of the hardest things I ever had to do. When I left the school I couldn't do anything to Mr. George to get even. I would carry that burning hatred and unresolved anger for the next twenty seven years. For the remainder of my life right up until I was 39 yrs. old I avoided social settings like it was the plague. All of the pain, the horror and the fear that took place in that room at Lower Post, will stay in that room forever. And it will go to my grave with me. Years later, in my ADR Hearing, I told part of what happened. What happened to me in that room instilled an uncontrollable hatred, an uncontrollable rage inside of me that I carried for over thirty years. I was not a physically aggressive person. I learned from the violence at home to keep quiet and not let my anger show so I kept it inside me and it all came out through an extreme addiction to anything that had the ability to change my feelings and/ or my mood. I could not figure out where this anger and hatred was coming from until I started my healing journey in 1994, thirty years later. That abuse scarred me so deep I felt dirty all the time. It was a dirtiness that could not be cleaned with soap and water no matter how much I washed. The scars of that abuse ran so deep I felt like I was marred with an irreparable scar. The feelings of pure unadulterated shame that was created in me by that abuse caused me to be depressed for many, many years. I covered it up mostly with alcohol but I would experiment with any kind of drug that was put in front of me, what did I have to lose? I was depressed all through my teens and into adulthood until I turned thirty nine and finally started to heal.

Throughout my whole life ever since my first trip to Lower Post, shame was my biggest enemy. From as far back as I can remember, shame kept me locked in a prison of negativity. It kept me locked in a prison of insecurity. A prison that made me look at anybody and everybody with envy in my eyes. I felt and believed with all my heart that no one, absolutely no one had a worse life than I did. I believed that everybody else had more than I had. They had more love. They had more happiness. And they had more to offer other people than I ever could. Shame drew a black curtain over my dreams. It locked me up in a doorless dungeon of despair, depression and desperation. It blocked out every shred of hope that tried to raise its head enough to grab a breath of fresh air. I did not feel worthy of anything in any way. In fact I felt the opposite, I felt totally worthless. All because of the guilt I was feeling. Later in my teen years I struggled with feelings of not being sure if I was queer or if I was straight. This made me even more self-conscience if that was possible. Shame made me withdraw deep into myself. So deep, I could not come out and be myself. It stripped me of my identity and brought me to the place where I did not know who I really was. I was faceless, felt worthless, I was homeless and loveless. Alcohol kept me alive. When I would crash (come down) from a heavy night of cocaine use, the depression would get an iron-grip on my heart again and it would form a lump in my throat that was so big I was certain it was going to choke me. And then old man suicide would start calling my name and he would whisper in my ear, "It ain't going to get any better Andy. You know it. Just end it. You know you want to. Go ahead, it's not hard. You can do it without pain." It was at those times that alcohol helped me get through the depression. I was not able to look people in the eye for any extended period of time when I was sober. I could only look people in the eye for an extended period of time if I was high on something or had some alcohol in me. I was afraid they might see the shame and the fear that was there. I was afraid they might catch a glimpse of one those scenes where Mr. George was taking advantage of me. These feelings of guilt and fear were always present with me and they loomed large, very large.

I noticed one day when it was getting closer to Christmas there was an unusual excitement in the air and in the boys. And then one day Mr. Roland came down the stairs whistling a happy tune with a list in his hand. As he pinned the list to the rec room bulletin board everyone rushed over to the list. The boys were pushing each other and jostling to get a look at the list. I asked my friend Walter, "What's this?" "That's the going home list," "Whatta' you mean going home list?" I had to know and grabbed his arm stopping him. "If you're name is on the list, it means you're going home for Christmas Holidays." "Oh," I said. "Are you going home?" I asked him, "Yes sirree boy!" he blurted out with a big smile. "I'm going to tell Larson." [Walter was from Cassiar and was a good friend of mine at the school. He left the school when he turned sixteen and a couple of years later he drowned along with his brother Willie, when they were trying to cross a river with a heavy load after hunting.] I walked up to the list eager to see if my name was on it. It wasn't. I had to stay behind at the school for the Christmas holidays. I later learned that your parents had to pay the bus fare for you in order for you to go home for the Christmas break and it was the same at Easter break.

During the Christmas break, the abuse continued. It was Christmas so we had a few more candies than usual and of course Mandarine oranges. I had lots of ice time just shooting the puck against the boards during the break. At Lower Post we had this great big slide that went up in the air about twenty feet or more. The sliding track was pure ice! It was a single track that they flooded with water to keep it icy. When you slid down this slide you went fast! *Very fast*! I have a natural-born fear of heights and used to have many dreams that I was falling off a cliff or a mountain as a kid. I still have a fear of heights to this day. But back then, when I first saw that slide, I was amazed! It was so huge! It was like looking at the Empire State Building to my ten-year-old mind! And the steps that took you to the top were straight up! I did not want to climb it but I sure wanted to try that slide! I would not have done it on my own, but when Robert dared me to, that was all I needed! After that first slide, you couldn't keep me off it! During the Christmas break, I was asked to fill in and do one of the Intermediate boys' chores. The chore was to sweep the main hall by the reception area. The same hall I walked down when I first arrived at the school. As I was sweeping, I noticed one of the doors was slightly ajar. The door led to a room where one of the priests lived. I could see through the crack in the door that an open suitcase was on the bed. Inside the suitcase I saw a package of Export cigarettes and a wallet. I was alone in the hallway and had been alone since coming up with my broom to sweep the hall. I quickly glanced back and forth to each end of the hall to see if anyone was around. The hall was empty. I pushed the door open and stuck my head in the dark room and asked rather quietly, "Is anyone here? Do you want your floor cleaned?" I listened for an answer while keeping one eye on the hallway. Convinced that there was no one in the room, I slipped in as quietly as I could. I closed the door almost completely shut. I walked over to the suitcase and laid the broom on the front of my shoulder. I stopped to listen if there was any movement coming from the washroom. It was silent. I picked up the pack of cigarettes and took out four cigarettes. I closed the package and put it back. I picked up the wallet and looked through the bills. I only took out one ten dollar bill. I didn't want it to be noticed that anything was missing. I wrapped the ten dollar bill around the four unfiltered cigarettes and shoved them down into the waistband of my shorts. I went back over to the door and peered through the crack as I listened for any footsteps walking in the hall. It was silent. I opened the door and stepped out into the hall. I did not feel nervous in the room, but started to feel nervous now. I had to get back downstairs. I looked at the pile of dirt I had accumulated from my previous sweeping and decided to pick it up and then leave. But no, I couldn't do that because it was plain to see that the rest of the hall needed sweeping. I took a deep breath and thought about the situation. Then it dawned on me that even if the priest came back, he probably would not miss the cigarettes or the money right away. I calmed down then almost smiling to myself. It felt good to be able to steal from these people who kept me as their prisoner.

I did not tell any of the other boys my age about the cigarettes or the money. I kept my stash to myself until I figured out who I could trust. It had not dawned on me that I needed matches in order to smoke the cigarettes. I was already smoking back home by the time I was seven. I was seven years old when I inhaled my first cigarette. I was quite used to smoking by the time I was ten. I had to take a risk and confide in one of the Senior boys about my stash. I never told anybody where I got the cigarettes or the money. I had to pay Roy a Senior Boy the ten dollars to get some matches and I also had to give him three cigarettes. I had no choice. He could've taken the whole thing and there would be nothing I could do about it. I smoked part of my one cigarette while out at Boys Town on a winter picnic outing. It made me so dizzy and sick I gave most of it to Roy. To this very day, whenever I smell cigarette smoke in the outdoor winter air, I am reminded of Lower Post and the day I smoked that one cigarette. During that Christmas break, I ate quite a bit of candy and I got to meet with the other boys and girls who didn't go home for Christmas. It was strange at the school because most of the students were gone for the break. It was quieter and lonelier. The students only went home for two weeks at the break, but it felt like two years to me. I found out who Louise was as she stayed at the school during the holidays. We really liked each other and had a crush on each other until the day I left there for good three years later.

When the students returned, it felt so, so good to see and be with them again. I was glad Christmas only came once a year. Then my teeth started hurting, especially the three in the front. I had never been to a dentist before and when they told me they were going to stick that great big needle in my mouth, I had never had to face fear like this before! Talk about a fear of needles! I cried as hard as I could possibly cry, thinking that if I cried hard enough they would find another way and wouldn't put that needle in my mouth! No such luck. They pulled three teeth in the front and one on the back. I stayed in the dorm out of school for three days until the gums healed up enough for me to eat soft food.

Summer finally came to Lower Post. It was nearing the end of the school year and I was getting ready to go home. I could not contain my excitement and neither could the other kids! We were all giddy and acted totally goofy and as silly as a happy kid could possibly be who was going home to see mom after nine months of separation. When the day to get on the bus to go home finally arrived, every single one of us had butterflies in our stomachs! We were saying "Good-bye," with great big smiles and Robert and I did the Chicken Walk like it was going outta' style! We were going home! I didn't care if my mom was an axe murderer I was going home to see her again!!! Yippee! She is going to be so happy! I could see myself running up to her and burying my face in her chest as we hugged forever! And I would give Liz and Margaret and Kim a great big hug and then I'll hug our dogs Trixie and Rex then I'd run over to visit my friend Daryl and Gary! I could not wait!

On the bus ride to Whitehorse the kids were going crazy laughing and wrestling and rough-housing. We made stops at Watson Lake to let kids off and at Upper Liard, then Squanga Lake and all along the way until there was just a few of us left when we arrived at Whitehorse. When we got to the Bus Depot in Whitehorse I was surprised because there were not very many people waiting there to greet us. And to my disappointment neither my mom nor any of my sisters were there! Maybe the school got the dates wrong or maybe my family got the time wrong and thought the bus was coming in later? I had all these questions running through my anxious mind. I did not have any baggage to carry other than a few drawings I made during the school year and after looking and waiting for my family to appear, it was clear no one was coming. I started to feel let down but then it hit me, I was free! I was free! No more Lower Post and no more Mr. George! And no more Bro Guy! And no more keeping quiet and no more eating that slop! Well, it's good that no one showed up! I'll surprise them! I said to myself. I started running towards Sleepy Hollow. It was so good to see Whitehorse again! So great to be walking on my old trails again and it was like heaven to see the Yukon River slowly flowing by in the middle of June on such a nice warm sunny day! I ran past Jamieson's Store, ran past Whitehorse Elementary School, past the old Army Buildings and only slowed down to catch my breath. It felt like I was home when I felt the dirt under my runners from our old familiar school trail that wound its way from Sleepy Hollow to school and continued uptown. I crossed over the railroad tracks and could see our house pretty clearly in the distance. As I approached the house running at full speed, I slowed down to a walk for a bit because it looked like there was no one home. I could see from a distance that our door was wide open. Trixie our dog was not in the yard nor was Rex our other dog. Something was amiss. Keeping my distance, I strained my eyes to see inside. It took a bit for my eyes to adjust from the bright sunlight to the dark interior of the house but after a second or two my eyes adjusted to the dark and I could see my mom at the table. It looked like she was passed out. There was a half-empty bottle of Lemon Gin on the table.

Fear quickly gripped my heart and pulled at my breath, was she dead? I snuck up as quickly as I could while being as quiet as I could and stopped just outside the doorway. I looked at her belly to see if she was breathing. Her belly slowly rose up and down. Once I realized she was alive, I got scared. A new fear took over. Would she wake up and grab me and hurt me? I glanced around the room to see if anyone else was there. I held my breath and listened. All I heard was the buzzing of a few flies fighting over whatever was in the pot on the cold stove.

I turned and ran as fast as I could to the railroad tracks where I sat down put my arms across my knees hung my head down and cried. A wave that felt like total abandonment formed at the bottom of my heart and almost choked me until it finally completed its journey as a river of tears gushing from my eyes. How could she do that to me!? Surely she must've known I was coming home today! How could she NOT KNOW? How could she DO THAT?? The hurt and disappointment overwhelmed me! That day, at that precise moment, loneliness took me on a new turn in the road. Loneliness became the ever-present beast that I hated more than anything else and the main emotion I would live with until the day I started to heal. I sat there crying until my eyes were puffy and my nose was sore from blowing it so much. Then finally my choking sobs subsided and I was so tired I felt like sleeping. But then I realized that I was free! Free from Lower Post! I was free from Mr. George and free from Bro Guy! No need to cry! I then wondered, where is Margaret and where is Liz, Kim and Frieda? I decided to head over to the Dawson's house to see if Gary or Maddy were home. As I walked into their yard, I could see Gary and Maddy had a bike over turned and they were working on it. I tried to sneak up as best I could but Maddy noticed me first and shouted in surprise, "Nieman!" Then Gary turned and when he seen me, his face lit up with a great big smile and he too shouted, "Nieman! Well I'll be a son-of-a-gun! Where'd you come from? Man it's good to see you!" That was the kind of welcome home from Lower Post that I wanted and it took the Dawsons to give it to me.

We talked and laughed and caught up on all that had happened over the past winter. The hours flew by. Then before we knew it, it was suppertime and May, Gary's mom, came over with a bowl of stew and while handing it to me said, "You're mom home?" I lied by shaking my head "No." "Where's all your sisters?" I had six sisters. I looked at May when she spoke to me because she was such a kind person. I did not look most people in the eye because of the shame the sexual abuse left in me. I liked May very much and respected her. She had lots of love in her heart and always backed that love up with action. I shrugged my shoulders at her to indicate, "I don't know." I hated lying to her. "Poor kid. You look so skinny. Finish all your stew and if you want some more Gary will get you some more." "Thank you Mrs. Dawson." "Call me May not Mrs. Dawson, I'm not your school teacher." All of us laughed at that one including May.

Around 11 pm that night May called us all into the house. She turned to Gary and said, "It's time for Andy to go home now. He's been here all day. Gosh, Mrs. Nieman must be worried sick about him. You and Maddy can walk him home. I don't want Mrs. Nieman mad at me she's a strong woman you know. I bet that woman could pick me up with one arm." She laughed after she said it. Gary then asked, "Can Andy stay the night?" It was almost as if Gary's dad Art, who was laying there watching TV in his bedroom could hear the conversation, he couldn't of course as the TV was blaring away. But we all heard his booming voice as he asked point blank, "Is that young Nieman boy still here? It's time for him to go home now, it's past eleven. His mom must be wondering where he is! You kids tell him to go home right now. Gary, you hear me?" Gary answered, "Yeah, yeah I hear you." Part of me wanted to go home so badly and part of me dreaded going home. I didn't want to go home because I was afraid mom would still be drinking. If she was still drinking it meant clearly that I did not mean anything to her. I did not want to face that reality. I would rather not know. I couldn't face the hurt of feeling rejection again. I decided that I was not going to go home. I mustered up the courage to speak, "Mrs. Dawson, I mean ahh May. Is it OK if I sleep over? My mom is drinking and I'd rather stay here until she's sober." "It's OK with me but I don't know about Art. I'll ask him." I did not like to put May on the spot because she was always so kind to me and rather than risk Art getting irritated with her I said, "Oh, that's OK May, I'll go home." "Are you sure?" she looked at me with concern clearly written on her kind face. "Yeah, that's OK. Thanks anyway." I wanted so badly to stay yet part of me wanted so badly to see my mom. Maddy and Gary walked me to the tracks in front of my place. I turned to them, "See you guys tomorrow." "See you Nieman," Gary said. "See you Andy" Maddy added. "Why don't we get together and go to the clay cliffs tomorrow?" Maddy asked. "OK!" I added real quick. "We'll pick you up then," Gary said. I knew my mom did not like me bringing any of my friends over to the house so I said, "I'll come over to your place in the morning and we'll go from there." "OK, we'll wait for you," Gary said looking at me and we sealed the deal when our eyes made contact.

I waited until they left and were out of sight then I bent down and slowly crawled up the small hill the railroad tracks were set on. I peeked my head over real slow and surveyed the yard in front of our house.

Someone was home. I could see our dogs Trixie and Rex laying in the front yard. There was smoke coming from the chimney. We had to use the wood cook stove for our meals even during summer. It was about ten hours now since I had noticed my mom passed out at the table after I ran all the way from the Bus Depot when I returned from Lower Post earlier today. I did not know what to do as I lay there. My eleven year old mind was racing in many different directions trying to think of a safe place to go. I could go to my friend Darrell's place and say that my mom was drunk again but it's too late at night to bother them. I could spend the night in Johnny Tom Tom's (RIP) old abandoned car that was a permanent fixture in our yard. I could just take a risk and walk in the door. As soon as that thought crossed my mind, my brain was flooded with memories of being trapped inside that house while my mom drunk on Lemon Gin beat me with anything she could grab. Memories of being dragged by my hair and having my faced pushed into the pillow to muffle the sound as I am being hit repeatedly all over my body by a block of wood. But what if she has sobered up now and has come to her senses realizing that this is the day I came home from Lower Post? I decide the best and the safest thing to do is to sneak up to the house, look through the window and if she's sober I'll go in, no problem. And if she is still drinking, I'll sleep in Johnny's Tom Tom's car. I don't want Trixie and Rex to bark and give me away so I stand up right where I'm at and get their attention by waving my arms. The plan works like a charm. They see me, it takes them a moment then they recognize me and once they recognize me they start runnng towards me with their tails wagging and a smile on their faces. I pet them and give them a hug then I start walking down the short dusty dirt road that leads to our place. I crouch down and make my way along the side of the building to my mom's window to her room. I slowly peek in and what I see makes my heart ache. My mom is eating something on a plate and in front of her on the table is a half a bottle of Lemon Gin and her big white tin cup she drinks out of. She is still drinking. I am heart broken, angry and scared all at the same time. I feel like this is the story of my life, I am constantly on the outside looking in. I don't feel like I am part of this family. I feel like I don't have a family at all. Well if that's the case, I'll live on my own. I'll take care of myself. I sneak over to our window and peek in to see if Lizzy, Margaret, Kim and Frieda are home. They are. They are all asleep. It hurts me deeply that they weren't waiting up for me. I go over and open the door to Johnny Tom Tom's abandoned car as I try to see through my tears. There is an old dirty blanket there and a small cushion from a couch. The back of the seats are torn and bits of torn foam lay here and there barely covering the seat springs that stick up here and there. The front seat is OK to sleep on. I move the blanket and the pillow onto the front seat. Trixie and Rex jump in the back. I lay down in the front seat and for the first time in my life, I realize that I would have to take care of myself if I was to survive in this unpredictable cruel world. As I fall asleep the smell of an old car, rubber foam and dashboard dust fill my nose. I didn't know it at the time but this experience of returning home from Lower Post only to be left alone by those who I expected to love me the most, created a deep valley of hurt in my heart that I never recovered from until twenty eight years later. Along with the sexual abuse that happened to me in that same year, I learned to shut people out. That night was the last straw. From that night on, I kept people at an emotional distance vowing that they would never hurt me again. I decided that I would not get close to anyone and I would not let anyone get close to me. As a result, I developed an emotional disability that prevented me from truly getting close to people even if I wanted to. And even to those that I love. I still feel the effects of this even to this very day.

CHAPTER NINE

THE GROUP HOME & SKAG WAY

"Trying To Hide"

Please come and heal my heart
Heal my mind and heal my soul,
I need to know I'm not alone
When happiness is just on loan,
Too long in darkness I have roamed
As songs drift from the radio,
Of love and joy that freely flows,
I wonder where the good times go,
I long for them I want to know,
I hold my head up with a smile,
While deep inside sorrows collide,
Don't look too close into my eyes,
There's something there I'm trying to hide,

A. Nieman

I first heard about the Group Home from my friend Mason. I was 12 yrs. old. Mason knew that I slept anywhere I could as a young boy. Now-a-days they call it "couch-surfing" to me it was just my way of life. One day Mason said, "You should give Barbara MacPherson a call and see if you can move into the Group Home." Barbara MacPherson was a Social Worker who worked with Child and Family Services in Whitehorse. Mason continued, "All's you need to do is tell her how rough it is for you at home. Just tell her the truth, that you're getting beat up all the time and have to run away to be safe and that you've sleeping all over the place." "Will she have to talk to my mom?" I questioned the idea. "Probably, I'm not sure. Want me to ask her?" "If she has to talk with my mom

85

then forget it, my mom won't let me." "Ya' never know!" Mason said trying to encourage me. Mason was one of my truest friends. He was big in stature and big in his sense of humor. Mason was very smart and extremely honest. So honest that he would never and I mean never come with me to do a "job" any illegal job that is. He had a unique outlook on life in that he would think outside the box. He had great taste in music and he liked to read a lot. He was also very mechanically inclined, so much so that I called him "Machine Head" once in a while. Mason was the first in our group of teenagers to own a car. He purchased the car when he and Gary were working at the Whitehorse Copper mine. If you owned your own vehicle back then you were supercool. Mason also introduced me to some cool bands and great music. It was quite common for Mason to pick me up first to go cruising with him. Many times I was the only one he let ride with him as we went cruising. One Friday night when he pulled up to my place and picked me up the song, "Tell Mama" by Savoy Brown was playing on his eight track player in the car. I fell in love with that song and that album and the band right from the first time I heard that song. He also introduced me to the band Chilliwack.

Mason said that he would ask Barbara MacPherson to contact me. I said, "No, why don't you just get her phone number give it to me and I'll call her?" I did not want a Social Worker to come to my house in case she showed up when my mom was drinking. That would really get my mom going and it would only bring the heat on me. "OK" Mason said. "We'll smell you later then!" "Yeah right," I told him as I smiled, "I'll smell *you* later!" He laughed and walked away. I met with Barbara MacPherson and she gave me a grand tour of the Group Home to see if I liked it or not. The first thing I noticed as we entered the premises was the smell of fresh bread baking. The second thing I noticed was a very, very pretty girl named Mary Jane as she was watching Tom Jones singing on the color TV. The third thing I noticed of course was the color TV. It was one of the coolest things I had ever seen to that point in my life.

We walked down a couple of short stair cases and into the rec room. One of the students there Patty, was singing along with the record player as Tommy James and the Shondells belted out, "Crimson and Clover". Patty had a very nice voice and she sang in perfect harmony with the song. I liked what I saw in this new surrounding and I liked it very much. I couldn't get excited though, not just yet. I did not want to set myself up just to be disappointed in the end if it didn't work out. Miss MacPherson asked me if I liked the place. My heart was saying, "Wow! What's not to like!?" but my mouth said, "Yeah its' OK I guess." I didn't want to show any sign of happiness after all, I was trying to convince her that my life at home was not very good. "Would you like to live here Andy?" she said in a gentle voice. She was very pretty and I had a secret crush on her already (just like all the other guys at the Home I would later learn). "Yes, it would sure be better than living at home," I assured her, trying to sound convincing. "Do you want me to see what I can do make it happen?" "Like what?" I was scared it would involve sitting down and talking to mom. I could see my mom in my mind's eye giving this pretty lady one of her meanest stares while she verbally abused her.

Barbara continued, "Well I'll have to check with your mother or your dad to see how things are at home. If what you told me is true about your home life and I believe you are telling me the truth, then I'll just need one of them to sign the paperwork." My heart sank. I thought to myself, "Mom will never do that! She'll never let me go!" Then Barb no doubt seeing the disappointment on my face said, "What's the matter?" "My mom will never let me go. It'll only make things worse for me if we ask her." "Well, we can ask your father then, what's his name, Paul?" "He's not home he's out in the bush cooking somewhere. He's never home," I said my voice heavy with disappointment. Barbara knelt down in front of me and took my chin in her hand, "Don't worry Andy, we don't have to ask for anybody's permission. We don't even have to ask for your mother's permission. We could go to court and that is all it would take. You don't have to face your mother. It will take a little longer though going through court." I knew about court. It sure didn't take them long when they dealt with me and sent me to Lower Post I thought. "I'll have to ask some questions and get some information to prove that you are not safe at home and then I can get things ready for court, how does that sound?" she asked. I knew everything was up in the air and I just nodded my head, "Yes" with not much enthusiasm. "Do you have a safe place to stay in the meantime?" she asked. I shook my head, "No". "OK. We'll get you a safe place to stay until we work this out. Do you have any questions?" again I shook my head, "No." I wound up staying at Mary House for a couple of nights. We went to court and in the month of December just after I had my 12th birthday on December 16th I was placed in the Group Home at 501 Howe St. in Whitehorse. In later years, the Group Home was turned into a Receiving Home and as of this writing 2012, it is a Boys Receiving Home.

Going to live at the Group Home was a welcome change for me. I was actually feeling quite happy to be moving in because my friends Gary, Maddy, Johnny and Mason were already living there. Some of the other students living there included: "Cookie," Peter, Jimmy, Charlie, David, Beverly, Mary Jane, Barbara, Rose-Marie, Corrina, Doreen, Patty and sisters Diane, Hazel and Margaret. Every one of us who lived there between 1966 — 1969 developed friendships to last a lifetime. The building was brand new and it was one of the most modern buildings in Whitehorse. It had a color TV, a Recreation Room with a pool table, a ping pong table and a record player. They took me shopping for brand new clothes. I got a brand new winter coat, new boots and brand new *boys* skates! I asked Barbara if I could sign up to play hockey at the Jim Light Arena. She said, "Sure." I signed up to play hockey and Barbara would drive me to the rink to play and she would sit through each game watching me play. I wanted so badly for my mom or my dad to come to a game, but it never happened. I played Defense. I remember one Friday night when I scored the one and only hat trick of my life I wanted so badly for one of my parents to be there because I felt so proud. Barbara was the only one to shout my name each time I scored. I was so glad that Barbara was there to see it happen otherwise no one would have believed me!

I had a bad habit of stealing and my bad habits didn't change at the Group Home. I would steal cigarettes, candy, gum and clothes. Basically whatever I could get my hands on if I liked it, I'd steal it! The times I got caught for stealing, which was a lot, I usually got grounded or I would get a spanking or I would get both. I was not the only one who was behaving this way, so were my friends, Gary, Johnny and Maddy. Johnny was the type who didn't just jump into things. He liked to think and analyze then make a decision. He was intelligent and very good at schoolwork, especially Math. He was a good fighter also just like Gary and would not back down from a fight with anyone. One time when we were at Camp Yukon, a guy from Skagway named Doug was stealing food from the guys in his cabin. Most of us kids in camp knew about it and the kids Doug would steal from were too scared to do anything about it. Johnny was in Doug's cabin and one day Doug stole something from Johnny. When Johnny confronted him about it we all stopped dead in our tracks! Doug was a big guy and nobody dared to fight him as everyone was too scared. Everyone that is, except Johnny. After Johnny told Doug that he wanted his stuff back and if he didn't have it back by supper, Johnny was going to take it back. The whole camp couldn't wait for supper to come that night so we could see what would happen. As it turned out Doug did not give Johnny his stuff back so the fight was on! Johnny gave Doug a black eye, won the fight and Doug never stole from anyone in camp again.

Johnny and Gary were the scrappers in our crowd back then and they would even fight each other every now and then. I only saw them fight each other once and it was painful to watch as they were both my close friends.

My stealing habits continued all the time while I was at the group home. It was usually Maddy and I who did all the stealing. Johnny and Gary just took what we shared with them. If I stole something I would usually share it with the other three and vise-versa. All four of us would get the blame evenly because we didn't "rat" on each other or tell where we got the stolen stuff from. Gary, Johnny and Maddy and I eventually got fed up with all the strappings and all the groundings. One night in June after school was out for the season and it was the summer holidays, the four of us were grounded on a Friday night. That Friday night we devised a plan to run away from the group home and to go to Vancouver, British Columbia where we could live any way we wanted to live with no one to boss us around!

Our plan was to sneak along the railroad tracks until we got to McCrae a truck stop about 3 miles from Whitehorse. At McCrae we would then get on the highway and hitchhike to Carcross. "I know a lot of people who would pick us up going to Carcross," Johnny ensured us. Once we got to Carcross we would walk on the tracks for about a mile and jump the train when it went by. Maddy said, "I saw how slow that train goes. You ever see how slow it goes Andy? We could catch it like nothing. We'll be good actors like Jesse James." We all laughed. Johnny said, "How you gonna' get past the Conductors they watch that train like a hawk so nobody sneaks on?" "We'll wait until the Conductors jump on board and when the train gets out of town a ways and everyone is seated, then we'll jump on!" I said, getting more and more excited about the prospect of the adventure. "It doesn't go that slow you have to run pretty fast to catch it," Johnny continued. We all listened with special interest to Johnny because he came from Carcross and the railroad tracks ran straight through town in Carcross. He had more knowledge about the train than any of us. "I think we can do it!" I piped up. We were all so excited about leaving the group home and going to Vancouver that nothing would have stopped us. Johnny continued, "Well, if you ask me, we are going to have to run really, really fast to catch that train once it leaves the station." "Aww come on Johnny," Gary joined the conversation, "You're a fast runner aren't you?" it was more like a challenge the way Gary said it. "I know I'm a fast runner, but what about these guys?" Johnny tilted his head towards Maddy and I. "Don't worry 'bout us," Maddy said right away, "I'm Frank and this is Jesse," he nodded in my direction, "the James brothers, we can catch any train pardner," and Maddy burst into a fit of laughter and I couldn't help but laugh too. You could tell Johnny and Gary were quite concerned about us and the situation because they didn't laugh. "Yeah right," Gary said, he was not impressed. The second part of our plan was to stow away on the ferry that stopped at Skagway and then go all the way to Vancouver from there.

We all agreed to leave the next night which was Saturday. After lights out and bed check the next night, we each climbed out the same window each carrying a little bag of clothes. We walked south towards the Robert Service Campground and at the edge of town we started walking on the railroad tracks. We walked to McCrae and caught a ride in the back of a truck all the way to Carcross. When we jumped out of the truck, I forgot my jacket and my bag of clothes in the back of the truck. We snuck through the bushes and made our way down to the beach. Johnny said, "We can go over to my Grampa's house, I think he's out on the hunt. Let me check first. We waited and Johnny came back chewing on a piece of dry meat. He gave each of us a small piece. I smelled mine and it smelled a little too spoiled for me so I gave it to Maddy. "Sheesh Nieman," Gary said, "why didn't you give that to me?" Maddy and I were the same age 12. Gary and Johnny were the same age 13 at the time. At the time, I was closer to Maddy than Gary or Johnny because Maddy was always willing to join me whenever I suggested a B&E or stealing a car or some other crime.

Johnny continued in between chews, "Grampa's not there. When we go in I don't want you guys to touch anything you hear me? I mean that. Don't touch anything! No stealing," he looked at Maddy and I. "That's my Grampa's house and I don't want you to take anything from him." We all nodded in agreement and Gary warned his little brother, "Yeah Maddy." We snuck along the beach and went into his Grampa's house. It was an old house with antlers hanging on some of the walls. It smelled like kerosene oil, dust and dried moose meat. There were a few pictures of his Grampa in a cowboy hat posing with some white men. A rifle hung on the wall. It was clean in the house. You could tell no one had been there for a while as there was a thin layer of dust on just about everything. Johnny gave us each a drink of water. He found a can of plums, a can of peaches and a can of Klik, luncheon meat. We all wanted to eat the can of meat right then and there but Johnny said, "No we're taking it with us." I told Johnny that

I forgot my coat and my bag in the back of that guy's truck. "Well, we'll have to leave it there," Johnny said, "we can't go get it." I knew he was right, we could not let anyone see us as the cops were probably looking for us right now.

We left the house after an hour or so and snuck along the beach until we got to the railroad tracks. As we walked on the tracks we came to a sign that said, Skagway, 67 Miles. We went a little farther and stayed in the bush that night waiting for the train to pass by the next morning. Even though it was June, I got cold that night and wished I had my coat. We said we would take turns watching through the night but there was no need to. Gary, Maddy and I were not used to sleeping out in the bush but Johnny was, so the three of us stayed awake practically the whole night. We could hear Johnny enjoying his sleep.

The next morning was very sunny and the forest was noisy and alive with the sounds of singing robins and a lone woodpecker at work in the distant background. We shared the can of Klik for breakfast and made our plans for how we were going to jump the train. Maddy and I would be on one side of the tracks and Gary and Johnny would be on the other side of the tracks. We took our places down by the tracks and waited. When we heard the loud clear sound of the train's horn signaling that it was leaving Carcross, we all looked at each other and let out a great big smile as we prepared ourselves. When the train got to us it was going so fast that the wind it created almost blew us over and we would have been knocked off of our feet if we did not grab some willows in time! Catch the train alright! If you were lucky and quick enough and stupid enough to even be able to grab a handle (which was a total impossibility), it would have easily ripped your arm right out of the socket! We had to step back and make sure we stayed out of the way or it was certain death! Each Passenger coach of the train was named after one of the lakes in the Yukon, Alaska and British Columbia and the lake name was printed in big letters on the side of the train. Well the train was going by so fast you couldn't read one word of that writing! The train was travelling we later learned, at approximately 45 miles per hour! The wind created by the speeding train made our clothes flap and our hair stand straight out sideways. When the last car finally passed, the four of stood there staring directly in each other's eyes in total disbelief at what we had just witnessed! Everything became quiet. When the reality of what just took place sunk in, we all burst into uncontrollable laughter at the exact same time and pointed at each other and laughed some more for being so stupid to think we could actually catch this speeding train that could have so easily killed us!

When we finally got through our bout of gut-wrenching laughter we settled down and considered plan B which was invented right there on the spot. It was an easy plan and an easy decision to make, we were going on. We would walk all the way to Skagway because it was: number one impossible to get lost (since one of us so deftly induced that all's we had to do was follow the tracks!); and number two it was summer time and number three I have a sister Eileen living in Skagway who really likes me and she'll feed us and give us money and four Johnny has a relative there who will do the same so it was game on! We started walking and it was fun. We kept a steady pace pushed on by Gary and Johnny,

Maddy and I wanted to stop and skip rocks on Lake Bennet. If Maddy and I had our way we would have never made it to Skagway there were just too many interesting things to do on the way! That first morning as we walked we sang songs, we told jokes and we acted silly! We were so totally FREE! We were in control of our lives and in control of our destiny! We were out in the wilderness and you can rest assured…no one, no one, knew where we were! This, my friend was heaven-on-earth! It all felt so great! That is, until the hunger pangs acted up! We did not plan on bringing any food because we did not want to be burdened down or draw suspicion on ourselves. We said we would just up and go! Our plan was to live on fish we caught out of the lakes, pick berries and kill ptarmigan along the way. At least that was the plan. We made very short work of the two cans of plums and peaches Johnny brought. That first afternoon after all the steady walking, we were four very hungry boys! The weather was nice and it was warm and sunny. As we walked in silence, we rounded a corner and surprised two ptarmigan that were in the middle of the tracks! With a loud flurry of flapping wings and a couple of loose feathers floating in the air, they flew off into the distance! One kept going and the other circled back and landed about 100 feet from us! Gary said, "Shhh, stay still you guys!" All of our eyes were riveted on the bird we dared not take our eyes off him! With a whisper Johnny said, "Slowly, you guys pick up a rock, real slow now, go." As if we had been practicing this together for some time, we all slowly reached down for a rock and when we each had one, we formed a perfect line like a firing squad. Johnny then said, "OK on the count of three, one, two three!" we all threw at the same time and the bird fell over flapping its wings in the last throes before death. "I got it! I got it!" Johnny shouted. "Good shot, you got that sucker Johnny!" Gary shouted and we all ran as fast as we could to grab the bird before it flew away. We all knew it was Johnny's rock that hit the bird. I saw my rock land way behind it. We were ecstatic! Food! We made a fire and we were all thankful that Johnny (the experienced bushman) had the presence of mind to bring a small pocket knife and matches. Johnny took good care of preparing the bird for consumption. It was like he didn't trust any of us city-slickers to touch it. He gutted it and made a spit for it and was in the process of cooking it when an argument broke out between us and Johnny. Johnny then threatened to keep all of the ptarmigan if we, "Didn't all just shut up." When he threatened to keep the whole bird to himself, Gary, Maddy and I felt insulted. We got mad and Gary said, "Well keep it then, you can have it all and you can travel all by yourself too! Let's go you guys. Come on Maddy let him keep his bird." With that we turned and started walking away. Johnny, sitting by the fire and tending to the bird as it cooked said in a casual voice, "Go ahead you guys, catch you later." That made us even angrier. I started running, "Let's leave him here then, come on you guys he can fight the bears and the wolves by himself!" We took off running as fast as we could and we didn't stop until we rounded the corner! We walked for a little bit and then had a change of heart. We all looked at each other and didn't even have to say a word, we knew, we couldn't leave Johnny alone out here in the wilderness. Gary then said, "Let's hide behind that big boulder up there by the tracks and we'll wait for him. "We sat behind the big boulder and waited as our stomachs took turns growling in hungry protest. About fifteen minutes passed and sure enough, here comes Johnny running down the tracks in full flight with the chicken on a stick and he shouted out real loud as if we were miles away, "Wait up you guys! I'll share with you, I was just kidding!" We were going to step out but Gary put his arm out and held Maddy and I back. He shook his head and moved his lips without talking and his lips silently said, "Just wait." Johnny went running right by. When he was about 50 feet ahead of us we got back on the tracks then Gary shouted, "Hey Johns, where you going in such a rush?" He was relieved to see us and we were relieved to see him and the chicken. We enjoyed that northern chicken together and it gave us some much needed energy. It is always nice to make peace.

We continued walking and stopped only to eat blueberries, go to the washroom and rest. Then we walked some more. We walked off and on through most of the night. It was June in the Yukon so it was daylight twenty four seven. When the train came by us in the morning, as soon as we heard it coming we went and hid in the bushes to make sure we were not seen. The beautiful country of the Yukon we walked through was breathtaking! It was also dangerous, wild, unforgiving country. The poet Robert Service captured some of its wildness and beauty in some of his poetry. Come to think of, Robert Service had to come over these very same railroad tracks we were walking on! After all, this was the same gold rush trail of '98 that we were travelling on. And Lake Bennett the very lake that we were walking beside is the same lake that hundreds of thousands of hungry gold seekers sailed on in their makeshift rafts. No doubt, there were many that lost their lives in these frigid ice cold waters. It was ice cold even in the heat of mid-June. Walking along Lake Bennett was like listening to a disc that had a scratch in it where the song would keep repeating itself stuck at that one spot. We would round one corner and just when we thought it was over there would be another corner. We would round that corner thinking it was the last one and there would be another corner! This went on for hour after hour after hour and what seemed like an eternity. And then finally at lunchtime of the next day we saw the train depot at Lake Bennett. It first appeared as a little dot in the distance and we would not have recognized it if not for Johnny. He was the first to see it and to announce it to us. We got super happy, hungry or not! It meant we were making progress!

As we got closer and closer to the Lake Bennett station we were careful not to be seen and made sure we didn't walk on the tracks. We noticed that the train was stopped at Lake Bennett and Johnny explained that the train always stopped there for lunch. Although hunger and food weighed heavy on our hearts and minds, we viewed the train as a means of fast transportation to our destination. It would take us all the way to Skagway! We decided to sneak on the train while it was parked. Johnny explained that we would have to hide in one of the ore cars otherwise we would get caught if we went inside the passenger cars. We broke into pairs. Maddy and I went together. Johnny and Gary went together.

We spread out, walked along the train where the big ore cars were and climbed on at different segments.

Once Maddy and I had climbed on, we noticed there was a tiny crawl space in between the ore bin and the rail car just big enough for two small bodies to crouch down in. Just as we were about to crawl into the opening, I noticed a keen eyed conductor about a quarter of a mile away and it looked like he spotted us! I jumped back real quick and told Maddy, "I think the Conductor seen us!" We quickly squeezed ourselves forcibly into the tiny space. We could hear the conductor's boots on gravel as he was running and drew closer to where we were hiding. Closer and closer and closer, until sure enough, he stopped right beside the ore car we were in and climbed up! In the crawl space we could barely look up it was such a tight squeeze and I guess that's why the conductor never thought to look there. However, he knew that we had climbed onto the train and as he was looking around for us, he rested his elbows on the railing right above where we were. JUST MERE INCHES above our heads! He was so ridiculously close to us, and yet did not have a clue that we were there! If the situation were not so serious, I would've laughed. He then proceeded to shout towards the other end of the rail car, "OK you guys come on out of there. I know where you are! You boys come out of there right now, do you hear me!?" He did not know where we were. And there he was, mere inches from our faces! We were looking straight up his nostrils. In fact, we were so close I found myself gazing at his nose hairs! And they were quite long nose hairs. Well that did it! (Have you ever been kicked out of class for pulling a prank, and you and your best friend were told to report to the principal's office? Meanwhile, as the two of you are walking down the hall you couldn't stop laughing, the prank was so funny? Then you stand there, before the principal, you know you're going to get a strapping, and the principal looks at the both of you and asks, "Well, why'd you do it?" And at that critical moment, that very serious moment when silence and suspense, hang heavy in the air. That moment when you know you've been given a chance to redeem yourself, and all you can do is try to keep from looking at your friend because you know as SURE AS SNOW, that if you just so much as glance at your friend JUST ONCE, you will both bust out laughing? And just as sure as the Yukon winter nights are long, cold and dark and the sun is yellow, you look up at your best friend. As soon as your eyes meet, the both of you break out into a loud, uncontrollable, belly-shaking fit of laughter! Has that ever happened to you?

Well, our situation on the train was very similar to that. The conductor was so ridiculously close to us and did not know we were there that it was downright comical! So comical that Maddy, who always found humor in any little thing, burst into laughter so loud and so forcefully, that he sprayed both the conductor and myself with a mouthful of spit! I don't know if that conductor was more scared than he was surprised, or more angry at being scared than he was surprised! The expression on his face was akin to that of someone who had just seen a proverbial ghost! He jumped back like the rail car had a bolt of electricity running through it!

Needless to say we soon found ourselves being escorted by the conductor, along the train, and as we passed the place where Johnny and Gary were hiding, I snuck a peek at them. I could barely see their eyes through the cracks in the rail car door, but what I could see was not a pretty picture. Both their eyes were searing with anger. Anger, not at the conductor, but at us for getting caught, for Johnny and Gary knew that they could **not** go on without us. I thought about our situation, what would the conductor do with us? Spank us? Lock us up or send us back on the train? I shot a fearful, quizzical look at Maddy. His desperate, scared eyes told me he was thinking what I was thinking. Our situation was indeed desperate! I was thankful the conductor was not a young man. He must have gotten tired of holding our collars so tight because the first mistake he made was to let go of our collars. The second mistake he made was to let us walk in front of him, because as soon as we realized he didn't have a hold of us anymore, Maddy and I looked at each other and bolted like two scared gophers who had just realized they were being engulfed by an eagle's shadow! It was no contest. The conductor didn't even bother to chase us. All's I heard as I ran was, "You boys are in a lot of trouble now! You won't get away with this!" We bolted off the train tracks and into the bush. Ahhhh safety, we kept running until we were sure nobody could see us.

The conductor was the least of our troubles. We had a lot of miles to cover yet. We were hungry. We were in untamed wild country, in the middle of nowhere and we still had Gary and Johnny to contend with. Well, we expected to get the third degree and sure enough it came. Gary and Johnny called us every name in the book and we didn't hear the end of it for the longest time. They constantly reminded us each time we ran into a hardship on our journey that, "If you guys didn't get caught, we wouldn't be here going through this right now, we would've been in Skagway long ago!" Like the time we came to a valley in between two mountains. Standing on the side of the mountain we got very discouraged when we noticed that the train tracks went alongside the mountain we were on for miles and miles and then went over a bridge to the other mountain and went alongside that mountain for miles and miles. Gary swore a very loud and long profanity and we all sat down to rest and to get ready for this next discouraging segment of our journey. Down the valley we could see what looked like a small creek. The whole side of the mountain going down to the creek was almost straight up and down. It had a few small trees here and there with lots of willows and shrubs cropping out. Maddy was the first to speak up, "Hey you guys why don't we just slide down the side of the hill and go across that creek. No sweat!" Johnny piped up, "That's no hill Duke, take another look that's A MOUNTAIN!" Johnny liked to call Maddy "Duke" after John Wayne. "Besides," Johnny continued, "I'll bet you ten dollars that's a river not a creek!" "Nah, that's a creek Johns," Gary said. I added my two cents, "Yeah that's a creek, we can get across that!" Johnny continued, "Maybe we could get across it no problem, but how we gonna' get down there? Do you realize how steep that is? We could kill ourselves!" He was right it was at least 500 ft. of sheer drop off! We considered our only other option, walking all those miles on the tracks just to get across a valley that seemed to be only a couple of hundred feet wide! Sliding down that mountain was certainly riskier but it would save us a lot of time and precious energy. We were so tired and hungry and I'm sure our young minds did not fully understand the danger and the risk of taking the shortcut down the side of that sheer drop off mountain. We looked down the side of the mountain and I said, "As we go down, make sure you grab onto the willows and bushes to slow you down." "Who's going first? Not me!" Johnny answered. Gary then spoke up, "Nieman you and Maddy are the youngest, you guys go first." "No way, you and Johnny go first you're the oldest!" I answered loudly as if to indicate that they had some responsibility for Maddy and I. Then Johnny said, "Here, I know what we can do," he bent over and pulled a few dry weeds from the ground. He broke them off and said, "We'll draw straws. The shortest one goes first and the longest goes last." Johnny held the straws in his hands. "Let me see those straws," I said, stepping forward to make sure the straws were not all the same length. "I'll hold them," I said. "Yeah let Nieman hold 'em," Gary added. "Yeah Johnny, let Andy hold 'em," Maddy jumped in. Johnny handed me the straws. Johnny, who was the brains behind the straw idea told me, "When you hold them, make sure all the tops that are showing are even," and he grabbed my hand to emphasize his point. I held the straws up and said, "Who's first?" Gary said, "I'll go first," and he picked one. Maddy picked one, then Johnny picked one and I got the last one. As it turned out, Maddy would slide down first, I would be second, Johnny third and Gary was last. Maddy sat down and went close to the edge. He then looked at us and smiled and said, "OK, here goes Geronimo. You ready Nieman?" I decided to stay close to Maddy and went right behind him. I said, "OK let's ride 'em Geronimo!" and we shoved off. I let Maddy get a little ahead of me before I went as I did not want to bump into him. Maddy let out a big yell as he went over the edge, "Yahooo!" Then I pushed off. I let out the very same yell, "Yahoooo!" and the fall was on! What a RUSH! At first we were able to hold onto the shrubs and willows but once you picked up speed you could not slow down! As we slid faster and faster my pants were forced right up into my butt cheeks and pressed against my testicles extremely hard! The small trees and willows went flashing by me on both sides! I could not stop myself if I wanted to! I could hear small rotten logs cracking as my hands hit them as I tried to slow myself down! I could see Maddy's little head bouncing up and down as he hit little bumps along the way and I was doing the same hitting those bumps too. Maddy went right over a wasp nest and dislodged it. The wasps came out in a swarm and Maddy kept going down the hill so fast none had a chance to chase him and then I plowed right through them before they even had a chance to realize what was happening. Maddy and I did not get stung but the wasps were wide awake by the time Johnny and Gary hit them and both Johnny and Gary got stung a couple of times each. We were going so fast when we reached the bottom that we would have broken our legs when we hit. The only thing that saved us was a big tree that had fallen over where the river eroded the embankment and where the roots of this big tree had been there was a deep pile of sand. When we hit that sand, each of us had to scramble out of the way really fast to get out of the way of the one coming behind us! It was all over in a matter of seconds! We looked at each other to make sure everyone was alright. We all had rosehip thorns stuck in our hands and other than a very sore butt and a realization that it was more dangerous than we thought we were all OK. No broken bones and other than Gary and Johnny's wasp stings we were in good shape. Johnny was the first to comment and point out how lucky we were to land where we did because all around us were big water smooth boulders except for that one spot of sand! When we gathered our senses and took a look at our surroundings, we were in for a big shock! Getting down the mountain we just came down was a cake-walk compared to what stood before us!

Johnny was absolutely, 100% right! The so called "creek" that looked so small when we were way up on top of the mountain was in reality a full-fledged, deafening, raging, category ten river of pure white water. This was no ordinary river! It's water was white and turbulent and unrelenting for as far the eye could see either way. There was NO WAY we were getting across this! We were stuck. There was no way we could go back up the mountain and there was no way to cross this raging, violent, continually deafening river. The constant spray of the river kept us soaked to the bone. Johnny said, "Looks like we'll have to walk along the river up to the railroad bridge." We decided that was our only course. We could not talk very much because the roar of the river drowned our voices out. Our clothes were soaked to our skin. As we followed the river, we realized we were in a canyon where the walls got higher and higher and it got to the point where it was impossible for us to go any farther. Then Gary got our attention over the roar of the river by whistling with his fingers in his mouth and motioned us over with his arm. As we all huddled closer together in the spray of the river, Gary pointed to a spot in between the canyon walls where two boulders jutted out of the side of the canyon walls one on this side and one the other side of the river. The boulders from where we were standing, looked like they were touching each other. Gary shouted as loud as he could in order to be heard over the roar from the river and said, "We might be able to get across down there, it's not too steep on either side of the canyon and those rocks look like they're close enough for us to cross." That was our only chance. We could not go back and we could not go forward, we had no choice. Johnny shouted at the top of his lungs, "Are you crazy!? One slip in that water and you're a goner! You fall in that water and those rocks will crush you like a rag doll. Once you fall in there that's it!" "What choice do we have Johnny? None! Look how close those rock are, we can do it!" Gary continued. Johnny said, "You're crazy Gary. That's all I got to say is, you're crazy." As we made our way down to where the two rocks were we realized that the rocks were a little farther apart than they looked at first. One rock was higher than the other and we could not just step from one to the other you had to jump! And we had to jump up to the other rock not down. The white water was rushing by so fast it created a wind which had such force our wet pants and our wet shirts stuck to us and flapped like paper in the wind as the white water became a blur underneath us. When Johnny realized we would have to jump in order to get across, he went and broke down a small tree to use as a balance. The rocks were slippery on both sides. We were all very scared. We knew the danger. One slip into that water and you were dead. We also knew we had no choice. It was necessity that drove us on that day not bravery. Gary decided to go first. Johnny shouted again in order to be heard above the roar, "Here hold this stick when you jump." Gary shouted back, "No it'll throw me off balance." Gary then took a couple of steps backward as far as he could in order to get a decent run. "OK, wish me luck," he shouted. With that, he leaned back, then bolted forward as fast as he could and sailed through the spray and the wind. For the sudden-death danger that was involved in the feat, Gary made it look easy as he cleared the jump with room to spare. Seeing that he made it with so much room to spare helped us all breathe a little sigh of relief. Relief that was short-lived as the danger of the situation quickly brought us back to the task at hand. Johnny handed one end of the pole to Gary and Gary grabbed it. Now we had the pole to use as a guide when we jumped. I was scared. Maddy was going to go next but Gary shouted, "No Maddy, let Nieman go next!" I think Gary knew I was scared and did not want me to go last. I shouted, "No you go ahead Maddy," I wanted to see how easy it was for the next person before I went. Johnny offered the pole to Maddy as a balance but Maddy just shook his head, "No." Gary shouted at Maddy, "Grab the   pole Maddy!" but Maddy was already getting ready to run. Gary and Johnny pulled the pole out of the way and Maddy jumped. His legs weren't as long as Gary's but he made it, just barely. He scrambled up the other side of the canyon to make room on the rock. Then it was my turn. I knew I was just as athletic as Gary and Maddy as we all had lots of practice jumping from one sternwheeler to another back home in Whitehorse. But realizing the sheer magnitude of the danger involved in this feat where one slip and my life would be over, I decided to use the pole as a guide when I jumped. When I got safely across I scrambled up that wall to safety as fast as I could! Johnny had no problem jumping across and did not need to use the pole. When we got to a place of safety we were totally soaked and with our adrenaline pumping we all let out a happy war whoop so loud it that would have shaken the laziest sleeping bear out of hibernation!

It was a relief to get back on the tracks again. The warm June weather dried out our clothes in no time and when we stopped for our first rest after crossing that raging river we fell asleep. When we awoke, there were new hunger pangs to deal with. We were using our energy fast from all this walking and getting hungrier by the minute. We had not seen any berry patches in quite a while and the temperature was dropping because the terrain was changing. We were climbing higher into the mountains. We began to see patches of snow here and there on each side of the tracks. The wind made it even colder. We came to a place called Log Cabin. It was a rest stop no doubt built during the gold rush of '98. As soon as we seen the building our stomachs automatically thought of food! We could hear gophers announcing our arrival as we drew closer to the old building. Peering inside, it was like a picture out of a western movie. The sun shone through the cracks in the wall exposing the dust and the spider webs. It looked like it hadn't seen human life since the gold rush! We all peered in and since it didn't look like a morsel of food could survive in such a place we just as quickly pulled our faces away from the cracks and looked away. I decided to take a peek inside this old decrepit building just in case there was something interesting like a knife and maybe something to keep me warm inside. No such luck. Just as I was about to leave, I noticed a great big jar sitting on the very top shelf high and almost out of sight. There was something inside of that jar but there was so much dust covering it I couldn't get a good look. I decided to use some of my precious energy and check it out. To my surprise and to my delight, it was a jar half-filled with dried raisins! As soon as I recognized what it was I let out a yell, "Hey you guys over here!" I took the jar down with such care you'd think it held the world's most precious treasure in there! Gary, Maddy and Johnny came running over to see what it was that I was so excited about! "I found some raisins!" I blurted out in excitement. Blowing off some of the dust from the top of the tin cover I wiped it clean and then struggled to get the top off. It did not come off easy but when I finally got it off we all dug in like ravished wolves and grabbed a hand full. As soon as we bit into the dried raisins they immediately turned to dust in our mouths and almost choked us! We gagged and spit and gagged and spit some more! I let out a stream of un-repeatable words and threw the jar against the wall breaking it into a hundred pieces! Maddy then said, "I've got an idea how we can get that gopher! Let's plug up all his holes and leave one open. He'll have to come out that hole and when he does we'll nail him!" So we gathered rocks and plugged up as many gopher holes as we could. We waited for what seemed like an eternity and sure enough the gopher poked his head out of the only hole he could, only to be greeted by a barrage of weakly thrown stones! He was gone back down the hole before the first rock hit the dirt where his head used to be! Gary said, "Let's go you guys." We all turned and started back towards the tracks except Maddy. Maddy picked up a boulder and stood right over the hole the gopher came out of and waited. Gary looked back and said, "Sheesh that Maddy, what's he doing now?" We all turned around and I yelled at Maddy, "Forget it Maddy, he ain't gonna' come back out for a long time, come on let's go!" We started walking and Maddy kept waiting. Finally, after about five minutes of waiting, Maddy came running up and said, "I don't really like the way gopher taste anyway, you Nieman?" I didn't answer. It was cold walking through the Summit, very cold even in June. The wind never stopped blowing, I just had a t-shirt on and part of a thin white sheet I found at Log Cabin. The guys took turns letting me wear their jackets to warm up. There were many lakes on either side of the tracks that we walked past. We could hear ptarmigan but never seen any. We saw ducks on the lake and our mouths watered at their sight. Then, as if sent by God Himself, we came across a work crew that was working a section of the railroad. The work crew used what is called a chassis to transport them and their tools to and from work. A chassis is a small car that rides on the track and may have a motor or can be propelled by a hand controlled pump. This chassis was like a small boxcar. Johnny explained to us what the work crew was. The first thing I noticed was that the work crew was working about two hundred feet away from the chassis. I could easily check out the chassis to see if there was any food in there. I told the other guys that I was going to check out the chassis to see if the guys had any food in there. I said, "They must have their lunches boxes in there, I'll go check it out." Maddy and Johnny said, "I'll go with you!" Maddy, Johnny and I snuck up to the chassis and sure enough there were lunch boxes in there. Maddy was so hungry he was going to just grab a couple of boxes and run! "No wait," I grabbed his arm. I found a bag and said, "Leave the boxes let's put some stuff in here, we don't want then to notice anything is missing." We quickly opened a few of the lunch boxes and began grabbing things. We grabbed a few sandwiches some apples and a couple of oranges. [Author's note: forty-five years later I met one of the men whose lunch we stole that day. I was conducting his wife's funeral and told him the story of our walk to Skagway. He remembered that day his lunch went missing and he said, "We blamed the ravens. We thought the ravens got into our food." End of Author's note] We made short work of what little food we managed to steal and could feel the energy it produced almost immediately! We then had to walk around the work crew going through the bush so they wouldn't see us.

After two and a half days of walking on the railroad tracks we finally reached Skagway. As we came to the outskirts of Skagway, we noticed a white van parked across the railroad tracks as if to block all on-coming traffic. We didn't notice it was the sheriff until he started walking towards us. We later learned his name was Sam. The people in Skagway called him "Sheriff Sam," he was a big fat man. His belly hung over and hid his belt buckle. His ring of many keys hanging at his side jingled as he walked. He always had a toothpick in the corner of his mouth. His face was red. His nose was redder than his face and it had little blue squiggly veins that stood out so much you had to force yourself to keep from staring at them. As he walked towards us we were so bone-tired and half-starved to death that running away never even came close to entering our minds. When the sheriff spoke, his southern drawl had the ability to stand out in any crowd. All he said as he walked toward us was, "There you boys are. Thought you were never gonna' git here. Where's the other one? Heard there was five of you critters?" Maddy shot back, "Must've been my shadow." We all laughed except the sheriff. The sheriff turned slowly towards Maddy and just casually stared at him. All of a sudden out of nowhere his hand flashed out and grabbed Maddy by the front of his shirt. He twisted the front of Maddy's shirt and made a fist. He stood Maddy up on his tippy toes and as if on purpose made sure just the tip of his toes dragged on the ground. Pulling Maddy's face up closer to his he said, "One more smart remark like that and you'll be wearing my boot on your butt, do you UNDERSTAND ME!?" This caught us all by surprise and Maddy just shook his head, "Yes." "Good. Now keep it that way!" The sheriff put us in the van and brought us all down to the jailhouse. He put all four of us in the same cell and it was quite crowded. He locked the cell then went over to his desk and pulled out some papers. The jail was in a small corner of a basement in an old building. It smelled like rusty iron and old mothballs. It was dark in the room and the only light was a dim light bulb that hung high over the sheriff's desk. "Which one of you is Andy?" I stood and went to the cell bars, "I am," I answered. "What's your last name?" "Nieman." "What is it?" "Nieman," I said louder. "How do you spell that?" "N. I. E. M. A. N." I took my time spelling it. "Which one is Johnny?" the sheriff rolled the toothpick from one corner of his mouth to the other. Johnny answered, "Right here." "What's your last name Johnny, you guys have family in town here?" Johnny and I answered at the same time, "Yes!" "What kind of family do you have here Johnny?" "My Aunt." Johnny answered quickly as he stood and walked to the cell bars. "How 'bout you Andy"? "I have a sister here, Eileen Roth," I said it loud and clear. "I know both your kin," the sheriff said without looking up from where he was writing. "What is 'kin' I thought to myself." I looked at Johnny quizzically, he just shrugged his shoulders. The sheriff picked up the phone dialed a number and when someone answered he said, "Two cheeseburger deluxe, two pieces of pie and two cokes over at the cells please. Apple pie. Thank you." He then came over and opened the cell door, "Johnny you and Andy go have a seat over there," he pointed at two chairs in front of his desk. He shut the cell door and locked it. Maddy got up from the bed and walked to the front of the cell, "What about us sir?" Maddy was curious. "What about you?" the sheriff seemed annoyed as he turned to look at Maddy, "Can we come out too?" "And do what"? the sheriff stared at Maddy obviously irritated that Maddy spoke up. Maddy didn't know what to say, "I dunno," was all he could muster. Gary then spoke up as if to relieve the tension and come to his brother's rescue, "Don't you want to know *our* names?" "Don't you get too worried now," the sheriff's voice was thick with sarcasm, "I'll get to you when I'm done with these boys if that's alright with you?" "Oh, I just wanted to know that's all," Gary said as he pushed Maddy back away from the bars. It appeared that the sheriff was finished with his paperwork so he turned to Johnny and I and said, "You boys have a whole lot of people worried over you, a whole lotta' people. What are you boys running from anyway?" Just then there was a knock at the door and the sheriff bellowed, "Come in!" It was the delivery guy from the restaurant. "Your order's ready Sheriff." "Good, just leave it on the table over there and put it on the tab along with the usual tip." "Thank you sir," the young man said as he held out the bill for the sheriff to sign. Immediately the room was filled with the strong smell of French fries and cheeseburger! All of my senses SPRUNG TO LIFE…FOOD! When the delivery guy left the sheriff took a quick look into the Styrofoam containers that held the food and then opened the cell door and placed both bags in the cell for Gary and Maddy. Johnny and I felt totally left out as the smell of food was so strong and we were so starved, we couldn't help but watch Gary and Maddy as they bit into their burgers. The sheriff then said, "OK let's get you two over to your folks, they've been phoning all day!" Johnny and I turned to Gary and Maddy and waved as we walked out while saying, "See you later." "See you guys," they both mumbled their mouths filled with hamburger.

Two days later they put all four of us on the train at the same time. As soon we all laid eyeballs on each other we pointed our fingers at each and we busted out laughing! So much for our great trip to Vancouver! Maddy said, "Ho, just like when the Two Gun Kid went to jail. The sheriff locked him up for two days just like us." With that we all burst into a new round of uncontrollable laughter! What we were really happy about was just seeing each other again! I thought I wasn't going to see any of them for a long time! On the train ride back we pointed out all the spots that meant something to us and as we recalled each incident we again burst into a fit of laughter! Some passengers on the train smiled at us as we made so much noise and others frowned. The train stopped as usual at Lake Bennett for lunch. The train was loaded with well-to-do, well-heeled, sophisticated-looking, elderly tourists. Most of them appeared to be of an aglo-saxon background. The conductor informed us that we would be stopping here for an hour and a half. We all filed off the train and into the dining area where waitresses guided us to our seats. Johnny and Gary went in a line that took them away from Maddy and I, almost to the other side of the hall. Maddy wound up sitting directly across from me. The setting in the dining room was clearly set for rich, well-paying folks. We knew that by the silverware, white-laced table cloths, silver candle holders, silver pitchers, but especially by the FOOD! There was mounds of steaming hot roast beef, steaming hot gravy, mashed potatoes, peas, carrots, pie and of course, hot fresh-baked sourdough buns! I looked at Maddy, he looked at me and with glee in our eyes, we both knew we had hit the jackpot! Our smiles clearly indicated what we didn't have to say verbally …*not bad for a coupleof natives from across the tracks.*

The meal was absolutely delicious! We were still not fully recuperated from our journey so our ravenous appetites were quite evident. Maddy and I were holding our own quite well with this high-fluting, clearly out-of-our-league crowd! Holding our own in terms of not making too many mistakes in front of all these fine, sophisticated white folks, by remembering or displaying, what little manners we possessed. As native people, we grew up being very shy of white folks and always felt somewhat uncomfortable in their presence. When native people eat together, this is a sign that one is very comfortable with the other people present. And even if you are comfortable or not, you could always simply get up and take your meal elsewhere to eat and no one would mind at all. But to be native and to be more or less forced to eat in front of non-natives (which is exactly how Maddy and I were feeling), that's a different story! However, being 12 years old and always hungry, we soon forgot our etiquette and began to just "dig-in."

In between bites, I happen to glance up to look at Maddy and he was already watching me (like he was waiting for me to look up). I could see that his eyes were mischievously dancing with what appeared to be laughter. I knew exactly what he was thinking. He was thinking how silly *I looked*. A little Indian boy trying to be so "prim n' proper" eating with all these fine folks, when I was nothing but a run-away thief, on the escape from a group home, who would just as soon steal from these folks as look them in the eye. And no one knew that reality more than Maddy and I! He knew THAT was exactly what *I was* also thinking about him, and as soon as our laughing eyes acknowledged and relayed that message to each other, Maddy with his mouth stuffed full of roast beef, couldn't help but burst out laughing! Only this time, his mouth was so stuffed that there was no place for his laugh to go except up through his nostrils, which, as if on cue, produced an ever-expanding bubble of light green mucous, that grew steadily out of his left nostril into a perfectly round, large bubble! A snot-bubble! As soon as Maddy noticed that he had produced this unexpected bubble, the sheer magnitude and humor of such an unlikely event ever happening, caught him totally off-guard. He found it so funny, that he busted out laughing uncontrollably! When he started laughing, the bubble broke, his mouth opened, and he deposited all of his food onto his plate. Well, to make a long story short, there went our meal! We both laughed so hard and so un-controllably, it was useless to even try to finish our meal! All this went on to the dismay of those tourists who were alert enough and close enough to catch the event. They promptly turned their heads, wiped their mouths with their napkins and with a few words of utter disgust graciously began to rise then left the table. One of the waitresses came over and with a concerned look on her face, asked, "Is everything alright?" as she glanced at the procession that was departing from our table. We were both trying to stifle our laughter as I mumbled something to the effect, "Yes, we're OK, thanks." Before Maddy and I left, we couldn't just up n' leave so much free food behind, so we promptly filled a few napkins and our pockets full with roast beef and sourdough buns. We got up and left the table. Just before we got to the door I looked back. As if on cue, Gary and Johnny got up and just as our survival instincts told us, it told them the same thing and I could see them stuff their pockets with roast beef and sourdough buns. They followed us out. We all got on the train and sat down. Gary sounded mad when he spoke to Maddy. He looked at Maddy but I knew he was talking to both of us when he asked, "How come you got kicked out?" Maddy thought Gary was going to hit him so he put his elbow up to protect himself and said, "I didn't get kicked out!" I automatically came to Maddy's defense and said, "We didn't get kicked out we just left because it was too embarrassing to stay there." "What do you mean too embarrassing?" After I explained what happened with Maddy's green bubble, Gary and Johnny cracked up laughing too. "You guys are crazy!" Gary shook his head. Maddy and I were trying to hold back our laughs while I was telling the story and when we saw them laugh, we burst out laughing even more!

On the train the booths were small and faced each other. I sat beside Maddy and Gary sat beside Johnny. I asked the whole group, "What do you think will happen to us when we get back to the group home?" "Well Mr. MacDuannah is going to spank all of us that's for sure." Gary said. "And we'll probably get grounded," Johnny added. "He better not lock us downstairs again" Maddy said with seriousness in his voice. He was referring to the time last winter when we all got picked up at a dance at the rec center and the police brought us home late. They locked us downstairs in the bathroom for two days with no food. All they gave us was water and a mattress. We all knew what Maddy was talking about. "I'll run away again if he does." Maddy sounded like he meant it. "I will to!" I almost shouted. And Johnny said in his low voice, "You guys will just get into more trouble. Just take your punishment get it over with and be done with it." We all settled back and retreated into our own thoughts no doubt all thinking about the impending punishment that was coming our way. When we arrived in Whitehorse the social worker met us at the train depot and drove us back to the Group Home. We each got a spanking and we were grounded for a month. I decided I was not going to stay inside and be grounded at least not in the summer. I ran away from the group home all that summer and lived on my own staying anywhere I could and sleeping mostly in abandoned cars. I couldn't go home because I was sure the social workers or the police would catch me there. That summer I learned to survive by my wits and by my wits alone. I kept to myself. I did not trust telling anybody anything about where I was or what I was doing. I was wild and free for that whole summer.

That's when I started stealing from the churches and their offering boxes. I would alternate between the Anglican Church, the United Church and the Catholic Church but mostly from the Catholic Church because that's who ran the Lower Post Indian Residential School. I was baptized a Catholic. I only went to confession in those days to check if there was a priest in the church. I stole when confession was taking place because then I knew where the priest was and no one got suspicious to see this little kid hanging around the foyer. I would check around to see if anyone was looking and when no one was around I would lift the lid on the little wooden offering box they left out in the foyer and steal the money. After a while, they got wise and put a lock on the box so it could not be opened. I simply pried the lock off the wooden box and took the money. Then they chained the wooden box to the wall. I pried the chain out of the wooden box and took the whole box. Then they changed it from a wooden box to a steel box and they put a bigger lock on it. So I had to steal the whole box including the chain after I pried it out of the wall with my hammer. I returned about a week later, only to discover they had drilled a hole into the floor and the offering box had now become a long brass tube that went clear through the floor and into the basement! The top of that brass tube had a little slit where people could squeeze their money through. At first I got so mad I kicked the tube as hard as I could! And then, almost immediately my criminal mind shifted into high gear. I had to smile in spite of myself. Instead of detouring me, this procedure fueled my determination and made it more of an adventure! They had now forced me to get a little braver. Now I had to go *inside* the sanctuary. This posed a risk as I was unsure if anyone was in there. They might have set up a trap for me. There might be a priest or two, hiding away waiting. Well, I've had to live with bigger risks at home, I thought to myself. They wouldn't beat me as bad as mom does. At least I hoped they didn't. Besides, they'd have to catch me first. I have runners on, they have priest shoes. I decided to go for it! I went into the church down the stairs into the CYO Hall to find where the brass tube ended. It ended inside one of the rooms downstairs and it was quite high off the floor. There was a padlock that went through two holes drilled in the brass tube. I looked around for something to break the padlock with and noticed a fire axe inside a glass case hanging on the wall beneath a rolled up fire hose. The glass case was locked. I was just about to break the glass to get the axe when I realized that I had no way of reaching the padlock, fire axe or no fire axe. I was beat and I knew it. I became furious! I took my anger and my rage out at them by destroy-ing as much as I could in their kitchen. I didn't care if anyone heard me or if any one came down. I never went back there.

While I was on my own that whole summer of my twelfth year, I got drunk for the very first time. It was while I was checking the offering box at the Anglican Church. In those days, the churches always left their doors open during the day. At the Anglican Church, they would collect the offering and leave it in a jar in a metal dresser where the priest kept his uniform, the wine and other things. I always made sure I did not take all the money so that no one would get suspicious. I would usually check it on Mondays after the Sunday service. This one particular Monday when I went to check it there was only twenty two cents in the jar! Two dimes and two pennies! Well that just insulted me and I got mad! I thought they had figured out what I was doing and had decided to empty the jar each Sunday so no one could steal it! Well I'll fix them I thought. I'll take some of their wine. I looked at the wine and thought to myself, so this is the stuff that makes my mom so crazy. At first I thought I better not. Then I thought ah why not? I took out a glass and filled it half full. I put the bottle back. I smelled the wine and it reminded me of home. I hated the smell. I put it to my lips and gulped at all down as fast as I could so I wouldn't have to taste it. I rinsed the glass out, put it away and got out of there as fast as I could. I didn't have to worry about being seen going in or out of the church, it was just when I stole something from there that I got nervous. As I was walking away from the church, I felt something real warm in my stomach and it felt good. My steps starting feeling lighter and I felt like I could almost float. I stopped in the Hougen's Store on Main Street and pretended to read the greeting cards. My stomach felt warmer and warmer and I felt like laughing. I liked this feeling! I didn't feel like myself, I felt like a totally different person. I felt like a new person all together! I wanted some more of this! I immediately went back to the church and everything was just as it was before, quiet and still. I went into the back of the church and into the closet and dug out the same bottle of wine. This time I filled it right to the top as full as I could get it. I filled the cup so full I had to bend over and sip some from the top to keep it from spilling. Then I gulped the whole glass down just like I did the first one! Again, as I was walking away, my stomach felt like it was on fire and it felt so, so, good that I thought I could take on the world! I wasn't afraid of anybody! Not the social workers, not the police, not my mom… NOBODY! The last thing I remember saying that day was, "I could even take on Samson with no problem!" I awoke the next morning in a pool of my own puke on the floor of the fort that my brother Buddy had built. My mom knew all about me getting drunk and wanted to know, "What kind of drink did you have and where did you get it from?" I told her, "Maddy and I found a bottle of wine at the Tramway and we tried to sell it but couldn't so we tried it." Funny, she didn't spank me or even get mad, I am sure she must've had a hangover, because she pulled out her stash of blueberries and made me some ice-cold blueberries with sugar and milk. I did not feel like eating anything, but not wanting to provoke her in any way, I ate as best I could in front of her so she could at least feel appreciated.

From that very first experience with alcohol I was hooked and every time I drank after that I always drank to excess and to the point of blacking-out. If I did not drink to the point of blacking-out then I considered it a waste. This would be the pattern that I would follow for the next 27 years. I drank to excess and my goal each time I drank was to reach that point of totally blacking out. At that early age of twelve, my life was already showing signs of unraveling and spiraling downward into a cesspool of trouble. One day while skipping out of school I went down to the basement of the United Church. I did not know where the anger and the rage was coming from that I felt so strongly in those days. I would learn twenty seven years later in therapy that the anger and rage stemmed from the violence I experienced at home and the sexual abuse I experienced at Lower Post. I went down into the basement of the United Church, where the kitchen was and just went completely berserk! I tore the whole place apart! I smashed dishes, spilled food and sugar and milk and all the foodstuffs in the fridge all over the floor. I spray-painted dirty, filthy curse words and graffiti on all the walls! I took a knife and cut swear words into the wooden walls. When I left there the place was a mess! Later in court before they sent me to Lower Post again, they showed pictures of all the damage I did. It looked much worse in the pictures.

From the time I was seven years old, every Halloween, I went on a rampage of breaking as many school windows as I possibly could. Then Maddy would join me and part of our regular routine on Halloween night would be a stop at one of the schools to break some windows. Then they put up screens over the windows at the schools. The police knew who did it they just could not catch us. So the next Halloween when Maddy and I were twelve years old, the police locked us up in the local adult jail the night before Halloween just to be on the safe side. There was no juvenile detention center in the Yukon at that time. When the policeman told us we would be with them for two nights we both cried and cried and cried as this was our first time in jail. We were scared and lonely and both of us lost our appetites until the next morning. They kept us in that jail for two nights. They held us in the women's section of the small jail. At that time, the police station in Whitehorse served as the main jail as well as the police station. On the second day of our time in jail, I went to the washroom and while I was in there, I noticed there was a small window that was open. I was curious and went to take a look outside. To my surprise, I noticed that the bars were wide enough for my head to fit through! I could squeeze through the bars and out the window then drop to the ground. It was quite high but not too high. I had to tell Maddy! When I got back to the cell and told Maddy, right away he said, "Let's go!" I said, "No just wait. I don't want them to get suspicious. I just came out of there so let's wait a while and we'll both pretend we have to go the washroom at the same time. Our plan worked like a charm! We both squeezed out the window and when we hit the ground running, I heard a lady with an Old Crow accent yell out, "Hey you boys, what you're doing?" we took off running as fast as we could! We made it as far as the graveyard on Steel St. A cop car came screeching to a halt behind us at the edge of the graveyard and two policemen jumped out and started chasing us. One of them yelled out in anger, "You boys stop right there!" We split up and ran in different directions. Maddy couldn't run quite as fast as I could and got caught first. I managed to just make it over a fence as the policeman's fingertips touched the back of my shirt collar. The policeman stopped and I took off running. I glanced back over my shoulder as I ran and noticed that the cop had stopped chasing me! I also noticed that Maddy was caught. "Run Andy run!" Maddy shouted. I slowed down to a walk to catch my breath. The policeman that was holding onto Maddy then shouted out, "If you keep running your friend here is going to pay for it! If you stop and come back right now, nothing will happen to either of you." Maddy then shouted, "Don't listen to him Andy it's a trick, RUN!" I decided to listen and gave myself up. When I got into the back of the police car with Maddy, Maddy was a bit mad at me, "Man, whatsa' matter with you? Why did you turn back? I would've kept running if I was you!" "Yeah, to where?" I said back to him defensively. When we got back to the jail and we saw that lady who told on us, we called her every bad name in the book. The police made sure there was a guard with us each time we went to the washroom after that. They didn't punish us. In fact the police actually got a kick out it! They were amused at how clever we were to be able to escape from the jail. They let us out the next day, the day after Halloween.

When I would skip out of school Maddy and I would steal bikes from the school bike racks. We would take a bike and go hide it down by the Reamy Gates at the north end of Sleepy Hollow. We would then steal another bike and we would cut the front end off of one bike and add it to a different bike to make a new bike that looked like the Dennis Hopper motorcycle in Easy Rider. This would make it harder for the owner to identify the bike. We would also spray paint the bikes. My second trip to Lower Post Indian Residential School came about because I was stealing so many bikes and because of the incident at the church basement. Going to Lower Post the second time was harder than the first. I don't know why, possibly because I now knew what lay ahead. This time I was not placed on a bus, but was escorted by a social worker in an orange and black government car. The social worker was a black lady. She took me down to see my family before the long trip to Lower Post. I tried to be brave, as I looked at my mom. She was sober. No hangover. I felt her love. Would someone please stop this scene and freeze it? I want more of this love! I don't want to go. There's a mistake happening here. Someone stop this scene! But no one could. I put on the bravest face I could. I wanted to be mom's brave little man. Yet I couldn't be. The tears gave me away. They flooded my eyes and ran like a river in big splashes to the floor. "You go now, Andy. Don't keep that nice lady waiting" my mom said. I knew I had to go. My heart told me I had no choice and my tears declared it. "See you Andy" Liz said ever so sadly. My sister Margaret repeated the same with a similar tone of sadness in her voice, "See you Andy". We didn't ever hug in those days. We never said "I Love you" either. None of us kids did. The only time we got hugs was when the unmistakable smell of alcohol fell on you from people's breath. The social worker gently took me by the hand and where the thought came from I don't know, but my mind was checking to see how hard or how loose she was holding my hand. It was not firm at all. I took some quickly fading comfort in that, as I was used to a grip (my mom's grip) that was iron-clad and impossible to break unless she was drunk. I felt a warmth in this social worker's hand but I could not bring myself to enjoy it because she was the enemy. I hated her. No I did not hate her personally I hated what she stood for, authority. In my mind and in my heart no matter how gentle she wanted or tried to be, I rejected her. As we were driving away, I thought about what I was leaving behind. I was thinking how nice it was going to be for Lizzy and Margaret. They were going to enjoy mom while she was sober. They were probably going to cook up some potato pancakes and have some rabbit soup. I could picture them smiling and enjoying themselves. My heart ached as these thoughts invaded my mind. The pain in my heart was only evident in my tears. I made not a sound. I would not let this cold, cruel person who was taking me away from all that I loved in the world, hear me cry.

As I mentioned, this lady that was escorting me to Lower Post was a black woman. She was tall, slim and very pretty. She was gentle and kind. I ignored her good qualities. She was trying to be kind I had to give her that. She made repeated attempts at trying to strike up a conversation. But that soon ended as my silence and lack of eye contact told her I wasn't interested and she eventually kept quiet. We drove in silence. I let my tears do their own thing. I did not want her to see me cry but it was oh so hard to be leaving my mom. The social worker was quiet for the longest time, probably realizing it would be best to just let me be, alone in my hurt. We came to McRae a little truck stop just out of Whitehorse. It was obvious that she was trying to make me feel better as she said, "Tell you what Andrew, I'll stop here and get you a treat. You can have a pop or some chips or a chocolate bar." I didn't want anything. I just wanted to go home. She pulled up to the restaurant and stopped. She shut the car off. "What would you like?" Then a brainstorm flashed through my skull. The car is stopped, we are close to town, I could make a run for it! I decided to see if I could get her to go into the store and leave me in the car. Would she actually fall for that? I then looked at her with my red eyes, "Can I get a Coke and some chips please?" "Sure, what kind of chips would you like?" "Just plain." "Would you like to come in and pick out a chocolate bar also or use the washroom?" "No, that's OK, I'm fine." "OK, I'll be right out." What? She's actually falling for it!

I watched her closely as she entered the store and went towards the back of the store where the racks of chips were. I waited just a second longer watching her and it was a good thing I did because she walked back to the window and looked out at me to make sure I wasn't going anywhere. I quickly turned my eyes away and put my head in my hands when I noticed she was about to look out the window at me. I peeked through the cracks in my hands and when I saw that she wasn't at the window any longer I flung the car door open and started running through the gravel parking lot towards Whitehorse! Both sides of the highway were extremely thick with bush and I had to run in the ditch if I was going to make any progress away from there! The going was slow as there was a lot of uncut bush in the ditch along with sharp broken willows with protruding tips that could easily stab you if you weren't careful or if you tripped! I turned to look back and noticed that the orange and black government car we were travelling in was just pulling out of the parking lot! She was coming after me! I decided to run through the bush, surely she wouldn't follow me there! I was wrong. She began to give chase the second the car screeched to a halt. There was a lot of dead fallen trees that made running extremely difficult and next to impossible for my short little legs. The trees looked like a scattered cord of uncut wood laying everywhere with each log about three feet off the ground. I could not jump over the logs so I had to scamper under. Every once in a while I would hit a small clearing and just when I was starting to hit a good stride more logs appeared. When I did hit one of those clearings, I looked back over my shoulder to see if she was still coming. It is amazing what the mind's eye can absorb in a split second! What I seen was like a picture out of an Olympic highlight reel! The social worker looked like an Olympic hurdler in full flight on a record breaking run as she bounded over those trees like they weren't even there! Elbows and legs were pumping in smooth, rhythmic, fluid motion. She had a panicked determined look on her face as she flew over those logs in perfect form as smooth as a gazelle in full flight! She crossed those logs like she had been practicing for this event for months! In no time flat she caught up to me and grabbed me by the back of my collar. I had escaped for all of five minutes! We both stood right where we were and caught our breath. "Not bad for such short skinny legs," she said still trying to catch her breath as we walked back to the car. She did not hold onto my collar for long there was no need to I was no match for her and she knew it. This was strange because I was a fast runner for a twelve year old and could usually outrun most adults that chased me. I was taken aback in amazement at this woman as I had never seen anything like the speed that I just witnessed! I had mixed feelings for this woman for the rest of the trip to Lower Post. Those mixed feelings consisted of respect and a deep loathing that came with the knowledge that I could not escape from her. She never gave me another opportunity to escape for the rest of the trip. We stopped at Teslin for lunch. I kept my eyeballs peeled for a chance to run. When she went to the bathroom she asked one of the people working at the restaurant to keep an eye on me. I spent the winter at the Lower Post Indian Residential School and did not come home until school was out in June. They put me back into the group home when I arrived back in Whitehorse.

CHAPTER TEN

THE PARKING METERS

"THE PAST"

A silent memory stole its way into my quiet heart,
And stirred to life a sleeping past that I kept in the dark,

My past got up, it stretched and yawned then looked me in the eye,
I saw its tears as it drew near real happiness was gone,

I felt a tear roll down my cheek, I said, "Please go away!"
He stopped and gently took my hand said, "Please don't be afraid."

"I'm part of you and I am true, you know all we've been through,
For we are one, no need to run, just make me work for you."

"When you share me you will be free, from all that unshed pain,
And someone who is going through, what
you survived may live again."

I realized my past was right he is a part of me
I took a stand and took his hand that's when I saw him smile at me.

A. Nieman

One day, when we were around fourteen years of age, in the fall time, my friend Rodney walked into the locksmith's office in Whitehorse. His mom had sent him down to get a key cut. When Rodney walked in, the locksmith was in the backroom working on something and did not hear Rodney come in. As Rodney looked around the room, he noticed a parking meter that was in for repairs, sitting right in front of him, with a key stuck in the slot. Rodney, not being one to pass up an opportunity and not being the most honest guy in the world at the time (and how could he be, he hung around with yours truly), casually reached over and made the key part of his own private collection by placing it in his pocket. He turned around and walked right back out. I'm not sure if he ever got his mom's key cut, but he soon sniffed me out and shared his secret. Now I might've been a lot of things in those days; untruthful, conniving, selfish, devious and so on, but one thing for sure, when it came to money, drugs or alcohol, I could be faithful to keep a secret. I was the first one Rodney told. I knew this because I questioned him and made sure there was no one else who knew. I felt both honored and excited that I was the only one Rodney told about this great secret. "Did you try it out yet?" I asked. "Well of course. " And he pulled out a handful of change as if to prove his point. I don't know if my eyes rang up dollar signs but they must have come pretty close because Rodney said "Looks good hey?" "I wonder if it works in all of them?" I thought out loud. "Yep, all of them" Rodney said. "It's the Master key". "Wow!" I blurted out. I could not contain my excitement. Rodney was a thinker just like me. I'm sure he recognized my excitement because he said, "We have to be careful no one sees us and I mean real careful". "So what are we going to do, wait until it gets dark?" I asked. "That would be the safest thing to do. You better not tell anyone about this Nieman! " "No way. You have my word, I promise", I told him in my most reassuring voice. "Not even Gary Dawson", Rodney warned.

"Not even Gary, you have my word". I looked him straight in the eye to let him know I meant it. Rodney gave me his half smile that told me he believed me. "What should we do now?" My question let him know that he was in the driver seat since he had the money. "Want to go to the pool hall and shoot a game?" He said it a little too quickly as if he was waiting for me to ask. "If you feel like losing, that's fine with me!" I said. "Yeah right, as if. You and what army?" he shot back. We jumped on our bikes and began riding. "You got the key in a safe place?" I asked. "I'll leave it at my place where it'll be safe. I've got a secret place to stash it", he said. We kept that key for over a year. It bought us LSD, marijuana, hash and alcohol. At first, Rodney kept the key and would not lend it to me. After a while he let up and let me use it. We had the key for about eight months and we were sure that the heat was being turned up and the police were no doubt on the look-out so we had to be careful. We only used it at night. We took turns using the key and whatever money you made you kept. In those days, the weather would stay at 40 below or colder for 3 to 4 months at a time. When it got cold like that I used the key more than Rodney did. One night in particular stands out in my memory. I decided go out at 2 AM in the morning when it was 40-45 below. I figured the police would never expect anyone in their right mind to be prowling around when it was that cold out. I stayed awake on this night reading Archie comics until I was sure everybody was sleeping. Then I slipped out of my warm bed as my mom and dad and my four sisters all snored as if in unison in the background. I pulled out my BIC lighter and lit the candle that I left on the table purposely for this reason. I ignored the mice that scurried from the light and quietly hoped they didn't rattle any dishes. I waited until my eyes adjusted to the dark and then I quietly put on my layers of warm clothes. I stopped to listen to see if there was a break in any of the snoring, there wasn't. I pulled out my dad's EverReady flashlight and checked to make sure the battery was working. It was. I then blew out the candle and used the flashlight to see. I put a dishtowel over it to block its brightness. I put my boots on and tied them snugly. I opened the door very quietly and the cold air created a cloud that rushed in and hung on the floor. I slipped out real quickly and hoped the cold air didn't wake anyone. I knew time was of the essence and that I had to move quickly. I headed into the night and into a thick ice fog. It seemed like I was walking through a London fog in a movie. Sherlock Holmes was popular back then and I pretended that I was him heading out to solve a case. There was absolutely nobody around. Nothing stirred. I walked past the McCormick's and the Darbyshires houses. All the lights were out. As I got closer to the edge of town, I noticed the only things moving were taxicabs. Oh yeah and me. One thing about living in the Yukon, you learned very quickly how to dress warm. I was oblivious to the cold. I walked on the railroad tracks. As I walked past the ship yards a dog started barking. This caused other dogs to start barking. I silently swore at them and quickened my pace. I kept a wary eye on the houses to see if any lights came on. None did. I arrived at the White Pass train depot on Main Street and hid behind a garbage can as I watched the Yukon security services vehicle drive by. I forgot about them and made a mental note that I needed to be watchful of them. I looked down Main Street as far as the ice fog would allow me to see. Nothing moved. The only sound I could hear was the dull buzzing of an overhead streetlight. It sounded oddly loud. I walked into the brightness of the streetlights and stopped in front of the first meter. As soon as I took my mitt off I felt the cold attack my hand. I dug the key out of my pocket as quickly as I could and the sweat from my hands made the ice cold key stick to my fingers. I had no problem pulling them loose and right away realized it could've been very serious. I put my mitt back on with the understanding that I had just dodged a bullet! That key could have easily froze right to my skin in this type of weather and that would have created a BIG PROBLEM for me as I knew I would have had to go to the hospital to get it removed. I clumsily held the key in my mitt and put it in the slot. I took off my other mitt held it under the meter, turned the key, opened it and let the change fall into my mitt. I closed the meter, pulled the key out and dumped the change from my mitt into my coat pocket in a matter of seconds. I started walking towards the next meter and as I glanced up to see if anyone was around, I noticed there was a buildup of ice on my eyelashes and on the outside of the scarf I wore around my mouth. This was my warning that the cold was catching up to me and catching up fast! There was no place for me to warm up between here and home. It was a good twenty minute walk. I wiggled my toes to see how they were doing. I could barely feel them. What to do? What to do? Should I keep going and risk freezing my feet or leave the money and go back home safe and sound? I couldn't leave the money I came too far to just leave it. I told myself I would check four more meters then go home. I also told myself I'd better hurry!

As I stuck the key in the slot of the next meter, headlights lit up the ice fog and a police car slowly inched its way towards me. I ducked down real quickly leaving the key in the slot and layed out on the ground. I then rolled myself slowly into the porch of Taylor and Drury's store and watched as the police car's headlights got brighter and brighter. I laid there very still daring not to move. My heart pounded in my chest and in my ears. Did they see me? Could they see the key? I would soon find out. I could hear their tires crunch the snow and they sounded very loud. Are they pulling in? I wondered. I dared not turn my head as I listened to see if they slowed down or stopped. If they stopped I was going to run, I already made up my mind. As I carefully listened to the tires I became aware of the cold. It cut through my clothing, all three layers. I could not stay here much longer. Much to my relief the police kept going. I turned my head in time to see them go around the corner and watched as the red tail-lights disappeared into the ice fog. I quickly jumped up brushed off the snow, turned the key in the slot and this time put my coat pocket right up against the meter and let the change fall directly into the pocket. I had two more meters to go. As I quickly made my way to the next meter I noticed my eyelashes were starting to freeze together. It was getting too hard to see. I took my hand out of my mitt and squeezed my eyelashes between my fingers. I could feel the ice melt and I could also feel the bitter cold stabbing at my fingers. I got the ice off my eyelashes. I could see clearly again yet I realized it would be short-lived. I had to hurry! When I got to the next meter I noticed a buildup of ice on my mitts and it was getting very difficult to hold the key. I couldn't get the key in the slot without taking my mitts off! Oh well here goes nothing I thought. I was just about to grab the key with my bare skin when I remembered at the very last second that the key just about froze to my finger last time! I caught myself in mid-motion and pulled my hand back into my mitt. Whoa! Too close for comfort! I then became aware of the cold with an awareness I never knew before. I was in danger. I fumbled with the key and managed to get it into my big coat pocket. I didn't care about the police anymore or the money. I didn't care about the security patrol either. I was facing a new danger now, a real danger. A 45 below danger. The cold had now become my number one enemy. I was in real danger of freezing my feet. If I froze my feet would I be able to walk on them, I wondered to myself. What if I froze my feet and couldn't walk on them? I would freeze to death and it wouldn't take very long in this bitterly cold weather. What can I do? Real fear began to formulate itself in my heart. I looked up Main street and noticed that the yellow cab dispatch office was open. I forgot about that. They were always open 24/7. Almost immediately I imagined the warmth that was in that office. I had used it many times in the past to warm up when Maddy, Gary and I stayed out all night in the middle of winter. The Dispatchers in those cab stands didn't really question us as to why we were there, somehow they seemed to know. They knew that life for us First Nation kids wasn't an easy one at home. But that was a long time ago. I am now fourteen years of age would their attitude be different? I then came to grip the reality that this was my only hope. I *had to* go to the yellow cab stand and warm up. It was the only thing open at this hour that was close by besides the police station. I really had no choice. But if I went to the yellow cab stand, questions would arise. Questions like what are you doing out in this crazy weather? And he or she would no doubt want to know my name. Would they call the police on me? I had to think fast. I stood in the porch way of Taylor and Drury store stomping my feet to try and keep warm. It was useless. The cold now had an iron grip on my feet, my hands (which I had bunched into a fist inside my mitts), my legs and my face. My feet were the worst. What can I tell them I wondered to myself? I have a very creative mind, always had and immediately I formulated a story. I would tell them that I was sleeping over at a friend's house and my friend's dad came home drunk and there was a party and a fight and I got scared and took off. I'll tell them I walked from Riverdale and I am on my way to Sleepy Hollow and that I just wanted to warm up for a bit and I'll be on my way. What if they called the police? Fear crept in again and I was caught between my fear and the cold. The cold won out as I realized that I had no choice. I had to go into the cab stand. My frozen boots on the crunching snow were the only things that made noise as I made my way towards the cab stand. As I pushed the door open I couldn't help but notice the heat that hit my face! The next thing I noticed was the light blue cloud of cigarette smoke that filled the room and hung in the air. When the strong smell of nicotine hit my nostrils, I enjoyed the smell. That smell reminded me of my dad and my Uncle Walter (RIP). This little room brought me warmth and familiarity and in a strange way felt like home.

I looked over to see who the dispatcher was. It was a woman with red hair in middle age. She had an unfiltered cigarette hanging from the corner of her lip. She didn't even remove the cigarette but spoke right through it and said, "Well, well, well what do we have here? What in heaven's name are you doing out in this God-forsaken weather darling? Do you realize how cold it is out there!?" I heard the real concern in her voice. The ice quickly gave way to the heat and disappeared from my eyelashes. I got a better look at her. Once I recognized who she was I quickly looked away. I knew her face but not her name. She *knew* who I was! I was hoping she wouldn't recognize me. I wanted to take my scarf and toque off because I knew I would warm up faster, but dared not to. I had to keep it all on in hopes that she wouldn't see who I was. All I mustered back at her was a quiet, muffled "Hello". She rose from her seat, came over to the counter rested on her elbows and leaned over checking me out. "Are you alright dear?" I could smell her perfume. I took a couple of steps backward and sat down on a chair. I wanted to relieve my feet from the pressure and the coldness and I also wanted to avoid making eye contact with her. No such luck. She opened the door that separated the dispatcher from the public and came over to me. "You look frozen. What's going on sonny?" She sat on her haunches right in front of me and gently pushed my scarf down, put her fingers under my chin raising my face to look directly at her. Our eyes met for the briefest second and I looked away as fast as I could. Too late, in that split second that our eyes met, face recognition passed between us and she said in a calm voice, "You're one of Paul Nieman's boys. It's OK, I'm not going to hurt you. She must've seen fear in my eyes in that split second as well. "Things not going well at home, is that why you're out this late?" My mother's physical assaults on my dad in public places was not hidden under the rug in those days, it was common knowledge in Whitehorse. Whitehorse was a very small town and every knew everybody else's business. I shook my head back and forth to signify no. Just then the door swung open and one of the cabdrivers walked in. He paused ever so briefly to quickly size the situation up then asked, "What's up Dot?" as he made his way over to the coffee pot. "That's what I'm trying to find out," she said back to him. I felt I had better explain and try to get out of there as fast as I could before they called the police and turned it over to them. I cleared my throat and said in a sad and disappointed voice, "I was having a sleep-over at a friend's place and his dad came home drunk and there was a party and a big fight broke out. I got scared and took off from there." I made sure I looked them both in the eyes as I explained. I had learned the importance of maintain eye contact when lying a long time ago. "Where did you walk from?" the man asked. "Riverdale," I said. "In this weather!" the man exclaimed sounding shocked. "You must be freezing! It's not fit for man or beast out there!" "It's not too bad," I lied. Then the lady jumped in, "Are you hurt?" "No," I said looking her in the eye. The man looked at Dot. It was as if a silent conversation had passed between them. "Yeah, go ahead," Dot said, as she walked back around to the other side of the counter. "He lives in Sleepy Hollow, Paul Nieman's place. I'll cover it," she sounded annoyed. The man looked over at me, "Come on young feller, I'll run you home." "But I don't have any money." The statement felt out of place as soon as it left my lips. "I'll cover it son," Dot spoke up. "Are you warmed up now?" the man asked me. Warm or not, I wanted out of there before the police came sniffing around. "Yeah, I'm good," I said quickly rising from the seat and heading towards the door. "Thank you very much Mame," I said looking at Dot. "You're welcome, stay inside and stay warm," she said without looking up. She had the dispatch receiver in her hand and spoke into it, "Car seven where you at?" I opened the door and my old enemy the cold, was right there to greet me. The cab was nice and very warm as we drove slowly through the ice-fog. I did it! I actually did it! I made it! No frozen corpse in the snow tonight! I felt giddy. I almost wanted to see a police car now, I felt so secure. The world of danger I just came out of seemed far away now. I couldn't wait to see how much money I got! "Can I get off by the tracks sir?" I asked the cabdriver. "I can take you right to your place, it's no problem," he said back. "Nah, that's OK, the tracks will be fine. I don't live far from there." "OK, if that's what you want, that's fine with me," he said nonchalantly. I thanked him before I got out of the cab and started walking home. I could feel the weight of the coins in my pockets. Funny, I never noticed it before but the coins felt quite heavy. I could see the lights were all out at the house as I approached. I slipped inside and stopped immediately after I closed the door to listen if anyone stirred or said anything. Nothing. I could feel the warmth of the cook-stove and I knew it was getting low on wood. It was OK for me to put more wood in it and it was

OK if anyone woke up while I was doing it. If anyone did wake up, I would get brownie points for getting out of bed and putting more wood on the fire. I filled the stove. Ahh, the warmth, life was good. I was in the safety zone now. I wanted to count my money but dared not to. Instead, I sat beside the cook-stove in the dark, soaking in the warmth. Small bits of light escaping through the tiny holes in the cook-stove from the flames of the crackling dry wood, shone brightly in the dark and lit up my face. I stared at the flickering flames. My mind drifted back to the events of that night and I just couldn't help but think of how close I had come to something terrible happening. That was the last time I went out in the middle of the night in the middle of a Yukon winter to use the key. My little sister Frieda's cat made its way through the dimly lit room and rubbed itself against the side of my leg. As soon as I picked it up to move it away it started purring. I didn't like cats then.

CHAPTER ELEVEN

DEATH AND MY FIRST BIRTHDAY IN JAIL

"LOOKING BACK"

Looking back I had to smile, our memories they stretched for miles,
The ups and downs the good and bad, so
many good times that we had,

Looking back I wiped a tear, I felt the times we held so dear,
Someone like you so hard to find, someone so real, someone so kind,

Looking back I had to sing, you gave to us your everything,
True love, true friends we faced it all, you
picked me up each time I'd fall,

Looking back I longed for more, but I know I must close the door,
Will we meet you there in eternity?
The love of truth, holds lock and key

A. Nieman

In that same year when I was fourteen years old, I kept going in and out of the group home because I kept getting into trouble with the police. Today, I walk into the group home and Patty is singing along with "Bad Moon Rising" by Creedence Clearwater Revival. She is singing loud and happy in that beautiful voice of hers. There were some new faces at the group home. Three sisters from Mayo had moved in and another girl named Doreen who was from Whitehorse. The three sisters from Mayo were very, very pretty girls. To me they were movie-star pretty. Diane, Hazel and Margaret were not only pretty they had beautiful attitudes to match. They were not stuck-up or snobbish but kind, gentle and quick to laugh. I knew Doreen from before the group home. Her family lived in the same area I did, Sleepy Hollow. We all became very good friends and were very close at the group home. Some of us lived there for years. I stayed there about three years in total. We were a family there. We played pool together, played board games, watched TV and were involved in different sports and other activities. Mason and I would play hockey on this tiny rink about two blocks from the home, until we were bone-tired and could barely walk home for supper. We spent hours and hours on that rink. Life at the group was up and down for me. I had this feeling inside of me that I was different that I was marred and dirty. I looked at others with envy. I had this form of extreme negative shameful thinking that was so persistent I believed I could never be free from it. In my mind, I believed that people could see right through my eyes and into my soul if I let them see my eyes for very long and all the feelings of doubt, hate and shame would be there in plain view for them to witness. I believed they could see it but were kind enough not to mention that they could see it. I lived on the edge of fearing that one day I would meet someone who would mention to everyone out loud what they seen in my eyes. I feared such exposure! This type of thinking made my palms constantly and consistently sweaty. I hated to shake hands with people because of this. My palms were sweaty all the time, except for that exact moment when I had a bottle of alcohol in my hand and then peace would start to make its way into my heart! My self-consciousness got worse later on when I started to get heavily into the hallucinogenic drugs of LSD (Acid), MDA, Magic Mushrooms and Crystal Meth. Not having any front teeth didn't help my cause any either and it bothered me something fierce. I also had to wrestle with the dark secret of the sexual abuse which made me feel that no matter how hard I tried, I could never be normal or innocent like I imagined all my friends were. As much as I pretended to be happy I was the opposite. I could act any part and I could act it almost to perfection. NOBODY KNEW how I felt. On the outside, I was this happy-go-lucky, energetic normal teen. On the inside there was a fierce battle raging as I fought to keep my demons of fear and my shame at bay. Heaven help me if anyone ever found out that I was a victim of sexual abuse! That would be the ABSOLUTE WORST possible thing that could ever happen to me! So I PRETENDED and I ACTED and I PUT ON my best and biggest smile for the whole world. While inside I was lonely and fearful and felt like I would NEVER FIT IN no matter how hard I tried. So the drinking alcohol gave me some relief from the acting and the loneliness. I drank every weekend and would not even remember how I got back to the group home. I woke up locked in the bathroom downstairs after a night's drinking. Blacking out from drinking too much was actually my goal and my intention. I did not believe in drinking socially, good grief are you kidding me! Get that sociable drinking away from me! I drank strictly and solely for the effect of the alcohol. I drank for an escape and to change how I was feeling. I looked forward to drinking. I looked forward to how it would take me away from myself and the misery of how I felt. However, in the end and on the mornings after, I always wound up with the same old me needing another drink to help me drown who I really was and to help me feel a little better. When I wanted to drink more, I simply ran away from the group home and did B&E's to get money to support my alcohol habit. But it was always apparent that I would wind up back at the group home one way or another. Drinking eventually became EVERYTHING to me. By the time I was fourteen I was a full-blown, full-fledged alcoholic and did not even realize it. I got grounded a lot at the group home as a result of my drinking. I would go to school hung-over and irritated. The only time I would stay in on a Friday night back then was when I was grounded.

On one of those Friday nights when I was grounded two of the pretty sisters Hazel and Margaret along with Doreen went for a ride with some guys from Carmacks. Back at the group home the rest of us and the girls were playing the Kissing Game where the girls would chase after one guy, overpower him (of course we pretended to fight our hardest) and the girls would each take a turn kissing him. The girls did this to all the guys so it wound up that all the guys got to kiss every one of the girls by the time the game and evening was over. The game only worked if the girls chased the boys it could not work the other way around. As the game went on it was getting later and later into the evening 10:30 pm came and went. On Fridays if we were not staying out for the night we had to be back at the group home by 11:00 pm and no later or we would get grounded. Diane was the first to notice the time that it was getting close to eleven and she began to wonder how come Hazel, Margaret and Doreen were not back yet. "They're going to get grounded," she said. We never thought much of it as there was always someone getting grounded at the home. The next morning as a couple of us were sitting at the table eating breakfast we heard Diane let out a loud piercing scream from the office. She cried out in a loud heartbreaking wail, "No! No! No!" We all knew something very terrible had happened and we looked at each other our eyes wide with fear. Diane continued to cry out, "No not Hazel! Not Hazel! No, No, No!" Hazel and Doreen had both been killed in a car accident last night. Margaret was in the hospital with undetermined injuries. The news hit our hearts like a ton of bricks! We held each other and cried and cried and cried some more. Our world collapsed! We were shocked! We went and tried to comfort Diane as best we could but Diane was more interested in going to see how her sister Margaret was doing in the hospital. We all wanted to go but Mr. MacDunaugh said it was best if just Margaret's family were with her at this time. He drove Diane to the hospital. Hazel and Doreen's favorite song that they always liked to play when it was their turn to use the record player at the group home was, "I Cry Like A Baby" by The Boxtops. We played their song over and over again all through the night as we sat in the rec room and truly cried like babies. It was devastating! Five people died in that car accident the night it happened. There were seven young people in the car, two survived, Margaret and a friend of mine named James from Carmacks. Losing Hazel and Doreen brought a cloud of heaviness that hung over the group home for weeks. Hazel was the life of the party. She loved to dance. She loved to sing. She had a bouncing bubbly full of life personality. She could light up any room that she walked into. Her beauty in itself was something to behold and she could turn every head in the room because of it both male and female. Hazel did not seem to be aware that she was so pretty. She liked to jump into any conversation and be a part of whatever was happening without being intrusive. She was not shy.

Doreen had fairly dark skin and was fairly quiet but carried herself in a mature way. She liked to think before she spoke and was easy-going. She also liked to have fun. Doreen took pride in the way she dressed and liked to look her best. Margaret was more the motherly, caring type. Margaret was very pretty. She had a great big smile and in that smile it was evident that her heart carried real love and real compassion. She was more the quiet and laid back type. Her voice was very soft-spoken like soft velvet petals floating on a gentle summer breeze. Margaret's voice was a very comforting voice. She had a true heart of gold. She survived the car accident with a hip injury that caused her to limp for the rest of her life but that injury did nothing to steal her beautiful smile or her love for life and for people. She was an inspiration and a very true friend to me. She was one of the first out of our bunch to give her life completely to Jesus. I later learned that she prayed a great deal for me I am eternally grateful for that. "Thank you so much Margaret." (RIP)

Margaret Smeeton (nee Alger) and her stepson Jonathan. I am baptizing Ruby Van Bibber in the Name of Jesus when this picture was taken.

There was always some loose talk going on in our little crowd of teenagers about getting out of Whitehorse and going to the big city lights of Vancouver, British Columbia. You could probably say and no one would argue that it was a dream that came naturally to every young person who ever grew up in Whitehorse. The thought of going to a great big city like Vancouver was fascinating, absolutely fascinating to a young mind! Such a topic had the potential to capture our full attention whenever Vancouver was mentioned and plans on how to get there were dreamed over and over again without ever losing its appeal. We talked about all the drugs we could have access to, the cheap price and each of us talked about the first drug we would get high on once we got there. We knew there was an endless supply of street drugs in Vancouver because of all the stories we heard from Yukoners who had been down there in the late sixties (1965-1969) and when they returned they always brought some drugs back with them. We did our best to devise various fool-hardy ways to travel to Vancouver and whenever someone came up with a plan on how to travel there, the rest of us did our very best to tear the plan apart by finding and poking holes in it. This was done so we could devise a fool-hardy plan that would actually work and get us to Vancouver. Every plan we devised failed, simply because it always took too much money. Then, I had a brain-wave or the brain-wave had me. I'm not sure which. Anyway, I actually came up with the best fool-hardy plan and it was so realistic and fool-proof we decided to do it! One evening, we bought three grams of hashish and decided to smoke it in the basement of my friend Sonny's parent's place. His parents were drinking beer and having a good time. I had to sneak in because Sonny's dad, Larry did not like me. His dad didn't like me because three years prior when I was 12 yrs. old, he caught me stealing cigarettes out of his car parked in front of the '98 Hotel (which is a popular drinking establishment). When I was twelve years old I used to carry two rocks in my pocket when I would look through cars for cigarettes and money or booze and if anyone chased me I would use the rocks to throw at them. At least that was the plan. The rocks were used more to give me a false sense of courage than anything else when I did my criminal deeds. I never intended to use them, besides I was a very fast runner and I had no intention of letting anyone catch me! They were fair sized rocks, to say the least. I only had to use the rocks once and it happened when Sonny's dad started to chase me that one day. Maddy was with me as I was "checking cars" for any valuables and I told Maddy, "Watch the door of the '98. If anyone and I mean if anyone comes out start whistling, OK?" He nodded. So Maddy stands over by the door of the '98 and "keeps point". Just then, I spot a pack of Export "A" cigarettes lying on the dashboard of a car and check to see if the door is unlocked. It is open. I glance around and notice there is no one coming. The car is about twenty feet from the front door of the '98. I nod at Maddy to get ready before I go in. He nods back. I quickly swing the door open, jump in and reach for the cigarettes. Well, it would just be our bad luck that Sonny's dad came through the door! He was a lean, mean truck driver and had a reputation as being one of the most honest, hardworking and toughest men in the Yukon back then! Unknown to me, while I was reaching for the cigarettes, Larry came out of the hotel and Maddy recognizing that it was one of the toughest guys around that suddenly appeared in the doorway got too scared to whistle and not only that, he was too scared to even say a WORD! Maddy froze! Now if Larry did not say anything he would've caught me dead in my tracks, but as soon as he seen me digging in his car he let out a loud yell that sounded so mean it could've stopped a bear, "Hey you little #★&?@# get the #★&?@# out of my car!" I immediately scurried out of the car turned and stated running! It was not a split second too soon as I felt the tips of his fingers brush against the hairs on the back of my head as he tried to grab the back of my shirt collar! He was running right behind me. I started to run as fast as I could and he had no problem keeping up with me! I dodged this way and I dodged that way and he dodged this way and he dodged that way and stayed very close behind me right on my heels! I couldn't shake him! I started to panic and then I became aware that the two rocks in my pockets were weighing me down and slowing me down! I could hear his heavy breathing so close behind me that I realized he was GAINING and just about to grab me! SHEER PANIC gripped me! Without even thinking and with my adrenaline going a hundred miles an hour I grabbed one of the rocks from my pocket and by some twist of fate was able to half turn as I ran, see my target and managed to throw the rock. It all seemed to happen in slow motion because I could see the whole scene take place as it unfolded. He noticed I was throwing the rock at him, his head went down and his hand went up just as I threw the rock but his hand came up a split-second too late! The rock caught him on top of the head and opened up a deep gash. The rock staggered him slightly. He stopped running almost immediately after the rock hit him! Just in time too because as soon as I released the rock from such an awkward running position I tripped and went skidding onto the pavement as the palms of my hands used about twenty sharp pebbles as brakes to bring me to a stop. Ouch! I didn't care about the pain though I was worried about my life! I immediately jumped up and with blood starting to flow from the pebbles stuck in my hand I ran as fast as I could straight for the Yukon river bank! All I heard behind me as my running feet barely touched the pavement was a stream of profanities that ended with the words, "You won't get away you little #★&?@#!"

Word soon got out in our small town and just about everybody knew about this incident. I made sure I stayed away from Sonny's dad from then on that is until tonight. That is why I had to sneak into the basement or at least make an attempt. The girls went into the house as it was too cold for them to stand outside with Sonny and I. Sonny and I both stood out in the freezing cold porch talking back and forth trying to figure out how I was going to get past his dad and into the basement. There were five of us there that Friday night looking to get high, Sonny, Maizi and three of us from the Group Home; Diane her sister Margaret (the one who was in the accident, she had a limp now as a result of the accident) and me. I was 15 yrs. old Maizi was 15, Diane was 17, Margaret was 14 and Sonny was 14. Sonny's parents and a couple of friends were sitting in the kitchen drinking beer and laughing up a storm. The door and the stairs that went down to the basement came directly out of the kitchen. When you came up from the basement you came right into the kitchen area. Sonny's dad was sitting right beside the door that led to the basement. It was no problem for the girls to make it downstairs, all they had to do when they entered the nice warm home was simply tell their names, where they were from, give a hug to those who asked for one and then they went downstairs. But there was NO WAY I could get past them without going past Sonny's dad who was still very sober and quite coherent. He sat right beside the door that I had to go through to get to the basement. I said to Sonny, "If he was a little drunker than he is he probably wouldn't mind or he probably wouldn't notice me but he looks completely sober.""Yeah.""Well, looks like I'm screwed," I said starting to weigh my options. Weigh my options? I had no other options! I needed to get high and there was no other place that I could go to do that except here! My heart sank. Sonny seemed to pick up on my despair and then with a wide-eyed light-bulb moment he comes up with an idea. An idea which he thinks is absolutely brilliant! Brilliant that is because there is no risk on his part and he pipes up with, "Why didn't I think of this before! That's it! I've got it! It's brilliant! I'm a genius! I've got it!""Got it? Got what?" I ask. "We don't have to wait for dad to get drunk at all in fact it's better that's he's NOT drunk!""What in the world are you getting' at?" I ask him. "That time you hit dad with the rock that was what about four years ago right?""Three.""OK three, four same thing. What my dad really respects are guys who have balls." Sonny was referring to guys who have courage when he said 'balls'. "So if you were to go in there and face him and show him that you have balls, that you're a man and apologize for what you did, he'll respect you for the rest of his life for being a man.""What?? Yeah right! Are you nuts Sonny!? No way! You just want him to throw me out and you guys will have all the hash to yourselves! And then to top it off he'll punch me out! No #&★@ way!" "No. Honestly. Listen Andy, I am telling you the truth! I wouldn't do that to you! Trust me I know dad. Just to make it safer for you, I'll call Maizi up and ask her to ride shot-gun for you that way if he starts punching you out Maizi can stop him. He listens to Maizi!?" "Oh great… 'If he punches you out' well thanks for the words of encouragement! I thought you just said you *knew* him?" "Well I can't predict the future!" We both fell silent. Sonny watched my face intently for any telltale signs of acceptance for his so-called 'brilliant plan'. I thought about the proposition for a moment and the freezing cold that was biting at my toes and our noses reminded me that time was running out and running out *fast*! Sure enough my need to get high and escape reality overcame my fear of being punched out and thrown out into the forty below weather. I looked at Sonny with an expression that told him I would do it. He responded with, "Good. I'll go get 'Gunna!' 'Gunna' was Sonny's short version of saying Maizi. I grabbed his arm and stopped him in his tracks as he started to quickly turn to go inside. He was getting cold too. "Just a minute," I said. I went over to the window and peeked in. They were all laughing and having a grand old time. As I peeked in and found Larry' face, my resolve to go ahead with the plan took a much-needed leap up the ladder of courage when I noticed the smile on Larry's face. Sonny watched me, "OK?" he asked. "Just a minute. You don't have to get Maizi I'll just do it.""OK, here's what we'll do. You wait out here and I'll ask dad if it's OK for you to talk to him.""Why don't we just walk in together?""No. I don't think that would be a good idea it'd be better to ask him. I know him he doesn't like surprises.""OK. Let's do it.""I'll come out and get you." I was so, so scared. I would have backed out right then and there as soon as Sonny entered the house but it was too late. There were only two things that kept me from running, one — the hash and two — the forty below freezing cold weather! As soon as Sonny entered the house I got as close to the door as possible and listened. All I heard was Sonny's muffled voice which I couldn't understand and then Larry's booming voice which we all heard loud and clear saying, "Well where is the little pecker? Tell him to come in!" When the door opened I felt as small as a church mouse dangling by the tail in the paws of a giant Cheshire cat about to get swallowed whole! Everyone else in the room faded into oblivion except for Larry and as I took a step just inside the door Sonny slammed it quickly shut. The smell of nicotine, spilled beer, fried moose meat and wood smoke quickly welcomed me into this warm reality that I wanted so badly to run from and yet wanted so badly to be a part of. I stood there extremely tense ready to defend myself from any type of blow that might come my way. I dared not look at Larry until he spoke to me or hit me one or the other. The calm that was in his voice captured the full attention of my spinning hyper-alert mind and brought it down to earth into full focus. "Come over here. Come closer," he said calmly. It was only then that I looked at him and I noticed a curious grin on his face. I then heard Sonny's mom in the background, "Oh that's Paul Nieman's son Andy. That's Sonny boy's best friend. Maizi and his sister Lizzy are best friends too. You don't bother him Larry. His mom used to be mean to him." I wanted to say, "Hi" to Sonny's mom and didn't want to be disrespectful but I couldn't I was too afraid of Larry and had to give him my full attention. I took two steps closer towards him and stopped. "Come over here, right in front of me right here," he said pointing to a spot on the floor directly in front of him. "I want you to see something." I grabbed the last thread of courage as it was about to leave from deep inside my heart and used it to pull both my feet towards Larry until I stood right in front of him not more than twelve inches from his face. He then bent his head down and said, "See that scar right there?" It was easy to see the scar as Larry always kept his head shaved into a neatly trimmed very short brush cut. I was like super-scared now! I thought to myself, "Oh, oh he's doing this to justify laying a beating on me! He did this to get me close enough to him so he could grab me!" To my surprise Larry continued, "Well, do you see that scar there?" "I'm sorry Mr. Profit, I am really, really very sorry." He slowly reached out and grabbed the front of my shirt. He made a fist with my shirt rolled up in his hand and he twisted it until it started to choke me. "You know what I ought to do with a little punk like you that likes going around stealing from cars and throwing rocks at people? I should turn you upside down right now stick your #&@ head in that garbage can and bang it up and down until I knock some sense into you! Whatta' ya think about that?" I was sure everyone could see me sweating and shaking. I froze with fear and never said a word, not even the slightest peep! "But because you were man enough to come and face me and had the balls to come over here on your own to apologize to me, I'm gonna' shake your hand instead. That's the kind of friends I want my son to have, not no chicken-livered punks. You boys get downstairs now, I don't wanna' see your faces for the rest of the night." I believe there was a world record set that night by yours truly for the fastest time going from freezing cold to sweating bullets! You wanna' talk about RELIEF! Right then and there, that night in that little house on Cook St., I became the happiest and the most relieved human being in all of creation! I was also very proud of myself as I had just faced one the toughest guys in Whitehorse. From that night on, Sonny was right, Larry had a respect for me that never wavered and still remains to this day. Years later when my good friend Sonny passed away, Margaret and I sang a special solo song at his funeral titled, "Where The Roses Never Fade." Larry approached me later at the supper after the funeral service and said, "If I go before you, I want you to sing that song at my funeral. Deal?" "It's a deal," I assured him. "Let's hope it's not for a long time yet," he said winking and smiling at me. I love Larry, he's a solid man. Now, back to the plan I devised for our travel to Vancouver.

Once we got down in the basement, I shared my plan with the others. The plan was simple and I explained that it went like this, "We steal a car that has a full tank of gas and we take turns driving it down to Vancouver. We just need enough gas to get as far as Lower Post because my brother Paul works there and I can get some money from him for gas. Once we get out of the Yukon it will be nice and warm in British Columbia and if we run out of money it will be easy to siphon gas." The more I spoke, the more the excitement started to build in me and I could see it was building in the others as well. I continued, "All we need is a hose and a jerry can. Sonny do you know where we can get a hose and a jerry can?" "Dad might have one somewhere, I'll have a look later." Maizi asked, "Now where you gonna' get a car with a full tank of gas? What about food? Where we gonna' sleep? And when would we do this? Don't you know it's forty below out there!" Maizi always had a sharp mind and she had the ability to think outside the box, she could think ahead and perceive things the normal person didn't. I liked her questions because it also meant we could problem-solve together and it meant if I came up with the right answers, Diane and Margaret would come along with us. I answered, "It's better that it's forty below out because people will keep their cars running and since it's almost Christmas there are a lot of people out shopping so the parking lots will be full, we just need to look until we find one with a full tank. For food, we just need to get some bread, some mustard and some sandwich meat. We can sleep on the highway as we drive." Margaret then joined in the questioning, "What about the police? The Group Home will phone the police as soon as we stay out past midnight?" "We'll be long gone by then, we'll be out of the Yukon." I answered. "Just think we could be in Vancouver two days from now!" I had no idea what I was talking about and nobody questioned that it would take such a short time to drive to Vancouver. There was silence. Minds were turning over the possibility of seeing the big city for the very first time. Diane was the first to let her imagination be verbalized, "Wow, can you imagine those tall buildings, the bright lights and all those people? They'll never be able to find us!" Sonny joined in with excitement clearly evident in his tone of voice, "And pushers on every corner!" Then Maizi always the level-headed one brought us back to reality and the task at hand which was step one by asking, "When would we do this? Who's going to get the vehicle?" That was the question that put our plan into motion and even though we didn't flat out say we were going to do it, our planning said we were already there. I took the lead, "I'll get the car. It's easy to get one from Tourist Services at the supermarket." "I'll go with you Andy," Sonny said looking serious. "It's better if I do it by myself it'll look too suspicious if someone sees two guys looking in cars. If the cops stop me I'll just say I'm looking for my uncle's car. You can wait for me in the porch at Tourist Services though I'll pick you up." I continued, "Tomorrow is Saturday and it will be real busy then so that would be the best time to do it." There was no objection so I went on, "Once I steal the car I can pick the rest of you up somewhere and we'll head straight out." The decision was made we would do it the very next day. The only person who wasn't sure about going was Diane. She kept saying, "I'm still thinking about it." The next day around 2 pm Diane, Margaret and I left the Group Home with just our winter clothes on we didn't take anything extra so we wouldn't draw any suspicion on ourselves. It was bitterly cold out at least forty below and we had decided last night that we would all meet at Sonny and Maizi's place today before I went to get a car. Diane decided that she wanted to walk down to the Shipyards area to Harold's place and that was where she would be for the rest of the day. Maizi, Sonny, Margaret and I met in the basement. All eyes were on me and all eyes were silently asking me, are you really serious about this? As I stared back there was no need for words they could see I was going through with it. Of course, Maizi who was always the responsible one, had to be the first to speak, "So what's the plan?" I jumped at the opportunity to take the lead, "It's almost dark now so now would be the best time. I'll go get the car and I'll pick you guys up in the alley behind here." "Do you want me to drive from here?" Maizi asked. We all knew that out of all of us Maizi was the best driver as she had the most experience and well, driving just comes naturally to a truck driver's daughter. "Yeah," I answered. I then added as a last minute thought, "If we get caught, remember I was the one who stole the car and did all the driving and it was all my idea. You guys just came for a ride because I told you that I borrowed my Uncle's car OK." They all agreed rather quickly and in unison said, "OK."

It was about four thirty in the afternoon and dark out as I walked over to the parking lot of Tourist Services. It was as easy as picking cherries because back in those days nobody locked their vehicles in such a small town as Whitehorse. In this freezing cold weather every vehicle in the parking lot was left running to keep the vehicle warm. After checking two vehicles I found one with a full tank of gas. I jumped in and drove it as carefully as I could out of the parking lot and parked it in the alley like we planned. Maizi, Sonny and Margaret were surprised that I was back so soon. We quickly piled into the car and Maizi took over the driving duties. She asked me, "Where to?" Margaret then asked before I could answer, "What about Diane?" "Let's go to the shipyards. We'll pick Diane up." I said starting to get a bit antsy because time had now become our enemy. We stopped outside Harold's place in the shipyards and Margaret went in to see if Diane wanted to come. The door to the small house opened and Diane peeked her head out and then quickly closed the door once she seen that we actually had a car. When Diane and Margaret got in the car we made our way straight to the highway and once we were on the road, the darkness swallowed us up and brought us some relief as we sped through the cold winter night heading to

Vancouver! All eyes were glued to the road ahead and we watched as the glow of the headlights illuminated our young faces and lit up the snow-filled trees on each the side of the road. Our young minds started to absorb and process the seriousness of our new found reality. We did it! We're doing it! We're going to Vancouver! Yahoo! Maizi drove and I let Diane sit in the front seat because she looked like a full grown woman and it would look less suspicious when we drove up to a gas station. Maizi, true to form, had saved about a hundred dollars and when we got to Teslin she said, "We better get gas here because we don't know how far it is to the next gas station."

Later that night we pulled into Lower Post, B. C. It was about midnight and it was still bitterly cold. Lower Post is a tiny village and it only had a gas station, a restaurant a small hotel and an off-sales window. I asked the guy at the off-sales window if he knew Paul Nieman. He did. I asked him if he knew where Paul was and he replied, "He's partying around here somewhere. You could check over at Tibbet's place he might be over there." "Where's that?" He gave me directions and we pulled up outside of the house. I knew some of the Tibbet family and went up to the door and knocked. Evelyn answered. The first thing she said was, "Andy Nieman what in the world are you doing here? Come on in! Who's that with you? Don't you know how cold it is out there, what you doing travelling?" I knew Evelyn from when I attended the Residential school there as a child and a teenager. I explained that I was looking for Paul. "He just went to Watson," she said, referring to Watson Lake a community in the Yukon that was just fifteen miles away. "I don't know when he'll be back or if he'll be back, he's partying with Dalton and them." She could tell I was deeply disappointed. "Who's your friends? Tell 'em to come in! Gosh, don't just leave them out there!" She invited all of us in, fed us and said, "There's only one bed but you guys are welcome to spend the night if you want. It's too cold to be out in this weather" We spent the night there and the next morning because we did not plug the car in to keep the engine block warm, the car froze solid and we were stuck! My brother Paul heard that I was at Tibbett's place and came over to see me. It was a Sunday morning the date was December 15, 1969 the day before my sixteenth birthday. Paul was still a little tipsy from the night before. "What are you guys up to now Andy? Who's car is that outside?" he asked. Diane surprised us all when she answered, "It's mine." "Who are you young lady and where you guys headed to?" "I'm Diane and this is my sister Margaret. We're going to Vancouver. We didn't plug my car in last night and it froze." Paul looked at me and the rest of us without saying a word. He turned to Diane, "You're dad's Fred…?" he let the question hang. "Yes." "I met him before. I think it was in Mayo if I remember correctly." "Probably Mayo, that's where we're from." "How'd you get tangled up with my little brother?" "Well I met him through my sister Margaret. I'm on my way to Vancouver and he asked if he could go along so I said sure why not." Paul turned to me, "How's mom? How's Lizzy and Margaret?" "They're good," I answered hoping he would stop asking so many questions. "I thought you were staying at a Group Home in Whitehorse aren't you still there?" "No." "Where you staying at then?" "Here and there, mostly at Sonny's." You got any money?" "No. I was gonna' ask you if I could borrow some." "Borrow," he said it mockingly. "Everybody wants to borrow and nobody wants to pay back. When you gonna' pay me back?" he was just joking, he knew I couldn't pay him back. "I'm just joshing you," he reached for his wallet, "So what are you guys gonna' do now?" he looked at Diane. "You car's frozen solid you ain't going nowhere until you thaw it out." Diane looked at me and said, "I don't know what we're going to do. What can we do?" Paul brought us all the relief we needed when he said, "You're gonna' have to have it towed to the garage to get it thawed out before you go anywhere. I'll get Johnny to tow it for you. It'll probably take a couple of hours." Paul took fifty dollars out of his wallet and handed it to me. "Why don't you guys go down to the restaurant and have something to eat and tell the waitress to put it on my bill? When your car is ready I'll come and get you at the restaurant." We all perked up at the mention of food and that started us into motion. "Thank you very much," Diane spoke first. Sonny and the rest of us spoke the same words, "Thanks Paul." Paul drove us down to the restaurant and after letting the waitress know that he would pay for our meal he said, "You guys can wait here and when the car is ready I'll have Johnny drive it over here." We all thanked him again. Paul made me feel proud that he was my brother. We finished our meal and were waiting around inside the tiny restaurant when Maizi noticed the police car pull off the main highway and turn into Lower Post. "Oh, oh," was all she said. "What?" I asked looking at her. "The cops just pulled off the main highway and drove by. They might be looking for that car." I reassured everybody, "Just remember, I told you guys that I borrowed my Uncle's car when I picked you up, that's all you have to remember. I'll take the rap so don't worry 'bout it nothing will happen to you guys." "But I told Paul that the car was mine," Diane was very concerned. "I shouldn't have opened my big mouth." I tried to calm her down by saying, "All you have to say is that you lied to protect me from getting into trouble with my brother." She still looked worried. No more than ten minutes passed and we all watched as the police car slowly pulled up outside the restaurant. Before the cop came in I said to them again, "Remember, I did everything, all the driving everything!" Needless to say, our trip to Vancouver was over. The police took us to the Watson Lake jail. My birthday was the very next day, Dec. 16. I turned sixteen in the Watson Lake jail and on my birthday Monday December 16, 1969, they fingerprinted me and charged me with Car Theft. Later that afternoon I sat in the backseat of a police car as they transported me back to Whitehorse for court. I'm not sure what happened to the rest of our crew I think the social worker drove them back to Whitehorse. I was thankful that I was the only one charged.

The police took me to Whitehorse Correctional Center (WCC) which is an adult jail. Back in those days, when you reached sixteen years of age in the judicial system you were treated like an adult. When I entered the jail they had me shower and the prison garb I changed into consisted of underwear, white canvas running-shoes, blue jeans and a green work shirt. They gave me two white sheets, a thin grey army-type wool blanket, a pillow case, a toothbrush, a razor, a round cake of shaving soap, a bristle shaving brush, a plastic cup, a pouch of Vogue cigarette tobacco, cigarette rolling papers and a pack of matches. I spent two weeks in Remand at WCC and then they sentenced me to six months in jail. I never dreamed I would spend my sixteenth birthday locked up behind bars with criminals from various walks of life. I also had no way of knowing that I would spend eight years in total behind the walls of WCC in years to come. In Remand I was placed in a cell with three other inmates. Remand was different than the rest of the jail and you had a few more privileges than other areas of the jail because you were not sentenced yet. You could sleep all day if you wanted, you did not have to do any chores other than keeping your area clean and they let you get an hour of fresh air each day. After I was sentenced to six months the same day that I returned from court they moved me into NCB. NCB is short for New Cell Block. NCB is where all newly sentenced inmates are held until they are classified. When you are 'classified' this means you are given a security rating and you are assigned to an area of the prison according to your security rating. NCB is not a nice place. You are locked in a single cell that has three walls of solid steel and one wall that is all bars with a slot in the door to pass your food tray through. There is an iron bed welded to the wall it is immovable and has no bed springs just a solid sheet of iron. On the back wall there is a stainless steel toilet with a sink above it that is all one piece. There is an unbreakable mirror set in stainless steel above the sink. The mirror is scratched and hard to see through. On the third wall there is a tiny iron table and a small seat both welded to the wall. Remand wasn't so bad compared to this place at least over there you could see the other guys and you could play cards with them. Here, you couldn't do any of that. You were more isolated. You could talk to other inmates but you couldn't see them. You couldn't really talk all that much either as sometimes there were inmates who were doing 'hard time' who didn't want to talk and out of respect you didn't push it. When someone was doing 'hard time' we had a name for that, "shaking it rough". If you couldn't handle your time you were "shaking it rough." Talking was also limited because some guys wanted to sleep. I didn't mind not talking, in fact I would rather not talk, But in jail if you don't talk, the other inmates will think there is something wrong with you and this might cause some unnecessary hardship for you. In NCB all you could do was read, write letters or exercise. In NCB I read "A Stone For Danny Fisher" and it was one of the best books I had ever read up to that point. Harold Robbins was my favorite author back then. Reading was my escape, poetry and reading. I could barely hear, "Spiders and Snakes' by Jim Stafford straining from the radio through a small speaker high up on the cellblock wall. I am hungry. You're almost always hungry in jail unless you work in the kitchen or you have money for canteen. Sometimes you were let out of your cell after supper to watch TV for a few hours, go for fresh air or go to the gym. When you first come to jail and those doors slam shut behind you, your choices have been cut down and become next to nothing. In jail your whole world changes. Everyone in your circle of family and friends is affected one way or another and it is usually 99.9% in a negative way. When you are locked up in jail you have a lot of time on your hands and you have a lot of time to think. As you lay there on your hard bed staring at the ceiling with the scratchy sound of a radio playing CKRW in the distant background, your mind starts to think. You are alone with your thoughts, alone with your failures, alone with your heartaches and your fears. While locked up alone your mind automatically drifts to your life out there, your life outside of jail. I tried to but I could never count my blessings. I couldn't count my blessings because I felt damaged and dirty from the sexual abuse and my thinking was warped and dysfunctional. All my mind would focus on, all my mind would think about were the lost opportunities, the regrets and the way things might have been IF ONLY. IF ONLY I didn't come from a violent alcoholic home. IF ONLY I didn't go to Residential School. IF ONLY my dad was home more. IF ONLY that pedophile wasn't there. IF ONLY I wasn't separated from my family so much. IF Only I wasn't born. If only. If only. If only things could've been different. And then, inevitably you wonder if you really matter to anybody. And if you matter to someone, you wonder how much you truly mean to them. Jail is the one true place where you will FIND OUT FOR SURE who your TRUE friends are, GUARANTEED! Some will promise you the world, others will say they will do this for you no matter what, girlfriends and boyfriends will lay down promises to wait for you and it is while you are in jail, that is where you will discover who is real and who the talkers are in your life.

While 'doing time' 99% of the inmates say they are innocent. This is a natural response. Anyone who is in jail and says they didn't do the crime, 99% are, in reality, just letting you know that they are still dysfunctional and in denial. They are not fooling anybody or hiding anything by saying this they are just giving others a clear indication that they still need healing. The other 1% who know they are guilty and admit to it are being either totally honest or are trying to get a parole. Jail was to become my home for ten and one half years not a day less. At the time, I would never admit it but the reality was jail was my home. On the street, I was an addict, a hopeless drunk, a thief, a bum, a wino, a nobody, a failure and in the eyes of society and the courts, a habitual criminal who would never change. Out there on the streets, I was a low-life who was not worthy of any respect and was not to be trusted no matter what. But in jail, I had instant respect. I was among those who were like me. This was a place where I felt like I belonged because I was accepted.

From the day I was sentenced and was told what day I would be released, I started counting the days and marking them off on the calendar. This is the worst way to do time. After becoming more experienced at doing time I learned that this was a definite no-no as it makes your time drag. I was placed in the kitchen as my workplace after two weeks in NCB. There were four of us inmates working in the kitchen and they had a separate dorm for the kitchen crew to sleep in. At sixteen years of age, I was the youngest one on the crew. On my second day in the kitchen, I noticed in the dorm we were out of toilet paper and was going to ask the guard for more. I turned to Dalton one of my co-workers and asked, "What's the guard's name?" "Clark." "Clark what?" "Clark Kent." "Yeah right," I half smiled. "That's true, funny hey. That's what we all said, 'yeah right,'" Dalton was serious when he answered me. "Clark Kent?" I asked again, I had already taken the bait. "Yeah, Clark Kent."

The guard's desk was right next to the kitchen dorm so I didn't have far to go to ask. The guard was sitting there reading a comic book when I approached him and said, "Excuse me Clark," he stopped his reading and looked at me out of the corner of his eyes, "What did you say?" "I said 'excuse me," "No, I mean what did you just call me?" "Oh, Clark. It's Clark Kent right?" Just as I said the full name the whole kitchen dorm erupted into loud uncontrollable laughter and I knew I was taken! "I knew it!" I said out loud. The guard slowly got up from his chair and walked over to where I was standing. The laughter started to subside. He stopped right in front of me and had to lean way over and look way down to look me straight in the eye. When our eyes locked he said, "My name is Mr. Hinsley, NOT Clark Kent!" When he said "Clark Kent" the whole kitchen dorm erupted into loud laughter again and this time I could not help myself for the life of me, I erupted into loud uncontrollable laughter right there standing in front of Mr. Hinsley! After a few seconds, I composed myself and Mr. Hinsley continued, "One more smart remark like that Nieman and it's Digger time for you, do I make myself clear!?" I made sure he heard the sir part when I answered with, "Yes sir!" He ended the conversation with, "Now get outta my sight before I change my mind." I went back into the dorm feeling like a fool, yet somehow feeling good about myself. Dalton was burying his face in a pillow trying to keep his laughter quiet as I closed the door behind me. "I'll never listen to you again Dalton," I told him. Dalton was a giant of a man who played guitar and had a great sense of humor. We became very good friends and spent many months together doing time at WCC. It was during this time my first sentence at WCC that I started to write poetry. I was inspired by a man named Clarence who was nicknamed "Smitty." Clarence was from the small town of Carmacks in the Yukon.

I had to do four months out of the six they sentenced me to and it dragged on. Back in those days when you did time at WCC they made sure you did every minute of! Once out of bed at 7 am you could not lie on or return to your bed until after supper. You had to button up your shirt completely except for one button from the top. You had to get a haircut. You had to tuck your shirt in and keep it tucked in. There was no talking in line. You could not sleep during the day even if you are sitting up. The guard would kick the bottom of your feet if he caught you sleeping while sitting up. The kick would wake you up and then he would write you up and give you a pink slip. You had to do your job assignment, (sounds a lot like the residential school huh?). If you violated any of these, you were written up and once you got three write-ups you would go to Isolation or what the inmates called the "Digger" or the "Hole". In those days in the "Hole" you lose all privileges which meant no phone calls, no visitors, no mail, no smoking, no canteen, no reading material except the Bible. The

"Hole" is a cold cement room with no mattress and no pillow. If you created a problem when you were in the Hole they could either hose you down or turn all the lights out until you are in TOTAL DARKNESS. If you have never been in total, total darkness where there is not even a sliver of light, you cannot imagine how quickly your mind will start becoming confused. I'm talking about TOTAL blackness where you cannot see your hand in front of you. After a while you can't tell if your eyes are open or closed. You start to hallucinate. You start to lose your sense of depth and it begins to feel like you are falling or drifting in space. It is very scary and one cannot take total darkness for long. One of the ways we used to keep ourselves grounded when in total darkness is to tear off a shirt button throw it in the air and then get down on all fours and find it. This exercise will pull all of your five senses together and "grounds" you and you feel better once you are stabilized. In those days, when you did Remand time and then went to court and were found guilty your Remand time did not count for anything you did not receive credit for that time. Out of my six month sentence I served four months and was released in April 1970.

CHAPTER TWELVE

THE DRUG LIST

"THE CURE"

I stuck the needle in my arm
Tried to kill the hurt and harm,
Tipped the bottle drained the wine
I watched my dreams leave me behind,
I took a pill I felt relief,
When I came down still had my grief
While smoking pot I ate a lot
And did my time when I got caught,
I found no glamor in those drugs
They can't replace true love or hugs,

A. Nieman

When I got back on the street after finishing my jail stint in April of '70, I did my best to fit in with my friends on the "outside". I laughed at their jokes. I talked like them. I even dressed like them. But inside I knew I was not one of them. And no matter how hard I tried, I could never be one of them. The abusive words of my mother that were burned and seared into my subconscious brain always found their way to the surface and would be so clearly echoed into my habits, "You rotten no good for nothing. You'll never turn out to be anything but trouble. You think you're something? You're nothing and always will be nothing!" I was damaged, dirty and doomed to live a lie. That was exactly what I was doing, living a lie. I would do anything even give my life to keep my secret and make sure nobody ever found out about the sexual abuse I suffered. So I put on my mask, did their dance and did my best to fade into the crowd of normality in a crippling attempt to bury, smother and hide the truth. As a result, whatever shred there was left of Andy Nieman's true personality became drowned and buried somewhere at the bottom of fantasy's graveyard and amidst thousands of empty bottles of booze. As the din of the party on my first night out faded into the background and my thoughts drifted inward, the question wouldn't go away. That simple but dreaded question which always asked, "Will I ever truly find a place to fit in?"

I made up for lost time by getting sloppy-eyed, fall down, drag-me-out, snot-nosed drunk! Whenever I drank alcohol and I mean *every time* I drank alcohol, I always, let me repeat that I *always* drank to GET DRUNK. I drank solely for the EFFECT that the alcohol had on me. I NEVER drank to be sociable. I never drank to make my food taste better. I never drank to impress anyone. I never drank for the taste. I drank because alcohol helped me to ESCAPE period! I could never drink one or two drinks and switch to coffee or tea, I drank for the sole purpose of getting plastered out of my mind so I could forget about life. Alcohol helped me overcome my self-consciousness, my anxiety, my feelings of hopelessness and the list goes on. I would buy it, borrow it, steal it, gulp it and seek it EVERY SINGLE DAY of my life! I LIVED to GET DRUNK. I didn't love it, I didn't enjoy it. It was a necessity. I HAD to HAVE it. It took away all my fears. It just magically erased them. It made me forget that I was a victim of a pedophile. It changed the feelings of shame I carried so deep inside of me. It gave me the courage (no matter how short-lived) to LOOK absolutely ANYBODY in the eye and for a short spell (as long as the alcohol lasted) I was just AS GOOD AS THEM and maybe even BETTER! (Now there's a real joke for you). Throughout my teenage years and throughout my adult life I stayed stoned on something or another *all the time*. The only time I wasn't high, was when I was at Wolf Creek Youth Detention Center or jail. I would do and take almost anything to get high. Here is a list of drugs that I got high on at one time or another in my life back then: Heroin, Cocaine, MDA, Sila Silum Mescaline, Magic Mushrooms, Hashish, Marijuana, Hash Oil, Thai Sticks, Purple Haze Acid, Blue Barrel Acid, Pink Barrel Acid, Blue Heaven Acid, Blotter Acid, Orange Sunshine Acid, LSD 25, Crystal Meth, T's and R's, Valium, Ativan, Mandrix, Tylenol 3, Aqua Velva aftershave lotion, Lysol, Ginseng Brandy, Chinese Cooking wine, Villa wine, Extra Old Stock wine, Private Stock wine, Bounty wine, I injected vodka and whiskey with a syringe, sniffed nail polish remover, sniffed airplane glue, took 15 Gravol pills and hallucinated the wildest and scariest scenes imaginable, smoked banana peels (which don't work) and drank cough syrup.

I was a turbulent, troubled, traumatized soul. To be truthful, I didn't know who I was. All's I knew was that inside...I was empty. Writing poetry helped me cling to life because I wanted my life to end so many times. Here I was only sixteen years of age and it felt like I carried the weight of the world on my shoulders with no way out except for the alcohol and/or suicide. Alcohol was my best friend and my worst enemy. There was no other way and no other choice of escape from my feelings or so I thought, that is, until I discovered Acid/LSD.

My very first encounter and the first time I got stoned on LSD was in June 1970, the summer I finished my first jail sentence. I wasn't looking for it but it seemed to be looking for me and it found me innocently enough. My older sister Eileen wanting to go to bingo that night asked me to babysit for her two children Larry Jr. and Tara until Buddy came home. Buddy was one of my two older brothers. Eileen said, "I wanna' try my luck at Bingo tonight Andy, I feel lucky. You'll watch them hey?" I hesitated in answering her as I wanted to go and see Gary. She noticed the hesitation and quickly said, "I'll give you ten bucks, if you do." That was all it took to make up my mind and I said, "Sure!" That was a case of beer. Gary and Mason could help me drink it, I thought. She went and got a ten dollar bill from her purse and gave it to me as if it was surety to seal the deal before I had a chance to change my mind. After about fifteen minutes, she said with a warning in her voice as if she could read my mind, "Don't try to take off with my money either Andy!" My good ol' big sister Eileen, almost knew me better than I knew myself. I was actually thinking about the possibility of just leaving with her money by telling her I was going to see Mason for a minute and would be right back. Thoughts of what and where to go and how to spend the money had already started to formulate in my mind when her warning shot my short-lived dream out of the air and brought my thought process back down to earth. It was about 2 o'clock in the afternoon and I thought she would leave around 5 o'clock. I secretly didn't want Buddy to come home until after she left so I could keep the money because if he came home, then she might ask him to watch the kids. For some reason, she didn't wait until 5 o'clock to leave. About twenty minutes after giving me the money and after she had finished cleaning up the house, she pulled out her curling iron and plugged it in. She set the iron on the edge of the table in a way to make sure when it got hot it couldn't burn anything. She set her eye lash curler on the kitchen table as well. She started to rummage through her big bag of combs, curlers, nail-polish, hairbrushes and who knows what else was in there (actually I did, because I thought she kept money in there and had "checked it out" last night). After putting her make-up stuff on the table, she proceeded into the most important task of her day thus far, "putting her face-on" as she called it.

Our kitchen table served as a substitute for a Hair Dressers Salon that afternoon. After Eileen put her face on, a car pulled up outside the house in a hail of dust and as if on cue honked its horn. A female voice shouted out, "Eileen you ready?" Just before she went out the door Eileen gave both Larry and Tara a hug and a kiss and threw a bag of suckers at me, "Give them one of these after I go," she said grabbing her purse. "I'll see you after Bingo," and with that she was gone. I wished she would have closed the door because Larry and Tara tried to follow her out the door and I had to run and block them. Tara burst out crying and Larry joined in. They both cried out together, "Mom!" as I held them back and they watched the car disappear down the road. I closed the door. I was left alone there with Larry and Tara. I cannot stand the sound of crying children or crying babies as it always triggers a sad feeling in me, even today. Both of them ran to the window in the first room to see if they could catch another look at the car. I dug out two of the suckers and gave one to each of them. I was thankful when the suckers did the trick and Larry stopped crying first then Tara. They both went over and sat down sinking into our old Mary House rummage sale couch and enjoyed their treat.

About an hour or so later my brother Buddy and Uncle Joe came home. When Uncle Joe and Buddy walked into the house Buddy immediately picked Larry Jr. up, gave him a big kiss on the cheek and threw him the air, catching him as he came down and started laughing. He laughed because Larry was caught off-guard and let out a gasp of breath, when he was thrown in the air all too suddenly. Buddy was tall, six foot four and his head came pretty close to the roof of our little home. Tara went running to Buddy and Uncle Joe cut her off and picked her up, "Where do you think you're going Miss Tara?" he said. Tara was comfortable with Uncle Joe and liked him. She let out a big smile. He put her back down and she ran to Buddy. Buddy picked her up and did the same thing he did with Larry, threw her in the air and laughed into her neck when he caught her. She let out a big giggle of sheer delight! Buddy asked me, "Did you feed them?" "No not yet, I was gonna' make them a sandwich." I replied. "Well feed them then, Uncle Joe and I have a surprise for you." What? A surprise for ME? That got my interest right away it was very unusual and totally unexpected that Buddy would have a SURPRISE for me!

I got very curious as to what kind of a surprise it could possibly be and started making the sandwiches quicker than I normally would have. After I gave the kids a sandwich each, I observed Buddy as he sat down at the kitchen table. He cleared a spot on the table and then went into mom and dad's room and came out carrying their round two-sided mirror. The kind of mirror that made objects look bigger on one side of the glass and normal on the other. "Where's my surprise?" I asked him not wanting to sound too demanding. "It's coming, just be patient," was all I got back from him. Buddy then reached into the watch pocket of his blue jeans and dug out some tinfoil that was folded into a small round ball. He opened the tinfoil and set it on the table. I watched very closely never taking my eyes off the tinfoil and was fascinated as Buddy displayed three tiny purple pills. Nobody spoke a word. Larry and Tara tried to poke their heads into our business to see what was going on and Buddy said in a serious voice to me, "Keep those kids away Andy! Take them outside to play." I was annoyed that I couldn't continue watching this fascinating process and hurriedly took the kids outside. I hurried back in just in time to see Buddy take a razor blade and cut one of the pills in half. He gave Uncle Joe one half and put the other half in his mouth. They swallowed the pill without any water. "Can I have my surprise now?" I was getting impatient. Buddy looked at me and smiled, "Oh, so you want a surprise huh," "Well you said…" I let the sentence hang. "Did you hear that Uncle Joe, your nephew wants a surprise," "Well give him a surprise then," Uncle Joe said looking at me with a smile. I was on the verge of getting annoyed thinking to myself, now they're gonna' say, "We were just kidding." "OK, since you want a surprise, I'll give you a surprise," Buddy continued. He cut another one of the little purple pills took it in between two fingers and said, "Open your mouth and stick out your tongue," I did as I was told. He placed the acid (LSD) which I later learned was called Purple Haze, on my tongue and said, "OK now swallow," I swallowed. "There, now you've got your surprise." I felt gypped. I wrinkled my forehead into a frown as I asked, "That's my surprise!?" my dis-appointment was clearly evident in my tone of voice. "That surprise cost ten dollars and THAT kind of a surprise cannot be bought in any store. Only certain people know where to get such a good surprise like that." Buddy said to me in an informative tone. "What's it good for? I don't need medicine," I made sure he couldn't miss the disappointment in my voice as I asked. Buddy let out one of his contagious laughs as he said, "It's not medicine that's Purple Haze! It's called acid. LSD! Just wait about half an hour and then tell me what you feel. It's going to make you smile and make you laugh and you won't be able to stop." "What do you mean make me laugh? This pill is supposed to make me laugh?" I asked incredulously, "Yeah make you laugh just watch you'll see," and he started laugh-ing again. I looked at Uncle Joe and Uncle Joe pointed at me and smiled then he pretended he was imitating me and said, "Andy's going to be like this," and he put his hand over his mouth and pretended to giggle while covering his mouth. "Yeah right," I thought to myself, "I'll make sure I don't look for any more surprises from you guys," I kept these thoughts to myself. Then I got curious and asked Uncle Joe, "How do you know, did you try it before?" He nodded his head, "Yes". Then he said, "Just watch you're going to start seeing things that aren't there just like they're really there and you're going to laugh away." "Maybe for you guys but not for me," I said. Again I felt gypped and I wanted to go and find Gary and get us a case of beer but I was a bit curious about this tiny pill and the talk I was hearing about it.

Sure enough, about half an hour later the acid started to take effect. I first noticed it by my thinking process. Something had changed in my thinking process and I wasn't quite sure what it was but I knew FOR SURE that some-thing was HAPPENING! I wanted to smile at the knowledge and the realiza-tion that this tiny pill was real and was actually having an effect on me! It was starting to take my thinking process to some place different and I realized I liked what it was doing to me for that very fact! And, for some reason I couldn't stop myself from smiling. It was weird what is going on? I thought to myself. I just wanted to smile and for no reason at all! Then I sensed there was a process now taking place that I no longer had any control over. I did not like the feeling at first, but I felt safe with my Uncle and with my brother there and I was in a safe environment. I knew my brother and uncle would not hurt or harm me in any way. I later learned that whether an acid trip was going to be a good experience or a bad experience had a lot to do with your emotional state at the time you take the acid. Uncle Joe was the first to notice and he said, "What you smiling about? "Nothing," I said as I made a feeble attempt to stifle my smile. "How come you can't stop smiling then?" he said in a teasing way. He knew. Then he said to Buddy, "Look, Andy's starting to get stoned." "No, I'm not." I said. I knew as soon as I said it that it was an obvious feeble attempt at a lie. "How come you can't stop smiling then?" Uncle Joe said quickly. Buddy looked at me and said,

"Come here, let me see your eyes." I looked at him trying to keep my mouth from smiling. And Buddy burst out laughing real loud, "What's a matter with your eyes then?" He kept laughing, "Look at his eyes Uncle Joe" Buddy said all the while laughing. When I looked at my nephew and my niece Larry and Tara they looked like they had shrunk two sizes smaller! They had all their same features but they looked SO SMALL almost like they were toys! I could not believe my eyes and started to laugh. "What you laughing at?" Buddy asked me, "What do you see?" I told him what I saw and both he and Uncle Joe started laughing too! Then Buddy and Uncle Joe went back behind the house where Buddy had his little shack and he and Uncle Joe stayed there most of the day and for most of the acid trip.

The laughing stage of the acid trip was just that, a laughing stage. It ended after the hallucinations started to take over. When the hallucinations got stronger and stronger they also became more and more weird. I saw the ground moving in waves in front of me. Colors were brighter and it was like I was looking through a kaleidoscope. At times I felt like I was taller than I actually was and other times it was like everything around me got bigger. I felt like I was all eyes with no body and got scared and had to actually look at my body to make sure it was still there! When I turned my head it was like the whole room warped in different directions along with each turn of my head. It was very hard to focus my eyes on one thing. Time lost all meaning as I was doing my very best to hold onto my sanity. I felt I was coming close to some kind of an edge in my mind but was not sure what that edge was. I told myself to relax and remain calm. When I moved my hand in front of my eyes I saw what looked like twenty versions of my hand following after my original hand through the air. I could hear echoes when people spoke and I had to pay extra close attention to what was being said in order to understand. I looked at the distant mountains far behind the flowing Yukon River and could not judge distance at all. This was a whole new world to me. A world I never could have imagined not in a million years! Even taking a drink of water was weird because my mind imagined what was taking place as the water travelled down my throat through my intestines and came to rest in my stomach. I could actually hear the water slosh around in my stomach with each step I took and it was very loud. What was this acid stuff? I wondered. I was mesmerized.

The whole universe had all of a sudden come alive all at once. I forgot about who I was. I forgot about my fears. I was amazed at all the details I could now see that never existed before. I walked outside and the sound of the birds singing was so loud it was like walking into a pet bird store! The trees and clouds were moving so fast that I thought a strong wind must be blowing but there was no wind, no wind at all. And then it all hit me as I came face to face with the reality of just how truly stoned and the danger I could potentially be in! I did my best to keep myself from panicking and did everything within my mental ability to stay away from thinking about this new reality that I now found myself in and the reality was THIS: what if I NEVER CAME OFF of this high and what if the drug never wears off and what if I never return to normal? What if I am the one person who does not take well to this drug? I felt a fear that was starting to get too big for me to handle and was bordering on panic! I had to have a question answered and Buddy or Uncle Joe were the only two who could answer it for me. I decided to go ask them but first I had to make sure Larry and Tara were still sleeping. They were. Then I told myself, I can't be that bad off I'm still thinking about and taking care of the kids, but deep inside in my heart of hearts I KNEW I HAD to HAVE THE ANSWER to this question that was so monumental and at the moment meant the difference between my sanity and the threat of losing my mind for good. I had to know HOW LONG does this drug last? I asked Buddy and both he and Uncle Joe had no signs of laughter or anything that resembled happiness on their faces when I approached them. The answer I got from Buddy was simple, "Eight hours," and he added as if he knew what I was feeling at that precise time, "it'll wear off you in about another hour, don't worry." That was PURE MUSIC to my ears! Few things in my short life to that point had sounded like a blessing to my ears, Buddy's words, "Eight hours," were the best words I could possibly hear! This was all so totally strange to me that it was both exciting and yet scary. After what must've been a couple of hours of hallucinating in wonder and in awe I did not really know how long it was, I began to come back to my senses and things began to mellow out. And not a moment too soon as Eileen came home from Bingo and right away asked, "How come you didn't cook supper for those kids?"

I could feel the acid for the remainder of the evening and drinking alcohol was the last thing on my mind. I did not want to go anywhere as I wasn't sure how long this acid stuff worked, or if you could tell that I was stoned or how long it would take to be completely off of it. I felt the effects of the acid all through the night and did not fall asleep until the morning light of a new dawn shone the first rays of sunlight threw the window. Although the high was enjoyable at the beginning and then mind-blowing and then some parts were scary real scary, I felt more like I had survived something special and in the process I had discovered a new found confidence in my mental capacity. I had come close to the edge of an unknown abyss and had survived. Something inside of me came alive! I found in acid, something that was adventurous, exciting and yet could be very dangerous. A whole new world of fascination and intrigue had shown its face to me and I wanted to see more. In fact I found that I longed to see more. Part of what I experienced on that first acid trip was a total release from the reality of who I was and it was *almost* a *total* escape from the misery of being a troubled teenager who the world only knew by drunkenness, criminal activity and a fake smile.

Acid took me to a place that was a million miles from reality. All of my senses were stimulated and amped up to the maximum. My hearing was magnified and listening to music any kind of music was a beautiful experience in itself! The hallucinations were beyond description. The colors and whatever I was looking at the design of the fabric or the wallpaper designs would be moving, twisting, floating out in wavy patterns that were so intriguing and amazing that I could stare at a wall, one single wall for hours and hours on end and never get tired until the acid wore off eight to twelve hours later. When I took too much acid or acid that was stronger than the last batch I could tell after about twenty minutes that, "Oh, Oh this stuff is stronger than the last stuff I've got to watch myself," and when that happened in my heart something told me that this could be the trip that I never return from. Sometimes the high was great and other times it took every last bit of mental strength I possessed just to maintain my sanity and to keep myself focused and grounded in the present in order to keep my mind from leaving this world and entering that place of no return. Many, many times I went to the edge of my mental capacity. I lived on the edge and was only one high away from being committed to a mental institution or from suffering brain damage on those occasions when I knew I took too much of the stuff. I've been on so many bad trips when stoned on acid and I saw so many strange and frightening things that it would be hard to believe if I explained them. Here is one example.

One time Rodney and I took some acid that was called, "Pink Barrel." The tiny tablet was in a cylinder shape (like a barrel) and it was colored pink with tiny red dots in it. As we sat in a restaurant finishing our lunch Rodney told me, "I bought some acid, two hits one for you and one for me. "It's called Pink Barrel." Want one?" He asked knowing it was a redundant question, of course I wanted one! I didn't normally take a whole hit of acid. I was using a fair amount of acid then and felt I could handle a whole hit. "Sure," I answered Rodney as I felt a twinge of excitement roll through my stomach, "Means we'll have to skip out of school this afternoon. Think old Mr. Fitch will miss us?" Mr. Fitch was our science Teacher. "Won't be the first time," "Probably won't be the last either," we both grinned and Rodney continued, "Goose will let us copy his notes." "Goose" was the nickname our whole class had for Monty a close friend of Rodney and I. "Keep an eye out for our buddy Falkingham," Rodney said in a friendly sarcastic tone. Falkingham was the detective who was now trying to be an undercover narcotics officer. I don't know why the RCMP picked him to be undercover *everybody* in Whitehorse knew him! Rodney reached into his jeans and pulled out the crumpled up tinfoil that had the two hits of acid in it. With both his hands under the table fumbling to separate the pills he casually looked around the restaurant as though he was just relaxing. When he had them separated he handed me one. I put it in my mouth took my glass of water and washed it down. Rodney did the same as quickly as he could. We ordered two more coffees and sat there making small talk as we waited for the acid to start taking affect. After about twenty minutes or so my palms started to get sweaty and I started to get mild cramps in my stomach. When you get mild cramps in your stomach from dropping acid it means (I am told) that there is a higher than usual amount of strychnine added to the acid and as a result your acid trip will have more hallucinations than normal. My palms got real sweaty and although my stomach was feeling the cramp more and more I soon forgot about it because I noticed that people's faces started to stretch and get distorted and then their bodies started to stretch and bend like they were standing in front of a trick mirror (the kind you see at a carnival or a circus). I looked at Rodney and he looked at me, "Pretty potent stuff huh," Rodney half-smiled. "You can say that again," I answered as I waved my hand in front of my face to see how many traces were following my hand. Looking at the traces following my hand is one of the ways I gauged how stoned I was getting. I was starting to feel nervous for some reason and couldn't quite put my finger on why I was feeling that way. I had to walk and move. I had to do something besides sit and watch people's faces get all distorted. "Let's go," I told Rodney, "Yeah good idea," he said as we grabbed our coats and walked out, "Where to?" Rodney asked. "Let's walk down to the river bank for a sec then we'll decide." I could feel the acid more and more and the sidewalk looked like it was moving in small waves. I felt like I was starting to stagger, "Whoa," I said as I looked at Rodney, "Feel that?" "Feel what, the sidewalk moving?" "Yeah, pretty wild stuff." We walked a short distance along the river bank, I looked up and the clouds in the sky looked like long stretched out flames of fire that were blowing in the wind. "Look at that," I told Rodney, "What?" "Those flames, those clouds they look like flames huh," "Oh yeah, neat." "This is pretty heavy stuff," I looked at Rodney, "Sure hurts the gut huh," he answered, "Yeah, lotsa' strychnine," at that precise moment we heard a car's tires braking sharply on gravel as a cloud of dust surrounded us ahead of the Narc's unmarked police car as it came to a halt behind us. Falkingham and another cop we had never seen before jumped out of the car so quickly you'd think they were about to bust one the nations ten most wanted criminals. "What are you guys up to Nieman, Rodney? Smoking pot? Put your hands on the hood and spread 'em! Now take everything out of your pockets slowly and put it on the car," Falkingham ordered. We did as we were told. They checked our stuff and quickly patted us down. We had nothing illegal on us and Falkingham said, "Put your stuff away. What're you doing down here, got a stash somewhere nearby? Where's all your marijuana?" "What marijuana?" Rodney asked, "Don't do that stuff." "Yeah right" Falkingham continued. "This here is Andy Nieman," Falkingham said to the new Narc poking his finger purposefully into my chest, "If there's ever a B&E chances are he's the guilty party, always check him out." I wanted to get a good look at the new "Narc" but when I looked at him I saw a big black maggot-like worm break through the skin on the side of his neck and then another one broke through and then another and finally I had to look away. Falkingham's voice droned on, "And this is Rodney, if he's hanging out with Andy Nieman better keep an eye on him too and make sure he's on your list of suspects to interrogate. Gentlemen, . ." Falkingham said through the gum he was chewing, "This is Constable Brown and you are to do as he tells you from now on or you will have to deal with myself or Corporal Gabb. Is that crystal clear?" I simply nodded my head, "Yes" and kept my eyes focused on the ground as I did not want to see those worms again. While looking down on the ground I noticed that Falkingham had stepped on a pile of human feces and there was poop curled up on both sides of his one shoe. I could not tell if I was hallucinating this or if it was real! I was hoping it was real but didn't really care I just wanted to get out of there away from the "heat". Falkingham continued in his holier-than-thou tone of voice, "Now you boys run along now and you know we'll be seeing you again so be good."

We weren't sure which way we were going to go so I started walking one way and Rodney starting walking the other. Rodney then turned towards me came over and quickly fell in step with me. I wanted to get out into nature and away from people and said, "Let's go to the tramway," the tramway was a trail that led through the bushes along the Yukon river up to where the dam was, "Why up there? Why don't we go shoot some pool I've got some money I'll buy you a game." I did not really want to go to the pool hall because on my last drunk I was told that Barnie the owner had to practically throw me out and he wasn't too pleased with me. It was a habit of ours (Gary and Johnny and Maddy and I and our friends) to stand around and watch our friends play pool on a cold wintery Friday night while we sipped on coke cans that were spiked with whiskey. Sometimes we would come up to the pool hall just to listen to music. We would go there stoned out of our minds on acid or MDA or Magic Mushroom or hashish or pot and put some quarters in the jukebox and listen to Rod Stewart singing, "Maggie May" or Alice Cooper singing "School's Out" or Deep Purple playing "Highway Star".

I told Rodney, "I got pretty gassed up last Friday and I heard that Barnie kicked me out for being drunk, I don't wanna' go there." "Barnie might not even be there it might be Rick working today. Tell you what, I'll go and check who's working if it's Rick we'll go up, if its Barnie then we'll go to the tramway, how's that sound?" I still did not want to go but said, "Go ahead then." As it turned out Rick was working so we went up. All the pool tables were occupied and it was probably a good thing as my hallucinations were getting more and more intense! Rodney bought me a coke and gave me some quarters to play the pinball machine while we waited for a table to open up. As I was playing the pinball machine, I could not tell which ball was the real one as I seen so many traces it looked like I was playing with ten different balls! Then the sounds from the pinball machine grew louder and louder and the balls on the pool tables sounded like thunder as they hit each other and everyone's talking speeded up to the point where they sounded like chipmunks and people kept staring at me and it felt like the police were going to come through the door at any second and arrest me in front of everyone and I started to sweat so much my clothes starting getting completely soaked! I felt like there were gigantic beads of sweat breaking out all over my body and on my forehead and I had to get out of there before people started to ask me questions! I walked over to Rodney and all I said was, "I gotta' go I'll see you later." I left him no choice to answer and quickly walked down the stairs. I had to get away and get somewhere quiet! I had to get home!

I made my way out into the street and as I looked around I noticed that everyone was looking at me! I wondered why they were all looking at me and then I saw that I had all these black beetles crawling on my arm and legs and they were spreading over my whole body! Where were they coming from!? I tried to tell myself, "It's just the acid don't worry about it it's not real." I got my bike and started to walk across main street with it and was just about to jump on when I noticed the black beetles were now on my handle bars and were starting to completely cover my bike! They got onto my bicycle seat and I decided to just ignore them and keep going. I had a tough time to get on my bike because the beetles covered the seat and I kept saying to myself in my mind, "It's just the acid, it's just the acid keep going." Then I started to hear this really high pitched ringing in my ears and I wasn't sure if it was a siren or what. It was getting louder and louder and I wanted to put my hands over my ears but could not I had to keep walking! I then forced myself to sit down right on top of the beetles that were on my seat and I started riding towards Sleepy Hollow. As I looked around I noticed that the beetles were beginning to spread everywhere on the ground! They were everywhere! I was riding over them! The ground was getting completely covered with them turning the ground black everywhere. As I continued riding I could hear them getting crunched as my bike tires ran over them and they would shoot out the other end of the tires all squished. I soon discovered that the only time I could get a bit of relief was when I looked up into the sky because the sky turned into a vast display of bright orange fiery flames that swept across the skyline for as far as the eye could see against a back-drop of crystal clear baby blue sky! It was so amazing I just wanted to keep staring at this magnificent sight! I kept my gaze on the sky as much as I could while doing my best to steer the bike. I peddled harder and harder and then I noticed that the faster I went the more the blackness on the ground turned into the color of brown and then green as the ground and grass started to appear somewhat normal! Also the faster I went the less I could hear the screaming siren in my head and then the bugs turned into normal ground. Yet the sky was still ablaze with flowing, dancing brilliant flames of fire that swept all across the sky! And then finally I saw my house come into view! I believed in my heart that if I could just get home the acid would start to wear off and everything would be OK. I felt like I had to get into surroundings that were familiar to me. That was the answer! I hoped my mom wasn't drinking. That would be all I needed! Her drinking was more of a hassle now and not the threat it once was because I was sixteen and not so small and helpless anymore. It was early Fall and school had just started the week before. Mom had just quit drinking about two weeks ago and had started attending revival church meetings in what we called the "Old Village." I saw a change in her but did not trust it to last long. To me, it seemed like she was putting on an act. She was always smiling and seemed happy about something but I could not figure out what it was she so happy about. I just couldn't put my finger on it. It didn't matter I did not trust her anyway. In our house back then seeing is believing and talk came cheap.

I pulled up and laid my bike against the house in its usual spot. The bugs had stopped yet the hallucinations continued. As I opened the door to our house the smell of frying pork chops told me that someone was cooking supper. It turned out to be my mom doing the cooking. She was sober and it brought me some relief to see her home. Her back was towards me as she stood over the hot wood stove turning a pork chop. There was a thin light blue haze of smoke in the room and I wasn't sure if it was the acid or if that really was blue smoke.

When she finished flipping the pork chops she turned to see who had come in, "Oh it's you, Lizzy with you?" "No" "How come?" "Guess she's walking home with Karen." "You see her?" "No." "How'bout Margaret?" "No, I didn't see her either." She turned back to her cooking. "I'm gonna' lay down" I said as I picked up a pillow and laid on the couch. It felt good to be home and to know that mom was sober but it did nothing to weaken the acid. As I lay on the couch I turned my back to the room and immediately the patterns in the material that the couch was made of started moving. The dark red patterns came out from the couch about six inches and they looked like they were waving under water in slow motion. The patterns were drawn towards my eyes as if my eyeballs were magnets. I had to close my eyes to stop them from boring into my head. The door opened and Liz and Margaret both came in. Margaret said, "There's Andy." Liz asked mom, "When did Andy get home?" "Just now, he just came in before you." Margaret asked, "Where were you Andy how come we couldn't find you after school?" Margaret's voice slowed right down and sounded like Darth Vadar in slow motion. Her voice and all sound started to fade into the distance as my mind drifted back to the pool hall and I recalled how I felt when the acid first started affecting me this afternoon and I thought about my horrible bike ride home. I looked at Margaret and I could see her lips moving but no sound was coming out. I looked over at Liz and mom and their lips were moving as they talked but no sound was getting through to my ears. I thought to myself as I began to panic, "Am I losing my hearing? Am I going deaf!? I CAN'T HEAR!" and then to my great relief just as the panic was about to get the best of me I heard Margaret's voice penetrate my silent panic, "Aren't you gonna' eat Andy?" Margaret's question brought me back to reality. "What?" I asked just to make sure I was actually hearing again. "Have some supper," Margaret said as she put her plate on the table and reached for the ketchup bottle. I could hear! Oh man what a relief! I CAN HEAR! I mumbled something about, "I'm not hungry." "What!? You're not hungry FOR PORK CHOPS!?" Liz turned to look at me in total amazement. "What's the matter?" My mom stopped to look at me in mid-step as she was making her way to her bedroom with a full plate of food and a full cup of hot tea. "Nothing," I said as I became aware that all three of them were now focused on me and genuinely concerned that there was something seriously wrong with me to not want to eat such a delicious meal. "I already ate uptown with Rodney," I surprised myself that I could still think and lie so quickly. All three of them turned back to what they were doing. I thought to myself, "Maybe the acid is wearing off now, I answered their question without even thinking." When I made it through this acid trip I reminded myself to stay away from Pink Barrel it had too much strychnine in it which causes an increase in hallucinations but also leads to more confusion and cramps your stomach muscles for a long time after. Again, I knew I dodged a bullet by gambling with my sanity. What would it take for me to stay away from the drug? I went to the edge of completely losing my mind on a number of occasions on acid. When I came too close to the edge from taking too much and I survived, I swore I would never touch the stuff again! Yet when one of my friends offered me some, I disregarded the bad experience of my last trip and went right back at it. The best thing I liked about acid was that it gave me a complete escape from reality and music always, without fail, sounded like it was sent from heaven. It captivated me. It was not always a pleasant trip when I took acid but I always went back for more.

For the next two years in between my stints of being locked up, every single chance I had I put all my money towards getting high on acid. From the age of sixteen to eighteen I went on more than two hundred acid trips. In reality it is more like three hundred acid trips but I want to be careful that I do not lie and so I am using a conservative number when I say two hundred. We were all into acid back then in 1970 those of us who hung together most of us from Sleepy Hollow. It was the era of the Hippy Movement. With Jimi Hendrix singing "Purple Haze" blaring in the background, the first time I had a needle full of drugs stuck into my vein was in 1970 at a Group Home on Hogue St. It was a Saturday night and Gary and I bought some MDA and Gary knew that our friend Larry had a syringe. Larry was staying at the Group Home at the time. Gary had already used the needle when he was down in Vancouver yet for me it would be the very first time. "Larry has a syringe let's go see if he's home." "Where's that?" "He's over at Hogue Street." "In the Group Home?" "Yeah." "OK. Let's go see him". I could feel a twinge of excitement and fear run through my stomach at the thought of putting a needle in my arm.

The Group Home was a long trailer that had a full basement. When we arrived at the Group Home the male worker stopped us at the door, "Who do you want to see?" I made sure I maintained eye contact with the worker to ward off any suspicion as Gary answered, "Larry." Gary answered like he had done this a hundred times before. The worker turned and yelled, "Larry! You have visitors!" A distant muffled response came back from the basement, "OK, I'll be right up," Larry shouted back. "Would you guys like a pop or something to drink?" the worker kindly asked. Gary and I answered the exact same words together in perfect unison, "No thanks." Answering in perfect unison like that caused all of us to smile. The worker then asked us more out of creating conversation than suspicion, "What're you guys up to tonight?" "Gary answered, "Not much, just gonna visit Larry for a spell." "You're Gary right?" "Right." The worker reached out to shake my hand, "And you are…?" "Andy," I looked him in the eye. He appeared quite young for a worker at a Group Home. Before he had a chance to say his name Larry came bounding up the stairs and entered the room curious to see who was coming to visit. Larry was a full-blooded First Nation young man who was my age (16). He always had a great big smile. He was very handsome with perfect white teeth and seemed to always keep himself in good shape. Larry seemed to have more of a purpose in life than Gary and I even though he still did some of the drugs and the dysfunctional things like drinking that we did. He wasn't into crime like I was. I was the Ringleader in that department. Once he recognized that it was Gary and I who were there to visit him, he flashed his big smile at us and said with a laugh, "Oh it's you two hooligans, come on in. Take your shoes off though or Chris here will kick us all out!" Chris responded with,

"I might not kick them out but I'll kick you out for sure." It was great to see that they had such a good relationship. Gary and I took our shoes off. Chris asked, "How long you guys going to be here?" Gary turned to face him, "How's an hour sound?" "An hour's fine, you can stay longer if you want." The three of us headed down the narrow stairs with Larry in the lead as Chris shouted after us, "Not too much noise now Larry!" "No problem," Larry shouted back. I admired Larry. He was cool. I was just a bit jealous because he had such great teeth and the girls always seemed to be after him. I was also proud though that he was my friend. This was the first time I had come to visit Larry at this Group Home. Back then, when you turned sixteen years of age you were considered an adult. The only thing you couldn't do when you were sixteen was vote or get into the bars. At sixteen years of age you could quit school, smoke cigarettes, leave the Group Home without anyone's permission and you would also be placed in the adult jail if you got into conflict with the law. I ran away from the Group Home on Hanson Street when I was fifteen years old and had to hide out until I turned sixteen. This was the first Group Home I was returning to since I left the one on Hanson Street. There were only two Group Homes in Whitehorse at the time.

When we entered Larry's room the first thing I noticed was the large black-light poster hanging on the wall of Jimi Hendrix playing his guitar. Below that was another cool black-light poster which depicted a large tiger seemingly jumping directly at you out of the jungle. Then I noticed Larry's record player and his stack of about fifteen records. I wanted to check out his tunes right away but decided to wait. We had more important things (like getting high) to attend to first. We all entered Larry's room and Gary and I sat down on his bed. "Close the door Larry," Gary gently instructed. "What're you guys up to?" Larry smiled as he closed the door. Gary half whispered "You got a syringe?" "For what?" "Andy's got some MDA." "You do? Cool," Larry smiled at me. "Yeah, I got a needle. How much 'DA you got?" It was my turn to join the conversation, "I bought three caps." "From who Bruce?" Larry asked. We didn't need to keep any secrets about drugs we trusted each other. "Yeah," I answered. "I heard he's got good stuff," Larry said as he turned and dug into one of his shoes in the closet. He retrieved a leather pouch. "Let's put some music on so Chris doesn't get suspicious," Larry was calm as he turned and smiled at me. As he was flipping through his record collection I watched closely to see what bands he had and noticed Alice Cooper, Led Zeppelin, The Rolling Stones, Black Sabbath then he stopped and pulled out Deep Purple's album, "Machine Head." He put the record on and the fast sound of "Highway Star" quietly filled the room. Larry turned it up just a touch and said, "Just wait here I'm gonna' keep Chris off our backs by asking him if the volume is OK. Sneaky huh," Larry smiled at me. I knew Larry respected me not only because I had the dope but because of the free-wheeling criminal lifestyle I lived. I was on my own and I wasn't afraid to partake in just about any crime that would fetch me some fast cash. I thought it was very ingenious of Larry to even think about going up to ask Chris if the music was too loud, it hinted that we had at least a shred of respect for him and would keep him from checking in on us. It worked like a charm! Larry returned with that great big smile of his, winked and gave us a thumbs-up sign, "It's cool," he reassured us.

The three of us went into the bathroom. Larry ever so gingerly unwrapped the glass syringe and filled it with water. He took out a spoon and placed it on the side of the sink. He looked at me with a questioning expression on his face as if I was holding the process up then asked, "Well, where's the dope." I pulled out the tinfoil with the three clear see-through caplets of MDA and handed one to Larry. "One each?" he questioned. I answered, "Yeah, one each." "You use a needle before?" he asked me. "No." "You gonna' do a whole one?" "What do you think?" "If it's your first time you should try half first." "OK. What do you think Gary?" I looked at Gary. "Half is good." Larry then asked me, "You wanna be first?" "No, you go first Gary." "I'll go first then," Gary had no problem with that decision. I watched as Larry emptied the whole cap into the spoon and added water. Once the drug was added to the water it was murky but quickly turned very clear. Gary pulled out an Export "A" cigarette and tore off a piece of the white filter. He rolled the small piece of filter into a tiny ball and upon Larry's consent dropped the tiny ball of cotton into the water which contained the drug. The cotton acted as a filter to catch any dirt and to absorb whatever the drug was "cut" with. Larry then pressed the needle into the cotton ball and began sucking up all of the water in the spoon. When the spoon was empty, Larry skillfully pulled the cotton ball to the side of the spoon just using the tip of the syringe and removed it from the end of the needle without touching anything with his hands. The process fascinated me and I watched with the anticipation of a man dying of thirst would watch someone pouring him his first glass of water after coming back from the brink of death. Gary rolled up his sleeve and twisted the cloth until it pinched off the blood circulation and the vein puffed out. He rested his hand in the empty sink bowl to steady it and held his arm up for Larry to put the needle in. Larry proceeded with the calm and cool of a practiced surgeon. I watched Gary's face for any sign of fear. There was none. Larry pushed the needle in and without the slightest flinch Gary received it. Once in the vein, Larry drew the syringe plunger back and as soon as there was a sign of blood in the syringe, he proceeded to push the drug into Gary's system. When the syringe was empty, Larry drew the plunger back one more time and drew some more blood then flushed it into Gary's vein again. This caused me to get a bit squeamish and I turned my head away. "Got to get every bit of that good stuff," Larry said. "You got that right partner," Gary chimed in. Larry removed the syringe and looked at Gary, "How is it?" "Ewww Good stuff," Gary smiled as he rolled down his sleeve. "Thanks Nieman." "How do you feel Gary?" I asked looking into his eyes to see if his pupils were dilated, (dilated pupils are a sure sign that one is high when taking a hallucinogenic drug). His pupils were gone. "I feel like Jimi Hendrix. Excuse me while I kiss the sky." Gary made us laugh with his comment. He was always so cool. I hated needles. I mean I was downright scared of needles! Yet, I had made my mind up a long time ago that when I got the chance to inject drugs into my vein I would do it no matter what. I made this decision simply because of the stories I heard of my friends getting high this way. I was willing to pay the price of facing my fear of needles if it meant I could get an escape and enjoy a little bit of freedom from the reality of my shameful life and since both Larry and Gary seemed so casual and so calm throughout the whole process of "shooting-up", this boosted my confidence. I WAS READY! I had total confidence in Larry's ability to handle a needle. Since I did not notice a big change in Gary as a result of taking a whole cap, I wanted to take a whole cap but both Larry and Gary agreed that I should do half because it was my first time. I went through the process without a hitch. Larry put the needle in my arm and it surprised me that it did not hurt at all. Once he injected me with the drug and as soon as I took the pressure off my arm the drug hit me. I was totally surprised and amazed at how FAST the drug took effect. It was instantaneous! I felt an energy enter my body as my mind went to place it had never been before. The high was a lot milder than I expected it to be. I felt a bit disappointed because it was so mild. It was nothing like acid. I didn't hallucinate but felt energized. And it wasn't until we went back into Larry's room that I started to notice that the drug was a lot cleaner than acid, meaning there were no cramps and no sweating. For my first time using the needle, everything went well. No too much and not too little. Just enough to get me hooked.

Gary was working at Whitehorse Copper for about six months and in June of 1970 he bought me a return ticket to fly down to Vancouver with him. His brother Maddy and our good friend Johnny all travelled together on the same flight and we were lucky none of us got bumped off because we were flying "stand-by." When we hit Vancouver it was a dream come true. Vancouver was everything we expected it to be and much more. For the first day it was a wonder we didn't get cramps in our necks because Maddy and I were totally amazed at how tall the buildings were. We just walked around looking up and kept saying, "Wow, look at that one!" and "Wow, look at that one!" Gary was our fearless leader because he had been down here before and stayed for a couple of months along with his brother Lance and a bunch of other Yukoners. We followed Gary like new born chicks would follow their mom. Gary took us down to Gastown and in those Hippie days when you walked down the street in Gastown, the sidewalk was very crowded and every second person dressed in their faded jeans with a leather pouch hanging on their hips, in tye-dyed t-shirts and long braided hair would be selling one type of drug or another and as you walked by them they would say, "Acid? Pot? Hash? Speed? Mescaline? Mushrooms?" We were amazed! Right here, right in the open people are selling drugs! Maddy and Johnny and I wondered, "Don't these guys worry about getting busted?" To our young minds, it was INCREDIBLE! This was like heaven! Johnny and Maddy and I kept looking at each other and laughing! We couldn't believe it! Alright! Vancouver! We're in Vancouver man! This is the BIGTIME! To make sure I didn't get lost when I passed out somewhere or got separated from the group I used Hastings Street and the big "W" high above Woodwards that you could see for miles as my anchor point. From there I began to learn my way around Vancouver and under Gary's guidance I soon learned the ropes. I started using the needle on a regular basis on that first trip to Van. Our drug of choice was Crystal Meth also known as "Speed" or MDA. I didn't trust myself enough in Vancouver so I stayed away from the Acid. I still could not use the needle on my own as I was not too sure of myself and I was still just plain too scared to poke myself. I left Vancouver after a month and went back to Whitehorse.

CHAPTER THIRTEEN

BUDDY

"MY TEARS SAY"

My tears say, "Love flowing from my heart"
My tears say, "It's hard to see you depart"
My tears say, "Together we walked some miles"
My tears say, "You made it easy to smile"
My tears say, "I don't know how to go on"
My tears say, "Yes, I can make it I am strong!"
My tears say, "You meant the whole world to me"
My tears say, "Love you can actually see"
My tears say, "I still miss you Buddy."

A. Nieman

There were three of us boys in our family, Paul Jr. was the oldest, then Buddy then me. Buddy was about four years older than me. He taught me so much. He taught me to skate. He showed me my first chords on the guitar and taught me to print my name when I was four years old. Buddy was a genius for building things and he could fix anything electric. He made a crossbow for me and I was the only one with a home-made crossbow in our family! Buddy built a cart for me that we used to race down the old Two Mile Hill Graveyard with. He also made a shoeshine box that had a built in compartment where you could store all your shoe polish and brushes and it had place for the person to place their foot on top while I shined their shoes. When I was eight and nine years old Buddy had me sit on Main street in Whitehorse with my little shoeshine box that he made and he told me to get more business just yell out, "Shoeshine, shoeshine twenty five cents! Come and get the best shoeshine you ever had right here, twenty five cents!" so that's what I did. He sat across the street watching me. He always kept most of the money of course for himself but I didn't mind because he always gave me just enough to keep me happy. I couldn't fool him either, if I tried to hold back any of the money he'd say, "Is that all of it?" "Yep" "Jump up and down then." I'd jump and down and if I was holding out, the jingle of the coins would give me away.

In the Fall of 1970, our family's life and especially Buddy's life would be changed forever. It happened one night when mom went to bingo and I was at home alone. My friend Rodney came down to visit me. As Rod and I sat there talking Buddy and his friend J. C. came into the house. They had a case of Pilsener beer and they sat down with Rod and I. J. C. was from Carmacks and he could play the guitar very well. Buddy usually had a guitar laying around somewhere. He hardly played it but he usually had one. Whenever JC came to Whitehorse he usually stayed out back behind our place in Buddy's little "Sugar Shack". He and Buddy were not drunk this night not by a long shot and they looked pretty bored. The four of us sat around making small talk. Rodney and I were drinking instant coffee and Buddy and JC were sipping on their beer. Buddy and JC were older than Rod and I and of course bigger so we didn't really feel too comfortable around them because they were drinking and kinda' treating us like we were kids. For some reason Buddy was trying to make Rodney drink a beer and Rodney didn't want to. Then Buddy got up and walked into my mom's bedroom and returned with a large bottle full of white pills. My mom was a diabetic and the pills Buddy had were for her diabetes. Buddy looked at Rodney and said, "You ever get high before boy?" I could tell Rodney was feeling uneasy and he looked scared and I knew he was scared when I heard him speak, "Ahh, no, no I haven't." and in one quick flash Rodney bolted for the door! Rodney got the door part way open just as Buddy stomped his foot on the floor and stopped the door from opening up all the way. There was just enough room in the open door for Rodney to squeeze his head threw and Buddy almost trapped Rodney's body half way in the doorway, but Rodney being as strong as he was, managed to hold the door open just enough to get his whole body through before the door slammed shut under the pressure of Buddy's six foot four body weight. I looked out the window and could see Rodney running as fast as he could towards home. I thought to myself, "Man, now he's going to be mad at me." I turned back to see what in the world was going on with Buddy and was going to ask him why he did that to my friend. Before I had a chance to ask him he said was, "Boy, he's pretty fast huh JC!? I bet you can't even run that fast!" and he started laughing. JC said, "Just like a scared rabbit with a wolf on his tail," upon hearing that Buddy let out another laugh louder than the first. I was mad at Buddy but didn't say anything. Buddy held up the bottle of pills and said to JC and I, "Who wants to get stoned with me, JC?" "Sure," JC said. Buddy looked at me, "Andy?" I was totally taken by surprise at all that had happened so quickly in these last few minutes and when it came to getting stoned I was game for anything, I answered without even thinking, "OK." Buddy continued, "OK. Here's what we'll do. I'll go first. JC you go next and then you Andy. First we each need a beer," Buddy opened a beer and gave it to me. "We'll take four pills at a time and wash it down with beer and we'll keep on taking the pills until we get stoned. You got it?" He looked at me again and I shook my head, "Yes.""You got it JC?" JC answered, "Got it." I didn't question what was happening. I respected my brother Buddy as someone who was smart and knew what he was doing when it came to drugs after all he knew how much LSD to safely give me for my first trip. I didn't ever question any of his judgments. All I asked was to look at the bottle of pills and after *only taking that one look*, I knew the spelling and the name of the pills and would never forget it. The pills were called; Tolbutamide.

Buddy started us off with, "OK, let's get stoned," and he took four of the pills and washed it down with a gulp of his beer. JC and I followed by taking four also. Buddy made sure we kept count of how many pills we took. We took the pills as fast as we could stand taking them. It's not easy swallowing four pills at a time. We kept checking with each other during the process of taking the pills and it became a common question between us, "Feeling anything yet?" and the answer was always the same, "No." I asked Buddy, "Did you ever take these pills before?" He said, "No." I stopped after taking sixteen pills. JC stopped at twenty and Buddy stopped after taking thirty six. The whole process took us about fifteen minutes. When it was apparent the pills weren't getting us high Buddy and JC took the rest of their beer and went to Buddy's shack behind the house. I only had one beer throughout the whole process and after Buddy and JC left I thought to myself, "What a rip-off." Then out of nowhere, I felt real dizzy. So dizzy that I felt like I had to lay down. Then I noticed that there was a buzzing sound in my head like that of a street light that is about to burn out and it would get loud and then fade away. Then I felt like I was about to fall over so I made my way over to the bed and laid down. The buzzing sound would get louder and then fade away. It felt so good to lay down and then I noticed that my mouth felt like it had cotton in it, it was the strangest feeling and I couldn't get rid of it. I did not like how I was feeling, it was nauseating. Then as I lay on the bed, my heart started to beat faster and it was hard to get a full breath of air into my lungs. I almost lost my breath a couple of times. All I wanted to do was close my eyes and fall asleep. If I could just close my eyes and sleep everything will be alright. I wanted this feeling to pass and I felt the sooner I fall asleep the sooner Id feel better. Now you can call it fate, chance, luck or divine intervention or whatever, but something told me deep in my heart that, "If you close your eyes and sleep, you will never wake up again." I knew, don't ask me how but I KNEW, that if I closed my eyes and went to sleep, I would never open them again. My body was getting heavy on me and I noticed it when I went to throw my legs over the side of the bed to get up. The buzzing returned in my head and I noticed that every one of the lights in the house had gotten brighter. I felt that I had to get to the hospital. I had to go and tell Buddy that I wasn't feeling well and wanted to go to the hospital. I half-staggered back to Buddy's shack and as I stood outside his shack I told him, "Buddy I don't feel well I need to go to the hospital," He answered with, "Yeah, we know. We wanna' go over there too." It was like I was walking through a strange land in a movie being filmed in the London fog. The buzzing in my head was now constant. The street lights had a dull glow to them and each one looked like it had a ball of cotton candy around it. My legs, my arms my whole body was getting heavier and heavier and it was harder and harder to walk. The three of us did our best to make it to Second Ave. so we could hitch-hike a ride. JC was helping Buddy as best he could trying to carry Buddy's six foot four frame as Buddy was slipping in and out of consciousness. I walked right out in the middle of the road and stood there in order to stop the first vehicle that came along. A pick-up truck stopped and picked us up and took us right to the hospital. The three of us rode in the back. I barely remember the ride to the hospital because I too was slipping in and out of consciousness. I do remember very clearly in between nods, telling the doctor the name of the drug we took. The nurse gave me a small paper cup filled with a black liquid that tasted like coke a cola made of thick tar. I drank all of mine and JC drank all of his. I asked the nurse what it was that, "Tastes like coke?" She just said, "It'll make you vomit so we can get the drugs out of your stomach." I said, "Make sure my brother Buddy takes his." She went over to give Buddy his cup but he laid there on his side completely unconscious with a large pool of foamy saliva coming out of his mouth. He never did drink his. He couldn't. He was out. The doctor came in and they quickly wheeled Buddy out of the room. For the remainder of that night, I slipped in and out of this hazy world where I teetered on the brink of trying to determine what was real and what was not real. The last thing I remember of being in Emergency that night was a nurse shouting at me, "Hey that's not a toilet!" and that's how I came back to reality, standing in the middle of a hallway in the hospital peeing into a plastic plant holder.

The next morning just after 7 am the RCMP gave Buddy and I a ride home. My stomach muscles were sore from throwing up so much. When we got home mom and dad tried to feed us but all we wanted to do was sleep. Buddy went out to his shack and I went and laid down on the bed. As I lay there, I heard the rattle of dishes as my mom got busy in the kitchen. Dad asked, "Did you see my gloves anywhere?" he was getting ready to go outside and do some work around the yard. I heard children's laughter coming from our neighbor's yard and a dog's playful barking as he was no doubt having fun with the kids. My mother turned the radio on and the Beatles sang, "Let It Be". I felt like I had come back from some faraway place and now that I was in familiar surround-ings; everything was going to be alright and it was now OK to fall asleep. And fall asleep I did. I slept until three in the afternoon. When I awoke I was feeling more like myself. My stomach was still a little sore and I was as hungry as a lion on the Sanhedrin. Other than that I was fine. My mother had a pot of stew on the stove and she told me to eat. She didn't have to tell me twice! I asked her, "Did Buddy eat?" "No." And the question that was inevitable that I knew was going to come eventually arrived at my regret and she asked, "What happened?" I realized the seriousness of our situation and I wasn't sure if Buddy was going to be OK or not so I told her everything. After I was done telling her all of it, she was silent for a long time. She had a front flap of a moccasin she was sewing in her hand and she kept turning it over and looking at it. I could tell she was in deep thought then I noticed a tear roll from her eye before she quickly turned her head away trying to keep me from noticing her tears. I had a feeling she was thinking about Buddy so I broke the silence with, "Want me to go see how he's doing?" She cleared her throat as she reached for a napkin and said, "Go ahead." I had never seen my mom cry before when she was sober. I witnessed her cry many, many times when she was drinking but this was the first time when she was sober. Somehow I felt like the situation was more serious than I expected. I had a feeling my mom and dad had already talked to the doctors and the police and might know about everything and probably knew more than I did. I walked slowly back to Buddy's shack thinking about this. I knocked on his door, "Buddy, are you awake?" there was no answer. I pushed the door open and it was very dark in his little one room shack and hard to see. I pulled back the covers from his face. He was still sleeping. I made sure he was breathing and then left. Back inside the house mom asked, "How is he?" "He's OK. He's still sleeping." "Are you sure?" with that question, I knew there was something not right. "Yeah why?" "Nothing I just wanna' know," was all I got from her. That was the end of that as mom went into the bedroom and I filled myself a bowl of stew.

Later that afternoon mom told me to watch (babysit) my little sister Kim. She said, "Lizzy has Frieda over at Karen's place." "Where you going?" I asked hoping she wouldn't say bingo. "Your dad and I are going to Bingo they're having a big Bingo tonight." I thought to myself sarcastically, "Big bingo alright, every night's a big bingo for you guys." I was angry at the thought of having to babysit and asked, "Where's Margaret?" "I dunno, she said she's going to visit Vera. I'll bring you guys back some Chinese food." "Yeah right," again my thoughts took off but I never said a word, "we'll never see any Chinese food if you start drinking." When she and dad left for bingo I found a couple of my dad's plain Export cigarette butts and rolled myself a smoke. I inhaled deeply and the tobacco was so strong that it burned my throat as it made its way into my lungs. I coughed a couple of times and through watery eyes I noticed that Kim was watching me. She said, "Why do you do that?" "Because I want to," was all I could answer. I decided to take Kim uptown with me to see if any of my friends were around so I could have a real cigarette. I dragged Kim around Main street with me for about an hour. I did not stay uptown too long as I didn't want too many of my friends to know that I was stuck babysitting on a Saturday night so Kim and I walked home along the railroad tracks. When we got to the house we couldn't get in the front door. Our front door was not a normal door with a handle on it. Our door was a homemade door that dad had built. It was made of two by fours and plywood. For a door handle he had a little tiny steel handle that was long and skinny and was held on by a screw at each end. You just pushed on it or pulled on it. Kim and I could get in the house as there was something blocking the door. To lock the door from inside we usually would just grab a couple of butter knives and push them into the door jam. If we really wanted to lock it we would use the big butcher knife. I banged on the door and was getting mad as I thought Lizzy was in there with some of her friends and yelled, "Is that you in there Lizzy? Open the door!" Silence. "Lizzy, I said open this door right now!" More silence. I start kicking the door. I could hear a radio or was that the TV playing on the other side of the door? Strange. Lizzy would have said something by now. I turn to Kim, "Go around and look through the window see who's in there and what's blocking this door." Kim comes running back around the corner yelling as she runs, "It's Buddy! It's Buddy!" "Whatta' ya' mean it's Buddy what's the matter!?" I ask as I run around to the window. When I look through the window I witnessed a scene that was instantly imprinted into my memory where it remains just as clear as ever to this day. Buddy is lying on his back with his head tilted to one side. The small black and white TV has been knocked over and is lying next to him on the floor. There is an overturned chair lying across the lower part of his legs. I look at his face. His eyes are closed and there is thick bright green mucuous coming out of both his nostrils and out of the side of his mouth. I immediately start to panic. I don't know if he is dead or not. I realize that time is of the essence! I run around and try to force the door open again but to no avail. I looked over at the neighbor's house and I see that their lights are on so somebody is home. I kneel down in front of Kim who is crying her eyes out by now and I take her face in my hands and say, "Buddy's gonna' be alright! I'm gonna' go get help for him. I want you to go over to Darbyshire's place and wait there for me OK?" she nodded her head, "Yes". "OK go! I'm going to get an ambulance and will be right back. Stay at the Darbyshire's until I get back!" She took off running and I took off running towards Tourist Services. It was the nearest phone that I knew of and it was about half a mile away. I ran with all of my heart just as fast as I could possibly run! When I got there I ran right into the restaurant and after I explained what was happening the lady picked up the phone. We did not have numbers on any of the houses in Sleepy Hollow and when the lady asked, "What's the address?" I automatically said, "Sleepy Hollow," then, "Dog Pound road," and realizing I was getting nowhere I blurted out, "just call the RCMP and tell them the Nieman's place, they'll know!" "OK got it!" she said as she dialed the police and requested an ambulance. Before she hung up the phone I bolted out the door and was gone running back to the house as fast as my feet would carry me. My heart was pounding a thousand miles a minute as I was running then I heard a siren in the distance and then I heard another siren. I pushed myself to run even faster! The police and the ambulance were already at the house when I arrived. The whole neighborhood lit up with the flashing lights of the police car and the ambulance. When I got there Buddy was lying on a stretcher and they were just placing him in the back of the ambulance. The police prevented me from going right up to Buddy and I asked the officer in a panic-stricken voice, "Is he alive? Is he alive?" "Yes, he's alive," the officer answered grabbing my arm and holding me. And to make sure I asked the ambulance attendant, "Is he?" "Yes he is. We have him on oxygen and he'll be OK." I sat down on the front steps of our house and caught my breath.

From that day on, the Buddy that we all knew who was so intelligent, who could fix anything and who loved to laugh was gone forever. The drug did irreversible damage to his brain and he was never the same. He came back home and it was a living hell for our family. I came to understand what it meant to live in a small community with a family member suffering from a mental illness. It is very, very hard on the family. My family and I constantly had people; friends, neighbors, relatives coming up to us and saying, "Buddy did this and Buddy did that. I saw Buddy and he was…" and they would explain the outrageous, weird and sometimes criminal things he did. We could not escape from this no matter where we went in Whitehorse. People would approach me anywhere and would start telling me what Buddy had done. It was shameful, embarrassing and made me very angry but there was absolutely nothing we could do about it. I read about his exploits in the paper and I heard it everywhere I went. It was a very hard time in our lives. My mother never gave up on Buddy though. No matter how crazy or scary the things he did at home were and in the community, she always went to whatever mental institution he was in and would get him out. Buddy spent the next nine years of his life in and out of mental institutions and the last time he came out he ended his life by shooting himself in the neck with a 22 caliber rifle at my mom's house and he died on Sept. 19, 1979. I'll always remember Buddy for his smile and his free flowing laugh. I could not cry at Buddy's funeral, I had too much anger breeding inside of me. And for the longest time after Buddy passed, I felt a lot of shame because I could not shed a tear at my own brother's funeral. JC and I dodged a terrible bullet the night we drank that awful tasting coke-like liquid.

CHAPTER FOURTEEN

VICTORIA AND OAKALLA PRISON FARM

"THROUGH OUT IT ALL"

Had time to smile and time to cry
Been times I'd laugh and times I'd sigh
I've sat in prison wondering why,
These blues won't ever say, "Good-bye"

Wore hard time holes beneath my soles
Wanted to die before I got old,
Life stretched for miles on a lonely road
Where I laid my head I called it home,

Had time to drink and time to think
Been times I'd float and times I'd sink,
But through it all one truth stands tall
God hears me cry each time I call,
Sometimes I run, sometimes I crawl
He walks with me throughout it all!

A. Nieman

I kept getting into trouble with the law in Whitehorse because I had to support my addiction to Acid. My brother Paul was living in Victoria, BC then and one time when he was in Whitehorse visiting I got into trouble for a B&E and Paul stood up for me in court and said to the Judge, "I think Andy is too easily influenced by his criminal friends here in Whitehorse. I think he'll do better in a different environment. If the court is willing Your Honor, he can come and live with me in Victoria and find some work." The judge had seen my face so many times already, he had tried so many different interventions, given me so many breaks and nothing worked. The Judge looked at Paul for a long time than looked at me and finally said, "What does Andy think about this?" Well, my head snapped to attention, my eyes locked in on the Judges' eyes and my ears couldn't believe what they were hearing! "You mean there is actually a chance this could happen?" I thought to myself. I couldn't believe it! I thought it would be WCC again FOR SURE! The Judge was looking straight at me and it looked like he was expecting an answer so I stammered, "Are, are you asking me?" My lawyer gently pushed on my elbow telling me with his nudge to stand up. I stood. The Judge kept staring at me and said, "I'm looking at you aren't I?" "Ah, what was the question again?" As soon as the words left my mouth I knew I should've said "Sir" at the end of my sentence. The Judge sounded firm when he said, "Do you think going to Victoria with your brother Paul here will make a difference in your life?" I couldn't believe my ears! Trying to contain the excitement that was starting to form in my mind at the possibility of avoiding jail I straightened up my shoulders and in my sincerest voice said, "Yes Your Honor." That's all it took, with that, I was off to Victoria the very next day sitting in the back seat of my brother's car.

In Victoria both my brother Paul and his wife Joan were working. He was a foreman with the City of Saanich and she was a nurse. I lived there with them for just over a month. I was left alone at their place during the day while they were at work and I was supposed to be out there looking for work, I did but not as hard as I could have. During the day, I would wonder the streets of Victoria on my own and before long I soon became bored. I didn't have any money other than what Paul and Joan gave me for a pack of cigarettes. My mind was constantly on Vancouver and I wanted to go there so badly. I kept seeing advertisements that some of my favorite bands were having concerts in Vancouver. Bands like; Led Zeppelin, Deep Purple, Jimi Hendrix and then it dawned on me that Vancouver was just a short ferry ride away! Well to say the least the temptation was too strong for me, I made up my mind; I'm going to Vancouver. Now, all I had to do was make some money and there was only one way I knew how to make money and that was to steal it! I walked through many different gift stores looking for an opportunity. I entered a fancy leather shop and when I went to the washroom I noticed that the main office was close to the washroom. Nobody was watching me so I quickly entered the room and as I dug through the desk drawers I found a wallet. I grabbed the wallet and stuck it in the back of my pants under my belt. I went out the back door. I walked away as fast as I could and went into a restaurant and straight to the washroom. I entered a washroom stall and opened the wallet. There was one hundred dollars in Canadian twenty dollar bills. I quickly stuffed them into my jeans. I looked in another compartment in the purse and to my amazement there was a whole bunch of American money! In American money there was three hundred and sixty seven dollars and in total with the Canadian money I had four hundred and sixty seven dollars. My heart started beating fast as I took the money out and threw the wallet in the garbage can wondering if anyone followed me. I dared not spend any of it and went straight home. I put the money in a sock and put it in my dresser drawer. It was a daily routine for Paul, Joan and I to sit and watch the local news on TV after supper and to talk about our day. To my amazement, the TV announcer reported on the wallet that I stole not even three hours ago! The reporter mentioned the location, the color of the wallet and the American money. And as fate would have it, Paul jokingly said, "What'd you do with that wallet Andy?" and he burst into one of his super loud laughs. Joan said, "Paauul, that's not very nice." All I said was, "Yeah right." Little did they know the money was sitting right here in this very apartment a couple of feet away! Life certainly is stranger than fiction!

Two days later I left a note on the kitchen table explaining that I was going to Vancouver then I took a cab to the Bus Depot in Victoria and bought a ticket to Vancouver. It was two days before my seventeenth birthday. When I got to Vancouver it was about eight at night dark, cold and pouring rain. I decided to walk to Hastings from the bus depot because that way, I could keep my bearings and I would know exactly where I was. I walked down to Hastings Street to see if I could find Gary or any other Yukoner. It didn't take long all I had to do was go to "Steam's Hot Dogs" a little café with Chinese owners right in the heart of Skid Row. I ran into Watson who is from Whitehorse and I asked him, "Have you seen Gary? Do you know where he is?" Watson said, "Have you checked the pool hall? He hangs out there quite a bit. Come on I'll show you where it is." It was only a couple of doors from Steam's. We entered the dimly lit, smoke-filled pool hall and sure enough Gary was there and Maddy and Johnny and Cecil. All of them are Yukoners. I felt like I had come home. With the money, I was the "Big Wheel" for a while and I only let Gary know how much money I had until I could not keep it secret any more. With the money I bought four ounces of Pot, a hundred hits (called a hundred lot) of Acid and twenty five caps of Heroin. The plan was to make some money by selling the drugs. Long story short when you have addicts in control of drugs they are addicted to, don't plan on making one penny of profit!

Back then Gary and I stayed at Howard MacIntosh "Big Mac" and Connie Ryder's place way up on Kingsway. Connie had a little sister named Lee who liked to hang out with us back then. Lee was like a little sister to me and we had a lot of great laughs together. One day Lee and I were standing outside Steam's Hot Dogs Café and there was a guy standing there doing his best to look cool. I think he was a drug dealer. Anyway Lee and I noticed him because he had pants that rode way above his ankles and it looked he was wearing his little sister's purple pants. His pants were way too small for him and here he was trying to look cool and make a sale. Lee couldn't help but laugh and pointed it out to me. She was laughing as she came over to me and said, "I don't mean to be rude but don't you think that guy's pants are a little too short for him!?" I looked over and said, "I'll say! It looks like he's waiting for a flood!" We both couldn't help it and cracked up laughing.

Gary, Cecil and I would stay at Big Mac's place for days on end and get stoned on Acid and then we started into the heroin. Once we started into the heroin it was our drug of choice. I sold all the Acid and used the money to buy more Heroin. One night in Gastown, Gary got busted with seven caps of my heroin and he went to jail overnight but because he had such a clean record he was out the next day. I was happy he got out but very mad because of my heroin. He wound up with a year's probation in the end. Heroin is like no other drug. It is in a terrible class of its own. The heroin high was better than anything I had experienced before. Heroin is one of the most addictive drugs known to man. It is very easy to get hooked on it because the high is both a body stone and the opium makes you dream which is called being on the "nod". The high is enjoyable but if you get addicted to it, the heroin withdrawal means you will go through a living hell. If you have nothing to assist you when you are withdrawing from heroin you would most likely shoot yourself if you had a gun. You get stomach cramps so bad it feels like someone kicked you in the stomach with steel-toed boots and then drove a red-hot branding iron directly into your stomach until it comes to rest on your spine. Your whole body aches and every bone in your body feels like it has severe arthritis. Your head and your respiratory system feels like you have the flu ten times over. Your nose runs constantly and you blow it until it becomes raw. Every pore in your body is sweating yet you feel like you are freezing in an icebox. Your hair and every bit of clothing gets soaked with sweat. Before injecting the drug you have to "cook" the heroin. Cooking the drug is easy, you just empty the powder into a spoon add water, put a match under it and heat it until it starts to boil. As soon as it starts to boil and not a second longer you stop cooking it. Once you inject the drug you will feel it even before the needle leaves your arm. At the beginning of use because you are not used to it and your body hasn't built up a tolerance yet, as soon as the needle leaves your arm and the drug is in your system your knees feel weak and you start vomiting if you are not used to taking the drug. The drug makes your skin itch especially your nose. You scratch and scratch and don't get any relief because heroin is a pain-killer and you will scratch until you develop sores, called "junk sores". Heroin is referred to as the "Dragon" and if you are going to "dance with the dragon" you are going to PAY one way or another! I have two Yukon friends who on their VERY FIRST encounter with Heroin, on the very first time they tried it, died. They paid the ultimate price. One smoked it on tinfoil and the other injected it.

Cecil and I got hooked on the heroin that I bought to sell when I arrived from Victoria. It wasn't long until we started hanging out at the Pender Café where all the junkies and heroin dealers hung out. The Pender Café was a tiny licensed Chinese food café and was known strictly as a junkie hang out. Cecil and I were hooked on heroin and all we looked for each and every day was to get that needle in our arms. We hung out at the Pender Café on a daily basis and walked the beat between Steam's Café and the Pender Cafe. Angel, who was a hooker that took a liking to me had a regular spot at the Pender Café and she was well known to everybody there, especially the dealer who always sold to her. When she was out making money I kept her spot warm at the popular junkie café. I felt like I was in a Humphrey Bogart movie like I was a "Big Shot" because I had a Hooker to supply my drugs and I didn't have to do anything for it. Each time I walked into the Pender Café my sense of smell was captured by the unmistakable aroma of chicken fried rice, nicotine and cheap beer. The tiny restaurant was shrouded in an ever-present hanging cloud of blue cigarette smoke. The sound of dishes being thrown into a rubber tub never seemed to end. Nobody noticed you walking in except the Chinese owners and the heroin dealers who constantly kept one eye on the door and the other on the deal they were making. The jukebox in the corner was usually playing "Black-eyed Blues" by Joe Cocker courtesy of Gary's quarter and "High Time We Went" by Joe Cocker or "Heart Of Gold" by Neil Young courtesy of my quarter

My addiction to heroin started to get the best of me and I had to have more and more. Heroin was so strong in the early seventies that four of us could get very high on one cap and the high would keep us in a "nod" for six to eight hours. That's how it was at the beginning. Now I was up to a cap a day habit. We shot up anywhere we could after buying a fix. One time Angel, Cecil and I went behind a school at 2 am to shoot up. None of us had a spoon so Angel had us look around for a bottle cap to cook the heroin. All the pop bottles and beer bottle caps back then were made of metal. I found an old beer bottle cap and we rinsed it out in the schoolyard fountain. It was hard to see. The only light we had was a dim 60 watt light bulb behind the basketball net at least 50 feet away. In those days there was no such thing as AIDS and nobody heard of Hepatitis C so it was common for us to share another junkie's needle if you didn't have your own. Back then, needles were very hard to come by. There was no Needle Exchange Program and they did not have plastic needles just the glass ones that doctors gave out to Diabetics through a local drugstore.

I wanted to get off the Heroin and I thought I could handle going through the withdrawals by getting drunk and staying drunk. It was Christmas Eve and the skid row bars were full as everybody on Welfare had just received their checks a couple of days ago. At 17 yrs. old I was too young to get Welfare but there was plenty of booze to go around. Well true to my form, I got totally drunk and blacked out. I woke up on Christmas day and did not know where I was, how I got there or where to go from there as I had never been in that part of Vancouver before. I was somewhere in the Kitsilano Beach area. My head felt like a concrete balloon. I felt totally embarrassed and got out of that house as fast as possible. It was pouring buckets out! I looked at the street sign and realized I was on West Broadway. I was so hung over and so hungry that I could barely walk. I knew it wouldn't be too long until I started getting "junk sick" from heroin withdrawal. I was broke and didn't have bus fare. I didn't know where most Yukoners lived. I just knew where Big Mac lived but that was miles and miles from where I was. I had no place of my own so I had no place to go. I didn't have an umbrella and got thoroughly soaked and cold in a matter of seconds. An overwhelming feeling of being abandoned, miles from home, feeling isolated and alone again reared its ugly head deep inside my heart as memories of my childhood stirred to life. I did my best to stifle the feelings and the memories. I was so far from home. And here it was. . . Christmas. I was on the verge of going through drug withdrawals, miles from any help. I was hung-over, cold and stuck. If my family knew my situation it would have broken their hearts. No doubt they would be enjoying a hot turkey dinner some time today. I tried hitchhiking and although there was lots of traffic, no one stopped. I decided to just keep walking as far as I could down to the Pender Café. As I walked, I came to a Denny's restaurant on Broadway. I caught the smell of roasting turkey. I glanced through the window of the restaurant in time to see a family as they were receiving their meal from the waiter. I stopped for a closer look. The waiter stood over them with a large tray filled with plates of turkey and all the fixings. I continued to stare for a brief moment. A lifetime passed in that moment for I saw a hard-working father who was a good provider. A father who put his family first and probably always would. He would see that they were well taken care of and protected. I saw a loving, caring mother and a faithful wife. She was there to keep her children happy and to give them the nurturing that nobody else could. She knew there was no one else who could ever take her place in that role so she did her very best to make the most of it. She was the only one to catch my eye. When our eyes met in that ever so brief second, I felt like she seen some of my sadness. It felt like my defenses were down. I quickly shifted my eyes from her and looked at the children. In the two children I saw happiness. It was evident on both their faces. They had a good life. They were safe and well taken care of. They were talkative, excited and full of smiles. It was probably one of the two that suggested they have this Christmas dinner at Denny's, I imagined. I envied them. I always secretly envied happy families.

Then my aching body brings me back to reality and I am reminded of the distance between my world and their world. We were eons apart. Their world was the one I wanted. My world was the one they shunned and would warn their children about. Their world was the one I could never have and my world was the one they would never want. I secretly longed for what they had. In fact, I craved it! Yet, no one knew about that craving. It was my secret. If only I could change my life. If only I could just tell someone who had the power to change it that I wasn't really such a bad guy. Sure I did some bad things and I made some mistakes, but I wasn't an evil person! But, what's the use? This is my life and there's no changing it. Get your mind off such foolishness, Andy.

Reality always had its way of jolting me back to the present. This all flashed through my mind in a matter of seconds. The rain reminded me that I had a long way to walk and the truth was I had miles to go. My hunger pangs reminded me that I was alone and the cold rain told me I needed some shelter. To ward off the disappointment that was trying to make a home in my heart and to keep from being reminded of my dismal situation, I remembered that in a restaurant like Denny's the patrons usually leave their umbrellas in a box by the entrance. I knew that because I had gone into one before and asked to use the washroom. I turned around and decided to walk back to check it out. What was the worst that could happen if they caught me stealing an umbrella? Jail? At least in jail I would be dry and I would have a bed and food. I went into the Denny's, went into the washroom and on the way out grabbed an umbrella from the box and never stopped to look back.

I had a long walk down to the Pender Café but somehow I made it. When I walked in the usual crowd of heroin addicts were there as Christmas meant nothing to us it was just another day. While Joe Cocker belted out, "Black-eye Blues" on the jukebox I wiped the rain from my forehead and scanned the faces in the smoke-filled café. Luckily Angel had just arrived there ahead of me and she fixed me up before the "junk sickness" really hit me. After I got some heroin into me and I could eat again Angel bought me some food and we settled into our usual spot at the Pender Café and nodded out.

A couple of days later Johnny (a friend of mine from Whitehorse) and I got caught for shoplifting some food in Woodwards. I had never been in a Vancouver jail yet so I had no idea what it was like. I had heard a lot of terrible stories from my friends about the Vancouver city cells or the "city bucket" as it was commonly called. Stories which I would soon learn to be very true. Like the guard nicknamed "Tiny". Tiny was anything but tiny, he was a big mean European guy who stood six foot six and easily weighed close to 300 pounds! It was clear that he hated every inmate. Tiny was the mean type who, all it took to get you in trouble with him was to make eye contact. The closest I came to Tiny was standing in line while he counted us and when he brought our meals around. I knew better than to get on his wrong side by getting him riled up and I never did look him in the eye. I've seen him drag some men who were very big men in their own right as he man-handled them like they were boys. He liked to put men in what they call, "The Phone Booth" for no reason other than looking at him the wrong way and he would only put them in there after he beat them up. The Phone Booth is a room where the walls are purposely built so that they can be adjusted to the point where you are not able to sit down and rest but have to stand as long as you are in there.

The police took Johnny and I down to the police station on Main and Hastings. They separated Johnny and I. The jail is old and if it had any heat I sure never felt any. It was downright cold! The beds are made of solid iron with no springs and no mattresses whatsoever. You get a thin wool blanket and that's it. The size of the cells vary some hold three people, some hold up to twelve and some are single cells. When you first enter the jail and they are gathering information from you the police ask specifically, "Are you a heroin addict?" "Yes" "How much do you use a day?" "A cap a day." "Pretty serious habit huh?" "I guess." "When was your last fix?" "This morning." "Need to see the nurse?" "Yes." The nurse is little help as she has no sympathy for heroin addicts. The inmates joke that she'll give you an aspirin and a band-aid no matter what your complaint is and tell you to use the band-aid and tape the aspirin over the place it hurts." Breakfast in the city jail is two pieces of toast and a Styrofoam cup of coffee. Lunch is a sandwich with just a piece of bologna or some other meat and a Styrofoam cup of soup. Supper is usually a meager helping of cold see-through meat, peas, carrots, potatoes and a Styrofoam cup of tea. Johnny and I are sentenced to fifteen days each at Oakalla Prison Farm in Burnaby. We have to spend a week at the city bucket before we go to court and are sentenced. In the city bucket you can spend up to a month in there and you do not get any amenities whatsoever. You can have visitors but must speak to them on a phone behind glass. You are allowed to keep your money as there is a chocolate bar vending machine there and a cigarette machine. In those days you could smoke anywhere and especially in jail if you could afford it. If you got hungry which we always did, you might get lucky if you had money and one of the guards was nice enough to let you out to buy a chocolate bar. The tough part of being in the city bucket when you had to spend a long time there was that you could not take a shower, you could not comb your hair, could not brush your teeth or wash your face or change your clothes and you went to court looking pretty rough.

The general talk among the prisoners at the "city bucket" is that going to Oakalla is a step-up from sitting in the city jail. All of the prisoners wait in anticipation for their name to be called for the bus to Oakalla. If your name is not called it means another night in the cold city jail with no sleep due to the drunks and various angry people coming in all hours of the night who are being charged for, "Something I didn't do!" It is quite common that a person would be picked up either half-drunk or stoned and charged with an offence. They also may be held pending an investigation and they are put in the same holding cell as you and a bunch of others. Many of these types come and it is a common occurrence for them to start kicking the door to get the guard's attention and they'll be demanding, "I want to speak to a lawyer!" or "I want to buy some cigarettes!" I've seen many fights break out as a result of this.

In the city bucket, the police can be very cold-hearted because they have to put up with so many bad attitudes. I have seen far too many times, where inmates with mental illness are placed in the same cells as the other inmates and the result is usually the same; the person with the mental illness would normally be beaten up by the other inmates so the guards would be forced to take them out. The reason being, those inmates who suffer with mental illness usually wind up in jail because they have not taken their medication for a while and their behavior escalates to the point where they are out of control. In jail, the inmates are already in a state of being worried, angry and nervous about what is hap-pening in their lives. To have a person with mental illness in your midst who is acting totally off the wall is not tolerated for very long at all by the other inmates and once they ask the guard to remove the mental patient and the guard refuses, the violence towards the mental patient happens. I've never participated in any violence to those with mental illness, because they reminded me too much of my brother Buddy.

At the city jail, the ones being transferred to Oakalla are handcuffed two by twos. The guards then lead us down the concrete stairs to a prison bus that is waiting in the alley. There are guards with guns all around us. It is cold and pouring buckets out. The prison bus looks like it came out of a James Cagney movie. It looks like a black and white school bus with steel screens over the plexi-glass windows. The windows are so scratched up it is all but impossible to see out of them. The seats are removed from the bus and in their place there is a sheet of iron which serves as a bench on each side of the bus on the floor. The iron benches are welded to the floor and there is an inch thick sheet of plywood bolted on top of the bench. I sat on those benches and have taken this same bus ride over forty times during my life of dysfunction. At the back of the bus, there is a section that is separated from us by a thick-wired screen that is so closely meshed together and painted over to make it purposely very hard to see or recognize anyone who is sitting there. All you can make out when you look back there are two seats that face inward. This area is for prisoners who are in Protective Custody. Protective Custody is called "PC". Those who go to PC are: rapists, child molesters and snitches (commonly called "rats"). You DO NOT want to EVER go to PC because once you go into PC you are labeled FOR LIFE. If you are labeled as PC, you then become a target for violence and/ or death no matter where you are, on the street or in jail. If someone who is labeled a PC and is put in with the general prison population and it is discovered that the person is PC he runs the risk of being killed and/or will FOR SURE receive a severe beating. Child molesters are hated so much by convicts because some of the convicts have themselves been victims of sexual abuse and most of the guys doing time have children on the outside. I witnessed many beatings of PC prisoners and there is one that stands out above them all. That beating took place at Oakalla in 1983. Let me explain how that came about and I will return to this point in our story after I give you a first-hand witness account of what happens when a child molester is caught in the general prison population. First I'll explain how I went to prison that time.

It is January 1983. My friend Mike and I are walking through the bars on skid row in Vancouver checking to see if there is any one we can rob or sell some bogus pot or acid to. It is pouring rain out on a Wednesday night and the bars are all but dead. Mike and I each took a valium that afternoon and drank a couple of beer. We are not stoned or drunk as the valium and beer only help to "take-the-edge-off" our hang-overs. In those days I always carried a knife on me because we sold a lot of bogus pot and had to be ready to defend ourselves if someone came back on us. So Mike and I walk through all the bars and it is absolutely dead. I then turned to Mike and said, "I know how we can get some instant cash guaranteed." "How?" "These cabbies always have cash on them." "Are you nuts? Everybody gets caught when they rob cabbies, you seen how many guys are in jail for that. It's a one-way ticket to Oakalla no way!" Mike sounded like he was insulted that I made the suggestion. I continued, "They get caught because they don't do it right." "Huh ugh no way." Mike said. I was persistent, "OK, tell you what I'll do. You don't have to do anything except one thing. Just sit in the front seat and when you see me put the knife to his throat, grab his dispatch radio and rip it out. That's all you have to do. I'll do all the talking and once I get him down a dark alley I'll get the money and we'll split. You just sit there and that's it! If we get caught, I'll take all the blame and all you have to say is that you had no idea I was going to rob him and I'll say the exact same thing." Mike reluctantly gave in saying, "You're crazy Nieman. Anybody ever tell you that? You're off your rocker!" We picked the first cab we came to parked outside the Marble Arch Hotel. The driver was an East Indian man with a blue turban on his head who appeared to be about thirty years old. He had a pitch black beard and his eyes were very attentive. Mike got in the front seat and I got in the back directly behind the driver. The car has a brand new car smell to it that is quite noticeable when we jump and close the door. Mike said, "Good evening." "Good evening. Where you guys going?" "You'll have to ask my friend he's the one paying," Mike said jabbing his thumb towards me and motioning with his head in the same direction. The driver looked in the rearview mirror and our eyes met, "Where to sir?" "I'm not exactly sure of the address I just know how to get there. It's just off Broadway." His accent was heavy, "Broadway and what?" he was not suspicious in the least as he eased the taxi onto the street. "Broadway and Oak," I knew that was a quiet area because my sister Margaret used to live in that area. The driver continued, "OK," then he picked up his radio and reported to the dispatcher, "Broadway and Oak."

We pulled up to a red light at Broadway and Oak. Traffic was rather light for a Vancouver street. At the red light with my left hand I reach over and grab the driver by his beard at the side of his jaw and put the knife up to his neck. When Mike seen me do that he ripped the dispatch radio out. The driver probably thought I was going to kill him because immediately he said, "I have a wife and three kids sir please don't hurt me I'll do anything!" I then said, "OK. Just do what I say and you'll be alright!?" "OK! OK! Whatever you say!" "Now calm down and follow my orders. Turn down this road." He followed my instructions. We drove on for a bit turning down this road and down that road because I was looking for a dark alley where we could get his money, jump out and run. The next alley we turned down, there was a taxi parked at the end of the street letting out some passengers. I have to give the driver who I was holding hostage credit for his amazing courage because as soon as we came around the corner and as soon as he saw it was another taxi, knife or no knife to his throat, he floored the gas pedal and took off at full speed straight towards the parked taxi! We are gathering speed at an alarming rate heading straight for the other cab and I thought for sure he was going to crash into it! I yelled out, "Stop you goof stop!" the driver didn't flinch he just kept driving as fast as the car would go! I thought for sure we were going to crash into the other cab so I took the knife away from his neck and braced myself for the impact! The lights from our speeding cab flashed on the surprised faces of the passengers who had just gotten out of the parked taxi as they looked helplessly at this car speeding so fast directly at them and then they realized they had no time to get out of the way! Then Mike leaned over in his seat and punched the driver on the side of his face as hard as he could! As soon as the punch hit the driver he slammed on the brakes! We came to a skidding halt mere inches from the parked taxi and the horrified passengers! We had the element of surprise on our side and Mike and I jumped out and started running before anybody knew what was taking place! It was raining buckets and for that we were thankful because then the police could not use the dogs to find us. As Mike and I were running Mike said, "Get rid of that knife." I took the knife out of my pocket and stopped beside an apartment building just long enough to push the knife into some loose gravel in a pot that held a fake tree then we ran some more. We tried to get into various apartment buildings but the doors were all locked. I spotted an outside balcony on the first floor of one the apartment buildings that had some thick trees around it, "In here Mike!" We got under the balcony and the trees hid us very well. We waited and waited and watched as police cruiser after police cruiser drove by us very slowly but because of the heavily pouring rain it was hard for them to see anything.

We watched as a couple more cruisers drove by us. The police were swarming the area. As we sat there as still as the statue of Liberty, Mike whispered in my ear, "I hope they don't have the dogs with them." Out of all that a career criminal has to put up with in terms of living dangerously and/or taking risks, police dogs attacks are at the top of the list of things you fear the most. As convicts, we have all heard the fearful stories of someone being attacked by a police dog. Sometimes the officer handling the dog will call them off and sometimes they won't.

Mike and I waited behind those bushes for what felt like hours. When we thought it was safe to come out and perhaps the police had moved onto another area, we started walking towards Broadway in the pouring rain. We were wrong. The police were waiting for us. As we walked, we went about two blocks and a cruiser quickly pulled up alongside of us. We were questioned and then taken down to the city jail and placed in the cells.

In the middle of the night the police came and I was taken from my cell and placed in a police line-up just like in the movies, where you have a bunch guys stand in a line up with bright lights shining on them and the victim stands in the shadows and tries to identify anyone in the line-up as the offender. I am identified as one of the offenders and after the line-up I am finger-printed and officially charged with Armed Robbery. Mike and I are both found guilty and I am sentenced to two years less a day (called a "deuce-less") and Mike is sentenced to six months. We are separated and Mike does his time in one of the easier jails in the Lower Mainland he goes to Allouette River Unit (ARU). I stay in Oakalla in the East Wing for six months until they send me to Mount Thurston Prison Camp, (it is called Mt. Thurston by all the prisoners).

It is while I am in the East Wing on Tier 5 waiting to go to Mt. Thurston that I hear about this child molester who has been placed in general population. The child molester is a man who had been caught sexually molesting his twelve year old daughter and apparently had been molesting her for many years before he finally got caught. He is placed in the cell right next to me! When he first arrived for two days I hear some activity going on in his cell but I'm not sure what is happening. I later learned after they took him off the tier that he was being tortured in a way that would not leave any marks. The ones torturing him had put a sock in his mouth to keep him from screaming as they hurt him and he did not report it as he was threatened with his life if he did. I learn of all this because one of the people involved in the torture is a friend of mine nicknamed "Wolverine." "Wolverine" was a friend of mine that I met when I first arrived at Okalla to start my "deuce-less". He was about ten years younger than I. He was a jovial guy whose hair was bleached-white blonde with eyebrows to match. He was a solid guy. He could be very funny and tell a joke as well as take one. He could also be very cold-hearted if you got on the wrong side of him. He liked fast cars and Harley Davidson motor cycles.

If you want to stay safe in jail you learn to develop the moto: "see nothing, hear nothing, say nothing." real fast. If you don't, you might as well check into PC. As I mentioned earlier PC is protective custody, where rapists, child molesters, and snitches go and PC's are marked for life. The prison grapevine is one that is alive and well on the streets as well, so there is no place to hide once you are branded a "PC case". One day Wolverine tells me, "Keep an eye open in yard today there's going to be some action. Primrose and I are going to take care of some business." Primrose is a big man six foot five and weighs two hundred and forty pounds. He is solid muscle as he works out on the weights every day. Wolverine is not too small either, six foot two and two hundred twenty pounds and he too is solid muscle.

That afternoon in yard all of us inmates and the guards know through the prison "grapevine" that something is going down. We all know that. We know this because Primrose and Wolverine come out to the yard with their steel-toed boots on and not their usual running shoes. Anytime either of these two comes out to yard and they have their steel-toed boots on, someone is going to receive a serious beating. We all know the child molester is the one who is going to be on the receiving end of a beating today. He is out in the yard walking around minding his own business totally unaware that he is a target. The child molester thinks everything is alright and takes off his shirt to get a sun tan. He sits on the hot concrete in the yard and rolls up his t-shirt into a small ball and places it like a pillow under his neck. He lays back and soaks in the sun rays. Primrose and Wolverine come out to the yard and all of our eyes follow them. They walk together around the yard once with their yellow-orange steel toed work boots overly obvious. The East wing yard in Oakalla is quite large and is big enough to hold a handball court and a tennis court in its compound. The child molester is lying on the far side of the yard. I am standing on the opposite side. Wolverine and Primrose go over to where the molester is laying and they stand on each side of him. Primrose kicks him first with a kick that is so hard that when his ribs break it sounds like a gunshot that I hear all the way across the yard! Wolverine then kicks the molester in the side of the head and he is knocked out instantly which is probably a good thing for him because they both then lay into the molester kicking him repeatedly. The guard looks away and busies himself with the clipboard he picks up. In a matter of seconds it is all over and the molester lays there motionless. Before leaving, Wolverine walks back, jumps high in the air and with both feet together he lands on the molester's head. I have no doubt in my mind just like the other 199 prisoners that the man is dead. There is dead silence. Primrose and Wolverine quickly make their way up the stairs and the guard opens the gate to let them out of the yard. The only thing that breaks the silence after that is the sound of the guard blowing his whistle to signal an emergency. In an emergency nobody moves. You stop and drop to the ground and lie flat on your stomach in the exact spot where you first heard the whistle and you do not move. The molester is taken out on a stretcher and the guard announces over the intercom, "Emergency clear!" and normal activity resumes.

About five minutes later a guard enters the yard with an inmate who is pulling a fire hose. The powerful spray from the fire hose blasts every last bit of blood to smithereens and washes the concrete completely clean. It is this same fire hose that can peel the skin off human flesh if one is too close to its spray. These fire hoses are used to quell riots besides putting out fires and oh yeah, to wash up blood. We learn later that the molester survived the beating with a number of serious injuries. I hear that he lost an eye, had multiple broken ribs, two punctured lungs, A broken jaw, a broken leg and suffered brain damage. This is only one of many, many similar beatings that I have witnessed in all my years behind bars.

Now we'll go back to the bus ride to Oakalla. On the prison bus and in prison, there is a wide variety of people and personalities from all walks of life. Jail is a reflection of society in that whatever personality type is found in society those same personality types are found in the prison system. People do not stop being people just because they come to jail. Some of the most common types of people one meets in jail are: alcoholics, drug addicts, drug dealers, murderers and career or habitual criminals. Career or habitual criminals usually engage in small-time crimes like Break and Enter, writing bad checks and stealing to support an addiction, this is the category I fell into. The habitual criminal will spend the rest of his life in and out of jail unless there is a dramatic change that takes place in their life. Habitual criminals have a saying, "I'm doing life on the installment plan." This type of criminal is "institutionalized". When a person has become "institutionalized," it simply means that the person has subconsciously developed a mental attitude of dependence on an institution where being in an institution is the only place where they truly; feel at home due to the familiarity of the surroundings. They thrive in such an environment and are at their best in an institution. It is here that they receive respect and acceptance, know their role and what is expected of them so there is no confusion. They know what the routine is going to be and are comfortable with it, they are not required to think for themselves in order to receive the basic necessities of life like being fed, clothed and attended to medically. I did not know it at the time but I starting to become institutionalized when I was at the Lower Post Indian Residential School for three years. In there, you didn't think for yourself, you were always told what to do, when to do it and how to do it and you had to do it whether you wanted to or not exactly like jail. From Lower Post I went to Wolf Creek a Youth Detention Centre, then to Whitehorse Correctional Centre for a total of eight years off and on. From WCC I went to other institutions like: Oakalla Prison Farm, Prince George Regional Correctional Centre, Allouette River Correctional Centre, Mount Thurston Prison Camp, Salvation Army ("Sally Ann") Adult Resource Centre, Vancouver Native Brotherhood Half-Way House and various other jails all over British Columbia's Lower Mainland. Oakalla was a very, very old prison that was built in 1912. It closed in June 1991. They used to hang people there until Canada abolished the death penalty on July 14, 1976. Okalla housed over 700 men and some 30 women at any given time. The men and women are separated of course.

From the outside, Oakalla looked like something out of an old gangster movie. It looked just like a prison should look. It was old, dirty, made of bricks and rock, had a big tower in the middle of it and you could actually see the bars on the windows from a distance. It was five stories high and had a barbed wire fence with razor wire that surrounding it completely. Around the whole perimeter of the prison property there is another fence with razor wire all around the top of the fence and a sign on the fence that reads: "WARNING ELECTRIC FENCE! DO NOT TOUCH AT ANY TIME." At the front gate there is a guard in an office that checks the identification of the bus driver each time he goes in and out. The bus driver signs the sheet on a clipboard an electric gate opens and we drive through. When I first walk into Oakalla the first thing that surprised me was how old this place is. It truly looks and smells like a dungeon. And then the strong, overbearing, almost offensive smell of bleach smashes into my nostril hairs and captures my full attention! It was almost like the strong smell of bleach was saying, "Welcome to your new world kid, it's time to leave your old world behind!"

I am placed in a large holding cell with about thirty other prisoners. These are prisoners that have arrived from communities and cities all over British Columbia and other parts of Canada. We are starting the process of being "admitted" into Oakalla and this is the holding pen. You see men in various stages of worry, fear and concern. A lot of them are first-timers who have never been in trouble with the law before. They are called "fish". Then there are Lifers who have come in from the penitentiary to attend court and are on their way back to the "Pen" they busy themselves by asking the local prisoners about their friends doing time at Oakalla and "Do you know how old so n' so made out in court?" Then you have the young guy who was trying his best to "go straight" but is constantly in conflict with the law who recently had a child with a girl and he is all concerned that he might lose both of them so he constantly gets on everyone's nerves by endlessly yelling and asking the guard, "If he can make a phone call?" And then there are the convicts who are institutionalized curled up and sleeping on the floor or on a bench or asking, "How long until lunch?" There is a lot of activity in this area and the din is continuous. Guards are constantly bringing in prisoners, unlocking their handcuffs and placing them either with us or in other cells. Heavy cast iron doors are constantly being slammed as prisoners are let in and let out. A prisoner is mopping the floor in one area and in another area the guards are busy processing files and doing the necessary paperwork as prisoners are being let out who made bail. There is a restless junkie clearly starting to feel the effects and symptoms of withdrawal. He paces the floor wrapping his arms around his aching body and his constant sniffling does nothing to stem the flow of his running nose. Toilets are being flushed about every three minutes and prisoners in different cells are talking back and forth.

Some have to yell to be heard over all the activity. Prisoners have cigarettes but are not allowed to smoke in this area and nerves already frayed get frayed a little more because of the lack of nicotine. Someone lights a cigarette and immediately the smell of cigarette smoke is noticed by everyone including the guards. Two guards come to the cell and open the cell door. The prisoner has already put his cigarette out by the time the guards arrive but it is totally obvious who he is by the long streak of black ash on the cell floor right next to his foot where he has extinguished the cigarette. He is quickly hustled out of the cell by two guards, has his pockets checked and everything is removed and he is placed in a cell by himself. The lingering aroma of cigarette smoke makes all of us want one. When your turn comes to be processed your name is yelled out and the guard comes over and opens the cell door for you. I walk over to a large showering area. There is steam in the air as there are men constantly showering during this process. The two people doing the processing are prisoners. They are sitting at a table and they have your file in front of them. A guard stands behind them watching every move they make. Without even looking up at me one of them asks, "Name?" "Nieman." "Andrew?" "Yep," "Put everything you have in your pockets on the table please." I hand over all my personal belongings: wallet, watch, lighter and jewelry. I have no money. While I am doing this another prisoner steps over and stands next to me at the same table and he goes through the exact same process. All of my belongings are placed in a clear plastic bag and I sign for them. I am asked, "What size pants?" "Waist twenty-nine." "Shirt?" "Medium.""Shoes?""Ten and a half." He points to a bench by the shower, "Step over there please." I step over to the wet bench and sit down. I am handed a small rubber tub that has clothes, underwear, a toothbrush, a towel, white canvas runners and a razor. I am told to, "Put your street clothes in here and when you're done showering bring the tub over to that window." "OK. Thanks." Not once had any of the prisoners doing the processing made eye contact with me. Just when I am about to step into the shower a guard walks over and hands me a wax paper cup that is half-filled with a thick green liquid, "This is for lice. Once you wet your hair put this stuff on and it'll kill them critters dead! Then you can wash with your regular shampoo." I hate showering in front of other men and my anger gets stirred up when the guard slows me down to give me the lice shampoo. I do not say a word because I am fascinated by the whole process I am going through. It is all so very new to me. I do my best to rush through the shower. I am surprised that the water is actually warm yet angry that I have to rush. My friend Johnny is not too far behind me in the process and we smile at each other when we first make eye contact.

After we are showered and cleaned up we hand our tubs in and are given our bedding in return. I am escorted to a different part of the jail and discover that the holding cell I am in is where I will be held until I see the Classification Officer. I am glad when I see that Johnny is being placed in the same holding cell as me and two other guys. We are served lunch there and coming from the city bucket the lunch portion looks gigantic! This picks my spirit up and I turn to Johnny and say, "Well at least they'll feed us good here," we both laugh. It is a totally new experience for Johnny and I. I am seventeen years old and Johnny is eighteen. We do not feel any fear and are ready to face whatever is coming our way. We are young, we can fight and take care of ourselves and we will be getting three square meals and a nice warm bed for the next fifteen days, so what's the big deal, bring it on! We thought we were big n' tough and as bad as bad can be that is until we found out where they would classify both of us to.

The Classification Officer knew that we were both from the Yukon and were friends and so he kept us together for the duration of our time. We found out we only had to serve ten days out of the fifteen. The Classification Officer sent us to be "Tier Cleaners" in the South Wing. The South Wing was where they sent the worst of the worst. I had heard bad things about the South Wing when I was awaiting sentencing in the city bucket. The South Wing of Oakalla was where you did not want to be. It was the wing where they kept those prisoners that were sentenced to federal time and the federal prisoners who were attending court from the penitentiary so that is where they kept the murderers, kidnappers, the criminally insane awaiting sentence and the most violent prisoners who were too violent to be kept in general population.

Johnny and I lived on the bottom floor which is the tier cleaners floor and the laundry workers floor. There are five rows called tiers in the prison that look like they are "stacked" on top of one another. Each tier has two sides to it. On one side is a row of twenty cells side by side and holds twenty prisoners one prisoner to a cell. On the other side of the tier is the exact same thing. One side is called the Left Side and the other side is the Right Side. At the front of each side of the tier is a door made of cast iron bars and it opens onto what is called a "Catwalk." The catwalk is the space in front of the cells that you walk down to get to your cell. On one side of the catwalk are the cells and on the other side is a row that has two iron bars about waist high running the length of the tier with a thick wire screen on the outside of the bars to keep you from falling over or from being thrown over the edge.

Part of our job as tier cleaners was to serve the prisoners their food. The prisoners would come down one tier at a time pick up their tray of food, take it back to their cell eat and then put the tray outside their cell. Also as tier cleaners it was our job to pick up their trays when they were finished eating and then sweep and mop the tiers. When Johnny and I were first receiving instructions on how to do our jobs and how to behave around such dangerous prisoners, we were instructed to never talk to or get engaged in ANY WAY with any of the prisoners. Why? Because some of these men are very cunning and have the ability to manipulate you and you will not suspect a thing until it is too late. We were instructed that while we were sweeping and mopping each tier, which had to be done every single day, that we were to stop at each cell and to hold up the broom and mop up as an invitation for each prisoner to accept or refuse, but at NO TIME are we to speak with them. Well it just so happened that one day while I was doing that very thing holding the broom and mop up to see if this prisoner wanted to clean his cell, that the prisoner noticed the pouch of Export tobacco I had sticking out of my shirt pocket and he didn't say a word but silently motioned like he was rolling a cigarette and with that motion was asking, "Can I roll a cigarette?" Now this prisoner was no ordinary prisoner in fact NONE of the prisoners in the South Wing were *ordinary* prisoners. And we as workers knew who each prisoner was and what he was in for, but this guy who asked me for a smoke was one of the worst if not the worst one in the South Wing! He was in for murdering a lady and then raping her after she was dead. I thought to myself, "I better not," but then I knew how it was to not have tobacco so I decided to help him out this one time. I quickly looked around to see if the guard was watching and seeing that he wasn't I handed him my pouch of tobacco. The guy took the pouch of tobacco and I kept on mopping the floor so as not to draw any suspicion on myself. I purposely left the mop bucket on the other side of his cell so I could come back for it and grab my tobacco at the same time. It worked like a charm. He left the pouch of tobacco on his cell door and I grabbed it as I walked by without saying a word. I finished cleaning everything up and left the tier. I sat down to enjoy a coffee and a smoke. When I pulled out my plastic pouch of tobacco I discovered the tobacco was ALL WET! And not only was it all wet, it was all wet with pee! The guy peed in my pouch of tobacco! That was all he wanted he didn't need a cigarette. Well I got furious and I immediately wanted to get revenge! That was all the tobacco I had until canteen four days from now! I told Johnny what had happened and Johnny said, "Better watch yourself, that guy's not all there mentally and he sounds like one dangerous dude." Well dangerous dude or not, I was totally insulted and to think that he did this to me after I was trying to help him out only added to my fire of anger. I then thought up the perfect plan to get even with him.

I never said a word to him when he came down to get his supper or the next day when he came down to get his breakfast. But when it came time for me to go by his cell the next morning as I was cleaning, I slowly pushed the mop bucket that was full of dirty water up to his cell and stopped outside his cell. He gave me the finger. I looked at the guard and the guard was busy reading a magazine, so I took the bucket of dirty water and spilled the whole bucket into his cell! It flooded his floor completely and he immediately ran at the cell door started shaking it and called me every name in the book and threatened to kill me ten ways to Sunday! The guard came walking down the tier as fast as he could and asked, "What in the world is all the racket about?" And I apologetically explained that I accidently tipped the mop bucket over when I was stepping over it and I slipped. The prisoner was hysterical and accused me of lying! Of course the guard didn't believe him but took my word over his and then transferred me from working on that tier to the tier below! That was my very first introduction to just how unpredictable life at Oakalla Prison Farm could be. When I got out of Oakalla after serving the fifteen days I returned to Whitehorse and continued in my excessive drinking and criminal activities. My mom was going to Revival Meetings down at the Old Village in Whitehorse and she became a Christian. She quit drinking, quit chewing tobacco, quit Bingo, quit swearing and she seemed so much happier. She would play Gospel music tapes all the time at home. She would also record the church services and listen to them at home and of course I would do my best to leave the house whenever she did. I was staying at her place then and would stagger in at all hours of the night and day in various stages of drunkenness. I was a real burden to both her and my dad through my drinking. I should have been glad that my mom was a Christian but the sad truth was, I still had a lot of unresolved anger towards her for all the violence she put me through as a child. In reality, the anger really should have been directed at my dad because it was his fault for never being home and never being there for me. I did not learn this until I started my healing in 1994. After my mom became a Christian she was always there for me. No matter how many times I came drunk or at what hour she ALWAYS LET ME IN. She never gave up on me. She would buy me clothes and different things that I needed but she would NEVER give me CASH when I was drinking. She would always come to visit me in jail whenever she could even taking a taxi in forty below weather. She would even come to visit me in jail as far away as Vancouver when I had just been sentenced to two years less a day in 1983. I could see that she had changed and that she was following God but I had no interest in any of that.

The first and only time I ever thought about God on my own was when I was an Altar Boy at the Lower Post Indian Residential School. I wanted to be a priest because I noticed at the young age of 10, that the priest was well respected and got a lot of admiration. Although I was a Roman Catholic, the last time I prayed to God was the night my Grandma Jessie Jack died. I remember that night clearly because a bunch of my Uncles and Aunties had come to Whitehorse as Grandma Jessie was in the hospital on her death bed. That night, my sisters Margaret, Liz, Kim and myself, knelt down in front of the cross of Jesus and prayed for Him to, "Please don't let grandma die." Well she died that night and that was the last time I prayed. The only time I read the Bible was when I was in the "hole" (isolation) at Whitehorse Correctional Centre. My opinion of the Bible was simply that it was NOT the word OF GOD but simply the words OF MAN. I was of the opinion that the Bible was made up by a group of men who invented these guidelines in order to keep people "in line." MY God was the sun because without the sun there would be no life. I had no fear whatsoever of God, Hell or the Bible. I didn't care about God at all! I had not the slightest interest in Him period! All I cared about was surviving and making it through the day. That all changed one day when my mom laid her hands on me and prayed for me.

To say I was troubled by my drinking would be a gross understatement! I was heavily burdened by alcohol and hopelessly addicted to it. I could NOT imagine life WITHOUT IT. In fact, I TRULY BELIEVED that I could NOT BE HAPPY WITHOUT alcohol. It was like having a ball and chain around my neck. I just COULD NOT for the life of me break free from it! It did not matter what I tried I could not STOP DRINKING! I tried Alcoholics Anonymous. In fact, I would sit in on AA meetings at every jail I went to and when I would sit in those meetings in my heart I KNEW I belonged there and that I was one of them; a true blue bona-fide alcoholic! Yet I could not for the life of me, take that step and admit it. I viewed admitting that I was an alcoholic as a weakness and

I shunned anything that appeared as a weakness in me. I went into alcohol and drug Treatment programs four separate times to no avail. On one particular night when I was about thirty years old, I did not know how I got home the night before but when I woke up I had two big black eyes, a swollen nose, a fat lip and sore ribs. I was hung-over and feeling totally down in the dumps. After getting some orange juice from the fridge I laid down on the bed and wallowed in my misery. I was living with my mom up in Hillcrest at the time and she called me into her room. She gave me a couple of her Aspirin and asked me, "Can I pray for you?" "What for?" "I'm going to ask Jesus to help you quit drinking and to help you change your life. You can't keep living your life like that Andy it's not right you know." She had asked me if she could pray for me many times before and I always said, "No." This time I hesitated and thought to myself, "Well I have nothing to lose and besides this is her house and I'm staying here for free." So I said, "OK." I knelt down in front of her. She put her hands on top of my head and started praying and almost immediately I started weeping like I had never cried before! I couldn't stop the tears even if I wanted to! I couldn't figure out what was happening and I started to feel embarrassed. Where were these tears coming from? They flowed out like someone opened a floodgate! And as soon as she lifted her hands from my head the tears slowed down.

She didn't say a word and I sheepishly got up from the floor and without saying anything, walked out of the room wiping my eyes. Ever since then, ever since she laid hands on me and prayed for me, I began to think more about God and Jesus and heaven and hell. I started to think about God when I was drinking. I thought about Jesus when I was pulling the needle out of my arm. And I thought about Jesus many nights when I laid in a jail cell staring at the ceiling wondering, "Where is my life going?" Each time I thought about Jesus while drinking or doing drugs I felt very guilty. Something in my heart changed and I wasn't getting the same results when I was drinking or when I was getting stoned. Yet feeling guilty did not stop me from continuing in my drinking, drug-ging and going to jail. One thing I know that changed for certain after my mom laid hands on me and prayed for me that day was this: every night and I mean every single night that I did time in jail and was not high, just before I fell asleep, I said the Lord's Prayer, 'Our Father who art in heaven…" and prayed for my whole family. I was not even aware that I prayed each night until my life changed and God reminded me of this practice. After my mom was sober for over two years I truly believed that she had changed and that the change in her was for real. She never did drink again after that or return to any of her old lifestyle habits. She remained faithful to God until her passing in 1991. My life went in the opposite direction.

CHAPTER FIFTEEN

ALMOST LOST MY MIND AND MY LIFE

"UP FROM THE GRAVE"

Lonely slowly led me away
To a place I do not want to stay,
To a place I do not want to say
Where many a soul has gone astray,
When from God's face I run and hide
A death inside my heart abides,
I cannot run from tears that slide
Downhill where hurt and pain collide,
What makes me fight on through the pain?
When life at best can feel so vain?
What makes me want to start again?
It's You O Lord, Who's love I crave
Who brought my soul up from the grave

A. Nieman

In 1983 when I received a Two Years Less a Day sentence and was waiting in the east Wing of Oakalla to be transferred to Mt. Thurston Prison camp on May 13 I got the news that my father passed away. He had cancer in his intestines and had ended his life with a gunshot to his stomach. And because I had such a notorious record for not showing for court which carries a Charge of Failing To Appear (FTA) and of which I had over twenty FTA's on my record they refused to let me attend his funeral. It was a very sad time for me. The very next year1984 while I was at Mt. Thurston my sister Elsie was involved in an accident and broke her back. She became a paraplegic and wound up in a wheelchair until her passing in 1996. That same summer in 1984 while I was still at Mt. Thurston and working in the kitchen, I got a note from the guard who was also my Caseworker and the note said, "Your mother wants you to call her collect ASAP." The guard says, "You can call now if you want Andy." "OK. Thanks." I walked to the office and making the call I ask my mom, "Hi mom what's happening?" "Are you sitting down?" "No, why?" "You should sit down." I got angry, "No I don't need to sit down what's the matter?" The line goes quiet then my mom clears her throat and says, "You know your friend there that Kane boy that you hang around with?" Right away I know something has happened to Ronnie, "Yeah." "There was a fire yesterday in Champagne they say him and his brother both passed away." Something hits my chest and my throat feels suddenly dry. "You OK. Andy? You don't do anything bad now," my mom is concerned. "I'll be alright mom I won't do anything." I feel like someone just kicked me in the stomach. Most of my strength is sapped from my body. "I'll call you later mom." I hang up. I am in shock. This is too hard to believe. "Everything OK?" my Caseworker asks. "I just lost one of my best friends." "Oh. Sorry to hear that Andy. If you want I can probably get you off work for the rest of the day if you'd like?" I am in a daze, "OK." "I'll meet you in your cabin to let you know." I head to my room and sit on the edge of the bed as the memories flow like they just happened yesterday. Ronnie was a very popular guy in our group growing up. He was an excellent musician. I loved his singing. We all did. I was very close to Ronnie. He and I had no teeth in the front and we used to tease each other about that. Ronnie would point at me with one hand and put the other hand one over his mouth as if hiding his teeth and tell me, "Eeewww Raggy. Girls don't want you Andy. You got no teeth. They want guys who have teeth!" And I would reply, "Eeewww, where's your teeth? At least go and get some falsies. Girls don't even want to look at you with no teeth!" and we would both crack up laughing! I was looking forward to seeing Ronnie when I got out. He was in my plans as one of the people I would treat when I got back to Whitehorse. As I sit there on my bed in shock, the guard returns and informs me, "Yeah, it's OK. Take the rest of the day off Andy." I'm thankful no one is there to see me cry. I put my headphones on press "play" on my Walkman cassette player and try to lose my sadness as my favorite band Lynyrd Skynyrd sings, "Simple Man". I lay back with my hands behind my head and let the tears and the memories of Ronnie flow. Again, I am not allowed to go to the funeral.

I get out of jail that August and on my first day out I drown all my grief and disappointments in alcohol and drugs. After visiting my sister Elsie in the hospital at Vancouver General, my mom and I go to visit my sister Frieda in Chilliwack, B. C. I stay there for a couple of months. My mom and sister Frieda are going to church in Chilliwack. I have a guy from the church come visit me and I say the Sinner's Prayer with him and he tells me, "Now that you have accepted Jesus into your life you are saved." I did not feel anything in my heart nor did I feel any different after I said the Sinner's Prayer and I wonder if God loves me like everyone says He does or if I am just too bad for God to forgive me. I go to church a couple more times just to satisfy my mom and after church I would pull out my marijuana and get high. If I wasn't getting high on "pot"

I'd be drinking wine. I returned to Whitehorse and I stay drunk on Villa wine for three straight months. I drank every single day and amazingly I managed to stay out of jail during that time. I stopped eating in the last month of that three-month drunk. My sisters Liz, Kim and Margaret would find out where I was drinking or staying and would bring me food. I would wait until they left and I would give the food away because I didn't want the food to take away from the effect the wine would have on me. My mother heard that I was drinking so much and would not stop so she came back to Whitehorse to see if I would go back to Chilliwack with her. I kept refusing to go on the bus to Chilliwack with my mom and kept on drinking heavily. Sourdough Rendezvous is an end of winter celebration that happens every February in Yukon and goes on for a full week. It is a time of partying, a lot of drinking and a time of engaging in various skills contests as well as crowning a Rendezvous Queen and then more partying and more drinking. At least that's how it was for me back in those days. During this Rendezvous celebration I am drunk every day and the alcohol is flowing freely. At the end of the celebration my sister Kim picked me up while I am still quite drunk and drove me to her place. I pass out on her couch. When I awake the next day my mouth is as dry as a tumble weed in the Sahara and I am very hung-over. My mom is very demanding that I go to Chilliwack with her at noon that very day on the Greyhound bus in fact she practically leaves me no choice, and says "I'll pay your way."

I hear that my nephew Kevin is also down in Chilliwack so I decide to get on the bus and go with her to Chilliwack to live with her and my sister Frieda. My sister Kim asks me, "Do you want me to drive you to the hospital to see if they'll give you some nerve pills?" I am too hung-over to do anything and look forward to sleeping on the bus ride down south. I tell Kim, "No that's OK." "Aren't you afraid of going snakey?" What Kim means by 'going snakey' is when an alcoholic drinks for an overly extended period of time and then suddenly stops the alcohol intake the person can go through severe and acute withdrawal. The scientific name for this is: Delirium Tremens and is commonly called the "DT's" or "going snakey". When a chronic alcoholic goes through this severe, acute withdrawal it is worse than hell on earth and can oftentimes be fatal! Now doctors and professionals can call it what they want, but I have been there and I know from first-hand, front-row experience that it is more than simply being a medical condition it is a spiritual condition where you are overcome by demonic forces that seek to end your life. It is a form of demonic possession because you not only get a supernatural, super-human strength but you can actually see and touch demons that manifest themselves to you. I was about to experience this for myself first-hand and today you get a front-row seat to such an experience. I had a friend about 30 yrs. ago named James C. who went through this process in the hospital in Whitehorse. It was near the beginning of November and winter was setting in. They had James locked up in a padded room area of the hospital and felt he was secure and would be alright. But because of a demonic influence that gave him supernatural strength he was able to break out of that room and he ran straight down and into the Yukon River where he jumped in and drowned.

They could not locate his body because the current in the river was too strong. They found what was left of his body after the animals had gotten to it later at Spring break up.

When Kim asked me, "Aren't you afraid of going snakey?" I turn to her with my blood-shot eyes and foolishly tell her, "No, I'll be alright." Kim makes us a bunch of sandwiches and packs some water for us and puts it in a bag. The trip to Chilliwack from Whitehorse by bus takes two days. It is time to leave for the Bus Depot and we pack everything into Kim's van. My mom buys us both tickets, we say our, "Good-byes" and mom and I board the bus. The bus is almost completely full. My mom finds two seats for herself near the back of the bus and I find two seats for myself a couple of rows ahead of her. About half an hour after we leave Whitehorse my body starts to sweat and I mean it starts to sweat PROFUSELY. I am sweating through what feels like every single pore in my body. Even my thighs are sweating! The sweat is pouring off me in buckets! All of my clothes are soaked in a matter of minutes! Strange, this has never happened to me before! What is going on here? The bus stops in the middle of nowhere and a Swedish lady boards the bus. She sits down right beside me and I catch the unmistakable smell of wood-smoke, pine needles and Patchouli oil. She introduces herself. The last thing I want to do when I am sick with a hang-over is TALK! I do my best to avoid talking to her then she turns to me and asks, "Are you OK? You don't look so good. Are you sick?" and she takes out some Kleenex and hands it to me. I wipe my forehead. The Kleenex is totally soaked in about one second and does next to nothing to stem the flow of sweat. She hands me more and I keep wiping until she runs out of kleenex. I say, "Thank you," and close my eyes. I turn my head away from her so she gets the message that I'm not interested in talking. There is a boy sitting in the seat directly behind me. He has earphones on and is listening to music on a Walkman. The music sounds very loud and I wish he would turn it down. As we journey on, the lady next to me falls asleep. I hear fiddle and guitar music coming from somewhere and it keeps getting louder and louder. I can't pinpoint where the music is coming from and then I remember that the little boy sitting behind me was listening to music. I turn around and was just about to ask him, "Can you please turn that music down," when I notice that he is not listening to music at all. He has put his Walkman away and is sleeping soundly. The music is growing louder and it is then that I get my first clue and realize, "Oh, oh something is not right here." I try to pretend that I don't hear the music but it is no use. I then hear the sounds of a bar, it's like I am sitting in the middle of a barroom! Glasses are clinking and people are laughing. I turn around to take a look behind me and it suddenly all stops just like that. The only sounds I hear is an odd snore and the shifting of the bus' gears as it gathers speed. Glancing around the bus I notice that most everyone on the bus is asleep. I think to myself, "Wow! What was that all about?" I get up and walk to the washroom. As I get close to where my mom is sitting I see that she is wide awake. She looks at me and asks, "What's the matter?" "Nothing" "You're sweating." "A little bit, I'll be alright." "You look like you're shaking," it was more of a question, "I'll be alright mom." I am shaking. My legs are weak and they shake under me because I have not exercised them in months and they suffer from a lack of nutrition, so they struggle under my weight. I go to the bathroom. When I come out of the bathroom I notice that we are arriving at Teslin, a small community about 100 miles south of Whitehorse. We stop there for a half hour lunch break. Mom and I stay on the bus. My mom calls me, "Andy?" "Yeah?" "Come here." I go back to her. She is digging through her purse and pulls out her wallet. "You going in there?" she asks me. "No, I wasn't planning to why you want something?" I dreaded going in there because I knew I looked a mess. She pulls out a twenty dollar bill and hands it to me, "Here, you go in there and buy yourself a "Mickey" (a small flask of alcohol usually whiskey or vodka) of whatever it is you drink and bring me the change." [Author's note: Dear reader, you need to understand something very important here in order for you to grasp and understand how truly serious my situation was on that bus. My mom, who was a true, bona-fide woman of God who followed God with all her heart and would not do anything against His word, would NEVER EVER give me MONEY if she knew it was going to be spent ON ALCOHOL. She was strictly and totally against that. Yet on this bus ride, it is and was the first and last time she EVER OFFERED me money for alcohol. She must've seen something in me that day that I was not aware of. End of Author's note]

Before I touched the money I looked my mom in the eye and I knew it was against all of her standards to offer me money for alcohol so I decided not to take it. I said, "No that's OK mom. You don't have to do that, I'll be OK. I'll have a coke though." Then she said, "You sure? You don't look very well." "Yeah I'm sure. I'll be fine mom don't worry 'bout it." She ended the conversation with, "OK. Bring me a bag of Cheezies when you come back and an apple juice." I got back on the bus and drained my coke in no time. I was a lot thirstier than I thought I was. Good thing I bought two. I notice that quite a few people have gotten off the bus at Teslin. The bus is quite empty. We leave Teslin and as we travel on it gets dark outside as night falls upon us. We are going up a steep hill that is very long and I notice that we are going quite slow, in fact we are going much slower than usual. I look out the window of the bus and I what I see in the forest terrifies me! Just as plain as day and just as real as the book you are holding right now, I see that the whole forest is lit up and comes alive with movement as a large group of Klu Klux Klan is marching up the hill in single file following the bus. They are carrying torches with black smoke rising from their flickering lights in one hand and in their other hand there are different sorts of fierce looking weapons. There is a long, long line of them and there are even children dressed in the long white gowns. Some carry a Grim Reapers scythe (a tool with a long curved blade used for cutting grass or corn). Others have machine guns, some have swords, others have knives tucked in the belt of their robes and there is not a sound being made. They move silently and with a steady gait. It looks like they are going to meet the bus at the top of the hill. I look around and it dawns on me that my mom and I are the only non-white people on the bus so the Klan must be after us! No wonder the bus is going so slow! I start to panic and get up from my seat. I walk to the front of the bus to confront the bus driver. I stand by the bus driver and ask him, "You're not going to stop the bus are you?" He replies, "Stop the bus? What for? Of course I'm not going to stop the bus we're in the middle of a hill." With the panic clearly obvious in my tone of voice I continue with, "Please, whatever you do, don't stop the bus!" The last thing I hear from the bus driver before I black out is, "Just go and have a seat sir I promise I won't stop." When a person is caught up in such a dimension and goes through this spiritual hell, you lose your sense of reality and you lose you sense of time because your mind blacks out and you don't remember a thing and then you "come to" and then some of the time you remember everything and some of the times you don't remember anything! Then you go into a black out again. When I come back from blacking out after seeing the Klu Klux Klan, I find

I am sitting back in my seat on the bus. It is still pitch black outside. I get up and go to the washroom. When I return to my seat I see that my seat is occupied by a dwarf sized demon that looks like an alien with greenish, dark brown skin that is shiny with slime. He is sitting with both his feet tucked under him on the seat and he has six-inch long sharp claws on both his hands and his arms are crossed. He pretends he is looking out of the window but he is looking at me through the window's reflection and I can tell he has big, bright red reptile eyes. I notice sticking out of the corner of his mouth are long sharp baboon-like teeth. I make a bee-line outta there and head straight back to where my mom is sitting. I explain to her what I just seen. She says, "That's just the devil trying to scare you, there's nothing there. You just tell him, "You're not real I rebuke you in Jesus' Name." She then took my hand and prayed for me. When she is done praying I gather and muster up as much of my almost non-existent courage and walk back to my seat. I shuffle into the seat and sit down pressing up against this dark little ugly demon. He is still looking out the window when I sit down and I say to him, "You are not real and I rebuke you in Jesus' Name." Then this foul-looking dwarf from hell turns his head towards me and says in a deep, low, Darth Vader-like voice, "Not real huh? How's this for not real," and he lifts up one of his claws and pokes me with one of his six inch long claws. I bolt out of the chair like it is suddenly on fire and I go to the back of the bus. I sit down trying to calm my nerves when I hear someone behind me call my name in a whispering voice, "Andy, whatcha' doing on this bus? I didn't know you were on here, trying to hide away from us huh? I thought we were friends?" Then I hear a lady's voice coming from the same area, "Yeah, Nieman are you too good for us now?" I recognize both of the voices. Their voices sound muffled like they have something covering their mouth. They are the voices of my friends Ivan and Karen. I am surprised that I did not see them get on the bus. I turn to make eye contact with them but it is just a little too dark to see them. "Come on back," Ivan says. It looks like they are sitting on the very last seat of the bus so I get up to go see them. When I get closer to where they are sitting what I see is two mummies wrapped from head to toe in dirt-stained bandages and there is pus and blood oozing from sores under their bandages. I can barely see their eyes and when they come into what little light there is, I see what looks like big canker sores on their lips. Ivan has his arms folded and I can't see his hands. I catch the smell that is coming from them and it turns my stomach. It smells like swamp gas! I stop advancing towards them and try my best to look them in the eye then Ivan continues, "What's a matter never seen anybody with AIDS before? This is how you're gonna look too 'cause I heard you've been fooling around with my old lady. And if you somehow managed to dodge the AIDS bullet these will take care of you," and he pulled out his hands to show me the long razor-sharp blades that he had for fingers and they looked exactly like Freddie Kruger's hands. I am amazed at the size of these weapons on Ivan's hands and want to get out of there as fast as I can! Ivan says, "But don't worry, I'm not in no rush. I know where you're going, Frieda's a friend of ours too. I want to see the look on your face the first time I sink one of these into you," he holds one of the long blades up for me to look at. I black out. When I "come to" we are stopped at Chilliwack and it is night. I start to walk off the bus and as I am about to take my last step off the bus I see some bushes move and it is Ivan hiding in the bush! He tries to duck out of the way before I can see him. I know he is after me and I feel like he is going to kill me so I start to walk towards a gas station. Ivan follows me through some bushes so I start to run and he starts to run. I run as fast as I can and I reach the gas station. I run up to the window and in a panic yell, "Would you call the police for me please! Hurry it's an emergency!" "What's the problem?" the shocked lady attending the gas station asks. There's a guy chasing me that's trying to kill me!" "Where is he?" "He's right over there hiding in the bushes, right there see him? Hurry!" "I don't see anyone sir." "No, you won't see him he's too smart for that. He's right there what's the matter with you? Just call the cops please!" "OK, if you say so." Then I see Ivan jump from the ground and with one leap he lands on top of a building. He then jumps from roof to roof one building to another. He stops on the roof of the gas station and stands there grinning at me with his hands on his hips. I tell the lady, "He's just landed on your roof!" and I run as fast as I can back to where the bus is just pulling out. My mom has a Yellow cab waiting there and the driver has just loaded everything into the trunk and slams the top shut as I arrive there. I am frantic! "Quick jump in mom, let's get out of here!" "Gosh, what's the matter now?" mom says as she gets in the cab. We start to drive away and only go about 25 feet when the police arrive and they stop the taxi. The policeman gets the address that we are headed to from the cabbie and follows us over to Frieda's house.

We arrive at Frieda's house and when the cabbie unloads my mom's big duffle bag from the trunk, I see the duffle bag move on its own and then it dawns on me that Ivan is hiding in there! With everyone standing around including the policeman I shout, "He's in there! He's in there! He's in the duffle bag!" and I black out. When I "come to" I am at the Chilliwack General Hospital sitting on a hospital bed in a hospital gown.

I am still terribly afraid that Ivan is going to get me and I tell the doctor, "You need to lock those doors because he is very smart and can get in any-where." The doctor sits there and listens to me tell him the whole story about the bus ride and AIDS and the Klu Klux Klan and the Mummies. The medica-tion the hospital administered to me does little to bring me to my senses or to stop the demonic attacks. They place me in the psychiatric unit of Chilliwack General Hospital and I would spend the next 15 days there going through hell. The doctor says that he has given me some medication and asks me to lay down on the bed so I lay down on the bed and black out.

When I come to, I am sitting at a table with a tray of food in front of me and there are other men and women sitting there with me and we are all dressed in hospital gowns. I think I am in jail and I say to one of the guys at the table, "Hey this is a pretty good jail they even have women in here, cool!" One of the women at the table says, "This is not a jail. This is worse than a jail!" I look around and see a couple of nurses. One nurse is sitting at a semi-closed in counter and another is standing writing on a clipboard. The one writing on the clipboard puts the clipboard down and starts walking towards me. She speaks in a cheerful voice as she gets closer to me, "Ahh Mr. Nieman you're back with us again." I just have one question for her, "This is jail right?" "What makes you think it's a jail?" "Well I've been in jail before and I know a jail when I see one." "No Mr. Nieman, do you prefer Mr. Nieman or Andrew?" "Andy," "OK, Andy, no this is not a jail this is a hospital. Notice there is no bars on the windows?" "I've been in jails where there were no bars in the windows." "OK, I understand but this is still a hospital." "How long do I have to be here?" "Well, apparently the doctor says that you are quite sick yet and when you are better than you can go home." "I'm better now. I feel OK." "When the doctor says you are better than we'll know you are better and we'll let you go home, until then eat all your food. We need you to get some of your strength back." I don't believe anything of what the nurse tells me.

I feel like I am walking through a dream. I don't know where I am. I don't know who I am and I don't know what I am doing here. I hate what I am feeling because everything is so strange to me and I feel like I have no control. I feel totally isolated. There is nothing around me that is familiar. They have a little outdoor spot at the unit with a flower garden, a few trees and a man-made running water brook. I go out and sit down by myself. I wonder to myself, "What in the world is going on here? Am I ever going to get out of this place? And where in the world IS THIS PLACE!?" This strange journey that I find myself on is heavier than any Acid trip I've ever been on and a hundred times scarier! On this journey, I am constantly taken against my will to places that get freakier each time. I witness the most horrifying, scary scenes straight out of hell that words will never truly be able to explain. Like for instance one time in the psyche ward I saw a spotlight out in the yard of the hospital that looked like one of those circulating lights you see at the top of a guard tower in a prison movie. Well, this was not a normal spotlight because this spotlight was able to shine right through the concrete walls of my room at the psyche ward! And each time the light came around to sweep past me, its rays would slice right into me and through me and cut me into paper-thin slices that stayed suspended in the air until the light passed by and once the light passed I would be joined back together again. And when the light cut through me it was very painful and I mean very, very painful. This is a living hell and to me it is ALL REAL! There was no place to hide from it and you knew it was coming around again very shortly. Somebody let me out of this living hell! No amount of medication is able to help ME during my time in the psyche ward. While I am going through this hell, I do not know what is real and what isn't. To me, IT IS ALL REAL!

Remember I told you that when a person is under the control of a demonic spirit that person can get supernatural, superhuman strength? One night I "came to" out of a black out and I find myself standing in the middle of a sidewalk in the pouring rain at night bare foot in my hospital gown and the bottom of my feet have a bunch of little cuts on them and they are bleeding. I look around and recognize that I am in Chilliwack and that I am not too far from my sister Frieda's place. I make my way over to Frieda's and throw a small rock at her window (there was no outside buzzer) to let her know I want to come in. She lives on the second floor and her kitchen window is open. My nephew Kevin looks out the window and I hear him say, "It's Uncle Andy and he doesn't look too good! Should I let him in?" Frieda peeks out the window and then my mom peeks out. I hear mom say, "Go down there and let him in!" When I am in the apartment I start changing my clothes and my mom asks, "What you doing here, how come you're not at the hospital?" "I'm OK now. I'm not sick or anything anymore." "You better go back. Policeman gonna' come look for you. I'll get you a taxi, you better go back there Andy. OK?" "Well, give me enough for cigarettes and I'll go back." "Call a taxi," my mom doesn't hesitate and as she gives Frieda that certain "look" that springs Frieda into action! Frieda calls a taxi. When I am in the cab I instruct the cab driver to go down to the store that sells off sale alcohol and let me off. I go into the off sales store and order a half gallon of Apple Jack wine. The lady puts the wine into a bag and sets it on the counter. I pay for the wine and ask the lady, "Can you give me some change for the cigarette machine please?" just as I am asking, out of the corner of my eye I notice a police car pulls up right in front of the store. I go over and bend down behind the cigarette machine trying to hide unaware that my feet and legs are in plain view! I hear a bell signaling that the door has been opened and a cop walks in. He says, "There you are Andrew, I've been looking all over for you Mr. Nieman." I come out from behind the machine and angrily say, "My name's not Andrew." "Oh yes it is, I have your picture right here." He holds up my police picture. "So what do you want with me?" I ask accusingly, "I haven't broken any laws?" "Well, I know you haven't broken any laws however…" "So what law did I break?" "I'm not saying you broke *any* law but apparently…" "Well if I didn't break any law, you can't arrest me." "Well apparently you're still a pretty sick man and I'm not taking you to jail I just want to give you a ride to the hospital." "Well, I'm not sick anymore. I was, but I'm all better now." "Well, not according to the doctor." "Well, since I didn't break the law I don't have to go with you." "OK. Here's the deal. One way or another you are coming with me. I'm going to either take you down to the police station and lock you up or I'll take you back to the hospital. The choice is yours, what do you prefer?" I grumble again about not breaking a law and choose to go back to the hospital. The officer gets my money back from the sales lady for the wine and he lets me keep my cigarettes

After the police officer takes me back to the psyche ward I change back into a hospital gown, lay down on my bed and fall asleep. The next morning a nurse comes into my room and after opening the window curtain she takes my temperature and says, "Quite a little adventure you had last night huh?" "Adventure? What are you talking about?" "We'll talk about it after breakfast." After breakfast I sit in the kitchen and have a cigarette. The same nurse who woke me up earlier comes over and says, "Can we have that talk now?" "OK" "How 'bout we talk in your room?" "OK" I put my cigarette out and we walk to my room. I sit on the chair in my room and the nurse says, "Actually I didn't want to talk to you I want to show you something." "Show me what?" "Follow me," I follow her and we walk into a room that is just down the hall from my room. When we enter the room I notice that the big window, which takes up about three quarters of the wall has a large sheet of plywood bolted over it. Obviously there was no glass behind the piece of plywood. The nurse pointed to the plywood and said, "See what you did?" I got defensive and started to get angry, "See what I did? What do you mean, 'see I did'? I didn't do that!" "Yes you did." "No I DIDN'T!" "Well, it's obvious you don't remember," "Yeah right. Don't remember? Don't blame me I DID NOT DO THIS!" "I'm not going to argue with you Andy, you did do this and clearly you don't remember. I thought seeing this might help you remember." "OK, how was I *supposed to* have done this then?" "Come here," she takes me into the washroom and points to eight screw holes in the wall where there used to be a support bar. The kind of bar that is very sturdy, fat, long and round which people in wheelchairs use to support themselves when they need to go to the washroom. "You pulled that bar off the wall and smashed out the window and took off!" I had not the slightest bit of memory of doing this and was still not convinced that I was to blame. The nurse obviously aware of this simply said, "It's no big deal that you can't remember. The main thing is that you are back safe and sound." With that she walked out and I went back to my room racking my brain but I could not for the life of me remember smashing that window. The only thing I remembered about last night was "coming to" on the side walk and the remainder of the evening since then. I went back into my room and into the washroom and looked at the support bar on the wall. I went over and tried to pull on it. There was absolutely no give to it and there was no way I could possibly move it on my own strength. I laid down on my bed, put my hands behind my head, stared at the ceiling and thought about the whole situation. WHY could I NOT REMEMBER a SINGLE THING about the incident?

While I was thinking, I heard the sound of shuffling feet like someone was moving their feet over gravel on a concrete surface and it was coming from right outside my window! I deliberately stopped breathing and held my breath so I could listen as clearly as I could. I knew there was more than one person and then I heard them whispering, "This is the one right here. He's in here just wait." Then a very clear voice coming from just outside my window said, "I've finally got you now Andy after all these years. I've finally got you! You thought you could get away from me but I've got you now! I've got you exactly where I want you and you are not getting away this time!" Something inside of me tells me that this is the voice of Satan. Don't ask me how I know, I know! I thought the door was going to slam shut at any second so I jumped up and bolted out of the room! I went right to the nurse's desk and told her what I just heard. She said, "Oh, it's just in your head. Those are just imaginary voices they are not really there. Go lay down on your bed on your stomach and I'll be in to give you a shot in about two minutes." I went back to my room and the nurse gave me a needle in my butt. The nurse left and I went over to the window to see if I could see any tracks. There were none. I laid back down on my bed and started to feel a bit better. Then out of nowhere the voice returns! This time the voice was not outside the window but right inside of my head and it said, "Nobody knows that I am here but you. There is no escape. Nobody can hear me but you because you are MINE!" When I went to the nurse this time and told her, the doctor came and they put me in a small padded room with walls there were pink. There was a mattress on the floor with a wool blanket and the door was a solid steel door with a little slot that slid back and forth when someone wanted to look in. As soon as they put me in there I felt like I was being punished and I asked, "How long do I have to be in here?" the only response I received was, "Not long" and the key turned loudly as the door was locked. I turned around and reached for the blanket so I could lay down. When I pulled the blanket back there were three rattle snakes that were under the blanket on the mattress and they were all poised to strike at me. Beside them crawling towards me were four black tarantulas and as I looked around the room the walls started filling up and were crawling with spiders! I turned around and started kicking the door as hard as I possibly could while yelling at the top of my lungs, "Let me out! Let me out!" The little slot in the door opens and then closes. I hear the key turn in the lock and I black out completely.

The next and final time I "come to" I open my eyes just as the nurse walks into the room. When I gather my senses I realize I am lying on a bed in the psyche ward. "Good afternoon Andy. The doctor said he wants to see you as soon as you wake up. How 'bout I take you down there now before he leaves?" "Can I use the washroom first?" "Why of course." I finish using the washroom and she wheels me in a wheelchair down to the doctor's office. The door is open. The nurse gently knocks on the door, "Excuse me Doctor Brown, Mr. Nieman is here he just woke up minutes ago." "OK, come on in," she wheels me into the room places me right in front of the doctor's desk and locks the wheels in place. She asks the doctor, "Would you like me to wait sir?" "No, that won't be necessary just close the door please. Thank you." "You're welcome," she closes the door.

The doctor sits behind his desk directly across from me. He has a file in front of him that he is reading from. Holding a page partially turned back so he can read the next page, he looks over the rim of his glasses and we make eye contact. His eyes scan my eyes for a moment as though he is seeking to draw a conclusion from them. He lets the open page slide from his fingers and he takes off his glasses tossing them onto the open file. He picks up an orange pencil and starts to gently tap the table with it. He takes the pencil, one end in one hand and the other end in the other hand and he leans forward on his elbows and twirls the pencil in front of him. He lets the pencil drop to the table and he looks at me long and serious. He is silent. He purposely lets the silence linger for what feels like a long time. He stares directly at me dead serious. He finally breaks the silence with, "You have no right to be sitting here right now. You should be dead. In fact, I can't believe that I am actually talking to you." I am silent. I have no clue what this man is talking about but I pick up that this is serious. I stay silent. The doctor continues, "You know why you have no right to be sitting here right now Andy?" I clear my throat and sit up straighter in my chair while keeping my eyes locked with his. I softly answer, "Ah, no I don't." "You shouldn't be sitting here because the other night we did everything we could to save your life and when there was nothing left that we could do, I told the nurses, "Let him go, there's nothing left we can do for him. I told them that because your heart was totally out of control. It was beating so fast that you were going in and out of cardiac arrest and no matter what kind of drug we gave you nothing was helping to slow it down! So I wrote you off and told my staff to step back we've done everything, there's nothing else we can do. Now, I'm not a religious man and I don't go to church but if there is *anything* to prayer, if there is anything to prayer, then you owe your life to your mother and to that Pentecostal Preacher who stayed with you and prayed for you all night the other night. Your mom, I'm told, stayed and prayed ALL night and that preacher stayed and prayed for half the night. Your mom would not leave until she knew you would be alright. You've been sleeping for two days." I could not believe what I was hearing. I had no recollection of what had taken place none whatsoever. The doctor continued, "I felt it was important for me to tell you this personally because I knew you would not be able to remember any of what happened the other night. Andy. You need to do something about your alcohol problem." All I had to say was a sheepish, "Oh. OK. The last thing I remember was being let out of the padded room." The doctor let out a long sigh then said. "I have no doubt that's when the beginning of the end started" I didn't feel any emotion I just sat there. I think I had too many drugs in my system to fully grasp the enormity of what this doctor was saying. I had just escaped and/or had been brought back from death!

The doctor went on, "You have a very serious drinking problem Andy and I mean very, very serious. You can't continue on your current path and expect to live past forty. You're how old now?" he checked my birthdate in the file. "You're only thirty one years old son, my goodness you've got a whole life ahead of you! Don't throw it all away in a lousy bottle!" I had nothing to say as I sat there with my head down. Both he and I heard a couple of hunger growls escape from my stomach which prompted him to say, "I'm sure you must be starving after all that sleeping and all you've been through so I'll let you go get some food in your stomach. I'll have the nurse come and get you any questions?" "No." "Just need some food huh?" I nodded, "Yes." He continued, "I am very serious and very concerned about your drinking. Please get some help! You need some help Andy! Do you understand?" "Yes. Yes I do." "Will you?" I fall silent. It seems like an eternity passes. The truth is, I don't know where to get help. My moment of hesitation in answering seems to say it all and he continues with, "Have you tried AA?" I hang my head and nod, "Yes." "Have you really given AA your best Andy? The program has helped millions?" I find no need to answer him so I stare silently at the floor. He senses that I am uncomfortable and he breaks the silence with, "OK. You need some food. I'll call the nurse."

I was never bothered again by another demonic spirit after the night my mom and the Preacher prayed for me. They kept me in the psyche ward for three more days after the doctor talked to me just to make sure everything was OK and then they let me out. For the first time in my life I started attending church on a somewhat regular basis after I left the psyche ward. I didn't read the Bible like I know I should have and I didn't keep going to church like I know I should have in fact I was not as serious about God as I knew I should have been. I would go to church and then smoke Pot after Service and justify it by saying to myself and to my sister Frieda that, "Well, at least I'm not drinking."

I stayed sober for three months after leaving the psyche ward and then returned to drinking on skid row. I couldn't quit the alcohol yet, because I was still so messed up inside. It would take me another nine years to finally be delivered from alcohol. When I returned to skid row after Chilliwack, I took to my old habits again. I returned to my former lifestyle and of course started hanging out with my old gang of friends from the Yukon. At one of our drinking binges down at the beach at English Bay, my friend Jackie just couldn't pass up the opportunity and said, "So Nieman we heard you were in the looney bin. We were gonna' come and visit you, but figured you'd get too embarrassed when we saw you playing in a sandbox with a big diaper on pushing around one of those toy dump trucks with a cigarette butt sticking out the side of your mouth and a three-day stubble of hair on your chin. Can you forgive us for that or what?" Every one of us cracked up at Jackie's wry sense of humor to which I feebly replied, "That's OK, I'm not going to visit you either when it's your turn."

That reminds me of another time that Jackie blessed us with a mastery of his unbridled sense of humor. Remember I told you a number of chapters ago about Angel this hooker that took a liking to me when I first got hooked on heroin when I was seventeen in Vancouver? Angel was a heroin addict and heroin addicts have a need and a craving for sugar and anything sweet that contains sugar. Because Angel was a heroin addict and had been one for many, many years she had some of the most decayed teeth I have ever seen on anyone. I don't mean to be offensive, but it is the truth. They were even worse than mine! And mine were bad! Angel really liked me and our relationship was strictly plutonic yet Jackie could never believe it was that type of relationship. Anyway, one day while we were sitting on the beach at English Bay, drinking a half gallon of Applejack wine, there must've been about seven of us, Jackie brought up the subject of Angel. Jackie was one of my closest friends throughout our whole lives and he was clearly the bluntest person in our crowd and no doubt on the face of the earth! So anyway, we are all sitting around drinking and Jackie mentioned something about my teeth because I was complaining about a tooth ache and somehow he started commenting on Angel's teeth. He called them, "Burnt matchsticks." He mentioned her teeth, or "matchsticks", as he so matter-of-factly called them now. He commented on our relationship, and I quickly reinforced to him that our relationship was strictly plutonic. "I've never gone to bed with her not once." I did my best to show him that I was sincere. To which he replied, "Yeah right! Like she just gives you all this money just to walk her to her favorite corner what cabbage truck do you think we just fell out of?" I knew it was no use to try and match wits with Jackie, especially when he's feeling the Applejack wine. Jackie could be, and was, one of the funniest people I have ever known in my entire life! And today was no exception. He was on a roll and he knew he had an audience, so he piped up with, "So Nieman, aren't you afraid one of these times when you two are kissing and slobbering all over each other, that she'll stick you with one of those burnt matchsticks, cut your lip and give you blood poisoning? Come to think of it, you've got a few matchsticks of your own hey! How do you two kiss anyway? Aren't you afraid you'll bust a couple of sticks? Or aren't you scared your matchsticks will get stuck together and you'll both have to walk down the street with your faces stuck together on your way to the dentist's office so he can dislodge you?" With that, we all burst into laughter myself included. Jackie's humor was so cutting-edge and so funny, that even the person he was insulting couldn't help but laugh, (most of the time). And when Jackie was on a roll, no one was safe from his sharp wit and dead-bolt words. We all knew he could back those words up, since he was one of the toughest and best fighters any of us knew. My friend Sonny was killing himself laughing as Jackie was ribbing me, when Jackie turned to him and said, "You shouldn't laugh Sonny. Every time I turn around you and Christine are kissing up a storm one minute and the next minute you want to fight every guy in town who looks at her. I wouldn't laugh at Nieman's girlfriend if I were you matchsticks or no matchsticks! At least Nieman's not jealous. He shares his matchsticks with any one." To which Sonny shot back. "Yeah Jackie, at least Nieman and I have a girlfriend, where's yours? If you'd stop stealing from them all the time, maybe one would stick around!" And we all cracked up at that one. It wasn't very often anybody put "one over" on Jackie, so when anyone did, we all took special plea-sure in the laughter. Even Jackie had to laugh at that one.

For the next nine years after leaving Chilliwack I continued drinking, drug-ging and going in and out of jail. Throughout those years I stayed at my mom's place off and on and she would pray for me and tell me that I had to get ready because Jesus was going to return and if I was not ready I would not make heaven my home. She had all kinds of little church tracts that she would bring home and would leave them lying around the house. There is one particular tract that stands out in my mind and in my heart just as clear as though I read it last night. In that particular tract, it shows a man who is a typical regular "Joe". He is married, has two kids, a house, drinks socially, parties, gambles and goes to work every day. One day he and one of his co-workers are on their way to a bar to have a drink after work and they walk by a Christian who is handing out tracts and the Christian asks him, "Would you like to know more about Jesus sir?" his response is, "Aww, don't bother me with that garbage. I don't believe in any of that crap!" and he keeps on walking. Once inside the bar he makes reference to the Christian who they can see outside the window and tells his friend, "The nerve of these idiots trying to feed this nonsense about life after death and Judgment Day, it makes me sick. Once you're dead, you're dead and that's it! There is no Judgment Day or life after death. When you're in your grave that's where you're going to stay… IN YOUR GRAVE end of story!" So a few years pass and the man dies. The tract then shows a side view of the man laying six feet under the ground in his coffin. All of a sudden there is a voice from heaven that commands him to, "Come forth!" The spirit of the man sits up in his coffin and says, "Hey stop! What's going on here! This can't be happening I'M DEAD!" And he starts to rise in spirit-form from his grave and he yells out, "Hey put me back! I'm dead! This is not supposed to happen! Stop!" The man then stands before God and God shows him a review of his life on earth and reminded him of all the times God tried to get his attention through different Christian followers and each time the guy made fun of those Christians who tried to reach out and talk to him. He remembered how he treated those Christian people so badly and told them, "Aww, don't bother me with that garbage. I don't believe in any of that crap!" And the tract ends with the man begging for a second chance and God tells him, **48 But all who reject me and my message will be judged on the day of judgment by the truth I have spoken. John 12:48.**

CHAPTER SIXTEEN

A PROPHECY WITH MY NAME ON IT

"MADE ME FREE"

I don't see what You see in me, yet what You see I long to be,
You threw away the prison key, the day You set me free,
No more lonely chains on me, now I'll be all that I can be,
Your love O Lord is all I need

No mountain high, nor valley low, You're there to guide wherever I go,
I know I'll never turn from You, You treat me great with love so true,
Now I know You're really real, You made me happy, You made me free!

A. Nieman

I was released from Whitehorse Correctional Centre on April 8, 1991 the day my mom passed away. April 8th is also the birthday of one my mom's favorite granddaughters Stacey Marie Asp (RIP). That very morning when I was released from jail, I heard that mom was still in the hospital but did not realize it was so serious. Due to my dysfunctional state of emotions immediately upon my release from jail that morning I went straight to the bar and bought a couple of cases of beer and some cigarettes and went to drink it at a friend's place. I was not quite drunk yet when the phone call came to my friend's place that my mom had just died at the hospital and that I needed to go and be with the family at the hospital! I was such an alcoholic and so messed in my dysfunctional thinking at the time that rather than cry for my mom's passing, I got mad because going to the hospital meant I would be missing out on my share of the alcohol! That, dear reader, is a very shameful state and hard for me to admit to and write about even after all these years. Later that evening our family gathered at my mom's place. This is the same place where I lived with my mom off and on. As the evening wore on, I was sobering up very quickly and I decided to step out into the back yard for a cigarette. The second I stepped out into the back yard I was hit like a freight train by a flood of memories! Everything and I mean EVERYTHING that my mom spoke to me about God flooded every inch of my brain, grabbed me completely by my heart and my ears were echoing with mom's voice just AS PLAIN AS DAY and I remembered every single word she said to me, "Jesus is coming back soon and most of the world doesn't believe it and you need to be ready Andy. You have a little angel on your right shoulder and a little devil on your left shoulder and you've been listening more to that little devil and not the angel. Everyone, everyone, doesn't matter what they believe EVERYONE is going to stand before God on Judgment Day. You think God doesn't see what you're doing. . .he sees everything! The day Jesus returns in the sky every eye will see Him and lots of people who did not believe and follow Him will know that He is real, but it will be too late. You hear me Andy? You have to be ready!" I have never had such an experience before or after as having the words of my mom speak so clearly to me as they did on the day that she died! Everything she spoke to me through the years about Jesus came flooding over me in such an overwhelming way! The impact of her words hit me like a hundred pound sludge hammer! After her funeral, I got into trouble again with the law and there was a warrant out for my arrest because I failed to show up in court. I decided to leave Whitehorse and go to Vancouver. Before I left, my sister Kim was concerned for me and said, "Why don't you stay here Andy and just deal with the charges, you don't have to go down there. You might not come back this time. You know how the drugs are down there." "I need to go down Kim. That's where I feel closer to Jesus and I want to find Him. I won't find Him here. There's too much drinking here and with all my alcoholic friends I can't stop. I have to go. I want to be closer to God." I got on the Greyhound bus and left for Vancouver.

When I stepped off the Greyhound bus in Vancouver it was in October 1991 and at 5:00 am there was a light drizzle of rain falling. As soon as I heard the sounds of rushing traffic, a police siren and caught the smell of rubber tires, gasoline, the ocean air and smog, I felt like I had come home. I felt a sense of relief come over me and a hint of freedom teased my soul. I didn't have to look over my shoulder for the police anymore and nobody knew my name. I could go here and I could go there and be just another unknown face in the crowd and it wouldn't make any difference to anyone. I felt good. I put my small bag of clothes in a locker at the bus depot and started walking towards the skid row area of Hastings St. and Main. I stopped at the nearest restaurant that was open and had breakfast. I had plenty of time to kill until the welfare office opened so I just sat there absorbing my new surroundings and enjoyed the realization that I was actually back in Vancouver again.

It was about 8:15 am when I started walking towards the welfare office on Main and Water St. As I walked past the White Spot restaurant on Hastings St. my mind immediately went back to the last time I was in that restaurant because the last time I was in there my mom was with me. The year was 1986 and I was living on skid row then and my mom had just come down to Vancouver from Whitehorse to attend a Revival meeting where someone with the last name of Shambauch was preaching. I don't know how my mom and Frieda found me on skid row but they did! I was very hung over when I ran into them. I was trying to get some money from my mom so I could get a drink into me to cure my hang over. She asked me to go to breakfast with her first and then she said, "I might give you twenty dollars." Well as soon as I heard the 'twenty dollars' I would have gone to Timbuktu with her! So she says, "We'll go down to the White Spot they have a good breakfast there." "OK, let's go then." "Here you carry this," and she hands me one her bags. She was always carrying a couple of bags because she had so many grandchildren and she always made sure she bought something for EACH of them.

When we got to the White Spot Harry Hunt was sitting there. I had heard about Harry. Harry Hunt was a Charismatic Pentecostal preacher who held a lot of great Revival Meetings throughout the Yukon starting in the early seventies. He had quite a miracle ministry and many, many people were delivered from alcohol and many people had experienced healings through his faith. My mom first became a believer because of Harry Hunt's ministry in the Yukon and it was while attending his meetings in the Old Village in Whitehorse that she was delivered from alcohol and started seeking after Jesus. I had heard a lot about Harry Hunt but had never met him before until that day in the White Spot. The first thing I noticed was his constant amazing smile and the bright sparkling twinkle he had in his eye. It was like he could never stop smiling and it was not a "put-on" smile he was genuine. The first thing he said when he seen my mom was, "Oh Sister Nieman, well Praise God, it's so good to see you Hallelujah!" and they shook hands. Harry, all the while with that big glowing smile on his face, after he shook my mom's hand said, "Hi Frieda," then he turned to me and put his hand out, "Hello young man my name is Harry, Harry Hunt." My mom spoke, "That's Andy my youngest son." "Oh so you're Andy. Praise God! What a pleasure to meet you. It's so nice to meet you. Come on you guys sit down, sit down here, it's so good to see all of you!" I was nervous and uncomfortable and sick. The last thing I wanted to do was sit down with a couple of Christians knowing I would never get a drink of alcohol here. So we sit down and the waitress comes to our table and asks, "Would you like anything to drink?" I order an orange juice. I am very restless and wish mom would just give me some money SO I CAN GO CURE MY HANGOVER!

Then out of the blue Harry Hunt turns to my mom and says, "Jesus has His hand on your boy here." "What boy? Don't call me a 'boy'!" I think to myself. Then he continues, "He's going to be a preacher man and he's going to preach to multitudes. Many gonna' be saved because of how God's gonna' use him. Hallelujah!" I'm thinking and saying to myself as he speaks, "Yeah right! You just want my mom to buy you breakfast that's why you're telling her all this. ME a preacher? Give it up Dude!" Then Harry continues, "He's gonna' be OK you don't have to worry about him no more Sister Nieman, he's in Jesus' hand." I am getting angry now because I feel like he's conning my mom but I don't say anything because I know my mom respects this man and respects him a lot. The waitress returns with our drinks and asks, "Are you ready to order now?" My mom looks at me and it is clear in her eyes that hearing what Harry just said about me has made her very happy. I give her a mean look that says, "Can I have some money now I need to go!" my mom knows what my look says and she asks me, "You gonna' have something to eat first?" I answer her with, "No, that's OK can I just get that twenty?" She gives me twenty dollars and I am just about to rush out of the restaurant when my mom grabs my arm and says to me, "Just a minute," she turns to Harry and asks, "Brother Harry can you please pray for Andy before he goes?" I get mad in my heart but again I don't say a word. I have the money so I have no problem letting him pray for me. Harry says, "Praise God, I believe that's why God brought us together today." And he prays for me. I thank him for praying for me and I tell my mom, "Thank you for the money. I'll call you. See you Frieda." I leave and head straight for the liquor store. Eight years after that day, I met Harry Hunt soon after I decided to follow Jesus completely and he was one of the very first people I ran into after I started following the Lord. I will tell you about that later.

So here I am walking past the White Spot processing the memories that have just been triggered and I run into George Robinson (RIP). George was in Whitehorse for many years married to a Yukon woman and now he was on his own living on "the skidders" as he liked to call skid row. George was a very, very good friend to all of us Yukoners. He was like a father to those of us living on the street. Some even called him, "Grampa George". He would let anybody sleep at his place. If he could help it, he MADE SURE nobody was stuck for a place to stay. George was a true survivor on skid row who "knew-the-ropes" inside out. Most of us called him, "Rubbyskins". George would always without fail, do the word puzzle in the Vancouver Province where you had to unscramble the letters to form four different words and then find the word that was formed at the end. I liked to do that puzzle too but George always beat me to it and already knew all the answers. I had to remind him to NOT tell me the answers when I got a newspaper where the puzzle wasn't done yet. He was very smart. I ask George, "Have you seen Gary?" meaning my best friend Gary Dawson. "You just get in?" "Yeah about five this morning." "I saw Gary about half an hour ago he was on his way to the Multi-Use Center to get something to eat. You'll probably catch him over there." "OK Thanks. What are you up to?" "Not much just going down to the soup line." "OK. We'll track you down later I'm going to see if I can get a welfare check." "Should be no problem." "We'll stop by your place later." "I'll be at the Carnegie." The Carnegie is a public library that is also a drop-in, multipurpose facility right in the heart of skid row situated at the corner of Main St. and Hastings St. Carnegie has free services for those who are on social assistance and can't afford things like English as a second language, upgrading one's education, reading materials, phone calls and it is also a place to receive mail or messages if you don't have a fixed address. I walk through the heart of skid row heading to the Multi-Use Center commonly called the "the forty-four". I am feeling right at home back on the beat.

Life on skid row is all about alcohol, drugs and broken lives. If you find your-self ending up down here and becoming a member of this lifestyle, the chances of you getting out and living an overcoming life is slim and next to none. Every day, people here live on the brink of death. With each drink of alcohol there is a dance with death that takes place. Every time a snort or a poke of the needle is taken, the dance with death continues. You just never know when that next shot will be your last. Skid Row was home for me. I felt like it was where I belonged. I was in a world of outcasts, misfits, criminals, addicts, drunkards, the downtrod-den, the homeless, prostitutes and everybody in between to whom life had dealt a harsh blow. Down here everybody who wasn't a cop was accepted. Nothing surprised the people down here and it was "anything goes". The only thing we feared was letting our defense down and allowing someone to get a glimpse of the shame that was in our hearts should our eyes give us away. I felt this could only happen when I was sober so I stayed high as often as I could and for as long as I could.

I ran into Gary at the Multi-Use Center. The Multi-Use Center was a facility similar to the Carnegie. It was a place where you could shower and have your laundry done for free. You could also eat there for a real cheap price. Gary went with me to the welfare office. I told the welfare that I just arrived and needed a place to live. They told me to go and ask for a room and bring the address back to them and they would make out a check to that address. It was a common practice in those days to sell your rent check for half price if you could find a landlord to buy it. It was not hard to find such a landlord in those days. I told Gary, "I want to sell my rent check. If I do can I stay at your place?" "Sure if you give me half the check?" Gary was just kidding and we both had a good laugh at that one. "Good one Gary," I replied. Then I asked him, "Where you staying at?" "I got a five star hotel it has everything you can think of!" "Yeah right, especially cockroaches huh?" "Cockroaches and mice are free. They're thrown in for good measure just in case you get hungry." We both cracked up laughing. I sure loved Gary he was the best friend I could possibly have in them days. "I'm staying at the Wonder Rooms. Ya' know why they call it the Wonder Rooms?" I knew there was a punch line coming, "No why?" "Because it's a wonder anyone can live there with all the cockroaches and mice!" "Thanks Gary, that's just what I needed to hear," I said as we both made our way to the welfare office. I found a place in Chinatown where the landlord agreed to buy my rent check for half the price. This meant I would not have a place to stay and would have to depend on my friends especially Gary and George for a place to live. I picked up two welfare checks that afternoon one for rent and one for food the total amount of the checks was $359.00.

After I cashed my food check and sold my rent check I bought a quarter ounce of "Pot" (marijuana) and a half gallon of Bounty wine. Gary said, "Let's go see if Dale the Whale is home." "Who?" "Dale the Whale," Gary repeated. "Dale Dawson," "Oh, OK." 'Dale the Whale' was the nickname for Dale Dawson, Gary's first cousin. Gary also called him "Dayo." I think Dayo got his nickname from Gary's dad Art, who used to sing that song, "Daylight Come And I Want

To Go Home", whenever Art was drinking. When Art would start singing that song his wife May would join right in. Some of you will know that song, the one that goes "Dayo! Daaayo! Daylight come and I wanna go home." Dale was a very good friend of mine and we spent a lot of time together as part of the same crew from the Yukon. Others who hung out in our Yukon crew on the skidders in those days included: Johnny and Kirk from Carcross, "Wally Mac", George and Albert from Dawson City, Gary's brothers Lance Dawson (RIP), Artie Dawson (RIP) and Willy Dawson (RIP), Mike and Steven (RIP) from Mayo, Jackie (RIP), Sonny (RIP), Mickey, "Chili", Cecil and many others.

Dale was always very good to me and helped me many, many times when I was stuck for a place to stay. He would get up in the middle of the night and throw his front-door key down to me and he would let me sleep on his floor. He never failed to let me in. If he wasn't home and I couldn't get into anyone else's place I would have to sleep either under the bridge called the Georgia viaduct, in a doorway, a park bench, a hotel bathtub or at one of the shelters. This was a year-round routine for me because I always sold my rent check for alcohol or drugs. I did not like to sleep at the shelters because it reminded me of being at the residential school or in jail. One of the best places to stay was at the Catholic Charities Hostel because it was clean and they gave you food vouchers each morning before you left. The food vouchers were in the form of what looked like play money and came in a check-book style where you could tear along the perforated line and pay the amount owed. Each little "check-book" contained seven dollars and fifty cents worth of food vouchers. Most of the restaurants on skid row accepted them.

**After selling my rent cheque this is where I
slept under the Georgia Viaduct**

This is my home today. Sure beats sleeping under the bridge!

Our kitchen. No line-up here!

From the period of 1991 — 1994 skid row was my universe. When I arrived there in '91 just after my mom passed, my drinking and drugging continued to spiral me downward. I tried to drink the pain out of my heart. I tried to drug the pain out of my heart and no matter how hard I tried I could never outrun the hurt or heal the deep-rooted scars of my abusive childhood. Most of us

196

from the Yukon were using needles then and the popular drug of choice was called "T's and R's". T's and R's are street names for a mixture of the prescription drugs Talwin (pentazocine) and Ritalin (methylphenidate). Which when injected together, Talwin, a painkiller, and Ritalin, a stimulant, produces a "high" similar to the effect of heroin mixed with cocaine. Because of this similarity and their low cost when obtained legally, T's and R's have been called, "poor man's heroin". I hated T's and R's because they always without fail made me sick to my stomach and I always vomited each and every time I got high on them. Yet, I would still push that needle in my arm because the bottom line was; vomiting or not it helped me to forget the misery of my life for at least a little while longer.

I have an addictive personality and it didn't matter back then what type of drug you put in front of me if it could get me high I was willing to give it a try. Back then between 1991 — 1994 I was high on one type of drug or another and the only time I sobered up or stopped drugging was when I wound up in jail. My drug of choice was alcohol. I did not think it possible for my life or my addictions to be able to go down any farther than I was, that is… until I ran into COCAINE.

I know it sounds like an age old cliché and most people who don't know, think it's a tactic to scare people away from trying it, but once I got my first taste of cocaine at the end of that syringe… I fell in love with it IMMEDIATELY! No two ways about it! This was THE HIGH to beat ALL highs! No question about it! The search for relief was over! Once I had drained all the cocaine contents into my blood stream and pulled that syringe out of my arm I was on cloud ten! I found what I was looking for! I finally found INSTANT and I mean INSTANT relief and an instant escape from myself and reality! When I pulled the syringe out of my arm immediately the drug made me feel like I was in another world where everything, I'm telling you EVERYTHING became BRIGHTER! The lights were brighter, the people were brighter, the environment was brighter, the streets were brighter and to top it all off my mind was as sharp as the proverbial tack! I could speak a mile-a-minute! I was floating in the Twilight Zone! I was the Master of the Universe! I was "Joe Cool" "JayZee" "Mick Jagger" "Valentino" and the "King of Rock N' Roll" all rolled into one and ALL AT ONCE BABY! WHAT? Ya wanna' talk with ME, the King of the Universe? Let's get it on BABY! I can TALK WITH THE BEST! My shyness went away. My rotten teeth went away. I wasn't an alcoholic anymore are you kiddin' me!? I'm the King of my universe I CAN DO ANYTHING!

Well, sorry to burst your balloon buddy and sorry to have to hit the "reality button" on you but it all lasted the grand sum and total of a whole fifteen minutes! And before you know it my rotten teeth were back, my confidence grew wings and flew out the window as shyness took over its spot and reality slapped me on the back and showed me his ugly face again. HEY! WHAT AM I DOIN' BACK HERE? GET ME OUTTA HERE! I DON'T NEED THIS DREARINESS! I WANT MORE! I NEED MORE! GIMME, GIMME, GIMME! I would spend the next three years day in and day out, endless days upon endless nights seeking to feel, seeking to just get a small taste of that amazing feeling just one more time, but it would never come to be. Nothing even came close to resembling that very first time I felt like the King of my universe.

I did everything short of selling my body to get money so I could get more "coke" so I could try with all my heart and try with all my soul to feel what I felt on that very first time I pushed cocaine down the walls of that syringe and into the mainline of my blood stream. Every time I chased that "high" it left me feeling cold in my soul and feeling "used". It left me feeling like a fool yet I COULDN'T STOP the chase. I HAD TO HAVE MORE. The drug DROVE me. It RULED me. It CONSUMED me. It PUSHED me to my physical, emotional and suicidal limits. It drove me to the place where I wanted the drug more than alcohol (now that's a story in itself), I wanted cocaine more than food, more than sleep, more than sex, more than money, more than any of my friends. When I was simply a practicing alcoholic at least my friends could trust me in their homes and with money and with other important things. Once the "coke" took over, it stripped me of every fiber of decency and of any shred of morality I had left. Even to the point where I lied, cheated and stole even from my closest friends. It got to the point where some of my friends wouldn't even allow me into their homes because they knew I would steal from them. I am sad to say that I have taken some of my friends most important sentimental valuables and sold them. That is the "grip" cocaine can have on a person.

Every dollar I made went to "coke", every dime and every penny. That was the "grip" it had on me. And any chance I got, I would increase the amount I put into my veins until I pushed even that to the limit. I can tell you personally and with all sincerity that I know it was God and God alone that brought me back from the brink of overdosing on cocaine many different times. There are three separate and distinct occasions where I can tell you in all sincerity that I was brought back from a serious overdose on "coke" simply because I called out the name of Jesus at the very last second of consciousness. I'll describe one of those times for you. It was on what we call "Welfare Wednesday" which is the last Wednesday of each month. That is the day welfare checks are distributed. I had just cashed my welfare check and bought two "quarters" (a quarter is a quarter of a gram), of cocaine from one of the "Bikers" at a local biker bar. Back in those days and no doubt still today, cocaine was very, very potent and especially the "coke" you got from the Bikers. I always made sure I bought my drugs off the same people once I found they were a reliable source.

A bunch of my Yukon friends were sitting and drinking in one of the bars and I asked a friend of mine John, "Can I use your room to do a "fix"? (shoot up drugs with a syringe). "Sure," he said digging in his pocket for his key. John had a great sense of humor and said, "Don't make a mess I just hired a maid and it's all spotless in there," "Yeah right!" I smiled at him. I got his key bought a six-pack of beer and went up to his room by myself. The room was the room of a typical skid row alcoholic. It was a mess. Empty wine bottles littered the room and the overflowing ash tray was an over turned metal lid from a tobacco can that had cigarette butts that had been rolled and re-rolled time and time again until the tobacco resembled black ashes. I brushed away some of the ashes on the table as a couple of cockroaches scurried for cover and cleared a spot big enough to set my quarter gram down. I took out my syringe and was just going to do half of one of the quarters but then I thought, "Ah, I'll do the whole thing," I had no idea how potent the drug was. I filled the syringe with the cocaine, pushed it into my vein and injected all of it. About two seconds after I injected the drug it started to hit me. As soon as I took the needle out of my arm at that very second I KNEW I had taken TOO MUCH!

I dropped the needle to the floor. There was a very loud screamimg high-pitched ringing that immediately assaulted my ears and completely drowned out any other sound. The only thing I can compare the ringing to would be if you had a set of headphones on and there was the sound of a police car's siren you were listening to and someone accidently cranked the volume up! I couldn't hear a thing except the loud ringing and it wouldn't stop! My heart started pounding faster and faster! Sweat started pouring like buckets out of my body and especially my face and I began losing my breath! For some reason I could NOT GET ANY AIR into my lungs! I tried and tried to force air into my lungs but I couldn't! I couldn't BREATH! I was getting dizzy and felt like I was going to fall over. I reached for the bed post to steady myself. I couldn't get no air in my lungs and I felt like I was going into cardiac arrest! My body started shaking uncontrollably. I was blacking out and as I felt myself starting to fall over in my mind I said, "HELP ME JESUS!" That's all I could do was THINK those words, "HELP ME JESUS!" and amazingly, as wild as it may sound, INSTANTLY, right instantly, I was able to breath! The ringing stopped and I clutched the bed post leaning over as AIR, WONDERFUL BEAUTIFUL AIR, poured into my lungs and my heart beat returned to normal. I sat down. I found a dirty old t-shirt and wiped the sweat from my face. I looked at the bloody syringe that I had dropped on the floor. This was the first time I had come so close to death in a cocaine overdose. In a fatal cocaine overdose death happens through cardiac arrest (a heart attack). In those days, dealers would "cut" (mix and add), to their cocaine different things like: Baking Soda, Icing Sugar or even Crystal Meth and other things to increase the amount or the effect of the drug. If you have a heart problem or are allergic to any of these ingredients the result could be fatal the very first time the drug is used.

I sat there staring at that bloody syringe thinking about what had just hap-pened and how close I had come to leaving this world for good. All I keep thinking to myself as the seriousness of what just happened caused me to stop and say in my heart, "Thank you Jesus! Thank you Jesus!" A person who is not an addict would normally think, "Well that experience should be enough to cause him to quit, I mean he almost died!" Yet I was in bondage to this drug and even a serious overdose like I had just experienced was not enough to make me stop. Such is the power of a cocaine addiction. I opened one of the beers and guzzled the whole bottle down non-stop. I put the other quarter of "coke" back into the change pocket of my jeans and decided I would give it a rest for a bit. I grabbed another beer and quickly guzzled it down. I went back down into the bar to join my friends. Sitting there with my friends I warn them, "Whoa, those Bikers have some good 'blow" (slang for cocaine), over at the Cobalt be careful how much you take. I just about did "The Chicken". Doing "The Chicken" is slang for a cocaine overdose. I experienced two more cocaine overdoses after that first one and as hard as it is to believe, the other two overdoses were a carbon copy almost to the word. The EXACT same thing happened and each time, it was only in my thinking that I was able to ask Jesus to help me as I was 'going under" and I am so very Thankful that He heard and helped me everytime.

As a result of my addiction to cocaine I lived off the avails of crime and without fail I inevitably always wound up in jail. The last time I did time was in 1993. I got sentenced to six months. They had built a new Remand Center on Main St. and that is where I landed after I was picked up for breaking into a car and stealing the tape deck. While I was there in remand as usual I liked to read to pass the time. I picked up a book that was about a cocaine addict who had given his life to Jesus and was traveling around in a van to spread the word of truth. As I was reading, I saw so much of myself in his story that it touched me deep in my heart. I began to cry. And I was both surprised and relieved at my tears. Surprised because I NEVER CRY when I am sober! And I am relieved because I am glad that I am in a cell by myself so no one else can SEE ME CRY! I take a fast glance out the cell door to see if the inmate across the way can see me. Nope. I quickly wipe away the tears and compose myself. Enough of that crying stuff. I finish the book and think to myself, "I wonder if that is a true story or not?"

The next day I am on the prison bus headed to Oakalla. At Oakalla after I shower and get my bedding they put me on tier 4 on four right twenty. I am back in all-too-familiar surroundings. The jail is a usual bustle of activity as a prisoner wanting to use the phone yells out, "Guard up! Tier five!" Another prisoner is yelling at a buddy to, "Send me some tobacco," while someone else asks, "Are you going out to yard this afternoon?" As I walk up the stairs with my bedding every eye that can see me is straining to look through the screen and the bars to see if they recognize who is coming in. With a loud "Clang!" the guard opens the main lock and pulls a lever that will only open my cell which is four right twenty the last cell on the right side of the tier. I walk down the narrow walkway past every cell without looking into any of the cells. When I get in front of my cell, the door which is made strictly of iron bars is still not open. The guard then cranks my cell door open by turning a wheel at the main control. I step into the cell. He then cranks the wheel again and the door closes behind me. The heavy iron gate clangs shut behind me and I sit down on my bunk. I get up and make my bed then I lie down and stare at the gray concrete wall. I look at the steel table welded to the steel bolts embedded in concrete. There is an iron plate with holes drilled into it that is welded into the wall. It is a radio. There are no controls for the radio except for a tiny black button that can be pushed to turn it on and pushed again to turn it off. I push it to turn it on. I can barely hear the strains of Brian Adams singing, "It Cuts Like A Knife." The song reminds me of where I was and what I was doing the last time I heard it play. It brings me a wave of melancholy. I think again about my life. Where is it going. . . besides nowhere? Coming to jail like this always caused me to contemplate and take inventory of myself and my life. I couldn't seem to get away from it. It was like a still small voice would whisper to me in my soul and say, "Time to take inventory Andy." Was I really an evil person incapable of change? Many, many times I found my mind traveling down that road of personal history. Memories of my harsh childhood. Memories of the physical, sexual, emotional, verbal and mental abuse. If only it had been different. If it had been different, how would things be now?

I do my best to sleep but I find I am wide awake at 3:00 am. I have no choice but to listen to the snoring of the other prisoners. All the lights are out except for that dim nightlight at the end, middle and front of the tier that never seems to burn out and never burns any brighter. In the distance, the far distance, is the distinctive faint sound of a train whistle. It is hard to hear but I find if I hold my breath long enough I could hear the ever so faint clickety-clack, clickety-clack of the railway tracks. I think to myself, "How ironic. Just like in the movies, the proverbial convict thinking about lost freedom as he hears the lonely whistle of a passing train." Something Johnny Cash and retired convicts might write about. Two days later I learn that I will be doing my time at a place that has a reputation as a "soft" jail and it is where they send most alcoholics, Allouette River Unit (ARU). When I first get there they put me in a place that is nice and clean and modern which is a far, far cry from Oakalla. On my first night there the strangest thing happens. Somehow, I feel very blessed to be where I am. I feel like I have been rescued. The food is good. They treat you with respect here. The place is nice and clean and I look out the window at the nice freshly mowed lawn. In my cell there is a wooden desk with a pen and a pad of paper and a small lamp. The strange thing that happens (strange to me then but of course not now), is this; I feel like God Himself is right there in the cell with me and HE is the One making me think about how fortunate I am and HE is the One Who brought me to ARU and HE is now reminding me that HE is BEHIND ALL of what is happening to me in terms of keeping me safe. I start to cry and I CAN'T HOLD the tears back! I don't say a word. Not one word. But in my heart and in my thoughts I tell God that I am starting to understand that You are real and that You are with me and I Thank You.

A week later they place me in the dorms with the rest of the prisoners and for the first time in my life all I want to read is a Christian book. The selection is quite limited but I find a couple of Christian paperback novels. I feel guilty reading the Christian material and hide it every time someone comes around. I started attending church services and would sit way in the back. During one Sunday Service there was a man who got up with a guitar and started to tell his testimony and I remember him saying, "Living for Jesus is better than any cocaine or heroin trip I have ever been on!" I thought to myself, "Yeah right! What could possibly be better than getting high on cocaine or heroin? Give me a break buddy!" Then he began to sing and play his guitar and secretly in my heart I wanted to be just like him. I wanted to be like that. To be clean and sober singing and playing the guitar for Jesus and talking about how great life is!

Trouble was, I couldn't play the guitar and I certainly couldn't carry a tune like he could and as for Jesus, well Jesus was just a word to me then.

I went to just about every church service in the four months I was at ARU and I was very close to getting serious with God but not serious enough. I told the people who put on the church at the jail that, "I was SERIOUS ABOUT JESUS!" and "Yes, I want a Bible Study when I get out!" and "Yes, I will stay in touch with you!" but "No, I do not want anybody to pick me up on my release date." When I got out I never contacted any of them. And on my very first day out I returned to sticking a needle full of cocaine back into my arm. Only this time I felt very convicted (felt guilty) even BEFORE I decided to buy the cocaine and I almost stopped because of the conviction I was feeling as I walked down to see the dealer. But just the conviction wasn't enough and I kept going and wound up getting high and feeling very guilty about it afterward.

After getting out of ARU I found myself in one of the most despicable places in my heart that I had ever come to. I had been out of jail (ARU) for just over three days. I had gotten a welfare check on my first day out and spent it all in one night buying drinks and doing "Speedballs." A "speedball" is where you mix heroin and cocaine together in the same needle and shoot it up. I was feeling very lost inside. I was hung-over, broke, hungry and lonely. I didn't know what to do with myself. I didn't want to drink anymore and yet I didn't like how I felt when I was sober. I just wanted TO BELONG SOMEWHERE. Where could I go where I could feel like I belonged and was accepted for who I was? Where could I go where no one would judge me or look down on me in spite of my past and my failures? Where could I go where I could feel respected without having to pretend to be someone or something I wasn't? The reality hit me. The only place I could get all of that was where I had just come from, jail.

I never ever thought it possible, but I found that I actually wanted to be back in there (jail). It not only shocked me, but it made me feel very strange that I would even think like that! I had NEVER THOUGHT LIKE THAT before! It's a hard feeling to explain. It was a cross between feeling lonesome and ashamed, to feeling angry at someone or something, yet I wasn't sure of what or who I should be angry at. I had heard other guys talk about it while I was doing time and had listened to them in disgust, as they spoke about wanting to COME BACK INTO JAIL after they were out for a bit. I remember thinking at the time when I heard them talk about it, "What a bunch of losers! You guys are nobodies! How could you even think such a stupid thing? Maybe YOU need the system to take care of you, but NOT ME! How could anybody in their right mind want to come back to this dump?" And now, here I was. I had become what I had despised in them. I was glad I never spoke of it to no one. I was glad no one, except you who are reading this now, ever really knew or found out that I had those thoughts and feelings coursing through my mind and heart.

As all of this was going on inside of me Gary and I were standing on the sidewalk, waiting for the light to change on Main and Hastings St. The "city bucket" I told you about earlier sits on the corner of Main and Hastings St. Others know it as the courthouse. When you are held in the "city bucket" there is a small barred window with a few small holes in it. If you stand on your tiptoes, you can peer out and see the exact spot on the corner of Main and Hastings where Gary and I were now standing and you couldn't see very much of anything else. I peered out of that window too many times to count in my past. The first time I peered out that window I was seventeen years old. And I remember thinking to myself at the time, "When I get out of here, I'm going to stand on that exact spot and I'm going to look back up here and laugh!" What really happened when I got out was the opposite. I wanted to leave this place and its memories so far behind me. In fact, I hated to give even a quick glance up to that window because I started to believe it would jinx me. I felt the jinx would be so strong that if I gave even the slightest glance up there, I would be looking out from there possibly even that night.

However, on this day, the shame of all my shames had become a reality. I found that I wanted to go back there. I wanted to go back to jail. So today, I looked up there and secretly in my heart, wanted the jinx to become real. On this particular day, I looked up there for the first time in my life. . .without fear. This thought was floating through my mind, "Now what crime can I do that won't get me "Pen" time?" As I was thinking this, Gary broke me out of my thought process and brought me back to reality with, "What are you thinking about so much Nieman? I asked you if you want to go and see Dale the Whale twice already and you didn't even hear me. What are you so worried about? You look pretty sad there chum, what's up?" "Oh nothing just thinking," "Come on Nieman, I know you better than that you've got something up your sleeve." I did not want to tell Gary what I was really feeling even though he was my best friend and I knew he wouldn't repeat it to anyone. I knew it would make him feel sad if I told him the truth so I said, "I'm thinking of how I can ditch you guys next time I make a score before you blow me in again!" "You blew yourself in my friend," Gary said as we started walking. We were making reference to how quickly I had spent my whole welfare check on one night. We went over to Dale's and were surprised to learn that he had just received a welfare check and had just returned from the liquor store. Once again, alcohol took away my sorrows temporarily, and I'm pleased to say I never ever had thoughts like that again and based on the upcoming events in my life, I would never do any more jail time again.

Let me take you back now to Victory Square where I left off when I started this autobiography. Gary and I had just finished the bottle of wine Gary had and he was playing his harmonica and I was thinking about the hopelessness of my life. Gary staggered back over to me and said, "Hey Bro. I'm feeling kinda' tipsy. I'm gonna go back to my room and lay down for a while." He left me no option to answer or to try and dissuade him from going home as he turned around and started walking. "OK Gary. Have a good sleep. Thanks for the "nip". I'll stop by your place later," he was already well on his way heading to his room.

After Gary left to go home and sleep I shuffled my way down to Pigeon Park. Pigeon Park is in the heart of Vancouver's skid row at the corner of Carroll St. and Hastings St. and it is a popular hang-out for the hardcore alcoholics living on skid row. Living on skid row you meet ALL kinds of people down there. People who came from well-to-do families but got into the drugs and from that first "hit" were hooked for life. There are people who could not recover from a divorce and just gave up on everything. Just about every second person has been a victim of one type of abuse or another in their childhood and just about everybody down there has experienced one type of trauma or another as a defenseless child.

I became close friends with a man who introduced me to Peking Brand Ginseng Brandy. We simply called it, "Ginseng". Ginseng is a brandy that is imported from China and it is used for medicinal purposes, cooking and other things in the Chinese culture. It is very high in alcohol content 40% and back then in 1993 it was only five dollars a bottle. It was a very popular drink among all the derelicts on skid row. Ginseng replaced Chinese Rice Wine (which is used for cooking and has alcohol in it). When you start drinking Ginseng you are considered to be a bottom-feeder and one of the lowest of the low in all of skid row. Ginseng drinkers are at rock bottom. It seemed only natural that I would eventually digress down to being a regular at Pigeon Park. When I first came to Vancouver as a sixteen year old, I had heard so much about how bad it was at Pigeon Park that Maddy, Johnny and I couldn't wait to see it for ourselves. The first time I saw it I could not believe how rough, ugly and smelly a skid row bum could be. Some had vomit and feces on their clothes. Others walked around with big wet stains on the front of their pants where they had pee'd themselves and many were passed out sitting up and laying down. The first time we saw the derelicts in Pigeon Park some common words we used to describe them were "gross", "sad", "wasted" and "disgusting". We used to joke and tease each other back then about, "That's you in ten years." And "That's you in three!" It took me twenty three years to wind up down there at Pigeon Park and I fit like a "dirty ol' shirt". The man who introduced me to Ginseng is Wayne Hyland. I'm not even sure if he is still alive today. The last time I saw him alive was when I was driving by Pigeon Park in a rented car back in June 2009. I was going to stop but he was in no condition to recognize me. The best thing I could do for him was pray and pray I did with tears in my eyes.

Wayne was from Ontario and he was as hardcore an alcoholic as you will find on any skid row in the world. All he lived for was to drink. Just like me. He did not do any other drug not even smoke marijuana. When I first met Wayne he was staying at the Stadium Hotel. Gary was also staying at the Stadium and had a room right across from Wayne. I liked Wayne the very minute I met him. He had piercing blue eyes and he smiled through those eyes. He was smart and quick-witted with a sense of humor that never failed to make me smile. He was part Scottish and Irish and as stubborn as they come. He was about 45 yrs. old but looked 65. Wayne hid his sad, bitter, lonely broken heart behind quick wit and original humor. As we sat in Pigeon Park sipping on ginseng, I noticed lately that he often had this distant, forlorn gaze on his face as though he was lost in thought. To me, it seemed like he was gazing off into the distant barren landscape of his broken dreams, wasted life and untreated emotional wounds. Dreams that were drowning at this very moment, in the bottom of a ginseng brandy bottle. It was as if he was silently grieving something as he sat there. "What's the matter Wayne?" I asked in a soft, concerned voice. As he came back to the present, after my intrusion into his private world, he simply shrugged his shoulders and straightening up saying, "Humph, don't you worry 'bout me mister. I've faced tougher men than you Bucko and walked right through èm! Worry 'bout yourself. There's nothing wrong with me, nothing a good shot in the yap wouldn't fix!" I both liked and disliked the bravado he always tried to display. I liked it because he was showing his mechanism for survival. I disliked it because he was also showing the reason for his failure — denial. I knew he was hurting, yet he would never admit to it. Denial is one of the biggest walls an alcoholic/ drug addict can put up. And it is one of the hardest to take down. It's a wall of pride and shame. It is also a wall of avoidance addicts use to protect themselves from the traumatic reality that drives them to drink and drug abuse. In denial, an addict will say that, "Everything is OK," and "I can quit if I want to, I just don't want to." All of us sitting in Pigeon Park that day no doubt were still living in denial. This was my world. The world of the down trodden beat-up, cast off lonely discarded souls. I always sold my rent check that the welfare gave me and I slept on the street. I slept in back alleys, under bridges, park benches, shelters and Wayne always let me stay in his room if he wasn't passed out and I could get in. It was Wayne who taught me how to panhandle effectively. We didn't use the weak phrase, "Can you spare some change?" I learned from Wayne to use a down and out hard luck story approach instead of just asking for "spare change." It was very effective so effective that I've had people give me a fifty-dollar bill on more than five occasions!

CHAPTER SEVENTEEN

A MAN NAMED RAUL

"THE TRAIN"

The train of pain rolled in again
And punched my ticket to memory lane,
In calm protest I did my best
To keep from seeing what I detest,
The train of shame called out my name

Held up a list of pent-up pain,
Then said, "I brought your ball and chain"
"I'm taking you back to prison again."

The train of blame struck up a flame
And burned away my peace again,
My tears they fell like pouring rain
The train was rolling to an early grave,

A. Nieman

Sitting and drinking in Pigeon Park with Wayne put my hangover on the run. After I felt the effects of the alcohol in the Ginseng Brandy the blisters on my feet didn't hurt anymore. Wayne was starting to pass out so I made my way over to the Salvation Army soup line. I got my meal and sat down to eat. A man came in and sat at the same table directly across from me and he prayed before he ate his meal and ended his prayer with, "I ask it in the Name of Jesus." When I heard him say, "Jesus," I said, "Hey, I believe in Jesus too!" He was a Metis from Alberta and he said he was in Vancouver to start a First Nation Men's Gospel Outreach project. He introduced himself and that is how I met Raul. I never did learn his last name but it was through this man that Jesus was letting me know that He was with me even as I lived on the bottom rung of skid row. There were many times when I would be on my way to my favorite back alley to "shoot up" some cocaine and I would run into Raul and he ALWAYS wanted to pray for me.

I would be standing at a red light waiting to cross the street with my cocaine in my pocket as I was itching to get that needle in my arm and I would hear, "Andy! Hey Andy! Wait up!" it was Raul running after me. "I've got to go Raul! I can't talk right now, I'm in a hurry! See you later!" "Just a minute Bro just give me one minute." "I really have to go Raul I'm in a hurry! I'll talk to you later!" The light changes to green and I start walking across the street real fast. He half-runs beside me. "I just want to pray for you Andy that's all. Can I pray for you? It'll only take a minute?" I'm irritated. We reach the other sidewalk and trying to hide my anger I say, "I've really got to go Raul maybe another time." "Just thirty seconds Andy. Thirty seconds!" "OK but I am really in a hurry!" We stop and I take my hat off exposing my greasy hair and I become self-conscious of just how dirty and unkempt I am and I feel ashamed and uncomfortable. Raul puts his hand on my shoulder and prays for me. I think to myself, "Good, he isn't putting his hand on my greasy dirty hair." When he is done, he gives me a big smile and shakes my hand and I rush off with, "See you later." "God bless," is all I hear from him as I hurry off with a quick glance around to see if there are any police and I head for the spot where I always "shoot up" my drugs.

A couple of days later the same thing would happen. I would be rushing to my spot after I bought my "fix" of cocaine and I would hear someone shout from across the street, "Andy! Is that you Andy?" Sure enough it HAD TO BE Raul! He was the last person I wanted to see right now! I turn my head and pretend I don't hear him. I quicken my pace. "Andy? That is you! Wait up!" He jaywalks across the street to catch up to me. "I really have no time to talk right now Raul. See you later!" I cross over to the side of the street he just came from. It is not where I am headed but I am trying to lose him as quickly as I can. He follows. I think to myself, "Ah man! Just LEAVE ME ALONE!" but I don't say a word. Again he half-runs beside me, "I only want two seconds just for one short prayer Andy. It won't take long I promise!" "I can't Raul. I really have to go, please!" We cross the street and he won't give up. "I ran into you for a reason Andy I really NEED to pray for you." Something tells me, "He is not going to stop so you might as well just let him pray for you." I stop right there and with a disgusted voice I say to him, "Man Raul! Go ahead and pray! Man oh man!" It was like Jesus Himself was following me. I couldn't get away! After Raul prayed for me he said to my back as I went rushing off, "Thank you Andy. God has good things in store for you!"

God had a way of always reminding me that He was with me and that I was on His mind in the last days of my life on skid row. When I had to walk the streets all night driven by my bondage to cocaine and when I could not find a place to sleep that night because someone else had taken "my spot" under the bridge, I would find Gospel tracts in the strangest places. They would always be carefully held in place by a rock to keep them from blowing away. I would find them on window sills, at bus stops and on park benches. It seemed like they were MEANT FOR ME because they had NOT been PICKED UP by anybody else! I always picked them up and would read them and then I started putting them in my pocket and keeping them. The Gospel tracts told me that I needed to stop sinning and to get ready for when Jesus returns. In my heart I knew what I was reading was TRUE. I knew I was NOT READY for THAT DAY and I KNEW I HAD to GET READY. I bowed my head and out of a totally sincere heart I asked God, "Please help me. I want to be saved. I can't stop sinning and I want to be ready for when You return but I can't stop on my own! I want so badly to be ready! If you have to cripple me and put me in a wheelchair to make me stop sinning then please DO IT!" I'm thankful He had another plan for me. My reality was this plain and simple…I did not know how to live life! From being in the residential school and all those years in jail, I did not know or learn how to make my life comfortable. I really did not know how to enjoy life in a healthy way. In fact, I didn't even know how to enjoy life period! That is, without alcohol or some other drug. Cocaine completely eroded what little ethical boundaries I possessed. Moral decay ran freely through my character. I was not to be trusted. You did not want to let me into your house, because I would steal from you. I would leave your house with something that was valuable and probably sentimental to you. I didn't care how it made you feel, how it might affect you because I was addicted to cocaine and the addiction was stronger than the slightest bit of compassion that dared to try and show itself in my hardened heart. I did not WANT to be like this and I hated myself for what I had become. I was sticking that needle in my arm fifteen to twenty times a day and I was drinking the lowest form of alcohol and living with the worst hardcore alcoholics on skid row! Back then, it was common for me to stay awake high on "coke" for four days STRAIGHT day and night with not a wink of sleep. I started to get into the Ginseng more heavily and my best friend Gary would get mad at me for, "Drinking that Rubby," as he so aptly put it.

Drinking Ginseng every day caused me to wake up in the strangest and filthiest places and I had not the slightest clue how I got there! There is nothing quite like a Ginseng Brandy hang-over. If you drink too much of it for an extended period of time something in the brandy causes your muscles to cramp up real bad. The Ginseng helped to curb ever so slightly my need for cocaine. But near the end of my life down there on skid row I was "shooting up" more than I was drinking. In fact, I slowed down a fair amount on my alcohol intake and actually got myself a room just off Hastings St. on Cordova St. as you will see later, it was in that room that God would pay me a visit. However, this morning luckily I wake up in my spot under the bridge. I know I look an awful mess. I am feeling very sick, very shaky and physically weak. I am nauseous and need to sit back down as I feel like I am going to have another bout of dry heaves again. My stomach is empty and my throat is thoroughly raw from throwing up everything inside of my intestines. Yet, my body still wants to throw up some more and is trying to do just that. Only there was nothing left in my stomach to bring up.

This made the retching that much more painful. My body kept insisting that I bring up everything in my system. My stomach muscles hurt from the unstoppable "dry-heaves" and the constant retching. My nose is running like a dripping faucet. My eyes are watery. I couldn't stop either of them from shedding water. What an ironic state! Here I am, with an unquenchable thirst yet I couldn't get enough water into me to quench that thirst and my body is getting rid of water like a garden hose with holes poked in it. I was hungry and undernourished. My body needed food. Still, I had to get out on the street and face the world. I HAD to get a drink into my alcohol-starved system! I had to get out there and beg some change. Even though I hated to I had no choice. I needed a drink! Nothing else mattered. Thank God, this is Vancouver, what would I do if it were anywhere else? I wouldn't have the nerve to do it in my home town. Here, at least no one would recognize me for what I really was and what I had really become. I was an insecure scared little boy in a grown man's body being forced by the demons of drug and alcohol addiction to exist on the lowest rung of skid row. A beggar on the street clothed in sadness, shame and loneliness always the loneliness. No matter who I was with, there was always the loneliness. No matter where I would go or how drunk I could get the loneliness always showed up at my heart's doorstep. It knew I had no choice. . .but to let him back in. I had come to that place again the place where my denial defense was weakened and my thinking started to catch up to me. Only to remind me of what a dismal failure I had become. I needed a drink this morning and I needed it badly. My hunger pangs were strong but my need for alcohol was stronger.

It is early Sunday morning around 8:00 a.m on September 12, 1993 and it is unusually warm. In fact it is quite hot for September in Vancouver. I am walking through Chinatown. The day is just beginning as a Chinese merchant starts his usual routine of putting out wooden crates full of dried seafood, fresh fruit, vegetables, dried squid, mussels and fish of all sorts onto the sidewalk. Inside the shops and restaurants, workers were hanging Bar B Que Duck, Bar B Que Pork, whole cooked chickens and the whole half sides of a pig. The sun is shining bright with not a cloud in the sky. It is hot already or is it just my hang over?

Not far from the man putting out the wooden crates, another Chinese man, a fellow employee, is busy spraying the sidewalk with a green colored garden hose. The water quickly forms a small muddy stream that runs downhill on the sidewalk and gets re-directed with the first crack in the sidewalk. The spray pushes bits of vegetables and fish scales into the muddy stream which flows into the gutter. I can hear seagulls squawking and can't help but notice a couple of them that are perched atop telephone poles. They are fully aware of the process that is taking place below them with the garden hose. The experienced, furtive eyes of the seagulls watch every morsel that is being washed away. Their angry squawks seem to protest the waste of such good seagull food. Another day in Chinatown has begun. For me, another day with a terrible hang over has begun. I walk by the merchant's store, doing my best to hurry. I don't want to catch a whiff of the stench of dried seafood that always seemed to flood the sidewalks in various Chinatown stores especially on a warm morning like today. The strong smell of semi-rotting seafood would make me gag. I like eating seafood, but this morning, as hung-over as I was, I couldn't stomach the smell. I hurried my pace, using what little precious energy I had trying to stay ahead of the smell.

I make my way down to Strathcona Park and panhandle three dollars. I start walking over to Gary's room to see how much money he has and I run into him half way there. He is with two other First Nation guys and I recognize Winston who is Cree but I don't know the other guy. They already have a bottle of Ginseng. Gary only drinks Ginseng when he has a really bad hang over and when there is nothing else to drink or he'll drink it if he is already half drunk. Since it is so nice and sunny out we decide to go and drink at Strathcona Park. It is obvious that Gary and his two friends are well on their way to "curing" their hang over and I am far behind in that department. We find an empty park bench and sit down.

As I sit on the park bench we pass the brown paper bag around. I make sure I take a big gulp and it burns all the way down to the pit of my stomach! What an AWFUL TASTE! My mind starts to wander and I think about how sick I am and how despicable my life is. Here I am over a thousand miles from my family. I have no home, no money, no girlfriend, I'm hooked on cocaine, I'm a severe alcoholic, my clothes and my feet stink and I feel like I have nobody that loves me other than my friend Gary. My mouth tastes like the whole Chinese army marched through it in their sock feet and each time I take a "drag" of my rolled up cigarette butts it burns my throat something fierce. I am alone in my thoughts when an Oriental man who is clean cut in a white shirt and a tie walks up and he asks, "Does anybody here believe in Jesus?" In my gruff, raspy voice plagued by too many cigarettes I answer, "I do," and Gary copies me, "Yeah I do too." Winston says, "No I believe in Native Spirituality," and the other guy says, "I don't believe in any of that crap!" Then the Oriental man takes both Winston and the other guy aside and he talks with them. He then returns to Gary and I and asks, "How's it going?"

Gary asks him, "You got a smoke?" he says, "Sorry, I don't smoke," and when the man looks at me I share part of my dismal life story with him. I tell him about jail, the cocaine and the alcohol and that I sleep under the bridge. When I am finished and there is a silence in the air, the man says to me, "Say can I speak with you in private for a minute Andy?" I think to myself, "He's a Christian so if I let him talk to me about Jesus he just might break down and give me some money after," so I say, "OK." We walk to the next bench and sit down and he says, "I can see you have leadership qualities in you Andy. You're not like those other guys. My name is James Lee. I am a Pastor from West Virginia. I am attending a church conference here in Vancouver and I was scheduled to preach this morning but as I was sitting on the platform, the Spirit of God moved on me and told me to come down here. I told an associate of mine to take my place preaching and the Spirit lead me here. I can see this is a very rough neighborhood. I have never been down here before this is my very first time. I believe God sent me down here FOR YOU." "You know Jesus was in prison just like you and He also knows what it feels like to be very lonely and He knows how it feels to be an outcast. And Jesus died on the cross for Andy's sins and everybody else's sins so that we could have a new life with Him. It was not a pretty sight when Jesus died on the cross. I know just about every picture of Jesus hanging on the cross shows Jesus as a handsome man with no marks on him and a crown on His head. But it was not that way at all. His face was black and blue, swollen with black eyes and His face was a bloody mess because He was punched and kicked and the Bible says they tore His beard out. He did that for you and I Andy so that we could have a brand new life in Him. You can have a brand new life with Jesus Andy. You are going to be used by God Andy to lead many of your Native people out of darkness. You are going to be a Prayer Warrior and God is going to answer your prayers." I think to myself, "I hope you're almost done because those guys back there are going to finish that bottle BEFORE I GET BACK!"

He digs into his shirt pocket and takes out a thin brown leather bound New Testament Bible (I still have it to this day which is a miracle in itself considering my lifestyle back then) and he writes in it; "To the Mighty Warrior of The Lord Jesus Christ Andy Nieman, may God's anointing be upon you always and shine His light to your people. Love in Christ, James Lee."

He hands me the Bible and after he prays for me he asks, "Is there anything I can do to help you?" Right away the sound of a cash register "Kaw-ching!" goes off in my brain and a panic-stricken voice yells inside my head, "MONEY! ASK FOR MONEY!" So I do my best to be calm and I say, "Can I borrow some money?" As soon as I say 'borrow' I hear myself say, "Yeah right *borrow* alright!" "How much?" he asks. Shocked, I think to myself, "Did he just say HOW MUCH!? HOW MUCH!??" I am not sure what to ask for as I've never had anyone ask me that question before! I don't want to ask for too much and I don't want to ask for too little so I hesitantly say in a questioning tone, "Twenty dollars?" He pulls out his wallet and digs out a twenty dollar bill, an AMERICAN twenty dollar bill! My hang-over almost did a back flip out the window but stopped just short of leaving because it needs alcohol in order to leave and then James asks me, "Would you like something to eat?" I quickly shove the twenty dollars into the deepest corner of my jeans pocket and take a side-eyed glance over to see if any of the other guys seen him give me the twenty. They did not. I answer James, "No I'm still a little too sick to eat yet," "Do you think your friends would like something to eat?" "Probably," "OK let's go ask them."

I'm already thinking about getting a ten dollar shot of cocaine and another bottle of Ginseng and then I'll go and see if Wayne has a hang-over so I can help him "cure" it. James and I walk over to Gary and there is just Gary and Winston sitting there. The other guy was walking away with a slight stagger to his gait. To my surprise there is still some Ginseng left. I take another big gulp and again it burns all the way down. Gary and Winston had their hang-overs cured and when James asked, "Would you guys like to get something to eat?" they both answered together with an enthusiastic, "Sure!" James took us across the street to MacDonald's and bought us all something to eat. I couldn't eat so while they were eating I took out a napkin and wrote him a poem it was my "Rap" song and it went like this: "MC Hammer has nothing on me! I like to swim in the deep blue sea, I like to laugh and live my life free, I come from the Yukon which borders BC and I live in Canada this great country!" I handed it to James not sure of he would take it.

James took the napkin and put it in his shirt pocket. After he finished eating he shook our hands and he was gone. I tried to look him up online years later but could not locate him. After he left I went and bought a "spit-ball" and another bottle of Ginseng. A "spit-ball" is a ten dollar hit of cocaine. It is called a "spit-ball" because the dealers wrap up the cocaine in a tiny plastic ball and they carry it in their mouth so if a cop comes to check them, they'll spit it out on the ground and pretend that it is not theirs so they won't get "busted."

About three weeks after that Sunday in Strathcona Park welfare Wednesday came around and I picked up my check. I had just walked out of the bank on Main and Hastings Street after cashing my check when I ran into "Smitty" a friend of mine from the Yukon. He was with a lady that I met many years ago when I was doing time in Prince George Regional Correctional Center in 1974. "Smitty" asked me, "What you up to Andy, want to come to a Biker party with us?" "Sure where at?" "It's out in Surrey we're just going to pick up some "smack" (slang for heroin) and head out there," "OK. I have to pick up some "blow" first and some "pot". When you heading out there?" "Probably in a couple of hours. Here I'll give you the address and if you get there ahead of us, just tell them "Smitty" invited you, you'll be alright. OK?" "OK. I'll be there. See you out there." My first stop was the Needle Exchange where I picked up a "six-pack" of syringes. I then picked up half a gram of cocaine and a quarter ounce of marijuana and got on the sky train to Surrey. The address was not far from the sky train and was easy to find. When I arrived at the party there were only about seven people there. As I entered the small house the smell of "skunk weed" marijuana was heavy in the air and evidenced by a thin light blue haze of smoke that lingered in the room. I noticed right away that there were a couple of people who had obviously started to shoot up but stopped when they heard my knock at the door. After they saw that it was me they pulled out their needles and continued.

"Smitty" was not there yet. I was offered a beer and asked, "Unless you want something stronger?" I said, "A beer will be fine," and I notice there are a lot of bottles of whiskey and wine on the kitchen counter. I rolled a few joints from my weed and as we sat around smoking them they asked me where I knew "Smitty" from and I tell them, "From back home in the Yukon." After I felt that I was accepted and everything was cool I pulled out my needle and did a shot of cocaine. One of the guys offered me a fix of his "coke" and I said, "Sure in a little bit," just then "Smitty" and Patricia walked in. "Smitty" and Pat went straight into the bedroom. After about ten minutes "Smitty" yells out from the bedroom loud enough for all of us to hear over the music, "Danny!" and Pat walks out with a syringe full of heroin and passes it to Danny. He takes the syringe and just as he is about to put the syringe in his arm "Smitty" yells out, "Mary Lou!" and again

Pat comes out of the bedroom with a syringe full of heroin and gives it to Mary Lou. Pat goes right back into the bedroom and "Smitty" yells out, "Andy!" Pat comes out and gives me a syringe that is filled with heroin. Although I've shot a lot of "speedballs" (heroin mixed with cocaine) I have not used any heroin in the last couple of weeks and my tolerance to the drug is quite low. In my mind I'm thinking, "It should be OK to shoot this whole syringe of heroin because I have so much cocaine in my system it should just balance out." I yell out, "Thank you Smitty!" and "Smitty" yells back, "No problem Bro!" I put the needle in my arm and inject all of the heroin. Before I can pull the needle out of my arm my jaw goes slack and falls open. My whole body and all my muscles are paralyzed and I CAN'T MOVE ANY PART of my body! I want to say, "Somebody help me I took too much!" but nothing comes out! I can't even move my mouth! I can't get out any sound at all! I am not able to send out an alarm to let them know I AM OVERDOSING! Then the sound of voices and the music starts to fade away into the distance. The voices and the music grow quieter and quitter and I realize I am losing my hearing! I CANNOT MOVE a muscle! Then the light in the room gets dimmer and dimmer and the sounds of life get farther and farther away. I am totally helpless and start to drift away. Then everything turns black and there is no sound whatsoever and I black out completely.

The next day I open my eyes and the first thing I see is the bright colored flower design on the back of the couch and I discover that I am lying on my side with my face pushed into the back of a couch! But MORE IMPORTANTLY I realize I AM ALIVE! AM I REALLY ALIVE!? I swing my feet over the side of the couch and sit up. There is nobody in the house except me and an old lady. She looks like a retired granny-type biker-chick and I'll never forget what she says to me because it is the first voice I hear since all the voices had faded out on me when I "went under" and she says, "Welcome back to the land of the living kid. You threw a scare into us last night. Thought we might have to dump your miserable carcass in an alley somewhere. You better lay off that "smack" for good sonny it's going to be the end of you! Would you like a drink?" "No, that's OK." I really did not want a drink. I was JUST SO GLAD to be ALIVE! "What day is it?" I asked her, "Thursday just after "Farewell Wednesday." "Farewell Wednesday" that was another name we had for "Welfare Wednesday."

She continued talking, "I've still got to go pick my check up and was waiting for you to get up before I did so I can lock the place up. Where do you live?" "Hastings," "Figured so. Do you have bus fare?" "Yeah," I reached into my pockets but my pockets were EMPTY! Someone had rolled me! I thought to myself, "You probably rolled me you old bag!" but I never said a word except, "Ah no, no I don't have bus fare." "Figured that too," she said as she reached into her tiny little purse hanging on a thin rope slung over her shoulder and rested at the side of her hip. She pulled out twenty dollars and handed it to me, "That should do ya," "Thank you. Thank you very much." Then she asked, "Sure you don't want a drink? There's plenty left over?" "No, that's OK. Is everybody gone?" "You're the last one," "Which way to the sky train from here?" she pointed. "Mind if

I use the washroom?" "Help yourself. "Smitty said your name was 'Andy' that right?" "Yes it is." I WAS ALIVE! I could NOT BELIEVE IT! ALIVE! I got up and went into the washroom. I had no hangover not even the slightest sign of a hangover it was weird! I just felt so good to be alive!

I said, "Good-bye," to the biker lady and thanked her again for the twenty dollars which I still felt was mine in the first place. As I was walking to the sky train it was like I was walking through a dream world. Everything WAS BRIGHTER! I knew I had come back from the brink of death! I just KNEW IT! I have never been so glad to BE ALIVE! When I got down to skid row it was like I was walking on a cloud! Like I was HIGH on FRESH AIR! Every person I seen down there that I knew it was like seeing them after a long time in the hospital and it felt I had just beaten a terminal illness! It felt so GOOD just to BE ALIVE I didn't need any drugs! I Andy Nieman just DODGED A BULLET of DEATH! I did not think to thank God because I WAS SO HAPPY to be alive! However, God reminded me after I gave my life to Him that HE was the ONE Who brought me BACK from the brink of death!

I didn't ride the happiness for surviving the overdose very long. I got drunk that night but did not touch heroin ever again after that. My cocaine use esca-lated to the point where coming down from the drug was now at the very serious stage that is known as a "crash." This is where those who are severely addicted to "coke" are coming down from a "coke-run" a binge where heavy cocaine use has been engaged in for say a week or a couple of days and the high wears off and you have no more cocaine. You then experience a "crash." A "crash" is where severe, heavy, almost palpable depression sets in and suicidal thoughts dominate your thinking. It feels like the whole world is against you and you are not able to find a shred of peace nowhere! Suicide at that point appears to be the ONLY OPTION that will END your discomfort.

I was experiencing a "crash" one day and I decided that I had had it with living and decided to end my life with a heroin overdose. I made up my mind that as soon as I made enough money to buy a paper of heroin I was going to end my life. That night, it was very slow and I had not made any money. It was pouring rain out on a Sunday night at 11:30 pm. I had no place to sleep that night other than under the bridge and I was just sick and tired of freezing under that awful bridge which hardly offered any real shelter. I determined in my heart that on this night I was going to just end my life with a heroin overdose. With these thoughts running through my head I felt a bit scared because I knew I was GOING TO GO THROUGH WITH IT! I had attempted suicide before in Whitehorse in 1980 and almost died but at that time, I really didn't want to die, I just wanted to know if anyone CARED FOR ME. My sister Margaret and Ruby Van Bibber found me that time at my dad's apartment in the Senior Citizen's home on Alexander St. and took me to the hospital. I had taken my dad's sleeping pills Mandrax, and the doctor told me, "Two more hours and if nobody found you Andy you would've died."

But tonight I stand in the pouring rain at the corner of Main and Hastings St. in front of Carnegie Hall. I have no umbrella I have no place to go, I have no way to feel better and I have nobody to stop me and I KNOW I am going to end my life. Just then on that empty street on a lonely Sunday evening with not another soul out in this pouring rain, a man walks up and stands beside me as I wait for the traffic light to change and he says, "Hi Andy, what you doing out in this rain?" I look over in the darkness and at first it is hard to recognize him because he is in raingear and wouldn't you know it! Who do you think it is that I see? Why none other than Raul himself. With his right hand he holds his umbrella over me, puts his left arm over my shoulder and says, "You don't look so good my friend. What's up?" And I tell him the truth. "Well there's no use going on. I mean I hear everybody telling me that 'Jesus loves you Andy, Jesus loves you,' well if Jesus loves me why am I at the bottom like this? I've asked Him to help me time and time again and NOTHING!" "Well Jesus IS REAL Andy and He DOES love you but He never forces anybody to follow Him. If you're running from Him maybe you have to hit rock bottom first." "Hit ROCK BOTTOM!? Raul I'm AT ROCK BOTTOM! I can't go any lower than this! I DON'T WANT to GO ON from here!" "Well maybe you're like Jonah. God had a plan for Jonah's life but Jonah decided to run from God and he wound up in the belly of a whale at the bottom of the ocean. It was only when he was as low as he could possibly go that Jonah finally said, "OK God here I am I give up what do you want me to do?" I thought about what Raul was saying and no doubt Raul could see that I was thinking about it and he said, "Where you staying tonight?" "Ah, nowhere. I'll probably just walk around all night." "Come and spend the night at my place it is too wet and cold out here." "No that's OK." "Why not?" "That's OK don't worry 'bout it." "No, tell me why you won't stay the night, just tell me the truth." "Well, I haven't changed my socks in weeks and my feet stink real bad." "Well we'll throw them in the tub and you can wash them. Stink feet or no stink feet, you're welcome to sleep over anytime!" I spent the night on Raul's floor and he prayed for me before I left the next morning. I never thought about suicide after that night and I never did see Raul again.

CHAPTER EIGHTEEN

A VISITATION IN MY ROOM

"BENDED KNEES"

Sorrow rolled in, tears rolled down,
Wearing my lonely like a bent up crown,
I will not run, I will not hide,
I'm scrapping these blues, taking them outside,

This heart's been battered, drained and bruised,
Sometimes so selfish, sometimes so used,
I've hid my tears in the pouring rain,
Cried while laughing and smiled in pain,

Been to the place where I wished it would end,
My soul felt sad like it never would mend,
I looked to heaven saw an empty sky,
Yet God still heard when I began to cry,

I cried in sorrow, I cried in pain,
I cried in anger 'til I lay there drained,
Then a thought it whispered like a gentle breeze,
"Real freedom is found on bended knees"

A. Nieman

The next month October, I got myself a room just off of Hastings St. at Cordova Rooms. It was infested with mice, cockroaches and the occasional rat but for me it was home. There was a shared bathroom down the hall. My room had a bed, a sink with no hot water and a beat up little old fridge that only got cold when it felt like it. The only heat in the building came from a skinny pipe in the hallway. The towel that hung on the towel rack when I first got the room had old blood stains on it that were not able to be washed out. I was just glad that at least I had a towel and a roof over my head! Before getting this room while I was living on the street I went two and one half months without a shower. I know, it's even hard for me to believe! And during the last six months I had been dumpster-diving (jumping right into the big garbage bins and digging out anything of value).

It is amazing some of the things I found dumpster-diving. Things like; fine antique English China cups and saucers with 24 karat gold plating, jewelry, watches, brand new clothes and food! Nothing like day old pizza! Lol. From all that dumpster-diving which I did on a daily basis I just flat out plain STUNK! It got to the point where my feet would slip around in my runners from all the "toe-jam" and my feet stunk right through my runners so bad that people moved away from me whenever I got on the bus.

**Front door of the hotel where I had a room
when my life changed forever.**

I continued to get high on cocaine every day and continued to drink. The drinking slowed down a little but I always managed to get enough for some "coke" each and every day. I panhandled, stole VHS videos and broke into cars. Once I got the room I was able to keep a little cleaner and would get some pretty decent clothes from the free food places. I discovered that if I dressed in CLEAN clothes when I went into a store none of the store detectives would follow me. I didn't look like a "rubbie-dub" so they left me alone. When I learned that they would not follow me, my latest scam became stealing AA batteries and selling them in the bars. I made enough money that way so that it kept me in the cocaine and alcohol each and every day. I lived off the free food places and if you wanted to get a nice HOT meal you would have to sit through a church Service and listen to a sermon. I soon found that GOD WAS TALKING DIRECTLY to me when I would sit through a service where you got a hot meal after. Jesus was getting my attention even when I was NOT TRYING to get HIS attention. I continued to find Gospel tracts in various places and when people were handing them out on the street I started taking them and bringing them back to my room with me. I remember one day after reading one of the tracks alone in my room, I bowed my head and closed my eyes and I asked Jesus as honestly as I could to, "Please help me. I want to follow You I really do. Help to be the way You want me to be. PLEASE save me!" I looked at my table and there was getting to be quite a collection of tracts. After saying that prayer I went and caught the bus up to the liquor store on Hastings St. by the PNE Grounds so I could panhandle for something to drink. There was nobody panhandling when I got to the liquor store and it didn't take me long to get enough for a bottle of Bounty wine. When I got the bottle, I went into the alley and sat down by a dumpster. I kept the wine in the brown paper bag and I took a couple of deep drinks. It was a beautiful sunny day in the middle of winter. As I sat there I looked over at the mountains in North Vancouver and admired the sunshine and beauty of those mountains. And I thought to myself, "If only God was real. If only God was real then I wouldn't have to be so all alone," and I began to cry. I sat there alone in that alley and I let the tears fall because I started to feel in my heart that God was not real. And if God was NOT real, then I had no hope whatsoever.

A couple of weeks later on January 30, 1994 I went up to Granville and Nelson St. and stood across the street from Kripp's Drug Store. Kripp's was one of the stores I shop-lifted batteries from. I noticed there were no customers in the store and I needed at least one other person in the store when I went in so I wouldn't be the only one they were keeping an eye on. I watched the store from across the street waiting for a customer to go in. As I was watching the store a man walked up to me out of the blue and asks me, "Do you believe in Jesus?" and I said, "Yes," he said, "Hi my name is Jerry," he then asked me my name and I said, "Andy," he said, "Well Andy can go on believing in Jesus all he wants but the devil will still rule in your life and you'll still wind up in hell. Andy has got to make a decision to invite Jesus into his life before Jesus will give you the power to change. Until you make that decision nothing will change!" Then he asks, "I'd like to pray for you. What do you need prayer for?" "Well you know the normal things for First Nation people. To stop drinking and doing drugs, to stay out of jail and to have a healthy life," "OK that's good," then he put one hand on my shoulder and took my hand in his other hand and he prayed, "Jesus, don't let Andy enjoy the alcohol anymore from this moment on. Don't let him enjoy the drugs anymore. Keep him out of jail, strengthen his heart and give him victory for a new life." He then dug into his shirt pocket and took out his written tes-timony gave it to me and he walked away. The streets were very crowded and I watched Jerry as he walked down the street and disappeared into the crowd. He never spoke to another person he just kept walking. I thought to myself, "Hmm I'm the only one he stopped for." I put his testimony into the back pocket of my jeans and watched the store again.

I stole some batteries sold them and I went to the Sunrise Hotel the bar where I always got my drugs from. I always bought my stuff from the same dealer to ensure I would not get ripped off. I bought two "spit-balls" of cocaine and a gram of "skunk weed" marijuana. I then made my way back to my room. I was anxious and desperate to get high. I pulled out the first "spit-ball" and I was so anxious and in such a hurry that I spilled it onto the wooden floor and lost all of it! Right then and there immediately, the words of that man's prayer came to mind, "Don't let Andy enjoy the drugs." I got angry. I carefully pulled out the other "spit-ball" put it in the syringe and pushed it into my vein but I was so angry from losing the first 'spit-ball" that it ruined my high! And then that's man's prayer came to my mind, "Don't let Andy enjoy the drugs." I'm getting angrier now and I think to myself, "I'll get high one way or another," and immediately, I rolled a joint of marijuana and began to smoke it. I took two tokes and I COULDN'T FEEL A THING . . . NOTHING! I picked up the gram of "pot" looked at it, smelled it and SURE ENOUGH it WAS SKUNK WEED! I took another big toke, held it down an extra-long time, let it out and STILL could NOT FEEL a THING! Then right at THAT PRECISE MOMENT, I FELT a very strong Presence in the room and something in my soul and in my mind told me, "It's useless to try and go against this Presence that you are feeling." And in my heart of hearts, I KNEW I was dealing with a Force that was bigger than me or the drugs. I knew it was useless to even try to continue going against this force.

So I got up from where I was sitting. I put out the "joint" that I was smoking and I took it and the rest of the gram of "weed" and went out into the hallway. When I got to the washroom I emptied what was left of the gram bag of "weed" down the toilet, threw the "joint" in the toilet as well and flushed it. I walked back to my room. As soon as I entered my room I could feel that very same Presence. It was still there and it was very strong. I knelt down at my bed right then and there and began to talk out loud, "Okay Jesus, if this is You help me! You know I believe in You. You know I want to follow You, but I'm an alcoholic, a drug addict, a skid row bum and an ex-con. If You're real, HELP ME! I can't help myself! If You REALLY LOVE ME then MAKE YOURSELF REAL and PROVE to me that You love me! If You really love me then make a bed for me at Detox. (at the Detoxes in Vancouver, you can't just walk in there any time because they are ALWAYS FULL as there are so many addicts in that city. I know it sounds ironic but you actually have to PHONE AHEAD and RESERVE a bed at least two weeks in advance). I continued talking out loud, "If You make a bed for me at Detox then I'll know You're real and I will follow You. But if You don't make a bed for me, then I'll know that YOU'RE not real, that the BIBLE is not real, that HEAVEN is not real and that HELL is not real and I'll have nothing to fear if I end my life. But I do believe that this is You and I'm going to go over to Detox tomorrow because I have faith in You." I then laid down on my bed and I could feel that my body needed drugs.

That night I tossed and turned as my body was screaming at me for more drugs. I was sweating profusely. Each time I closed my eyes I seen an explosion of colors and it felt like I was a meteor falling through space at the speed of light! I turned the light on and the mice and cockroaches scurried for cover. I sat at the side of my bed and hung my head in my hands to try and take the dizziness away. I chased a cockroach off the sink and poured myself an ice cold drink of water. I was extremely weak and I leaned on the edge of the sink for support. After I drank the cup of ice cold water I got very cold and lay back down on the bed. Every part of the bed was soaked from my sweat and the sheets were cold to the touch. I kept all my clothes on and shivered through the night. The mice and cockroaches seemed to know that I was helpless and they lost their fear of me and started running onto and over me on the bed throughout the night. I drifted in and out of sleep all night and FINALLY MORNING CAME.

I got up. My clothes were soaked through with sweat. I took my wet clothes off and picked out a change of clothes from my pile of dirty laundry lying on the floor in the corner. At least they were dry. As soon as I changed, I knelt down by my bed and again I spoke out loud, "Jesus I believe in You. And I'm going to take a step of faith and I'm going to walk over to the Detox. If You make a bed there for me, I PROMISE You, I WILL FOLLOW You." I grabbed my plastic bag full of cigarette butts that I had collected the day before, put a few of my dirty clothes in a small bag, locked up my room and walked over to the Detox. I stood outside the Salvation Army Detox on Cordova St. and rang the buzzer. I waited and no one came. I rang the buzzer again holding it down to let it ring longer. After a few more minutes of waiting I was just about to turn away and leave when a man opens the door and says, "Yes can I help you?" "Do you have any beds?" "Man, are YOU LUCKY! Some guy just left TEN MINUTES AGO, there's ONE bed LEFT, come on in!" I knew it was NOT LUCK, Jesus had ANSWERED my prayer.

I was still in very bad physical shape when they booked me into Detox. Sitting there as they fill out my paperwork I am not a sight for sore eyes. I have very long hair reaching down to my butt that is greasy and dirty and it is pulled straight back Steven Siegal style into a ponytail. I use five elastic bands to keep it in a ponytail. My eyes have dark circles under them and they are sunken into the sockets. My teeth are missing in the front on top and on the bottom and the ones that remain are black with decay. I do not like to talk because of my teeth when I am sober. I am underweight by at least thirty pounds. After they booked me in I was so weak that I had a hard time standing just to take a shower and almost fell over a couple of times! When I was finished my shower the VERY FIRST THING I asked for was a Bible. I could not eat anything yet because of my alcohol and drug withdrawal and could barely keep water down. However, my thirst now was not for water but to see what was in God's Word, the Bible. I did not know how to find scripture verses in the Bible and did not know WHERE to START reading but I heard a man say one time, "If you want to hear from God, just open up the Bible and put your finger down wherever your finger lands start reading!" That was the only way I knew to read the Bible so that is exactly what I did. I opened the Bible up and put my finger down and I read; **"For I know the thoughts that I think toward you, saith the LORD, thoughts of peace, and not of evil, to give you an expected end. 12 Then shall ye call upon me, and ye shall go and pray unto me, and I will hearken unto you. 13 And ye shall seek me, and find _me_, when ye shall search for me with all your heart." - Jeremiah 29:11-13**.

God is telling me that He is NOT MAD AT ME. Deep inside of my heart I always felt that because of my life of crime God was mad at me and waiting to hit me with a lightning bolt. He was also telling me that if I wanted to find Him I would have to do it with ALL MY HEART. I was willing to do it with all my heart because I had made a promise to Him. I flipped to another spot in the Bible and put my finger down and read; **"A new heart also will I give you, and a new spirit will I put within you: and I will take away the stony heart out of your flesh, and I will give you an heart of flesh."(Ezekiel 36:26).** I NEEDED a NEW HEART because my old heart was FULL of anger, bitterness, resentment, hatred, un-forgiveness, loneliness, shame and the list goes on. Because of the past abuses in my life and because they forced us to never shed any tears at the residential school I hardened my heart with hatred and it was very hard for me to cry when I was sober. I had to have some alcohol in my system before I could shed a tear. But now God was telling me that He could give me a BRAND NEW HEART! YAHOO! There is HOPE for ME after all! THAT is EXACTLY what I need to hear.

I randomly turn to another part of the Bible and put my finger down and God says; **"If we confess our sins, he is faithful and just to forgive us _our_ sins, and to cleanse us from all unrighteousness." (1 John 1:9).** God was willing to forgive ALL my sins not just SOME of them but EVERY LAST ONE! I put my finger down and continue to read; **"And ye shall know the truth, and the truth shall make you free." (John 8:32).** So it is THE TRUTH that is going to MAKE me FREE, not AA, (Alcoholics Anonymous), not NA (Narcotics Anonymous) not CA (Cocaine Anonymous) but the TRUTH! But WHAT is the truth? I flip the pages, put my finger down and come to; **"Jesus saith unto him, I am the way, the truth, and the life: .." (John 14:6).** Ah ha, OK so JESUS is THE TRUTH and He is the One Who will make me FREE! So, I was looking in all the wrong places for my freedom! My finger goes down and comes to, **"If my people, which are called by my name, shall humble themselves, and pray, and seek my face, and turn from their wicked ways; then will I hear from heaven, and will forgive their sin, and will heal their land. (2 Chronicles 7:14).** OK. Now THAT is some deal! If I turn and stop my sinning God will not only forgive but He'll HEAL me! Awesome! I'm willing Lord just show me what to turn from. I put my finger down for the last time that night and God tells me; **"Therefore if any man _be_ in Christ, _he is_ a new creature: old things are passed away; behold, all things are become new." (2 Corinthians 5:17).**

I lifted my head from the pillow and sat up with my legs hanging over the side of the bed. I begin to think about what God is saying TO ME. I let His words "sink" into my heart as I ponder the reality of what I just read. How could I refuse what He was offering me? He was offering to forgive me of every one of my sins. He was offering to give me a brand new heart. He was offering to give me a whole new life and telling me that the old things or my old hurtful past will be "passed away." He was telling me that that I could get a BRAND NEW START and that HE was the ONLY ONE Who could give me that brand new start IF… I was willing to FOLLOW HIM with ALL of my HEART! I WANTED what He was offering me. It was EXACTLY what I NEEDED! But, there was one problem. I was on the verge of severe alcohol and cocaine withdrawal and there was a danger that I might go off the "deep end" and fall again into the hands of those demonic spirits that had tried to kill me once in 1985. So I bowed my head as I sat there on the edge of that bed and I prayed, "Dear Jesus I want to follow You but I am sick and I am on the verge of DT's. If You heal me and do not let me go through the DT's then I'll REALLY KNOW You're real and I WILL REALLY FOLLOW You!"

I went back over to the bookshelf and looked for more Christian material to read and I found a magazine that had people's personal testimonies of how Jesus had made them free and changed their lives. I fell asleep reading that magazine. When I opened my eyes the next morning the magazine was still lying on my chest and I was in my pajamas with my housecoat on sleeping on top of the bed covers. I swung my legs over the side of the bed and then the realization hit me; I SLEPT! Not only did I sleep, but I slept through the WHOLE NIGHT! And usually when I am coming off a "crash" from cocaine and alcohol I can't sleep for a couple of days and I certainly can't eat for another 5 days! Sitting there on the bed I had an overwhelming feeling of peace that flooded over me. It was a peace that I had never ever experienced before and I JUST KNEW I just KNEW that EVERYTHING was going to BE ALRIGHT from NOW ON. I knew it because AGAIN Jesus had ANSWERED my prayer EXACTLY the WAY I asked Him! It is January 31, 1994 the day I started to believe that there really was hope for me after all. I went and had breakfast. For breakfast I had coffee, cereal, toast and a banana. When I was done breakfast I did not realize it until I was walking out of the dining hall and on my way back to my bed and it dawned on me! I JUST ATE! Not only did I just eat, but I DRANK COFFEE! This is UNREAL! Because as I mentioned earlier when I am coming off a "crash" from cocaine and alcohol I can't sleep for a couple of days and I certainly can't eat for another 5 days! I realized right then and there that God had completely HEALED me of ALL of my withdrawal symptoms! No wonder I was feeling such peace. No wonder I was feeling that everything was going to be all right because GOD IS WITH ME! I couldn't WAIT to read the Bible again I wanted to learn more about what God's promises are in His Word. I wanted Him to teach me more about WHAT HE WANTED me to do so I could obtain that brand new life with Him! But first, I had to have a cigarette. I went back to my bed and pulled out my pouch of cigarette butts and rolled a cigarette. I walked out into the Common Room and sat down with the other alcoholics and drug addicts and I was feeling good! I thought to myself, "These guys need to know that God IS REAL and He is the ANSWER to their addictions. He can give THEM a brand NEW LIFE too! And the first thing I noticed was that every one of these addicts were staring at the TV. Every one of them! Then the thought hit me, "None of them have their minds on God because the devil is keeping their minds focused on the TV and it's through the TV that he is keeping their minds from the truth that God is real! I lit up my cigarette and took a drag. I kept thinking to myself, "The devil sure is doing a good job by lying to these men through the TV nothing on there is real it's all make-believe!" I was just about to take another puff of my cigarette and I thought, "Yeah, the devil has been lying to me about these cigarettes too! He's been lying to me by telling me that I am going to have a nervous break-down and it might kill me if I quit. When the truth is, I will live better if I quit. I then realized the truth and the truth is, I have been doing the devil's work all this time by smoking because I am killing myself through them and that is exactly what the devil wants! The truth is I have been listening to the lies of the devil and obeying him all my life! Well I was sick and tired of doing the devil's dirty work. I put my cigarette out and I bowed my head right then and there. I closed my eyes and without saying a word out loud deep in the depths of my heart I prayed, "Lord, I don't want to do the devil's work anymore. I'm sick and tired of that. I want to do Your work and I want to follow You. Please give me the faith to follow You. Please give me the faith to stop smoking, take away my cravings for alcohol and cocaine heal my broken heart and take away my anger. I ask it in the name of Jesus, amen." And you know what dear reader? I have never gone back not even once to alcohol, cocaine or any other illicit drug and I have never had not even one puff of a cigarette since the moment I said that prayer.

The next day Feb. 1, 1994, was my first day of totally repenting from alcohol, cigarettes, cocaine, heroin, marijuana and all other illicit drugs and I have been totally clean and totally sober right to this very day that I write this Aug. 31, 2012. A couple of days later I asked around to see if there was a Bible-Based Alcohol and Drug Treatment Program in the Lower Mainland. I soon learned there were a number of them. I chose to attend the Treatment Program offered out of the Union Gospel Mission a Baptist church affiliation. I chose that place because I was hungry for the Word of God and one of the addicts told me when I was enquiring about which treatment program to take said, "Oh you don't want to go to the Union Gospel Mission they teach too much Bible there, " and that is EXACTLY what I wanted MORE of the Bible! The same day that I made arrangements to attend the Union Gospel Mission, I was sitting in the Common Room at the Detox looking out the window and I saw many of my addict friends doing the same old they've always done; rushing here and rushing there as the devils of cocaine drove them to and fro and they had no idea whatsoever how to be ever break free. I knew that I had found the answer by doing what God's Word said to do. As I was watching them I heard a voice inside my head that said, "What do you think you're doing Andy? Do you think you're better than them? You're a failure just like them. You'll always be a failure. You're an alcoholic and a drug addict and always will be. You belong out there with the rest of those addicts. You tried treatment before and it never helped you. It'll be no different this time!" Then out of the blue, immediately following the voice I just heard I don't where they came from or if I read them or if I ever heard them before but these three scriptures came floating through my mind and those three scriptures became the PILLARS of my faith as I started walking this new road to freedom. Those scriptures are: 1. **"I can do all things through Christ who strengthens me." (Philippians 4:13);** 2. **"...If God _be_ for us, who _can be_ against us?" (Romans 8:31);** 3. **"Ye are of God, little children, and have overcome them: because greater is he that is in you, than he that is in the world." (1 John 4:4).** While I was at the Detox I wanted to find a church that held the most church services during the week because I couldn't get enough of God's Word! I found a little church right in the heart of skid row at Abbott and Hastings St. called "The Revival Centre." They held church EVERY NIGHT of the week and twice on Sunday! THAT was exactly what I was looking for! I attended every single night. I was so happy hearing the Word of God. I had never felt or known such happiness! Not in my entire life! At the Revival Centre I learn that the church is originally from Chilliwack and they are Pentecostal. At the time, I had no idea whatsoever that there was more than one type of Pentecostal church and that they do not all believe the same. I just wanted to HEAR the WORD OF GOD!

CHAPTER NINETEEN

A NEW ROAD

"A BRAND NEW DAY"

Today I'm given a brand new day
I'm looking to put old things away,
I have some choices only I can make
At times I feel like my soul is at stake,

I look upon this life of mine
Where tears and love stroll through hard-times,
And no one knows me when I'm blue
Yet God's sweet love still pulls me through,

Is there anyone out there singing my song?
Did you know Jesus felt He didn't belong?
Yet He kept on going though they bruised His face
Now we all can live in a better place,

Today I'm living a brand new day,
Only God can give it...and take it away

A. Nieman

After a week at Detox I was given the address to the Union Gospel Mission. It was located on Cordova St. just a couple of blocks up from the "Sally Ann" so I walked up there. When I arrived there I filled out the necessary paperwork, they gave me my bedding and put me in a dorm with six other men. It was a Men's Program there were no women. The attendant who gave me my bedding and checked me in told me, "Pastor Russell, he's the Manager of the program wants to see you in his office when you are done making your bed." "OK, thank you," "You're welcome." After I made my bed I went down to the office. Pastor Russell gave me a hard firm handshake and said with a big smile on his face, "Well Mr. Nee-man, welcome aboard!" "Thank you it feels good to be here." "That's great to hear. Have you ever been to treatment before?" "Yes, but never to one where they teach the Bible." "Oh I'm sure you're going to enjoy it. It'll be a battle but with God on your side you'll have the victory! And your first name is Andrew right?" "Andy," "Andy, OK. So have you accepted Jesus as your personal Savior yet Andy?" "Have I what?" "Accepted Jesus?" "What do you mean?" "Oh, I see you haven't OK well first things first," he reaches for a Bible and turns to **Romans 10:9-10** and shows me as he reads; **"That if you confess with your mouth, "Jesus is Lord," and believe in your heart that God raised him from the dead, you will be saved. 10 For it is with your heart that you believe and are justified, and it is with your mouth that you confess and are saved."** He closes the Bible and asks me, "Would you like to accept Jesus as your Savior?" "Sure. How do I do that?" "Well, all you have to do is believe with all your heart that Jesus Christ died upon the cross to forgive your sins like we just read and repeat the Sinner's Prayer after me and you will be saved." "OK." "OK bow your head, close your eyes and repeat after me," he stops every once in a while after a few words so I can keep up with him and we both say, "Heavenly Father, have mercy on me, a sinner. I believe in you and that your word is true. I believe that Jesus Christ is the Son of the living God and that he died on the cross so that I may now have forgiveness for my sins and eternal life. I know that without you in my heart my life is meaningless. I believe in my heart that you, Lord God, raised Him from the dead. Please Jesus forgive me, for every sin I have ever committed or done in my heart, please Lord Jesus forgive me and come into my heart as my personal Lord and Savior today. I need you to be my Father and my friend. I give you my life and ask you to take full control from this moment on; I pray this in the name of Jesus Christ. Amen."

"Well Praise the Lord! That is wonderful! Congratulations you're now a Christian! You're ready for heaven! Once saved always saved." "Once saved always saved?" I ask, "That's right, it's called Eternal Security meaning once you accept Jesus as your personal Savior you can never lose your salvation. Romans chapter 8 and versse 38-39 tells us that nothing can separate us from the love of God." "Thank You Jesus, Thank You Jesus!" is all I can say. "As a result of your conversion I have a gift for you Andy." He walks over to a bookshelf and takes out a brand new Bible from a stack of new Bibles. He hands me the New International Version Bible and I FEEL SO GOOD to have my OWN BIBLE. "Thank you Pastor Russell. Thank you very much." "Why you're very welcome son, it's my pleasure!"

I didn't know being saved was so easy and that I get even MORE HAPPIER than I was already. During the treatment program, I was falling in love with God's Word more and more each day and I couldn't wait to attend church each night! I still did not know how to find scripture or where to start reading in the

Bible but I noticed that there were 31 Chapters in the Book of Proverbs and since I wanted to read the Bible every day and knew there are 31 days in the longest month that is what I did, I read a chapter a day of Proverbs. Whenever I would read Proverbs and something in the chapter would STAND OUT for me or hit me like a ton of bricks, I wrote the scripture on the fleshy part of my thumb in pen and by that simple gesture, I was able to stand up to every temptation and overcome them by the Word of God. To get to the church I was attending I had to pass right by my old stomping grounds, my old friends and all the drug dealers who knew me like the back of their hands. There was no way to avoid them because the church was right downtown! When my old friends saw me walking by going to church they called out my name and invited me to join them as they sat there drinking and laughing like they were having a great time and when I felt weak and very tempted to join them, I would read the Proverbs scripture I had written on my hand and it always, ALWAYS gave me the extar boost I needed to say, "No thank you," and to continue on my way.

For the VERY FIRST TIME in my life I FELT FREE! WHY? Because I was learning that as long as I DID (not just believed in but actually DID), what the Word of God said to do I would be alright. I was not smoking, I was not drinking or taking any drugs and I LOVED to go to church and hear God talk to me! As part of the treatment program I attended AA Meetings and the others in the AA Meetings would say, "I thank God," and I would say, "I thank JESUS!" I went to my first NHL hockey game the second week I was at Union Gospel Mission and sitting way up there in the "nose-bleed" section watching the Chicago Blackhawks play the Vancouver Canucks, I was ON CLOUD NINE! Then one night two weeks after I had arrived at Union Gospel Mission as I was pulling off my socks getting ready for bed this thought hit me, "I can't believe how amazingly awesome everything is going in my life! Is it too good to BE TRUE? What if this is NOT GOD? What if this is JUST ME? What if this is just a dream, just my imagination and my bubble is about to burst? What if it's not God at all?" The lights go out. I sit there in the darkness with my legs over the side my bed and put my head in my hands. I feel scared and very discouraged and I start to worry. I get up and look out the window at the beautiful city lights of Vancouver at night. I watch as a car stops to talk to one of the "hookers" standing on the corner of the Mission. The Union Gospel Mission is located in a "red-light district" of Vancouver and "hookers" surround the Mission constantly and especially at night. I know exactly what is going on in those streets and I DO NOT want to go back there. I know that Jesus is my only hope but what if Jesus is not real? If He is not real then I have no hope whatsoever of succeeding and will inevitably wind up going back to that filthy life.

I lie down and miraculously fall asleep right away. I have a dream that night that is a most unusual dream. In the dream I am walking down the street in a residential area and I see a little old man who is a dwarf with a long, long white beard sitting on a picket fence. Did you hear that, He is SITTING on a PICKET fence and he is saying, "**Isaiah 45:45**." He catches my attention because I think to myself, "That MUST HURT sitting on a sharp fence like that," so I look at him again. And again he says, "**Isaiah 45:45**," and I wake up from the dream. I look over at the clock on my bed-stand. It is exactly 2:00 am and "**Isaiah 45:45**" is running through my mind. I pick up my Bible and I look for **Isaiah 45:45** but there is no **Isaiah 45:45**! Then **Isaiah 45:4** and **5** comes to mind and I turn there and this is what it says and in this scripture God Himself is speaking and he says, "**For the sake of Jacob my servant, of Israel my chosen, I summon you by name and bestow on you a title of honor,** though you do not acknowledge me. **5I am the LORD, and there is no other; apart from me there is no God. I will strengthen you, though you have not acknowledged me,**" (Isaiah 45:4-5). God KNEW EXACTLY what I was THINKING and EXACTLY what I was FEELING and He was letting me know that He was IN THIS ALL THE WAY. After that, whenever I thought about going back to my old lifestyle I thought, "Well I've let my mother down in the past, I've let my family down, I've let girlfriends down, I've let my friends down and I was able to run from all of them, but I just can't LET GOD DOWN because He sees everything I do and I want to show Him that I respect and appreciate Him!

Walking up Hastings St. one day two months into my sobriety as I was returning to the Union Gospel Mission, I saw Harry Hunt (RIP) and Peter Hager (RIP) standing on the corner of the Courthouse on Main and Hastings St. passing out tracts. Remember Harry Hunt? He was the man in the White Spot restaurant who eight years earlier told my mom that I was going to be a Preacher. Peter was in a wheelchair and Harry as usual had that shining smile on his face and Harry recognized me right away and he says, "Well Praise the Lord! Look who got saved Andy Nieman! Well praise God! It's so good to see you Brother Hallelujah!" Harry introduces me to Peter and then asks me, "Can I buy you some lunch?" "Actually I'm just on my way back to the Union Gospel Mission I have to be back for program." "Well can I buy you breakfast tomorrow morning?" "Sure, what time?" "You see that little restaurant right there on the corner?" he points, "Yes," "What time can you meet us there nine o'clock?" "Sure nine o'clock is good." Harry takes one of my hands and with both his hands he holds it and says, "Oh it' so good to see you Brother! I'm so happy for you. You're mom's prayers are finally answered! She's dancing in heaven right now!" I meet him and Peter at nine the next morning and we have breakfast. During the meal, Harry gets up and goes over to the payphone on the wall. He makes a phone call and I hear him say, "Guess who I'm sitting with? Andy Nieman, he got saved, praise God!" After breakfast as I am about to leave Harry tells me, "Sit down for one minute brother," I sit down. He takes out his wallet, licks his finger and separates five twenty dollar bills and he hands them to me, "Here that's for you," "No that's OK Harry I don't need that," "No you take it that's filled with the love of Jesus just for you." "OK. Thank you very much. Lord bless you guys and thank you for breakfast." Harry ends our conversation with, "Everybody is happy in Whitehorse to see you got saved, Hallelujah!" We both smile and laugh at each other. I shake both their hands and leave. The treatment program at Union Gospel Mission is three months long. It is a great program and every one treats me very well there. I phone my sister Kim and let her know that things are going great in my life and that I have decided to follow Jesus. She starts to cry on the phone and tells me that she remembers going into the washroom one time at her place and praying for me and God told her that I was going to be alright. Through the teachings in the Bible I learn to always be honest and truthful. To never run anymore from my problems but to stand, admit and face my fears head on. One day when it is my turn to work in the kitchen doing dishes, I see all of the workers there checking their Lottery tickets and I think in my heart, "Christians are not supposed to gamble. That's not the kind of Christian I'm going to be, I'm going to do exactly what God says to do." I see in the Bible that it is a shame for a man to have long hair in **1 Corinthians 11:14** so I get my hair cut. The first haircut I've had in over three years. Once you complete the 3-month program you are eligible to stay on and rent a room at the Mission. That is what I do. I enroll in an Upgrading course at Carnegie Hall on Main and Hastings. I know I need to get an education so I can learn a trade in order to become a productive member of society. I still have a shop-lifting charge that I have to deal with in Vancouver and I have a warrant out for my arrest in the Yukon. I am going to come clean with everything in my life and deal with all my charges in an honest way. I know I am guilty of the crimes that I am charged with and I make arrangements to plead guilty to everything. I try to waive my charges down to Vancouver from the Yukon so I can deal with every-thing at once but they won't allow me to. I go to court in Vancouver and plead guilty to my charges. I write a letter to the Judge explaining that I am turning my life around completely and if he decides to send me to jail I am still going to continue the path I am on. I have no idea but on that same day that I am attend-ing court and reading out my letter to the Judge there is a man named David Jobson sitting in the audience praying for me and he prays, "Jesus, keep Andy on the right path and lead him to the truth." Years later God would cause Bro. Jobson and I to meet to each other at Canada Conference in New Westminster. Bro. Jobson approached me at the conference and says, "I remember you! I was in court the day you read that letter and I prayed for you," God, as usual had someone there to pray for me. The Judge gives me a Stay of Proceedings.

When I arrive back at the Mission there is a message for me to phone my sister Margaret and another message for me to phone Northern Native Broadcasting Yukon (NNBY). NNBY are interested in doing a television docu-mentary on Yukoners who are living on skid row and they are wondering if I am willing to be in the documentary and would I show them around skid row? I agree to do the documentary and the title of the documentary is, "LIFE DOWN HERE" (the DVD can be ordered by phoning 867-668-6629). I phone my sister Margaret and she informs me that she is getting married and invites me to her wedding on July 2, 1994 in Haines Junction, Yukon. I take the bus back to the Yukon and attend Margaret's wedding. While I am in Whitehorse, I stay with my sister Elsie (RIP) and attend the same church my mom was attend-ing when she was alive, First Pentecostal Church, an affiliation of the UNITED PENTECOSTAL CHURCH INTERNATIONAL, pastored by Pastor Ted and

Margaret Wagner. Pastor Roger Yadon Sr. and Sis Willow Yadon are involved in the church as Associate Pastor. At that time the church in Whitehorse had been sold to make room for a Senior Citizen's complex and church services were being held in the gymnasium of Selkirk Street School.

While I am in Whitehorse I meet some of my old drinking buddies and I lead some of them in the Sinner's Prayer and tell them they are saved. I tell them once they accepted Jesus as their Savior they have eternal security and cannot lose their salvation. I tell them, "You don't have to do anything for salvation just believe in Jesus." I was about to learn that what I was teaching them was not truth and was not the biblical plan of salvation and I have asked God to forgive me. I noticed there is no change in their lives and why would there be, if 'once saved always saved' there would be no need for change. I am about to learn the truth about what JESUS TAUGHT on the PLAN of SALVATION. However, it would take me some time to learn and for my spiritual "eyes" to be opened to the truth. I'm thankful God is in control of all things.

CHAPTER TWENTY

EVERY SIN WASHED AWAY

"THE LIGHTHOUSE" (Con't from ch 1)

And then a light came shining through,
I heard a brand new song,
That told me Jesus has the love,
I'd need to make me strong,

I talked to Him and turned from sin,
Got baptized in His Name,
He filled me with the Holy Ghost,
And I've never been the same,

My sun's not setting anymore,
There's a lighthouse in its place,
With a brand new light and a brand new life,
I know I'll win life's hardest race,
With a brand new light and a brand new love
All I need comes from above

A. Nieman

One Sunday after church Pastor Wagner and Sis. Wagner invite me over to their house for supper along with Pastor and Sis Yadon and Sis. Margaret Smeeton. Sis Smeeton was with me in the Group Home when we were teenagers and she is very happy at the changes that are happening in my life. Sis Smeeton's husband Kirk was working in a mine somewhere in the Northwest Territories then. As we sit down to dinner, I am excited about the people that I have lead through the Sinner's Prayer and I tell Pastor Wagner all about it during supper. There is a fairly long silence in the room after I finish explaining what I have done. Then I pull out a list of names of those who I have lead in the Sinner's Prayer and I ask Pastor Wagner, "Can you please follow up with these people after I go?" Pastor Wagner takes the list. I break the silence by explaining all the wonderful things that are happening in my life since I decided to follow Jesus. After supper Pastor Wagner asks me, "When are you going back down to Vancouver?" "On Thursday," "You're going by Greyhound?" "Yeah." he checks his calendar and says, "I'm going to be busy tomorrow and Tuesday, what are you doing on Wednesday?" "Not much that I know of," "I'd like to buy you lunch if you'd like?" "OK," "Where would you like to eat what kind of food do you like?" "Chinese," "OK, you're staying at Elsie's right?" "Yes," "OK, why don't I pick you up there and we'll go get some Chinese?" "OK," "OK good I'll stop by at 11:30 on Wednesday would that work?" "That'll work."

Pastor Wagner picks me up at 11:30 that Wednesday and after I get into his car he asks, "Is there a particular Chinese restaurant you want to go to?" "No not really," "OK I know where we can go." We go to the Family Oriental restaurant and Pastor Wagner brings his Bible in with him and sets it on the chair beside him. After we finish eating Pastor Wagner takes out his Bible and before opening it he asks me, "You haven't been baptized in Jesus' Name yet have you Andy?" "No," "And you probably haven't received the baptism of the Holy Ghost either huh?" I answered with a question mark in my voice, "The Holy Ghost?" "Yeah, the Holy Spirit," "Yes I have the Holy Spirit," "Did you speak in tongues when you received the Holy Spirit?" "Did I what?" "Speak in tongues?" "No, what's that?" "Well when we are filled with the Holy Spirit the Spirit will cause us to speak in a language that we do not understand the Bible calls it 'speaking in tongues'. And when we speak in tongues this is the sign that we have received the Spirit of God and we will know FOR SURE that we HAVE RECEIVED IT because of this." "I was told that I received the Holy Spirit as soon as I said the Sinner's Prayer and accepted Jesus." "OK were you shown that in the Bible?" "No." "OK well let's look and see what THE BIBLE SAYS about the plan of salvation, the Holy Spirit and what we need to do to be saved is that OK?" "Yep." "OK the first two things we need to know are first of all THE BIBLE SAYS that God came to earth as the man Jesus; **"And without controversy great is the mystery of godliness: God was manifest in the flesh, justified in the Spirit, seen of angels, preached unto the Gentiles, believed on in the world, received up into glory. (1 Timothy 3:16).** This fact is stated clearly in; **"...and of whom as concerning the flesh Christ *came*, who is over all, God..." (Romans 9:5).** "So right away we learn that Jesus was fully a man, a human being with flesh and blood like all other human beings, yet He is also fully God. Now the second important thing we need to learn FROM THE BIBLE is that there is ONE Plan of Salvation for ALL of humanity. There is not a "special" plan of salvation JUST FOR First Nation people and there is not a "special" plan of salvation JUST FOR the Orientals nor for any other race, there is ONE PLAN FOR ALL. God tells us this in His word;" **"*There is* one body, and one Spirit, even as ye are called in one hope of your calling;**

5 One Lord, one faith, one baptism, 6 One God and Father of all, who *is* **above all,…" (Ephesians 4:4-6).** "OK. Now we learn that Jesus is God and that there is ONE PLAN of salvation. Now let's see WHAT is involved in THAT ONE PLAN and we'll learn it from Jesus, from God Himself."

So as we sit in that little Chinese restaurant I learn that being "Saved" (being spiritually born again and ready for the return of Jesus, for heaven and for Judgment Day), is more than believing in and accepting Jesus as my Savior, it involves being born of the water and of the Spirit just like Jesus said; **"Jesus answered and said unto him, Verily, verily, I say unto thee, Except a man be born again, he cannot see the kingdom of God. 4 Nicodemus saith unto him, How can a man be born when he is old? can he enter the second time into his mother's womb, and be born? 5 Jesus answered, Verily, verily, I say unto thee,** Except a man be born of water and *of* the Spirit, **he cannot enter into the kingdom of God." (John 3:3-5)**

Pastor Wagner went on to explain that being born "of the water" is to be baptized in the Name of Jesus and when I do this all of my sins will be washed away just like it says in the Bible; **"Arise and be baptized, and wash away your sins, calling on the name of the Lord." (Acts 22:16).** Then he shows me another scripture on baptism where Jesus again is talking and Jesus says; **"He that believes and is baptized shall be saved;…" (Mark 16:16).**

I looked at Pastor Wagner a bit confused and trying to wrap my head around baptism but not wanting to appear disrespectful I ask, "So we have to be baptized in order to be saved right?" "Right." "OK. I was baptized as a Catholic when I was a baby so I'm OK right?" "Well no Bro. Andy and I'll tell you why. Nowhere and I mean NOWHERE in the Bible will you find a record of a baby or an infant being baptized do you know why?" "No why?" "Because babies are innocent. They do not have any sin and are not even aware of sin they are totally innocent! They have no need to be baptized as a baby because there is no sin in their life whatsoever. I mean they're BABIES! It is when they get older and become AWARE of what sin is and it is only AFTER they KNOW they have been involved in sin and want to make things right with God then THAT is the time to be baptized. And when biblical baptism takes place it HAS TO BE in the NAME OF JESUS. It's THROUGH the Name of Jesus that our sins are forgiven and removed. Here I'll show you IN THE BIBLE don't just take my word for it I'll show it to you in the Bible." I am totally captivated by what I am learning and SEEING in the WORD OF GOD I had NO IDEA that all this was in there! Pastor Wagner turns to and reads from **Acts 19:5; "When they heard** *this***, they were baptized in the name of the Lord Jesus."**

This is ALL NEWS to me. I did not have a CLUE that I NEEDED to be baptized again and that baptism HAS to BE IN THE NAME of Jesus in order to have my sins washed away! I am not totally convinced yet though because I was taught differently. It seemed like Pastor Wagner knew what was going on in my head because he said, "Still not convinced huh?" "Well," I hesitated, "You know things have been going so great in my life, I have a lot of joy, I am happy and I know God has been blessing me…and well, if I was wrong why would

He be blessing me?" "Yes He has been blessing you Bro. Andy and that is great. He will continue to bless you and once you get baptized in His Name you will have MORE JOY because every one of your sins will be washed away and you will be closer to God than you have ever been!" "I don't know, I feel pretty close to God now and I already have LOTS of JOY!" "Well you'll have more joy!" "I don't think I could possibly have more joy than I do now." "Believe me, once you are baptized in the name of Jesus and all your sins are washed away you WILL HAVE more joy." "OK, if you say so, I just don't think it's possible!"

"Here Bro. Andy, let me show you one more scripture and then we'll go. If you want to know how to be saved the whole plan of salvation is right here in this one scripture in three simple steps," he flips through a few pages in the Bible and when he finds what he is looking for, he holds his finger on the scripture, hands the Bible to me with his finger at the place he wants me to read and says, "Here it is in three simple steps," and I read the scripture for myself and this is what I read; **"Then Peter said unto them, Repent, and be baptized every one of you in the name of Jesus Christ for the remission of sins, and ye shall receive the gift of the Holy Ghost." (Acts 2:38).** I want to be absolutely sure I understand so I turn to look at Pastor Wagner and I ask, "What are the three steps?" "Well we have to number one; REPENT which means to turn from our sin and turn to God and two; we have to get BAPTIZED in the Name of Jesus for the remission of our sins," I interrupt him to ask, "What does 'remission' mean?" "Remission means for the forgiveness of our sins," "Oh, OK," he continues, "And three; RECEIVE the GIFT of the HOLY GHOST which is the Holy Spirit of God. And once you receive the Holy Ghost you will speak in tongues and then you are BORN AGAIN and you will be ready for heaven." We get up from the table and Pastor Wagner pays for the meal with his credit card and we jump into his truck. He turns to me and asks, "So what do you think?" "Think? About what?" "Being baptized." "Oh, ah, yeah I wouldn't mind." "OK that's GREAT Bro Andy! That's GREAT! When would you like to be baptized?" "I don't know, when?" "Well you're leaving tomorrow right?" "Right," "Why not today?" "Today?" "Sure how about this afternoon?" "OK. Where?" "Well we can do it at the church or we can do it in the Yukon River or we can even do it in a bath tub which would you prefer?" "The Yukon River." "OK that's great! How 'bout two o'clock?" "OK. What do I bring?" "Just a change of clothes, I'll have Sis Wagner bring some towels." "OK." "That is just great Bro. Andy!" Pastor Wagner picked me up at my sister Elsie's place at 1:30 and we went down to Rotary Park a small park on the bank of the Yukon River. And right in front of the exact spot where I used to drink wine on the riverbank with my friends, Pastor Wagner baptized me in the Name of Jesus and every one of sins were washed away! As soon as I came out of the water, I looked up to heaven and said, "There mom! What do you think about that!?" The date was Wednesday July 13, 1994. That evening, Pastor Wagner said to me, "Bro. Andy when you get down to Vancouver it would good for you to seek the Lord for direction in your life." I thought to myself, "SEEK THE LORD? How do you SEEK the Lord?" I didn't say anything though and Pastor Wagner continued, "If the Lord directs you back to Whitehorse just give me a phone call and we'll pay for your ticket back here." "OK." "OK we'll see you then Bro Andy, Lord bless you."

On the bus the next day heading to Vancouver I remember Pastor Wagner telling me that once I am baptized in the Name of Jesus I will be closer to God. As the Greyhound bus sped down the highway I looked out the window at the trees speeding by. I thought to myself, "Just think God knows everything. He knows how many trees there are out there and not only that, He knows HOW MANY little pine needles are on EACH BRANCH! And if He KNOWS that then He knows EXACTLY WHERE I am at ALL TIMES and THAT means that I'll NEVER have to BE ALONE again from now on!" and the tears came flowing out of my eyes like big drops of rain and I HAD NO CONTROL over them whatsoever! And THIS was the VERY FIRST TIME that I cried tears of joy when I was SOBER and it went to prove that God was true to His Word when he told me, "A new heart also will I give you, and a new spirit will I put within you: and I will take away the stony heart out of your flesh, and I will give you an heart of flesh." (Ezekiel 36:26). Chronic, toxic loneliness packed up his bag on that bus ride back to Vancouver and walked out of my life and has never returned. Because Jesus is God and God is real and He is everywhere I know I will never be alone again.

As I stepped off the bus back in Vancouver I had a lot of thoughts running through my mind. Thoughts like how am I supposed to "seek" the Lord as Pastor Wagner had mentioned for direction in my life? How long can I stay at Union Gospel Mission? What am I going to do with my future? I did not know how to live a healthy life. The only way I learned to live a healthy life was by reading and doing what the Bible said to do. That was my roadmap to success. It was my foundation. As long as I did what the Bible said to do I would not fail. And that is exactly what I did and that is exactly what kept happening in my life I met with success after success after success. And it is still happening in my life to this very day! Now I knew that when I did what the Bible said to do; my life, my health, my outlook on life, my expectations, my faith, my treatment of people and get this… NEW DREAMS and NEW POSSSIBILITIES poked their heads into the scattered boneyard where my old broken dreams lay and truth picked up those old dreams, blew the dust of hopelessness off and handed them back to me. They were brand new. They now had REAL POSSIBILITY! I now KNEW deep inside my heart this REALITY, **"…with God all things are possible." (Matthew 19:26)**.

I began to "seek" the Lord for His direction in my life. I wanted to KNOW what it was that HE wanted me to do with this new found freedom that He was giving me. The only way I knew to "seek" the Lord was to get on my knees and pray and bring it all to Jesus. I just knew I had to be totally honest and that being totally honest was the only way for me to communicate with God so I said, "Lord I don't want to miss whatever plan you have for my life. I want to be absolutely SURE I am doing YOUR WILL and not mine. I will go wherever You want me to go and do whatever it is You ask me to do. If you want me to stay here in Vancouver I'll stay. If you want me to go to Whitehorse I'll go to

Whitehorse." Well after "putting out a fleece" (for a definition you can look up "putting out a fleece" on the Internet), it was clear that God wanted me back in Whitehorse. As soon as I know that I am to go back to Whitehorse I phone Pastor Wagner and he buys me a bus ticket. I say my, "Good-byes" to the people at Union Gospel Mission and on August 14, 1994 I get on the bus headed for Whitehorse, Yukon my hometown.

CHAPTER TWENTY ONE

SCHOOL AND THE HOLY GHOST

"ALL THE WAY"

Tore down the wall I stand here free
I'm going to be all that I can be!
Made my heart clean for eternity
Totally sure of my liberty,
I ran from life and lost my sleep
Past fading love I could not keep,
I felt a touch that touched me deep
Never knew love could be so sweet,
I looked to see Who's love it was
I had to look up, it flowed from above,
Made up my mind going all the way
I'll obey You Jesus 'til my dying day!

A. Nieman

I arrived back in Whitehorse and started attending the First Pentecostal Church where Pastor Wagner is pastoring. Two of the biggest obstacles any alcoholic or drug addict will face when they decide to pursue a life of sobriety are: LONELINESS and TIME. If an alcoholic or drug addict learns to deal and address these two things he/she will be on their way to successfully staying sober. Loneliness comes as a result of exchanging the people they use to associate with (drinking buddies) for new ones. It is rare for a chronic alcoholic to have healthy sober friends so they will have to find and make new friends. This is a very lonely process. The other issue, the issue of time is quite evident. The addict will find him/herself with an enormous amount of free time on their hands because in the past all their time was spent in the bar drinking. Now with all this free time on their hands they'll need to find something healthy to occupy their time. In my situation, the church helped me to overcome the loneliness and going back to school helped me with the time. One of the good and healthy things about the loneliness of sobriety in my case is that I learned to cry in a healthy way. In the past when I was dysfunctional and I got lonely instead of dealing with the feeling in a healthy way I drank. Now, being sober and following God I learned the value of shedding tears.

Throughout all that was happening in my life of sobriety and following Jesus up this point was nothing short of FANTASTIC! However, I was soon to learn that old scars don't automatically disappear just because a person believes in and decides to follow Jesus. I was about to learn just how dysfunctional and institutionalized my brain really was. More than anything else and second only to being a true Christian, I wanted to help other alcoholics and I WANTED SO BADLY to become a qualified Alcohol and Drug Counselor. I learned to my dismay that in the Yukon there was no such training available. One day when I was at Skookum Jim Friendship Center talking to a Training Counselor I learned about a pilot project program that was being started at Yukon College for First Nations students called Community Services Preparation Program (CSPP). The program was put together to assist students who were starting out on sobriety and wanted to further their education. The program had a Life Skills component to it as well as an Academic component. Through this program, a person could go to school to heal and learn at the same time. It was like this program was tailor-made for a former skid row alcoholic just like me. It was like God had orchestrated the program because He knew that was exactly what I needed. And yes, it WAS EXACTLY what I needed! I filled the application out at Skookum Jim Friendship Center went for an interview and then received a phone call that I was accepted into the program.

Well, on the first day of school when I walked into Yukon College it was the first time I was walking into such a big institution and it immediately reminded me of jail and it triggered me. It is a strange thing when the traumatized brain is triggered. The brain AUTOMATICALLY goes to a place where IT WANTS TO GO and the person has no say and no control over it. In jail a convict is continuously under surveillance by a video camera and as convicts we are constantly aware of this fact. When I walked into Yukon College my brain automatically without any help from me went into "jailhouse mentality" and I DID NOT EVEN KNOW IT! By 'jailhouse mentality' I mean that it feels like I am constantly on surveillance, like I have a camera watching me and recording me twenty fours a day seven days a week just like jail. I enter the college and as I am walking down the hall my brain gets "triggered" and in my thinking, I believe there is a camera and a guard is watching me to see if I mess up. Now in reality at that time 1994, there ARE NO CAMERAS in the school at Yukon College. Yet in my world, in my reality (unknown to me), at that time my brain is triggered and it thinks it is back in jail. I have this POWERFUL FEELING to RUN! I just NEED to TURN AROUND and GET OUT OF HERE! But no, I have learned to FACE MY FEARS because the Word of God says, **"For**

God has not given us a spirit of fear, but of power and of love and of a sound mind. (2 Timothy 1:7). So I GO AGAINST what I AM FEELING and I force myself to walk down the hall and I stop outside the Student Lounge. I lean on the doorjamb and peer in and I MAKE SURE I DO NOT ENTER because IN MY MIND I am IN JAIL and ON CAMERA and I don't want to MAKE A MISTAKE because there's a guard watching me. So I peer in and look at the other people sitting in the Student Lounge. Just then a young man looks up at me. When our eyes meet I make sure I keep his attention by raising my hand and ask him, "Am I allowed in here?" "'Scuse me?" I say it louder, "Am I ALLOWED in here?" "Do you go to school here?" "Yes," "Then you're allowed in here this the Student Lounge." "Oh. OK, Thank you". RELIEF! I go in and sit down on one of the nice big soft chairs. I sink into the comfort of the chair and I process what just happened. I think to myself, "Wow! That was too strange! That was weird! That was too close for comfort! I've got to slow down. Thank you Lord for Your Word." This episode only serves to solidify my resolve to ALWAYS FACE MY FEARS and NEVER RUN FROM them NO MATTER WHAT, because God IS with me.

It was at church in one of the services that I met a wonderful lady named Estelle Godbout, who has been in the church for over ten years at that time. She started talking to me about needing the infilling of the Holy Ghost in order to be saved and she backed up everything she was talking about by showing it to me in the Bible. I thought I ALREADY HAD the Holy Spirit because that's what I was taught. I did not know that it was one of the MOST BEAUTIFUL EXPERIENCES available to humanity! And then God clearly showed me that I NEEDED His SPIRIT inside of me in order to truly BE HIS CHILD and IF I DO NOT HAVE His Spirit I am none of His; **"But ye are not in the flesh, but in the Spirit, if so be that the Spirit of God dwell in you. Now if any man have not the Spirit of Christ, he is none of his." (Romans 8:9)** God also showed me that when I DO RECEIVE His Spirit inside of me I WILL KNOW I HAVE RECEIVED IT because I will "speak in tongues" (an unknown language) just like it says in the Bible, **"All of them were filled with the Holy Spirit and began to speak in other tongues as the Spirit enabled them." (Acts 2:4)** (NIV). Once I saw all this in the Word of God and began to understand that I NEEDED the Holy Spirit as part of the New Birth experience and to make it into heaven, I made it a priority to seek after it. And true to His Word God filled me with the Holy Spirit and I spoke in tongues on November 17, 1994!

Now up to this point in my life God had made Himself real to me in so many ways; through my dreams, by answering my prayers and talking to me through His Word the Bible and it was like well, like I knew He existed, but it was as if He existed way out there IN SPACE SOMEWHERE. However ALL that changed WHEN I received His SPIRIT (the Holy Ghost) that was THE DAY I KNEW with ALL my HEART, WITHOUT A SHADOW of a DOUBT that GOD IS REAL! Because NOW…He has COME to LIVE INSIDE of me through His Spirit and THIS is the ONLY REAL WAY that any of us can be ABSOLUTELY CERTAIN that God IS REAL while we are on this earth! The moment I received His Spirit I started speaking in tongues and when I HEARD MYSELF speaking in tongues I HAD JOY UNSPEAKABLE for the FIRST time in my ENTIRE LIFE! It is called joy unspeakable because even though I may have a gift for words, I am still NOT ABLE to DESCRIBE HOW BEAUTIFUL that experience REALLY IS! The Bible itself says, **"...ye rejoice with joy unspeakable and full of glory:" (1 Peter 1:8)**.

Dear reader you have read this far for a reason. You did not stop when you arrived at the places where I mentioned the Word of God and you did not toss this book aside and label it as an interesting autobiography. You know why? Because God has caused my life to cross paths with your life and it would be the means by which He would get your attention. His reason for getting your attention is the most beautiful reason of all. He wants you to know the GENUINE LOVE He has JUST for YOU and He is showing you how to MAKE HEAVEN YOUR HOME.

What you believe is VERY IMPORTANT and you have the FREEDOM to CHOOSE and believe whatever you want to believe. But having read what you have read so far and the scriptures of truth in God's Word that you have SEEN with your OWN EYES, you have now become accountable and there is a REAL CHOICE for you to MAKE. You can TAKE what you have read as truth and ACT upon it or you can LEAVE it, do nothing and go on with your life as you always have. If nothing changes nothing changes. God is not going to force you to follow Him. Yet, no matter what you CHOOSE to do or choose not to do Judgment Day is still coming for both of us and for every other human being that has ever lived on planet earth. And THAT is ONE APPOINTMENT that NONE of us will MISS... "For it is written, *As* I live, saith the Lord, every knee shall bow to me, and every tongue shall confess to God. 12 So then every one of us shall give account of himself to God." (Romans 14:11-12). You may say, "Well, I have never really harmed anyone and I would help anyone I can. I give to the poor and I am active in my community." That is all good. In fact, that is great! Maybe you have never bent your elbow to take a sip of an alcoholic drink. Maybe you have never raised or let the stain of a nicotine cigarette touch your lips. It could very well be that you have never ever touched an illicit drug or slept in the wrong bed... yet you still need to be born again in the only way possible (of the water and of the Spirit) and by the only One Who can give you that brand new spiritual life in order to be ready for Judgment Day, His name is JESUS.

Ever since the night when I was filled with the Holy Ghost that JOY has REMAINED and now eighteen years later it is just as strong, just as beautiful and just as pure as it was that November night. If not for the Spirit of God I would not be here today. If not for the Spirit of God I would have given into temptation years ago and who knows where I would be. I married my lovely wife Estelle on May 10, 1997. I graduated from the University of Regina in June 2000 with a Bachelor of Social Work Degree. I received my Local Minister's License in 2000. I started my own business in 2004. I started a church daughter-work in Carmacks,Yukon. I was Ordained with the UNITED PENTECOSTAL CHURCH in June 2009. In December 2009 I became an Officer of the Legislative Assembly as the Yukon's first ever Child and Youth Advocate a job I am still doing as of this writing. I Pastor the A. C. T. S church in Carmacks and I'm involved in reaching other Yukon communities with this Glorious truth. God has been and is so good to me.

I am 5 yrs. old with my little sister Frieda at our home in Sleepy Hollow

Buddy made this crossbow for me. I am 7 yrs. old. That's Johnny Tom Tom's old car behind me that I slept in many times.

Drinking

**My "baby-sister" Frieda and her son Richard.
I think this was taken in Chilliwack.**

This is my mom and I. Frieda took this picture. This picture was taken two days after I got out of the psyche ward in Chilliwack. I have some life in my eyes and I am happy to still be in this world!

My sister Liz "Lizzy" and husband Roland and their daughters (L) Brenda and Stacey Marie (RIP). We've come through a lot together.

CHAPTER TWENTY TWO

EPILOGUE

"THE BEST I'LL EVER HAVE"

I am so happy and so glad,
You're the best Friend I'll ever have,
You live inside me, made me free,
Sin had me blind You made me see,
My sweet Lord Jesus, no one knows,
what we've been through the seeds I've sown,
Yes, some were evil some were good,
didn't always live the way I should,

You took me back when I have strayed,
and You forgave each time I prayed,
There's nothing now I'd rather do,
then what You ask, that's loving You,
I know my life on earth is short,
please help me strive to do Your work,
The road is rough not always smooth, but with
Your love I'll make it through,

Someday I'll stand in eternity, all disappointments behind me,
Your loving face I'll finally see, how Thankful on that day I'll be!
I am so happy and so glad You are the best Lord, I'll ever have!

A. Nieman

I pulled up to a red light on Main and Hastings St. in my Honda five years after I left skid row. This was the very first time I had been back there since

I left in August 1994. I had my six year old grandson Peter sitting with me in the front seat. As I was waiting for the light to change I looked over to the place where I used to stand on the corner of Main and Hastings in front of Carnegie and I looked at all the addicts there. I COULD NOT BELIEVE how DARK and DIRTY and FILTHY they LOOKED! And when I realized that I used to BE ONE OF THEM, I had no control over my tears and I began TO WEEP! I started to weep because BACK THEN when I was ONE OF THEM I had NO IDEA how DARK and DIRTY and FILTHY I really was! I was brought back to reality by a car's horn honking behind me and when I started driving Peter saw my tears and asked me, "What's the matter Poppa?" "You see all those guys over there Peter?" "Yeah," "Poppa used to be one of them." "You mean you used to drink beer?" "Yup. Drank beer and took bad drugs and stole from innocent people and was in and out of jail and did a lot of bad things," "And then you met Jesus?" "And then I met Jesus Peter and I have never been the same since." "I'm glad you don't drink beer any more Poppa." "I'm glad too Peter, you know why I'm glad?" "Why?" "Because I wouldn't have met you otherwise." "And you wouldn't have met Estelle!" "Right! And I wouldn't have met Estelle."

I have the utmost respect for Alcoholics Anonymous because they have helped so many people and still do. In their program they have a saying and that saying is this, "Once an alcoholic always an alcoholic." As much as I respect the people and their program I just have to TELL THE TRUTH and the truth is this; you might start out as an alcoholic but once you are BORN AGAIN of the water and of the Spirit ACCORDING TO GOD'S WORD you become a NEW CREATION! HOW do I know? I know from first-hand, front-row, I've-gone-through-it experience! Here's PROOF. My wife Estelle and I were invited to a supper by Christiana a friend of Estelle's. As it turned out it was a dinner party and there was alcohol being served. As soon as Estelle and I arrived at the dinner we sat down at a counter that was just big enough for the two of us. About two minutes later one of Christiana's friends came over and placed a full bottle of wine right in front of my face along with two glasses! The bottle was almost touching my nose! I pushed the bottle back from my face then Estelle turned and smiled at me and said, "Well obviously they think we're drinkers." My wife had never been drunk not even once in her entire life and here she was married to one of the Yukon's biggest former hard-core alcoholics who was now two years sober. I looked at the bottle and although it was wine, to me it looked like it was nothing more than "freshee" or "kool-aid."

The bottle sat there in front of us for about fifteen minutes. While it was sitting there I turned to Estelle and said, "You know, if I did not have the Holy Ghost and if I was back where I used to be and trying to stay sober, I would not be able to leave that full bottle there because I would be breaking out in a cold sweat, my hands would be sweaty and shaky, my heart would be pounding and my mouth would be getting mighty dry and I would be using all my strength and concentration to KEEP MYSELF FROM REACHING for it! I would NOT be able to stay sitting here! But now that I'm not an alcoholic anymore it just looks like soda pop and I'm as calm as calm can be." "Praise God, it's a miracle!" she said. It was easy to see the joy in my wife's eyes!

At Mount Thurston Prison Camp in 1983, I was working in the kitchen trying to do my time as best I could. I was 29 yrs. old and I was in the best shape of my life. I bet a guy there named Terry that I could quit smoking cigarettes for good but alas I only lasted 30 days. I could bench-press 250 pounds, I was jogging, playing soccer, drinking lots of eggnog and I was reading stacks of Psychology books looking for a way to straighten out my life. I was on a big "think positive" trip back then and it was one of the few times in my dysfunctional life that I dared to dream yet dream I did. In my dream I am a successful writer making a living writing poetry. I am sitting at my desk with a cup of coffee in my hand and a pencil behind my ear. I'm sitting beside a wall that is made mostly of glass on the second floor of a nice home overlooking a beautiful lake. I put my feet up on the desk lean back and look out the window and enjoy the scenery that is calm, quiet and as I ponder the serenity, I am content. Then the dream ends. It is a short dream but it is my dream and it is a dream that is still yet to be realized and it is a dream that is now possible because I never dreamed I would come to know God as I know Him now and with God all of my dreams are possible. Yet, my BIGGEST DREAM of ALL is this…all I want from God is to please let my life be used to its fullest potential so that as many people as possible and especially you who are reading this will be saved and come to know the truth. Then it dawns me as I put the last few finishing lines on this project of my life-story…that my GREATEST dream of all will only come true with YOUR participation when YOU RESPOND and are BORN AGAIN of the water and of the Spirit.

P. S. If you want all that God has for you and would like to know HOW to be BORN AGAIN and about the PLAN OF SALVATION that will MAKE YOU FREE and READY for the RETURN of Jesus and for Judgment Day go to: http://www.upci.org or visit a UNITED PENTECOSTAL CHURCH near you. Or you might want to contact me personally through my website: www.freemanwalking.net Lord Bless you.

"THE WAY OUT"

I lived in a valley all shadowed in doubt, I lacked me the courage to
find a way out.

The world beat me down, and laughed in my face, I lived as an addict,
in shame and disgrace,

I worked everyday in the "Mine of Lost Dreams," digging up
sorrow... from sad memories.

I made me some friends called, "Lonely & Fear", who *always* told me,
"You'll never, leave here."

The walls of this valley seemed too hard to scale, To find the good life,
I *always* would fail.

With walls of despair I built me a house, A soul forced to live in the
"Valley of Doubt".

One night I laid down and wiped away tears, I cried, "*Dear Lord, are
you really up there?*"

"*I can't take this shame, this sorrow and pain, Lord, if You're real*, please *show
me the way!*"

I then met a man with scars in His hands, He stopped me and said, "*I
understand.*"

He said, "*I have heard, everyone of your prayers, I've come now to show you,
just how much I care*".

"*I'll show you the way, out of all your despair, I'll give you a future, your life can
be spared*".

"*You'll need to repent of all your old ways, Turn from your sins, My words to
obey*".

"When you are baptized in My Holy Name, everyone of your sins,
will be washed away".

"*I'll give you my Spirit, you'll speak with new tongues, I'll write down your
name, in Life's book with love*".

I took His advice, began to obey, all of the words this man had to say,

From that moment on, things started to change, I found a new
strength, to live every day,

Today, I look back on the "Valley of Doubt," I now have the Truth I've found The Way Out.
I'm living the life, I've longed to enjoy, A life of TRUE Love, real PEACE and real JOY.
No longer do I have to fear life, or death, God's given me life, that life is the BEST!
I've found The Way Out, God's given to me, The love of one man has set my soul free.
That man's now my Friend, He's taught me to smile, When I asked Him His name, He said "*JESUS,...my child.*"
I've found The Way Out, it's so plain to see, God's love from above, has set my soul free!
I've found The Way Out, it's so plain to see, a Friend such as JESUS,... is all, that we need!

Andrew Paul Nieman

ABOUT THE AUTHOR

I am Northern Tutchone, (pronounced "Two-Show-Nee") a member of the White River First Nation in the Yukon Territory, Canada. I never ever dreamed I would draw a sober breath long enough to actually matter to anyone. Today, I am completely delivered from the horrible loneliness violence and pain of being a former convict, skid row alcoholic and a cocaine/heroin addict. I am now 18 years clean and sober as of Feb. 1, 2012.

After God cleaned up my life, I went back to school and eventually earned a University Degree in Social Work. I ran my own therapeutic counselling business for 6 years and on December 10, 2009 I became an officer of the Yukon Legislative Assembly. I was ordained a Minister with the UNITED PENTECOSTAL CHURCH INTERNATIONAL on June 29, 2009. Looking back on my dangerous, traumatic, exciting, sad, happy life, I only have one regret. I regret that I did not give my life to Jesus sooner…because the life He gives back is the absolute BEST LIFE there could possibly be!